D1208004

INVISIBLE
EMPIRE

The Story of the Ku Klux Klan
1866–1871

PATTERSON SMITH REPRINT SERIES IN
CRIMINOLOGY, LAW ENFORCEMENT, AND SOCIAL PROBLEMS

A listing of publications in the SERIES will be found at rear of volume

ORIGINAL FLAG OF THE KU KLUX KLAN

The "Grand Ensign" of the original Ku Klux Klan of Pulaski, Tennessee, the birthplace of the organization. The flag, measuring five feet in length and three feet in width at the staff, is hand-painted, with a black dragon on yellow material bordered with red scallops. (The artist has run together the last two words of the Latin motto.) The flag is owned by the Tennessee Historical Society at Nashville. *(Photograph by courtesy of the Tennessee Historical Society.)*

PUBLICATION No. 81: PATTERSON SMITH REPRINT SERIES IN
CRIMINOLOGY, LAW ENFORCEMENT, AND SOCIAL PROBLEMS

INVISIBLE EMPIRE

The Story of the Ku Klux Klan, 1866-1871

BY STANLEY F. HORN

ILLUSTRATED

Second Edition
Enlarged by the Author

PATTERSON SMITH, MONTCLAIR, N. J.

TO
B. W. H.

AUTHOR'S NOTE

THIS IS JUST what its sub-title represents it to be — a *story* of the Ku Klux Klan. It is historically accurate (at least every precaution has been taken to make it so), but it is told in narrative form because that seems to be the clearest and most vivid way of presenting this incredible chapter in American history.

An organization such as the Ku Klux Klan could have been organized and sustained only in such circumstances as prevailed in the South following the War Between the States. Its birth, its life, and its death were shrouded in mystery; no complete story of its existence has ever before been told. It is the purpose of this book to tell that story, to clear away some of the mystery which hangs about the Ku Klux name.

To avoid interruption to the flow of the narrative, there are no distracting footnotes. Every statement, however, is fully substantiated. In the Appendix is a bibliography of basic works of reference, the reading of which has been supplemented by intensive personal research throughout the South over a period of several years, including the painstaking scanning of old newspaper files and numerous interviews with surviving members of the Klan.

An acknowledgment and an expression of appreciation are

due to all those who have so generously assisted me in preparing this work, but they are so many in number that an enumeration of their names might weary the reader. Among the institutions and organizations to which I owe thanks are the National Archives and Library of Congress at Washington; the New York Public Library; the Department of Archives and History of Tennessee, also the similar department of Alabama; the Tennessee Historical Society; the Buffalo Historical Society; the Nashville (Tennessee) Public Library; the Howard Library, New Orleans, Louisiana; the Cossitt Library, Memphis; the Virginia Historical Society; the Library, Duke University, Durham, North Carolina; and many others.

CONTENTS

Prologue

PART I

The Growth of the Empire

PART II

The Realms of the Empire

PART III

The Decline of the Empire

Appendix

INVISIBLE
EMPIRE

The Story of the Ku Klux Klan
1866–1871

PROLOGUE

'THIS IS AN INSTITUTION of chivalry, humanity, mercy
and patriotism; embodying in its genius and its principles all
that is chivalric in conduct, noble in sentiment, generous in
manhood and patriotic in purpose.' So ran the opening declaration in the official 'Prescript of the Order of the * * *' adopted
early in 1868.

Late in the same year the Reconstruction legislature of
Georgia passed an anti-Ku Klux law, declaring the need for
protection from the depredations of 'a secret organization of
men who, under the cover of masks and other grotesque disguises, armed with knives, revolvers and other deadly weapons,
do issue from the place of their rendezvous ... generally in the
late hours of the night, to commit violence and outrage upon
peaceable and law-abiding citizens, robbing and murdering
them upon the highways, and entering their houses, tearing
them from their homes and the embrace of their families, and,
with violent threats and insults, inflicting on them the most
cruel and inhuman treatment ... disturbing the public peace,
ruining the happiness and prosperity of the people, and in
many places over-riding the civil authorities, defying all law
and justice.'

At first blush it might appear that the 'institution of chivalry,
humanity, mercy and patriotism' would provide an ideal

mechanism for protecting the people from the outrages of this
secret organization which was committing violence and outrage
upon peaceable and law-abiding citizens. Strange as it may
seem, however, the band of lawless desperadoes referred to in
this legislative enactment were one and the same with the order
whose declaration of purpose was of so lofty a nature. The
* * * of the Prescript was the Ku Klux Klan of the punitive law;
and the wide gulf between these descriptions demonstrates the
impossibility of evaluating the Ku Klux movement by means
of sweeping generalities.

The story of the Ku Klux Klan is bound up, of course, with
the whole tragic story of Reconstruction. It is a story of political
involutions, corruption, duplicity, abuse of power, misrule and
violence, impossible to relate in a few paragraphs. For a brief
summary, however, it is difficult to improve on the minority
report of the 'Joint Select Committee to Inquire into the Condition of the Late Insurrectionary States,' which in 1871 made
the extensive investigation and voluminous report which is now
embalmed in an official government publication embracing
thirteen forbidding volumes of fine print commonly called the
Ku Klux Report. There were twenty-one members of this committee, carefully chosen to preclude any possibility of bias in
favor of the South, and a majority of thirteen brought in the
condemnatory report expected of them. The minority, however, sharply took issue with the majority and said bluntly:

'Had there been no wanton oppression in the South, there
would have been no Ku Kluxism. Had there been no rule of
the tyrannical, corrupt carpetbagger or scalawag rule, there
would have been no secret organizations. From the oppression
and corruption of the one sprang the vice and outrage of the
other. . . .

'When the testimony taken before us is analyzed, and the
ignorance and degradation of the Southern negro is understood;
when, as General Grant shows in his report of December, 1865,

they believed that the property of their former masters of right
belonged to them and was not entitled to any protection; when,
as all the testimony shows, the carpetbaggers, Freedmen's
Bureau agents and Loyal Leaguers who went to these states
took as the theme of their harangues the wrongs the negroes had
suffered and the right they had to take whatever they pleased
of the property they had labored to acquire for their masters;
when, in secret, sworn organizations hatred of the white race
at the South was instilled into the minds of these ignorant people by every art and wile that bad men could devise; when the
negroes were formed into military organizations and the white
people of these states were denied the use of arms; when arson,
rape, robbery and murder were things of daily occurrence;
when the great mass of the most intelligent whites were disfranchised and the ballot was put into the hands of the negro
by the government at Washington; when every promise made
and every law enacted was broken and disregarded by the
Federal authorities whenever it suited their purpose to do so;
when even the courts were closed and the Federal officers, who
were made by Congress absolute rulers and dispensers of what
they called justice, ignored, insulted and trampled upon the
rights of the ostracized and disfranchised white man while the
official pandered to the enfranchised negro on whose vote he
relied; in short, when that people saw that they had no rights
which were respected, no protection from insult, no security
even for their wives and little children, and that what little
they had saved from the ravages of war was being confiscated
by taxation and rendered valueless by the debts for which men
who owned nothing had pledged it, and saw that all their
complaints and remonstrances, however honestly and humbly
presented to Congress, were either wholly disregarded or regarded as evidence of a rebellious and unsubdued spirit, many
of them took the law into their own hands and did deeds of
violence which we neither justify nor excuse. But all history

shows that bad government will make bad citizens; and when the corruption, extortions and villainy of the governments which Congress has set up and maintained over the Southern states are thoroughly understood and made known, as we trust they will be some day, the world will be amazed at the long suffering and endurance of that people.'

AN INTRODUCTION IN PICTURES
to the story of the Ku Klux Klan

Photograph by Roberts Studio, Pulaski, Tennessee.

An evening in December, 1865. Six young men are sitting around the fireplace of Judge Jones's law office in Pulaski, Tennessee. The war is over. They are bored. Somebody suggests forming a club —

Illustration from 'Harper's Weekly' of February 19th, 1868, showing two Army officers posed in Ku Klux uniforms captured at Huntsville, Alabama.

The object of the society being purely amusement, they invent for themselves grotesque names and outlandish costumes —

Uniform worn by an officer of the Ku Klux in Marshall County, Tennessee. It is of red calico, with white trimmings; the head-dress of red flannel, with white mask ornamented with red stars. (From the collection of Lucius E. Burch, Jr., Memphis, Tennessee.)

which are at first simple, but later elaborate and brilliant —

A Carolina Ku Klux, as illustrated in 'A Fool's Errand.'

and ride about at night, terrifying insolent negroes, who believe they are ghosts of dead Confederate soldiers. Soon the plaything has become a dangerous weapon —

WHAT DOES IT MEAN?—The following mysterious "Take Notice" was found under our door early yesterday morning, having doubtless been slipped there the night previous. Will any one venture to tell us what it means, if it means anything at all? What is a "Kuklux Klan," and who is this "Grand Cyclops" that issues his mysterious and imperative orders? Can any one give us a little light on this subject? Here is the order:

"TAKE NOTICE.—The Kuklux Klan will assemble at their usual place of rendezvous, "The Den," on Tuesday night next, exactly at the hour of midnight, in costume and bearing the arms of the Klan.

"By or of the Grand Cyclops.

G. T."

On March 29, 1867, the editor of the Pulaski *Citizen*, Grand Geni of the local Den, publishes the first story on the Klan —

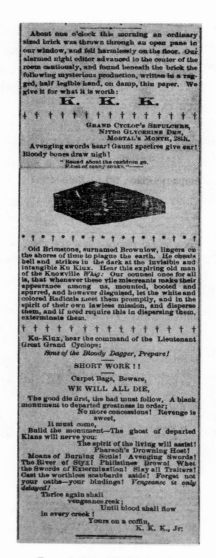

About one o'clock this morning an ordinary sized brick was thrown through an open pane in our window, and fell harmlessly on the floor. Our alarmed night editor advanced to the center of the room cautiously, and found beneath the brick the following mysterious production, written in a ragged, half legible hand, on damp, thin paper. We give it for what it is worth:

K. K. K.

✝ ✝ ✝ ✝ ✝ ✝ ✝ ✝ ✝ ✝ ✝ ✝ ✝ ✝

GRAND CYCLOP'S SEPULCHRE,
NITRO GLYCERINE DEN,
MORTAL'S MONTH, 28th.

Avenging swords hear! Gaunt spectres give ear! Bloody bones draw nigh!

"Round about the cauldron go.
Fillet of fenny snake."——

✝ ✝ ✝ ✝ ✝ ✝ ✝ ✝ ✝ ✝ ✝ ✝ ✝ ✝

Old Brimstone, surnamed Brownlow, lingers on the shores of time to plague the earth. He cheats hell and strikes in the dark at the invisible and intangible Ku Klux. Hear this expiring old man of the Knoxville *Whig*: Our counsel once for all is, that whenever these vile miscreants make their appearance among us, mounted, booted and spurred, and however disguised, let the white and colored Radicals meet them promptly, and in the spirit of their own lawless mission, and disperse them, and if need require this in dispersing them, exterminate them.

✝ ✝ ✝ ✝ ✝ ✝ ✝ ✝ ✝ ✝ ✝

Ku-Klux, hear the command of the Lieutenant Great Grand Cyclops:

Sons of the Bloody Dagger, Prepare!

SHORT WORK !!

Carpet Bags, Beware,

WE WILL ALL DIE,

The good die first, the bad must follow, A black monument to departed greatness in order;
No more concessions! Revenge is sweet,
It must come,
Build the monument—The ghost of departed Klans will nerve you:
The spirit of the living will assist!
Pharaoh's Drowning Host!
Moans of Burning Souls! Avenging Swords! The River of Styx! Philistines Drown! Whet the Swords of Extermination! Slay all Traitors! Cast the worthless scabbards aside! Forget not your oaths—your bindings! *Vengeance is only delayed!*
Thrice again shall
vengeance reek;
Until blood shall flow
in every creek !
Yours on a coffin,
K. K. K., Jr.

From the Memphis 'Avalanche.'

Friendly editors print Klan notices in the guise of news items —

"He was seen on his knees praying."

Ku-Klux Mode of Torture.

From a pamphlet published in Hartford, Connecticut, in 1872, purporting to relate the 'Experience of a Northern man among the Ku Klux.'

Since the times are rotten-ripe for it, the Klan spreads like wildfire. Imaginary stories circulate concerning its gruesome activities; some of these will appear later in Northern papers —

PRESCRIPT

OF THE

* *

—————— •••• ——————

What may this mean,
That thou, dead corse, again, in complete steel,
Revisit'st thus the glimpses of the moon,
Making night hideous; and we fools of nature,
So horridly to shake our disposition,
With thoughts beyond the reaches of our souls?

—————— ••• ——————

An' now auld Cloots, I ken ye're thinkin',
A certain *Ghoul* is rantin', drinkin',
Some luckless night will send him linkin,'
          To your black pit ;
But, faith! he'll turn a corner jinkin',
          An' cheat you yet.

Title-page of the Original Prescript of the Ku Klux Klan. (Originally owned by Captain A. T. Fielder of Dyer County, Tennessee; now in the collection of Mr. Hallum W. Goodloe, Nashville.)

The thing is getting out of hand. To control it, a formal constitution or 'Prescript' is drawn up by General George W. Gordon, Grand Dragon of the Realm of Tennessee.

The cabalistic three stars appear on General Gordon's gold badge, with the motto 'In hoc Signo Spes mea' (In this sign is my hope) —

The Cabarrus County, North Carolina, Den has its own proud banner —

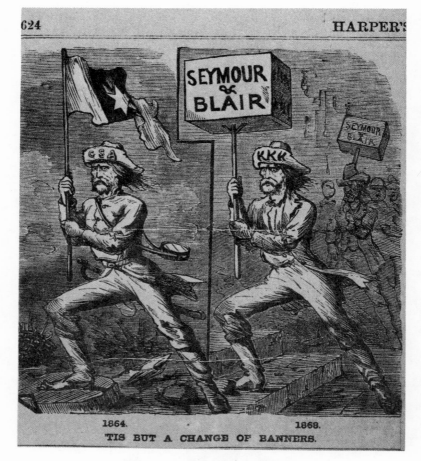

1864.   1868.
'TIS BUT A CHANGE OF BANNERS.

Political cartoon in 'Harper's Weekly.'

By the time of the Presidential election of 1868, the Klan is
a factor in national politics, used by the North to discredit the
Democratic candidates —

Warning sent to an offender in Alabama. (Introduced in the testimony before the Congressional Investigating Committee.)

Continuing to grow, the Klan uses threats more often than force. Warnings are often grotesquely embellished —

A PROSPECTIVE SCENE IN THE CITY OF OAKS, 4TH OF MARCH, 1869.

Inflammatory cartoon printed in the Tuscaloosa (Alabama) 'Independent Monitor,' September 1, 1868. The editor of the 'Monitor' was Ryland Randolph, Grand Cyclops of the Ku Klux Klan in Tuscaloosa.

Carpetbaggers are told what is in store for them —

A threatening letter, signed 'Ku Klux Klan,' sent to Thaddeus Stevens in 1868; probably the work of some crank or prankster, as it differs from the type of warning used in the South. It will be noted that although the letter was dated in New Orleans it was actually mailed and postmarked in Washington. (Photostat from Library of Congress.)

Thaddeus Stevens himself gets a warning —

THE TRIAL IS AT HAND!

The appointed day and hour will soon come!! Fail not——
& if thou dost—— ... *the stars will be ... o'clock*
   At night when the clock strikes *to ... o'clock* be ye faithful
unto your trust—nor wind, nor hail, nor rain, nor storm,
nor conscience, nor craven fear, shall excuse.

Dost Hear! Dost Heed!

Thus now do I call, and yet ONCE AGAIN, and if ye heed
not, ...

☞ K.X.R.T.E.H.Y. ✠✠✠ ☜

CYCLOPEAN, Secretary.

By order of the GRAND CLYCOPS!!

A rare Ku Klux broadside warning, printed and posted in Tuscaloosa, Alabama.
(Courtesy of Edward Eberstadt, New York City, N.Y.)

The work of the Klan goes on —

The 'Ku Klux Klan Waltz,' published in Nashville in 1868, authorship attributed to 'Gustavus Dolfuss.' The lurid illustration, printed in red ink, gives a good idea of the popular conception of Ku Klux proceedings at the time. (From the collection of Kenneth Rose, Nashville, Tennessee.)

Even song writers play on the morbid interest in its name —

Illustration from a broadside said to represent the trial and near-execution of one John Campbell of Big Poplar, North Carolina. It was stated that the proceedings were interrupted and the whole party of Ku Klux arrested, this woodcut being made from a posed photograph taken later, using the captured regalia. (Courtesy of Edward Eberstadt, New York City, N.Y.)

While Northern editors print their ideas of its murderous activities —

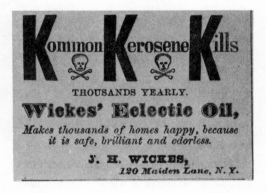

From 'Harper's Weekly,' January 6th, 1872.

Finally, after the true Ku Klux Klan had dissolved, merchants used its dread initials to call attention to their wares —

Uniform of one of the officials of the Pulaski, Tennessee, Den No. 1, of the Ku Klux Klan, now in the museum of the State Teachers College, Florence, Alabama. The robe is red, with white trimming, and is made of calico. The cap is flannel, with trimmings of white calico around the mouth and eyes.

Its brief life over, the Klan becomes a museum curiosity.

PART I

The Growth of the Empire

I. THE ORIGIN OF
THE KU KLUX KLAN

During the lifetime of the Klan there was widespread speculation as to its origin, and there were many theories advanced — most of them far from the mark. Aside from the wild guesses proceeding out of pure ignorance, the problem was complicated by the repetition of absurd and misleading stories deliberately put in circulation by the Ku Klux themselves for the purpose of throwing inquisitive people off the track. Many a Ku Klux herring was drawn across the trail as investigators ran around in circles. One Northern newspaper carried a story from an 'authoritative' source revealing the alleged fact that the Ku Klux Klan was organized in New York City 'by well-known Conservatives from Tennessee.' One imaginative editor even went so far as to charge that the Klan was headed by no less a personage than President Andrew Johnson; and there were numerous other equally erroneous guesses and speculations from time to time. One newspaper stated that it had been started by the Confederate prisoners on Johnson's Island during the war; but this was a muddled confusion with the secret society which was actually formed there, known as the 'Seven Confederate Knights.' This short-lived and fruitless organization had a skull and crossbones for its insignia; but it had no connection whatever with the Ku Klux Klan.

What was evidently a deliberately misleading and jocular

explanation of the origin of the new order's fantastic name was embodied in an article appearing in the Memphis *Appeal* which, without cracking an editorial smile, said: '"Ku Klux Klan" is a Hebrew term; and, if not found in the Talmud, is met with in a very old Jewish work entitled "A True and Authentic History of the Great Rebellion of the Hebrew Against the Ancient Egyptian King Pharaoh, B.C. 2000." In this work the orthography is thus: "Cu-Clux Clan," and is interpreted in the English language the "Straw Club," which is supposed to allude to the fact that Pharaoh required the hod-carriers to furnish their own straw, and also to the proverb, known to be of ancient Hebrew origin, "Straws show which way the wind blows."'

Perhaps the most ridiculous of all these current newspaper 'exposures' of the order's origin was one printed in the Richmond *Whig* early in 1868. This story, most probably inspired by some mischievous member of the Ku Klux himself, attributed to the organization an Oriental origin! 'The name,' said this article gravely, 'is not of American origin nor the whim of a wag; but, like the order itself, originated in China among the merchants engaged in smuggling opium into that Empire. It was introduced into America by Hon. Humphrey Marshall on his return from the Celestials. Marshall organized the first band in Room 94, Brown's Hotel, Richmond, intending it for a sort of hilarious social club. There are now 4000 Ku Kluxes in Richmond, and 700 more waiting admission. Each hundred has a captain, each fifty a lieutenant, and each twenty a sergeant. Only able-bodied white men are admitted, and all must be of manly stature.'

The outline of the plan of organization was suspiciously close to the facts; but the estimate of 4000 members in Richmond was probably a gross exaggeration and intended merely to inspire fear on the part of credulous readers. The attribution of Oriental origin was entirely imaginary. As a matter of fact, however, the Ku Klux Klan did originate as a 'hilarious social club,' although the place where it was conceived was far away from Richmond or China and neither Humphrey Marshall nor the opium smugglers had anything to do with it. Its entirely aimless and innocent beginning grew out of nothing more sinister than the ennui and idleness of six young men who lived in Pulaski, Tennessee, a short distance south of Nashville — Captain John C. Lester, Captain John B. Kennedy, Captain James R. Crowe, Frank O. McCord, Richard R. Reed and J. Calvin Jones. They were all men of the highest standing in their community, with unblemished records for good behavior. Most of them were college graduates, and none of them at any time was ever accused of any offense against the law of even the mildest sort. It is significant of their impeccable reputations for good conduct that when the Ku Klux investigation was held by the government a few years later none of them was summoned for examination by the inquisitors.

These six young men had all been in the Confederate army, and after they got back home and while they were adjusting themselves to the new conditions of life, time hung heavy on their hands. On an evening late in December, 1865, they were sitting around the fireplace in the law office of Calvin Jones's father, Judge Thomas M. Jones, idly discussing the dearth of amusements and possible ways and means of supplying the lack. As might naturally be expected under such circumstances, somebody suggested that a club or society of some sort be formed. This idea met with general approval, and after some discussion they dispersed to meet again in the same place the next evening. At that time a loose sort of temporary organization was formed, a chairman and secretary were elected, and committees were appointed to select a name and to draw up a set of rules and a ritual for the initiation of members, agreement being made to meet a week later.

During that intervening week it happened that one of the

prominent residents of Pulaski, Colonel Thomas Martin, went
on a trip to Columbus, Mississippi, taking his family with him,
and he asked Captain Kennedy to sleep in the house during his
absence to protect it from possible marauders. This circumstance provided the budding young society with an ideal secret
place for the carrying out of their plans, and Captain Kennedy
arranged for the next meeting to be held there. The organization was perfected in Colonel Martin's house and all of its
earliest meetings were held there; but it is stated in Pulaski that
Colonel Martin upon his return from Mississippi was not informed of what had been going on in his house during his
absence and that he died without knowing that his home had
been the birthplace of this history-making organization.

The objects of the new society being purely amusement and
relaxation, all of the original plans and arrangements were decidedly on the burlesque and grotesque side. The names of the
officers, as specified in the report of the rules committee, were
unusual and unique, the prime consideration being to get as
far as possible away from familiar military or political titles.
The meeting place was to be known as a 'Den,' and the chief
officer of the Den was to be called the 'Grand Cyclops.' The
officer corresponding to vice president, the assistant of the
Grand Cyclops, was the 'Grand Magi'; and there was a 'Grand
Turk' who was to greet all candidates for admission. The
secretary was the 'Grand Scribe'; and there were two 'Night
Hawks' who acted as messengers and two 'Lictors' who constituted the guard. The members in the ranks, not holding
office, were to be designated as 'Ghouls' — although at first
there were not quite enough members to fill all the specified
offices and everybody had a resounding title. The titles had no
meaning or significance, being selected arbitrarily and solely
for their weird and supposedly impressive sound. It was just
another local secret society of fun-loving young men looking
for an outlet for their unemployed energies such as has been

formed hundreds of times in the past without any particular purpose. In all probability it would endure but a short time until the attention of the members was directed along other channels.

Aside from the condition of affairs and other factors involved, the thing that caused the new organization to attract attention and later to spread beyond any dream of its organizers was unquestionably the impression created and the curiosity aroused by its mysterious, sonorous name. It was the kind of name people liked to repeat, just to hear the sound of its sinister syllables. Even the initials, in their alliterative attractiveness, were an asset. But this wonderful name was also solely a matter of chance.

When the organization meeting was held in Colonel Martin's home, the committee appointed to select a name reported that it had not been able to agree on a recommendation. They wanted something distinctive, something different from the 'Merry Six' or the names so tritely familiar as the entitlement of such organizations. That was a time when every educated young man's training embraced the study of Latin and Greek, also it was when the Greek letter fraternities were enjoying their first popularity in the colleges. So, as they sat around and cudgeled their brains for a suitable but unusual name for their new club, it is not surprising that some one of them should turn his thoughts to the Greek vocabulary. Finally Richard Reed suggested that they call it the Kuklos, from the Greek word Κυκλος, from which our words 'circle' and 'cycle' are derived; and this suggestion met with immediate approval. They repeated the word over a few times; and Captain Kennedy, having an ear for alliteration, suggested that they introduce another 'K' sound in the name by adding the word 'clan.' The alliterative sound was further improved by changing Kuklos Clan to Kuklux Klan; and from this it was later but a natural step to the now familiar style, Ku Klux Klan, with the impressive in-

itials, K.K.K., which were to develop such a terrifying significance within such a short while. This is the story of the origin
of the name as told by surviving charter members; and its
authenticity seems beyond question.

That the use of this particular Greek word in this connection
was not entirely unprecedented is indicated by the testimony
before the Congressional Committee of Daniel Coleman of
Athens, Alabama (strongly suspected of being a Ku Klux
leader there), who stated that he was first led to look into the
Ku Klux organization by reason of the similarity of its name
to the name of a society to which he belonged when he went
to college — the Κυκλος Society.

In some of the articles about the Ku Klux which were printed
in the North it was stated that the name 'Ku Klux Klan' was
derived from a supposed similarity to the noise made in cocking
and discharging a firearm. In the words of one writer, who
signed himself 'Carpet Bagger': 'The name "Ku Klux Klan"
is said to have been suggested to them [the organizers] by the
sound made in the act of cocking and firing the rifles and shotguns carried by them — the first two syllables being repeated
in a subdued tone of voice, as "Ku Klux," representing the
cocking of the piece; while the last syllable, "*Klan*," being
repeated with emphasis, betokened its discharge.'

This fanciful and far-fetched yarn was probably told the
gullible Mr. Carpet Bagger by some of the Carolina members
of the Klan with whom he came in contact, as it was a part of
the Ku Klux technique to surround all their activities with as
much blood-and-thunder mumbo-jumbo as possible and paint
in just as lurid a background of suggested terror as the credulity
of the hearer would admit. The gun-cocking story sounded in
character and people liked to believe it; and so it gained considerable credence. It made a good story; but, like so many
good stories, it was totally lacking in factual foundation. Long
years afterwards, however, this baseless theory was given wide

circulation when it was repeated by Sir Arthur Conan Doyle in his famous story of the Ku Klux, 'The Five Orange Pips.' Another ingenious theory as to the origin of the name was advanced by Mr. W. B. Romine, now editor of the Pulaski *Citizen*, in an interview in a Nashville paper in 1934. Mr. Romine, recalling the large number of volunteer troops who went to the Mexican War from Tennessee, says it is not unreasonable to assume that some of these soldiers during their sojourn in Mexico may have become familiar with Mexican mythology. Significantly, he says, the god of light in ancient Mexico was called Cukulcan, and he goes on: 'The fact that members of the Ku Klux occasionally referred to themselves as "sons of light" suggests the idea that some of them may have learned the story of Cukulcan from their fathers or uncles who were soldiers in Mexico, and with slight changes created a word which admirably served their purposes.'

Bubbling over with the excitement of their new-found plaything, the young members of the new Ku Klux Klan decided to make a public manifestation of themselves; so, borrowing the familiar idea of the easy Hallowe'en disguise, they wrapped themselves in sheets, mounted their horses and galloped through the streets of the little town, greatly enjoying the sensation they created — particularly the alarm and dismay of the negroes, to whose superstitious minds the sight of white-sheeted figures suggested nothing but spirits risen from the grave, and who accordingly fled to their homes in panic-stricken terror.

The successful effect of this entirely fortuitous costume was so satisfactory it was adopted as the official regalia of the order, and each member was required to provide himself with a suitable robe and mask and head-dress, the latter being built up of cardboard and designed to add to the apparent height of the wearer. 'It looked like he had an up-turned churn on his head,' one witness said in describing the appearance of one of the sheeted band.

The organizers of the new society were out for fun, but it was fun of an innocent and harmless variety they had in mind; and one of the original requirements of new members was that they be of good character and standing and not addicted to the intemperate use of intoxicants. The only other requirement of members at that time was a blood-curdling pledge of secrecy — not that there was anything in particular to conceal aside from the details of the elaborate horse-play of the initiation ceremonies, but it was felt that the edge of the fun would be blunted if the initiate had any inkling of what was going to happen. Then, too, the idea of secrecy carried an undertone of mysterious things to come which was very attractive and made it possible for the imagination of the new members to conjure up some serious, important objective which was entirely lacking in reality.

The perpetration of the initiation was really the principal object of the order at first. Most of the organizers had attended college and were familiar with the boisterous and elaborate flummery which for so long has made college secret societies and fraternities attractive to young men, and most of the original Ku Klux initiation was borrowed from this source. An idea of the schoolboyish nature of the proceedings in those early days of the Ku Klux may be had from a glimpse of the climax of the initiation which, in later years, was revealed by some of the aging members.

The preliminaries consisted of leading the blindfolded candidate around from one officer to another, where he was heaped with solemn admonitions and subjected to the rough buffoonery common to such proceedings. The big moment came when the Grand Cyclops in a deep voice gave the order: 'Let his head be adorned with the regal crown, after which place him before the royal altar and remove his hoodwink.' The regal crown was an oversized hat ornamented with two donkey's ears, and the royal altar was a large mirror. When the candidate's blindfold was removed and he beheld his ridiculous image in the glass before him he was greeted with howls of laughter and derision. This was the climax. It sounds silly now, but it provoked great merriment among the young Ku Kluxes of 1866; and every initiate was glad to observe his pledge of secrecy so that he might help enjoy the next victim's discomfiture.

As the order grew in popularity and gained in membership it was soon necessary to find a new meeting place, and one had been providentially prepared by Nature which ideally suited their purposes. On the top of a hill on the western outskirts of the town there stood the ruins of the home formerly occupied by Doctor Benjamin Carter. This house had been demolished by a cyclone in December, and there remained only a wing of three rooms, with a cellar beneath. The grove surrounding the house had also suffered in the cyclone, and the house was almost obscured from view by the fallen trees and broken branches, the surviving wing being covered over with the débris from the demolished part. On the whole it presented a most satisfactory spooky and eerie appearance and, inevitably, immediately acquired the reputation of being haunted. It was just the place for the home den of a group of white-robed, night-riding horsemen whose principal stock in trade was mystery — and the new Ku Klux Klan quickly and gleefully adopted it as their headquarters.

One strict rule of the society from the first was that nobody should be solicited to join. They wanted new members, of course, since without new members there could be no initiation; but it was thought that a mysterious air of reserve would best attract candidates for admission, and there was always the desire to be able to say to any malcontent that his membership had not been sought but that he had applied voluntarily. In instances where the membership of some particularly desirable person was sought, it was customary to solicit him by indirection. A member would engage him in conversation and bring

the talk around to the subject of the Ku Klux. Finally, in a
burst of confidence, he would say: 'It looks to me like a good
thing, and I've about made up my mind to join it.' If this
admission provoked the other to the expression of a desire to
join the Klan, the member would confide that he had investigated the matter to a point where he had learned how to go
about joining, and he would suggest that they meet at a given
place at a specified time and they would join together. Approaching the den in the blasted Carter house they would be
met by the outer Lictor, brandishing the spear of his office,
and after questioning them this Lictor would blow his whistle
as a signal to the inner Lictor to come out and receive the
candidates. When the genuine candidate was blindfolded, he
thought that his companion was receiving like treatment, and
he learned no better until the initiation ceremony was at
an end.

Undesirable candidates for admission received treatment of
different kinds — all effective. The ordinary means of subtly
hinting to a young man that he was not wanted in the Klan
was by means of the old 'snipe-hunting' dodge. He was blindfolded and with great ceremony conducted to some remote
place in the woods and seated upon a convenient stump or
log and told to wait there until he was called. He was, of
course, never called; and, after so long a time, it generally
dawned on him that his application for membership had been
delicately but definitely rejected. If an applicant for admission
was suspected of ulterior purposes, or thought to be entering
the order merely to learn its secrets, he was treated a little
more roughly. Such as these were generally stuffed into a
barrel and rolled down a long hill, their discomfiture being
equaled only by the merriment of the howling young Klansmen.

In later times, when the Klan had assumed more serious
objectives and its members had been proscribed by the Brownlow government in Tennessee, the intrusion of a spy was a

matter of life and death, and suspects were treated more rigorously. One such applicant, whose true identity and purpose were known, was received with every appearance of cordiality and led to believe that he would be initiated. But, after being blindfolded, he was taken to the woods and strung up to the limb of a tree with his feet barely touching the ground, from which uncomfortable predicament he was not rescued until the next morning.

The fate of another who did not escape so lightly was told in a Nashville newspaper in 1868: 'One bold fellow in the service of Governor Brownlow proposed to join the Ku Klux in order to discover their secrets. He was encouraged to believe he would be received, and was taken to the appointed meeting place where he was beguiled with soothing words and then taken to the woods where he was stripped of his clothing and shamelessly mutilated. In this shocking condition he was dismissed, weak and bleeding, and told to report to Governor Brownlow that he had been initiated in the first degree of the Ku Klux Klan. The fiends knew his business as well as he did, and he gained not the slightest knowledge of them.'

Another Brownlow spy who tried to get into the Nashville Den was given the barrel-down-the-hill treatment, with one important difference from the Pulaski procedure. In the Nashville episode the barrel was rolled down the wharf into the Cumberland River, and the Klansmen were in such a hurry to get somewhere else that they neglected to stay and rescue him from the river's muddy depths.

But these acts of defensive violence did not come until later, in 1868 and 1869. In those early days of 1866 there was no thought of violence, no need to fear the state authorities. Everything was innocent and harmless. Passing negroes might be frightened at the sepulchral appearance of the ghostly Lictor who stood by the side of the road at the gate of the driveway leading to the old Carter place; they might be terri-

fied by the flickering lights to be seen in the shattered and
deserted house on the hill or hastened on their way at night
by the shrieks of unearthly laughter which reverberated through
the storm-stricken grove — but this was merely a by-product
of the Ku Klux activities, not their original purpose.

Even though this had not been its purpose, however, the
terror created among the negroes by the new and mysterious
Ku Klux Klan soon began to create talk. It was noticed that
prowling freedmen who encountered the ghostly horsemen at
night were afterwards more inclined to stay at home after
dark; and this gave birth to the idea that perhaps the Klan
might be used as a means of subduing the undue bumptious-
ness and the nocturnal prowlings of some of those who seemed
incapable of using their new-found freedom discreetly. Parties
of Klansmen took to calling on such recalcitrants occasionally
in the dead hours of the night, taking full advantage of their
victims' superstition to give weight to their warnings.

At this stage of the Klan's development its visits were purely
admonitory. Sometimes, when visiting a victim, they did not
utter a word, trusting to the negro's superstitious fear to accomplish the desired result. Sometimes there were terrifying
threats of what would happen to the offending negro if he
did not behave himself. But they relied on threats and fear
alone to do their work; and fear, superinduced by superstition,
was at first sufficient. At this stage the barking Ku Klux dog
did not bite. It was not until later that his victims felt his teeth.

The white-robed Lictor before the Carter house had been
accustomed to telling passing strangers who inquired as to
his identity that he was the spirit of a Confederate soldier killed
at Chickamauga. Pretty soon the Ku Klux were being referred
to generally as the 'ghosts of the Confederate dead,' and a
negro preacher in Tennessee electrified his congregation by
telling them that he had seen one of the spirits rise from the
grave of a murdered Confederate soldier who was buried near

his church. As a matter of fact, there might have been some basis for this fantastic story, as graveyards were a favorite meeting place for rural Ku Klux, the old-fashioned box tombs providing an ideal hiding place for their regalia.

The theory that the Ku Klux were Confederate ghosts was readily accepted by the negroes generally as being entirely reasonable and credible, and when the Klansmen started to making moonlight visits of a regulatory nature they took their cue from this. The leader of the Klansmen would tell the negro visited, in a hollow voice, that he was thirsty and wanted a drink. When the negro brought out the water bucket and drinking gourd, the thirsty Ku Klux would cast aside the inadequate gourd and, raising the bucket to his lips, to the pop-eyed astonishment of the negro, would drain it to the last drop — with the assistance of a funnel inside his mask connected by a rubber tube to an oilcloth bag under the flowing robe.

'That's good,' he would say, smacking his lips. 'That's the first drink I've had since I was killed at the Battle of Shiloh; and you get mighty thirsty down in Hell.' This became the favorite and standard joke of the Ku Klux everywhere during those early days; it was almost the hall-mark of a Ku Klux raid — none genuine without it.

Another awe-inspiring performance was for one of the Ku Klux to wear his robe over the top of his head, surmounted with a false head (consisting generally of a large gourd with a mask attached) which could be removed in the negro's presence. 'Here, hold my head a minute,' the Klansman would say, thrusting the masked gourd at the negro, which never failed to reduce the victim to a state of quaking terror. Sometimes one of the sheeted riders would insist on shaking hands with all the negroes he met, the hand he extended them in greeting being made of wood in simulation of a skeleton's. 'Have you got a mattock?' one Mississippi negro was asked by one of the ghostly visitors. 'My head-stone is so close to my

head I can't rest good in my grave, and I want you to come
to the graveyard with me and move it.'

But all this innocent frolic and horse-play on the part of a
few small-town youths constituted merely the first stage in the
existence of the Ku Klux Klan. Its fame began to spread
beyond the bounds of Pulaski. As the supply of local membership material ran out, visitors were initiated into the mysterious order; and when they went home they talked about it
and frequently started similar groups in their own localities.
Trouble with obstreperous negroes was prevalent throughout
the South, and the white population was acutely conscious of
the need for some means of correcting this evil. The effectiveness of the Ku Klux as a medium for the pacification of the
lawless element among the negroes in the Pulaski neighborhood
began to attract attention, and the citizens of near-by counties
and states began to make inquiry as to how they could set up
Klans of their own to handle their local problems.

Through the fall of 1866 and the winter of 1866–67 the Ku
Klux Klan outgrew the confines of Pulaski and Giles County.
Also it began to take on a more serious purpose wherever it
had been established. It had grown out of its swaddling clothes
and, almost before its organizers realized what was happening,
they found it on the eve of branching out as a force of regulation
which was to affect the destiny of the whole South. Pulaski,
however, remained the nerve-center of the Ku Klux movement. Here was dropped into the pool the pebble whose
ripples spread so far.

II.   THE GROWTH
OF THE KLAN

The time being rotten-ripe for it, the growth of
the Ku Klux Klan was steady; but it was also irregular, un-
directed and altogether undisciplined. As the organization
spread, all the new Dens owned a sort of loose, informal
allegiance to the parent Den at Pulaski; but there was no
official, constituted authority vested in anyone, no recognized
rules or regulations — nothing but a common governing idea
that the Klan could be used as a sort of mysterious and effective
vigilance committee, depending mostly upon its mystery for
its effectiveness. It had no definite program and, worst of all,
no machinery for regulating itself. The activities of each new
Den were dependent entirely upon the inclination of the
members. If they committed excesses, there was no power to
rebuke or restrain them. Thus it drifted along for a year or
more, new Ku Klux dens springing up here and there, with
nobody in authority to guide or control them.

One of the factors contributing to the spread of the order
was the abundant newspaper publicity. The editor of the
Pulaski *Citizen* was the Grand Geni of the local Den, and
although there was not a word about the Ku Klux in his paper
for several months after its inception, the *Citizen* published
frequent notices during 1867 telling of the wonderful doings
of the mysterious new order that had sprung up in Giles

County — all as hearsay, of course: the editor knew nothing about it himself. 'What Does it Mean?' was the heading over an item in the issue of March 29 — which was, by the way, the first newspaper reference to the Ku Klux ever to appear in print. 'The following mysterious "Take Notice" was found under our door early yesterday morning,' the article stated, 'having doubtless been slipped there the night previous. Will anyone venture to tell us what it means, if it means anything at all? What is a "Kuklux Klan," and who is this "Grand Cyclops" that issues his mysterious and imperative orders? Can anyone give us any light on the subject? Here is the order':

TAKE NOTICE. — The Kuklux Klan will assemble at their usual place of rendezvous 'The Den,' on Tuesday night next, exactly at the hour of midnight, in costume and bearing the arms of the Klan.
  By order of the Grand Cyclops.

                                                    G. T.

Once begun, the publicity continued without abatement, and in the next issue of the *Citizen* appeared another notice headed 'Kuklux Klan' in which it was stated that another mysterious communication had been received from the Grand Cyclops, which it proceeded to print:

EDITOR OF THE CITIZEN: — You seem to express, in your last issue, some surprise and curiosity in regard to the Kuklux Klan, whose boldness and effrontery should so startle you. That they should dare send forth their imperial edicts; or that the GRAND CYCLOPS should presume to dispatch his Grand Turk with orders to his faithful followers, or that they should dare come so near your editorial sanctum as to leave one of their orders under your door. Now, sir, it is not to be wondered at that you should express feelings of astonishment that after night has spread her dark drapery over this sinful earth, when balmy sleep *should* enfold in her loving embrace all who have a clear conscience, and when all earth's innocent creatures should be enjoying happy dreams, and the hideous fiends of darkness and night are holding high carnival over a world that is all their own. We say, sir, that we do not wonder that you, together with this community, should express surprise at this; and we are not offended at your astonishment.

But seek not to know the object and designs of our 'Mystic Klan' or to impeach the authority of our Grand Cyclops to issue his mandates, for your efforts will be fruitless. If you see proper to publish our orders, and will do so, we thank you; but more of the Kuklux Klan you *cannot* know.

By order of the Klan.   G. S.

In the next issue of the *Citizen* this notice appeared:

KUKLUX KLAN

The Grand Turk will assemble the Klan at the Den, precisely at half past nine on Saturday night next. He will see that none come or be admitted without their costume, arms, etc. The Grand Bugler will not sound the 'assembly,' but the members will come simply from the notification of the Grand Turk.

By order of the Grand Cyclops.

G. S.

The appearance of these notices in the Pulaski paper created a buzz of comment in the little town, but everybody professed profound ignorance of the Ku Klux. Encouraged by the stir created by the appearance of the notices in his paper, the editor-Geni in his next issue printed a communication alleged to have been delivered him by a mysterious robed stranger. This letter was dated at 'Rendezvous No. 2; April 17th, 1867,' and said:

'"The public" seems not to comprehend or appreciate the high-toned objects and designs of the "Kuklux Klan," and are disposed to associate it with things vile and corrupt, mean and low. "The public" should not too hastily jump at conclusions at this *particular* time. Condemn not the object until you are sure it deserves condemnation. True, we hold our meetings in secret places. We have our reasons for that; and we have our secrets, signs, costumes, and mystic rights, and we entrust those to faithful breasts only. We have our reasons for that and, doubtless, "the public" can appreciate the importance of the Klan pursuing such a course.

'This is no joke either. This is cold, hard, earnest. Time will fully develop the objects of the "Kuklux Klan." Until such a development takes place, "the public" will please be patient.'

These 'communications' — really the official orders of the Grand Cyclops to the local Klansmen — were printed regularly in the Pulaski paper throughout the year. One notice enjoined the members to be prompt in assembling at the meeting on the following Saturday night, as the Cyclops was 'unwilling to encroach on the Holy Sabbath by transacting business after 12 o'clock.' In one notice dated from the 'Rendezvous in the Forest' it was stated that on account of the growth in membership it was necessary to abandon the former place of meeting (probably Colonel Martin's house) and that future meetings would be held at the forest rendezvous. Later notices were dated 'Rendezvous Under the Hill'; and still later, after moving into the blasted Carter house, notices were headed 'Den in the Ruins.' In May a notice was printed saying: 'The Klan will assemble at the "Den in the Fallen Forest" at the usual hour on Saturday night next, in full Klan costume and equipage, to meet the representatives of neighboring Klans from Elkton, Lynnville, Columbia and Franklin, and for the transaction of other important business.'

All this propaganda in the Pulaski paper was eagerly reprinted in other papers throughout the state and elsewhere, as evidence of some new and mysterious power astir, and editorial comments began to blossom out. Some of those who wrote about the Klan professed to consider it all a joke: others treated it seriously as a powerful and sinister force for evil which should be stamped out. Other friendly papers emphasized its benevolent purposes and deeds, one of them printing a story of how the Ku Klux visited the home of a poor widow there whose two sons had fallen in the Confederate service, leaving on her doorstep a package containing a generous purse of money and a supply of groceries and dry goods. But, however they treated it, the continued newspaper comment kept the public's interest alive, and encouraged the establishment of other Klans.

Throughout the early part of 1867 the Ku Klux began to attract public attention as the foremost topic of discussion. In fact, so much interest was manifested in the new and mysterious order and so many people indicated a desire to form local chapters, that the Pulaski *Citizen* finally carried the following advertisement for the order in the shape of an editorial:

'In answer to numerous correspondents from far and near, making inquiries of us in regard to the Ku Klux and how they must proceed to obtain a charter, we make the general reply that we can not give them any information positively, but we suggest to them that perhaps similar inquiries made through the post-office of the Great Grand Cyclops, who it is said makes his headquarters here, might receive a more satisfactory reply. We don't know how he would get the communications, as no one pretends to know who he is; but, after reading the numerous accounts of the wonderful things performed by the Ku Klux, we begin to believe that there are very few things impossible with them.'

Aside from all this free advertising, another reason for the instantaneous popularity of the new secret society was that it promised to fill what was coming to be recognized as a deeply felt need. This was the time of the development and growth of the secret organization among the negroes of the South known as the Union League or the Loyal League. This was a totally unrestrained and disorderly form of group activity in its Southern manifestation, used by low-grade white men as an instrumentality for organizing the negroes politically and keeping them unified by a steady infusion of inflammatory propaganda by imported flannel-mouthed orators. They were drilled in a formal catechism which taught them to hate and mistrust their former white friends. Bands of League members, armed to the teeth, prowled the country at all times, particularly at night, and the white people were increasingly terrified. Writing in later years, one of the negro leaders of that time frankly said: 'The fears of the whites with reference to these Leagues was well founded, for the men who controlled them had really nothing in view but public plunder.'

The part played by the Loyal Leagues and similar organizations in provoking the Southern people to defensive expedients was recognized by fair-minded Northern newspapers, and when in April, 1868, General Meade issued an order of suppression directed at the Ku Klux, the New York *Herald* commented: 'The order of General Meade providing for the suppression of the Ku Klux Klan will meet with the approval of all who espouse the cause of order and good government. But the General must not exercise his power on that organization alone. He must rigorously suppress the secret "Loyal Leagues" of negroes; for they are equally, if not more, pernicious in their influence than the white men's society. The arrogance of the negroes and their attempt to reduce the whites of the South to political vassalage by means of their "Loyal Leagues," and the many other outrages that have been committed by these same Leagues, are equally as dangerous to the peace and safety of society as are the retaliatory actions of the Ku Klux Klan.'

An Alabama paper in an editorial denouncing the Loyal League said: 'The League is nothing more than a nigger Ku Klux Klan'; going on to say: 'Of course we deprecate the appearance of ghosts in Tuscaloosa. But if Loyal Leagues continue, and negroes insist upon being insolent, we fear that some Grand Cyclops or other chief among the Ku Klux may visit our quiet community and put things in a topsy-turvy condition. Let Captain Heitburg break up the League and thus remove all temptation from the Kluxes to come here.' As the author of this editorial was himself an officer of the Ku Klux Klan, it provides further evidence that the negroes' Loyal League was a primary cause for the white men's Ku Klux Klan.

Aside from the menacing threat created by the setting up of these secret organizations of armed, irresponsible negroes, there were enough actual overt acts to convince the white citizens that their fears were by no means groundless. It was the usual practice for the Leagues, when they held their meetings, to throw out armed pickets in all directions about the building in which the meeting was being held, and they would not permit travelers and passers-by to walk in the road in front of the building. In Gainesville, Alabama, when some of the white people indignantly protested against such high-handed treatment, the negroes replied that 'they had the charter from the government at Washington, right direct, and they had the right to guard and they intended to do so.' As one of the residents later said: 'The negroes acted here just like an invading army after they had conquered everything and were going rough-shod over everything. They thought they were the big dogs in the ring.'

The importance of the psychology of the times cannot be overemphasized. Deeply rooted in the mind of every resident of the slave states was the latent fear of negro insurrection and race war. It was the chronic Southern nightmare. The bloody history of San Domingo was constantly in the white man's mind. He felt that he was living on a smoldering volcano of racial animosity; and he had an inherent fear of negro insurrection that was almost pathological. The sight of armed negroes meeting in secret conclaves filled him with a shuddering fear; and the thought of his own defenselessness was terrifying to him, especially when he thought of his wife and his children. Even so prejudiced an observer as the carpetbagger Judge Tourgee said: 'There is no doubt but this feeling, taken in connection with the enfranchisement of the blacks, induced thousands of good citizens to ally themselves with the Ku Klux upon the idea that they were acting in self-defense in so doing, and especially that they were securing the safety of their wives and children thereby.'

The newly freed negroes at that time were fond of repeating exultingly the old rural saying: 'The bottom rail's on top.' The white men remembered and were guided by the principle of another classic rustic aphorism of the South: 'Whenever two men are riding the same mule, one of them has got to ride in front.' The white people found themselves mounted on the mule with the negro; they meant to make it plain to him that they were going to ride in front.

Aside from the physical menace of the armed and truculent negroes, the principal grievance of the Southern people at this time was the quality of the office-holders under whose rule they were forced to live without having a voice in their selection. The almost unbelievable ignorance and incompetency of some of the negro officials foisted onto the people by the Reconstruction régime was well illustrated by a specimen of a release written by a North Carolina deputy United States marshal which was introduced in the testimony of one of the witnesses appearing before the committee in that state:

Linconton November the 2 day 1871

This is to surtifi that *John Doe* was Rain By Mea Beefore the
u. s. comishner R. P. Vest at the coat Hous at Lincoton of
Bein Berlongin to the inviserl Emphire and was Dischard of the
vilatin of the act of Congress charged in the With in Warrant.
This 2 day of November, 1871.

THOMAS W. WOMBLE, D. P. Marshall.

It was asserted that these 'indulgences' were for sale at the
time at prices ranging from five to ten dollars, depending on
the victim's capacity to pay, and that the suspected Ku Klux
who was willing to invest this much in one of these official
documents was safe from prosecution, at least temporarily.
This was an extreme case; but the general character of public
officials — black and white — was of a very low order. In-
competence and ignorance vied with dishonesty as a qualifica-
tion for office, and the plundering reached unprecedented
pinnacles as the audacity of the grafters grew with their realiza-
tion of their autocratic powers and their opportunities.

In such a state of affairs, it is not surprising that the white
people should come to feel that some sort of organization for
self-protection was needed, and throughout the South there
began spontaneously to spring up local defensive groups,
generally in the form of secret societies, designed primarily
to offset the aggressiveness of the Loyal Leagues. Sometimes
these groups had formal organizations and names, but generally
they were merely isolated bodies of alarmed citizens preparing
to protect themselves from whatever mischief might flow from
the secret meetings of the armed negroes. As the Ku Klux
Klan, with its awesome name, began to gain in fame, these
scattered, informal local organizations began to see in it the
possibility of a widespread secret society which could carry
on this defensive work in the South in a most effective manner;
and gradually these local groups became units in the network

of the Invisible Empire, as its sphere of influence increased.

Such methods of relief from unbearable official oppression are by no means rare in the annals of history. There have been numerous instances of it in our own country on a small scale, dating as far back as when the outraged citizens of Boston staged their historic tea party. It was, of course, an act of criminal outlawry for these men to disguise themselves and board a ship and destroy private property. If they had been apprehended and arraigned before a British jury they unquestionably would have been sentenced to prison terms; but history has been generally lenient with such criminals and the illegal form of their protest against oppression.

The members of the Boston Tea Party — and the members of the Ku Klux Klan — were but following a precedent set for them in earlier days in other lands. England had known the Moss Troopers, who took drastic means of manifesting their disapproval of the iron rule of the Normans; the misrule of Louis XI of France had resulted in the formation of that powerful and mysterious organization known as the Free Companions; Italy had its Carbonari during the Napoleonic wars. Freedom-loving people everywhere, when overwhelmed by oppression against which they had no other defense, have never hesitated to resort to secret and, if needs be, violent organizations for relief.

The Ku Klux Klan, from a casual and frivolous beginning, was destined to grow into perhaps the most powerful and extensive organization of the kind that ever existed. A thoughtful and observant Englishman named Robert Somers toured the United States in 1870–1871, and when he got back to London he published a book called *The Southern States Since the War* in which he had this to say about conditions in the South as he found them: 'A great terror reigned for a time among the white people; and in this situation the "Ku Klux" started into being. It was one of those secret organizations which spring up in disordered states of society, when the bonds of law and government are all but dissolved, and when no confidence is felt in the regular administration of justice. But the power with which the "Ku Klux" moved in many parts of the South, the knowledge it displayed of all that was going on, the fidelity with which its secret was kept, and the complacency with which it was regarded by the general community, gave this mysterious body a prominence and importance seldom attained by such illegal and deplorable associations. Nearly every respectable man in the Southern States was not only disfranchised but under fear of arrest or confiscation; the old foundations of authority were razed before any new ones had yet been laid, and in the dark and benighted interval the remains of the Confederate armies — swept, after a long and heroic day of fair fight, from the field — flitted before the eyes of the people in this weird and midnight shape of a "Ku Klux Klan." '

As a natural and almost inevitable reaction of effect to cause, the Ku Klux Klan in Tennessee had soon found itself operating as an active and effective protective organization of regulators. Before long it came to be that its principal activities were in the direction of discouraging the depredations of the Loyal Leaguers; and clashes between the two antagonistic groups soon got beyond the point of mere threats and warnings and developed into violence and even bloodshed.

As was unavoidable in meeting lawlessness with lawlessness, in combatting violence with violence, the performances of some of the members of the Klan began to overstep the bounds of prudence and discretion. As one of the originators of the order wrote later: 'The danger which the more prudent and thoughtful had apprehended as possible was now a reality. Rash, imprudent and bad men had gotten into the order.' Radical newspapers began to indulge in denunciations of this despicable secret society which, according to their professed belief, threatened a re-enslavement of the negroes, a disruption of the Union and other dire events.

Leading spirits within the Klan, although appreciating its effectiveness as a means of taming the insolent and vicious negroes, also began to recognize the fact that the thing was getting out of hand. They had set in motion a more powerful machine than they had ever expected; and, having started it, they felt an implied responsibility to attempt to guide that force in a proper direction. There was also a growing apprehension that the horrors of Reconstruction were likely to increase rather than diminish, and that the people of the South, in the absence of protection from the government, would have need for some sort of organized, controlled protective system of their own.

Accordingly notification was sent out to all the known Dens of Ku Klux instructing them to send representatives to a meeting to be held in Nashville in April, 1867. The immediate cause for this call is not known, but it is probably more than a coincidence that it followed closely after the enactment by Congress of the drastic Reconstruction Act which, in the boastful words of James A. Garfield, 'put the bayonet at the breast of every rebel in the South' and left the work of reconstruction in the hands of a hostile Congress 'utterly and absolutely.' The meeting, according to local tradition, was held in Room 10 of the Maxwell House, Nashville's big new hotel. This room was even larger than the usual spacious hotel room common to that day and time, and was amply large enough to accommodate representatives of all the Ku Klux Dens then in existence.

The purposes of the Nashville convention were enumerated as follows: 'To reorganize the Klan on a plan corresponding to its size and present purposes; to bind the isolated Dens together; to secure unity of purpose and concert of action; to hedge the members up by such limitations and regulations as are best adapted to restrain them within proper limits; to distribute the authority among prudent men at local centers and exact from them a close supervision of those under their charge.'

The principal order of business at the Nashville meeting was the adoption of an official constitution or, as the Ku Klux called it, 'Prescript.' The drafting of this formal statement of the purposes and basic laws of the order was entrusted to General George W. Gordon, an ex-Confederate officer then practicing law in Pulaski, who had been one of the first initiates into the original Den.

General Gordon's law office in Pulaski was just across a narrow passage from the office of the *Citizen*, which facilitated the job of having it printed after he had written out the first copy of it in longhand. A loose brick in the wall of the *Citizen* office concealed a hole which served as a secret post-office box for communications passing between the Klan and the printers so that there need be no contact between them. In this repository one morning Editor McCord found an unsigned letter asking how much it would cost to print a certain number of a small pamphlet of twenty-four pages, $3\frac{1}{2}$ x $5\frac{1}{2}$ inches. Mr. McCord wrote a letter to his unknown and mysterious prospective customer quoting a price of $100. The next morning he found in the hole the manuscript for the Prescript, attached to a hundred-dollar greenback, and the work proceeded. The printing was done at night, the type being set and the presses run by printers who were members of the Klan; and the pamphlets were stitched and folded by hand, being trimmed with a sharp-bladed shoe knife on the floor of the attic of the printing shop. The name of the order was nowhere mentioned. Wherever the words 'Ku Klux' were called for in the text there appeared merely the cabalistic symbol * *. In place of 'Klan' there was *.

In the first sentence of its preamble the Prescript stated: 'We recognize our relations to the United States government and acknowledge the supremacy of its laws.' Then there followed a list of the titles of the officers and their duties, the division of the territory in which the order was to operate, provision for election of officers, a tribunal of justice and other miscellaneous provisions including the obligation to be taken by new members.

The Prescript provided that the whole territory covered by the operations of the order (the Southern States) should be called the Empire; that the Empire should be divided into Realms (corresponding to states); each Realm into Dominions (groups of counties, approximating congressional districts); the Dominions into Provinces (counties); and the Provinces into Dens.

The officers, it was provided, should consist of a Grand Wizard of the Empire (the supreme official), to be assisted by ten Genii; a Grand Dragon of the Realm, with his eight Hydras, for each state; a Grand Titan, with six Furies, for each Dominion; a Grand Giant, with four Night Hawks, for the Provinces. The chief officer of the local Den was still styled the Grand Cyclops, with two Night Hawks; the other officers of the Den being a Grand Magi, a Grand Monk, a Grand Exchequer, a Grand Turk, a Grand Scribe, a Grand Sentinel and a Grand Ensign. 'The body politic,' it was specified, 'shall be designated and known as Ghouls.'

The care and precision exercised in drawing up this set of rules and regulations for what was now recognized as being at least potentially a powerful force for good or evil is evidenced by the elaborate and minute specifications as to the duties of the officers. Taking the Grand Wizard for an example, his functions are set forth as follows:

'Art. IV. Sec. 1 — It shall be the duty of the Grand Wizard, who is the Supreme Officer of the Empire, to communicate with and receive reports from the Grand Dragons of the Realms, as to the condition, strength, efficiency and progress of the *s within their respective Realms. And he shall communicate from time to time, to all subordinate *s, through the

Grand Dragon, the condition, strength, efficiency and progress of the *s throughout his vast Empire; and such other information as he may deem expedient to impart. And it shall further be his duty to keep by his G Scribe a list of the names (without any caption or explanation whatever) of the Grand Dragons of the different Realms of his Empire, and shall number such Realms with the Arabic numerals, 1, 2, 3, &, *ad finem*. And he shall instruct his Grand Exchequer as to the appropriation and disbursement which he shall make of the revenue of the * that comes to his hands. He shall have through his Subalterns and Deputies power for the organization and establishment of subordinate *s. And he shall have the further power to appoint his Genii; also a Grand Scribe and a Grand Exchequer for his Department, and to appoint and ordain Special Deputy Grand Wizards to assist him in the more rapid and effectual dissemination and establishment of the * throughout his Empire. He is further empowered to appoint and instruct Deputies, to organize and control Realms, Dominions, Provinces and Dens, until the same shall elect a Grand Dragon, a Grand Titan, a Grand Giant and a Grand Cyclops in the manner hereafter provided. And when a question of paramount importance to the interest or prosperity of the * arises, not provided for in this Prescript, he shall have power to determine such question, and his decision shall be final, until the same shall be provided for by amendment as hereinafter provided.'

In the section covering the election of officers it was provided that 'The Grand Wizard of the Empire is hereby created, to serve three years from the First Monday in May, 1867, after the expiration of which time, biennial elections shall be held for that office.' All the officers above those of a Den were to be elected every two years; but the Grand Cyclops and other officers of the Den were to serve only six-months terms.

The Prescript also provided the oaths and obligations. Any candidate for admission to the Klan was required to take this preliminary obligation before he could be taken to the Grand Cyclops for examination. 'I do solemnly swear or affirm that I will never reveal anything that I may this day (or night) learn concerning the * *. So help me God.'

If the Grand Cyclops looked with favor on the candidate's qualifications and he was permitted to advance to the point of the initiation ceremonies, he was then required by the Prescript to take this oath:

'I, ——————, of my own free will and accord, and in the presence of Almighty God, do solemnly swear or affirm that I will never reveal to anyone, not a member of the * *, by any intimation, sign, symbol, word or act, or in any other manner whatever, any of the secrets, signs, grips, pass words, mysteries or purposes of the * * or that I am a member of the same or that I know anyone who is a member, and that I will abide by the Prescript and Edicts of the * *. So help me God.'

There seems to be nothing more impressive or permanently binding about this obligation than there is about a number of other similar oaths taken by initiates into any secret order; but one of the most notable things about the Ku Klux was that its members were in some way given an ineradicable conviction that this oath superseded and vitiated all other oaths they might take. Certainly there were large numbers of the members of the order caught in the net spread out when the Federal Government conducted its South-wide investigation; but although they mounted the witness stand and took the oath prescribed to tell the whole truth and nothing but the truth, they obviously considered their Ku Klux oath as entitled to greater consideration. Even long years after the Ku Klux had disappeared as an active force, old men were reluctant to discuss its affairs, feeling still bound by that bond of secrecy; and even when they did in their old age weaken to the point of dropping a few morsels of information, they always did so with a stealthy and guilty air.

Aside from the printed obligation there was a printed 'Interdiction' providing that 'The origin, designs, mysteries and ritual of this * * shall never be written, but the same shall be communicated orally.'

For the purpose of communicating Ku Klux messages in code, setting the time of meetings, etc., there was a so-called 'Register' which specified adjectives to be used in place of the customary designations of the months, days of the weeks and hours of the day. The symbols for the months were: January, Dismal; February, Dark; March, Furious; April, Portentous; May, Wonderful; June, Alarming; July, Dreadful; August, Terrible; September, Horrible; October, Melancholy; November, Mournful; December, Dying. White was the code word for Sunday; Green for Monday; Blue, Tuesday; Black, Wednesday; Yellow, Thursday; Crimson, Friday; Purple, Saturday. The hours of the clock were also covered by the code: 1 o'clock would be the Fearful Hour; 2, Startling; 3, Awful; 4, Woeful; 5, Horrid; 6, Bloody; 7, Doleful; 8, Sorrowful; 9, Hideous; 10, Frightful; 11, Appalling; 12, Last.

This edition of the Prescript opened and closed with impressive poetic quotations, vaguely signifying the mysterious purposes of the order. On the title-page was printed '*Damnant quod non intelligunt*' (They condemn what they do not understand), a challenging retort to the critics of the Ku Klux; and at the top and bottom of each page was a more or less pertinent Latin phrase, some being quotations from Homer and Virgil, which gave some idea of the impelling principles of the organizers: 'Let there be justice, though the heavens fall'; 'Truth is mighty and must prevail'; 'Justice sometimes sleeps but never dies'; 'The cause having ceased, the effect will cease'; 'No one harms us unpunished.' On the last page was this L'Envoi: 'To the lovers of Law and Order, Peace and Justice, we send greetings; and to the shades of the venerated Dead we affectionately dedicate the * *'; followed by the Latin phrase: '*Ad* *unum omnes,*' the classical equivalent of the famous slogan of d'Artagnan, 'One for all and all for one.'

Some time in 1868, probably in January or February or the early spring, there was adopted and distributed what was denominated on its title-page a 'Revised and Amended Prescript of the Order of the * * *.' This revised and amended edition followed the same general·form of the original, one important difference being the inclusion of a declaration of the 'Character and Objects of the Order' in these words:

'This is an institution of Chivalry, Humanity, Mercy and Patriotism; embodying in its genius and its principles all that is chivalric in conduct, noble in sentiment, generous in manhood and patriotic in purpose; its peculiar objects being

'First: To protect the weak, the innocent, and the defenseless from the indignities, wrongs and outrages of the lawless, the violent and the brutal; to relieve the injured and oppressed; to succor the suffering and unfortunate, and especially the widows and orphans of Confederate soldiers.

'Second: To protect and defend the Constitution of the United States, and all laws passed in conformity thereto, and to protect the States and the people thereof from all invasion from any source whatever.

'Third: To aid and assist in the execution of all constitutional laws, and to protect the people from unlawful seizure, and from trial except by their peers in conformity with the laws of the land.'

A significant change in the revised Prescript was the elimination from the Grand Wizard's duties of the obligation to take steps looking to the 'rapid and effectual dissemination and establishment of the * throughout his Empire.' Presumably there was no longer any necessity for this provision, the Klan having been thoroughly 'disseminated and established' since the adoption of the original Prescript.

The new Prescript also had more detailed and elaborate

specifications for the setting up and conduct of the 'Judiciary,' the last section of this article providing that 'The several courts herein provided for shall be governed in their deliberations, proceedings and judgments by the rules and regulations governing the proceedings of regular Courts-martial.'

Another noteworthy change was that the revised Prescript definitely mentioned the names of the states embraced in the Empire. 'The territory embraced within the jurisdiction of this Order,' it said, 'shall be coterminus with the States of Maryland, Virginia, North Carolina, South Carolina, Georgia, Florida, Alabama, Mississippi, Louisiana, Texas, Arkansas, Missouri, Kentucky and Tennessee; all combined constituting the Empire.'

It was specifically provided in both the original and the revised Prescripts that the Grand Cyclops should govern his Den 'in accordance with and in conformity to the Provisions of this Prescript — a copy of which shall in all cases be obtained before the formation of a Den begins.' The Prescript was the sacred book of the Order.

The article covering 'Eligibility for Membership' was considerably amplified and elaborated, notably by the inclusion of a list of interrogatories to be asked prospective candidates immediately following the preliminary obligation:

'1st. Have you ever been rejected, upon application for membership in the * * *, or have you ever been expelled from the same?

'2nd. Are you now, or have you ever been, a member of the Radical Republican party, or either of the organizations known as the "Loyal League" and the "Grand Army of the Republic"?

'3rd. Are you opposed to the principles and policy of the Radical party, and to the Loyal League, and the Grand Army of the Republic, so far as you are informed of the character and purposes of those organizations?

'4th. Did you belong to the Federal army during the late war, and fight against the South during the existence of the same?

'5th. Are you opposed to negro equality, both social and political?

'6th. Are you in favor of a white man's government in this country?

'7th. Are you in favor of Constitutional liberty, and a government of equitable laws instead of a government of violence and oppression?

'8th. Are you in favor of maintaining the Constitutional rights of the South?

'9th. Are you in favor of the re-enfranchisement and emancipation of the white man of the South and the restitution to the Southern people of all their rights, alike proprietary, civil and political?'

If the candidate successfully ran the gauntlet of this searching interrogation he was carried on in the initiatory process. If he gave the wrong answers to any of the questions he was not regarded as proper timber for membership and he was forthwith discharged and dismissed 'after being solemnly admonished by the initiating officer of the deep secrecy to which the oath already taken has bound him, and that the extreme penalty of the law will follow a violation of the same.'

For some undiscoverable reason there were several changes made in the lurid adjectives signifying the months and the hours and the colors representing the days of the week. Perhaps there had been a 'leak' which destroyed the value of the old code; at any rate, the changes were made. To the Register was also added the code word 'CUMBERLAND,' which appears to have been provided as a means of using letters of the alphabet to stand for figures, the letters in the word CUMBER-LAND standing successively for the numbers 1, 2, 3, 4, 5, 6, 7, 8, 9, 0.

If the Grand Cyclops wished to call a meeting of his Den for say, Thursday night, July 25, at nine o'clock, he would post in some prominent place or advertise in the paper specifying the Purple Night, Painful Moon, UE, Awful Hour, and every Ku Klux would know what was meant.

Another noteworthy change made in the style of the new Prescript was the use of three stars instead of two in the blank space left in the name of the order in the official title, this marking the change from the two-word title 'Kuklux Klan' to the later three-word style 'Ku Klux Klan.' Another interesting detail was that before printing the second edition of the little book the Pulaski printing shop had evidently augmented its font of type and was able to use stars throughout the book in the blank spaces where the name of the organization was for purposes of secrecy omitted. In the original edition Mr. McCord's supply of stars was exhausted before the last page was reached, and in setting up the last line of the Final Obligation it was necessary to indicate the omission of the name by the use of that familiar printers' ornament, the dagger, in place of the stars. When a copy of this Prescript fell into the hands of the Congressional Committee later, they sought to make a mare's nest of this detail by suggesting that the daggers were used at this particular point as an indication of the tragic fate which would befall a violator of the obligation. This gave a sinister touch to the proceedings, but the prosaic fact was that the typographical change was due to nothing worse than the inadequacy of the Pulaski *Citizen's* supply of type.

III. HOW THE
KLAN OPERATED

D URING THE PERIOD of its active existence the Ku Klux
Klan was a secret society in the strictest sense of the word;
so much so, in fact, that there were even doubts expressed as to
whether such an organization actually existed. At the time
there was no information whatever available as to its form of
organization and its methods of procedure. Ku Klux and
mystery were synonyms.

In the absence of any accurate and reliable information,
the magazines and newspapers of the time vied with each other
in printing the 'revelations' and 'confessions' of alleged members;
but these were, almost without exception, wholly spurious.
During the Klan's declining days there were some actual confessions obtained from genuine members which threw real light
on the workings of the Ku Klux organization; but these so-called
confessions of the earlier period of the Klan's lifetime were
generally the product of some gifted writer's highly developed
imagination, highly seasoned with the blood-and-thunder
touch and more than a dash of the gruesome. They were designed
to pander to the popular conception of what the wicked Ku
Klux did, how they looked and how they operated; and they
accomplished this purpose in the most thorough and effective
manner.

An outrageous, but characteristic, misrepresentation of the

facts was an alleged eye-witness's account of a Ku Klux initiation which was printed in the New York *Illustrated News* in May, 1868. The author of this shameless fake told of how he had interviewed an individual, identified merely as 'L. G. W.,' who had been initiated into the order and who was so revolted by the gory nature of the proceedings that he felt justified in violating his oath of secrecy and pouring his horrid story into the willing ears of the *Illustrated News* writer.

'According to L. G. W.,' the story went, 'he upon the initiatory night was first conducted into the interior of a rude cavern, fitfully lighted with flaring pine knots, and filled with men in the usual ghostly disguise adopted by the Order under like circumstances — black mask, graveyard shroud, etc. Behind a small table, bearing the simple but suggestive garniture of a human skull, stood the Grand Cyclops, a gigantic man, naked to the waist, with a dagger in his right hand, and the whole upper portion of his body smeared with warm, smoking blood. The walls of the cavern were also lined with rows of grinning skeletons. At a signal from the chief, several of the assassins proceeded to a small sub-cavity in the darkest corner of the cave and brought therefrom a lusty negro, securely gagged and bound, whom they placed at full length on a sort of rude altar, immediately in front of the chief's little table. The wretched negro rolled up his eyes and quivered with terror in every limb, but could not move. Then the novice was informed that, before he could be admitted into the order, he must prove his fearlessness of murder by striking the victim to the heart and staining his hands in the gushing life blood; and the knife was placed in his hand for that purpose. The candidate at first drew back in horror at such a proposition, but the fierce glare of the eyes and the ominous clicking of firearms around him convinced him that his own life would be the forfeiture in case of refusal. So, closing his eyes, he rushed forward desperately and dealt the fatal blow. Then, after all the members had dipped their fingers in the gushing blood of the human victim, the oath was administered, the constitution signed and the ceremony of initiation rendered complete.'

This article is not without merit as an extreme example of the hair-raising school of writing so prevalent in the cheap magazines of the time, but it should be read and evaluated on the basis of what it is — highly imaginative fiction and not history.

\ Fortunately we are not dependent upon such raw-head-and-bloody-bones stories for a knowledge of Ku Klux affairs, as it is possible at the present time to present a fairly accurate account of the Klan's methods of operation, its oaths, disguises, passwords, etc., based on the accounts of witnesses before the Congressional Committee and the confessions of recusant Ku Klux in the courts, amplified and corroborated by the stories cautiously told in later years by surviving members of the organization.

In its system of procedure the Ku Klux Klan presented a strange combination of discipline and irresponsibility. They did not recognize the existence of any legal authority to which they were properly subject; but within their own organization they had rigid rules of conduct which, in the beginning at least, were firmly enforced and obeyed. It should be borne in mind, of course, that the Klan changed complexion with the times. Not until it had been in existence a year or more did it take on the self-conferred police powers which came to be its principal function. It was organized as a social and benevolent organization, and that it actually operated along those lines in its infancy is shown by this item which appeared in a Nashville paper early in 1868:

'The Franklin *Review* of yesterday related that the Ku Klux a few nights since visited the home of a poor widow whose two sons had fallen in the Confederate service, leaving on her doorstep a package containing one hundred dollars and a quantity

of domestics, calicoes and other dry goods. A widow lady of
Williamson County, with three children dependent on her for
support, was the grateful recipient of a similar package, inside
of which she found one hundred dollars in currency and a letter
which stated that the writer was formerly an intimate companion and fellow-soldier of her only son who was killed while
a member of a Confederate regiment.'

Admittedly the Ku Klux soon outgrew this stage of harmless
knight-errantry; but even in its more violent days there lingered
about its proceedings an incongruous reminiscence of this early
courtliness which lent a grotesque air to some of its doings.
A carpetbagger who was whipped by the Ku Klux in Mississippi
voluntarily commented on their discipline and generally good
behavior when they honored him with their attention. 'They
treated me very courteously,' he said, 'except the beating they
gave me; but otherwise I was not insulted or treated unkindly
at all. One of them commenced to curse; he began "God
damn ——" when the captain stopped him and said he should
not do that. They were civil in their manner.' It is difficult
to understand how the sting of the lash could in any degree be
ameliorated by the polite manner of the flogger; but this victim
seemed to appreciate being whipped in a 'courteous and gentlemanly manner.' Similar testimony was given by a North
Carolina scalawag who was disciplined by the Ku Klux. When
an excitable and impulsive member of the band began to
heap abuse on the victim, suggesting that he should be killed,
he was rebuked by the leader with a stern 'Remember your
oath: Justice and humanity,' and, the abusive member having
been reduced to a proper gentlemanly state, the whipping
continued in the proper manner.

Some explanation of the incongruity of this may be found
in the fact that the Ku Klux did not regard themselves as law-
breakers but as law-enforcers. As one of them said to a prospective member in Mississippi: 'We have got an organization

that is to whip out everything; and all the damned scalawags, carpetbaggers and nigger-equality men will have to leave the country. We are going to restore law and order.' The time was out of joint, and they were born to set it right. They went about their business in a manner which was sometimes violent; but they felt no more sense of personal turpitude than does the executioner who springs the fatal trap of the gallows. They were instruments of justice, and they felt a sense of obligation to carry out their system of punishment in as orderly a manner as was possible under such disorderly conditions as then prevailed.

Preposterous as it may seem, the Ku Klux considered themselves as something equivalent to an entire system of jurisprudence compressed into one body, combining the functions of prosecuting attorney, grand jury, trial judge and executioner. Until the days of the Klan's degeneration this power was not generally abused. On the contrary, in the proceedings of the individual Dens there was generally pretty close adherence to the prescribed policy of having a council or committee which decided all matters involving raids or punishments to be meted out to alleged offenders against the principles of the order. In the open meetings of the Den suggestions would be made as to persons who were thought to be in need of the Klan's ministrations; but it was the council which considered these matters, deliberated over them and decided what should be done. If it were concluded that a raid should be made, the individual members to take part in it were designated and the nature of the punishment prescribed. The council was in the nature of a grand jury. If it reported 'no true bill' that was supposed to end that particular case.

The respect for this phase of the Klan's mode of procedure, even among the most disorderly elements participating in its activities during its declining days, was shown by an incident in North Carolina. In 1871 four overzealous members of the newly organized Young's Mountain Den, impatient to get to work at their new profession of Ku Kluxing and unwilling to wait until they were detailed by the council, went to a neighboring still-house where they partook freely of its product and then decided on their own initiative to make a visit of remonstrance to a widow, Mrs. Murphy, who had a negro man living on her premises with whom they suspected her of being 'too thick.' Accordingly they put on their new disguises and called at Mrs. Murphy's home where, in the words of one of their fellows, 'they cursed her right smart and rode her horse and her mule off up the road about two miles and then turned them loose in the road.' One of the raiders, rendered careless by his inebriation, unwittingly left his calling-card at Mrs. Murphy's, dropping in her yard his hat with his name written in the inside. As a result of this, all four of the volunteer regulators were arrested and lodged in the Marion jail.

The next meeting of their Den considered their case, and it was proposed that the members storm the jail and release the prisoners, this being a part of the usual Ku Klux procedure in such instances. The other members of the Den, however, balked at the idea of exposing themselves to the danger of an attack on the jail for the purpose of rescuing brethren who had been arrested for an entirely unauthorized and unofficial raid, and they refused to take any part in the proposed rescue work. The Cyclops, however, felt that the honor of the Ku Klux was at stake; and so he called on a neighboring Den in South Carolina to send a rescue party to Marion, which the South Carolinians obligingly did, and the four prisoners were released and managed to make their escape from the country.

In sending to a neighbor Den for assistance, the Cyclops of the Young's Mountain Den was following the regular Ku Klux plan. Ordinary visits of threat or admonition were attended to by each Den in its own territory; but when there was more serious work afoot it was generally arranged to have it done by a band of Klansmen from some other community. This had a two-fold purpose: The raiders, if accidentally exposed to view, were less likely to be identified, being among strangers; and the local boys who were suspected of being (and were) members of the Klan were able to show themselves in public while the raid was taking place and thus establish ironclad alibis. This system of interlocking co-operation was practiced throughout the Invisible Empire, and was highly effective in preventing detection and identification.

The members of the Young's Mountain Den who made the unauthorized raid on Mrs. Murphy were violating one of the fundamental principles of the Klan's code. The individual members, the 'ghouls,' as they were officially designated, were like the privates in an army. They were supposed to obey the orders of their superiors; and action on individual initiative was severely frowned upon. In at least one known instance in Tennessee a Klansman was tried and executed by the members of his own Den because he whipped a negro for personal reasons while wearing his Ku Klux disguise.. In the organization of local Dens it was customary to place the official positions in the hands of men of maturity and responsibility, with some degree of executive ability and leadership; and, between the ghouls and the officers, the personnel of the local Klan generally represented the major part of the active men of the community. Newspaper editors made especially valuable members, as that gave the Ku Klux a mouthpiece and advertising medium; and it is remarkable how many editors in the South were members of the order or popularly understood to be such.

The Klan also had a system of auxiliary non-members, somewhat similar to the 'fellow-travelers' of the modern Communist Party, composed of those who were worth more to the order outside of it than in. A typical instance of this was supplied by a well-to-do planter who lived on a farm in Tennessee not far from the Kentucky line. One day he was visited by a

friend of his, a prominent doctor from a near-by town, who led
the conversation into a discussion of the parlous times in which
they were living and ascertained beyond any doubt that his
host was a true-blue anti-Radical. Before leaving, the doctor
intimated to him that he might be called upon to be of service.

'Don't ask any questions,' he was warned, 'no matter what
strange things may happen; just keep quiet. If you get any
messages signed with three K's, like this (showing him the
proper arrangement), do whatever is asked. If it is something
that involves you in any expense, make out your bill by merely
marking down the amount on a piece of paper — no heading
nor items nor statement, just the figures — and present it to the
president of the bank in town and he will pay it. But say nothing and don't ask questions. Then if you should be called on
by the Radicals why you know nothing about the matter, and
you can't get in any trouble.'

The next day after this visit the farmer received a note, signed
with the cabalistic K K K, saying simply: 'Supper for six men,
feed for six horses, at the old schoolhouse, nine o'clock tonight.'
The farmer dutifully sent the suppers and the feed to the
schoolhouse by a white man who worked for him, the doctor
having assured him that this hired man 'could be trusted,' which
was presumed to mean that he was a member of the Ku Klux.
At any rate, he performed the task assigned him and manifested
no surprise at being asked to do so. That night at a village in
Kentucky, twenty miles away, two particularly objectionable
carpetbaggers who had been preaching social equality to the
negroes were visited by a party of Ku Klux in disguise and
given a severe whipping. The farmer, the next time he was in
town, went to the bank and without a word presented to the
president a piece of paper on which was written '$3.' The
banker, also without comment, handed over the indicated
amount, and the transaction was closed.

The next week he received a note saying: 'Have your roan

mare left saddled and bridled under the cedar tree in the corner of your south pasture tonight at midnight.' That night a bumptious officer of the offensive Brownlow militia was shot. One of the natives of the town was strongly suspected of the shooting, but that night he disappeared. How he made his escape was a mystery, as he had no horse and none of the horses in town were missing. A few days later the friendly farmer was asked to send to a little deserted cabin in the near-by woods sufficient provisions for one man for a week; and he found his mare one morning in her stall in the stable innocently munching her oats.

Similar assignments were frequently carried out, the thrifty farmer always presenting his terse invoices to the town banker and always being paid without question or comment. When the Ku Klux investigation was being carried on this man was called as a witness and bombarded with questions: Had he ever belonged to the Ku Klux Klan? Why, no; certainly not. Had he ever seen a Ku Klux? No. Had he ever seen men in disguise? No. Had strangers ever stopped at his house? Had suspicious characters been about? Had the Ku Klux ever asked him to help them? No; no; no; he truthfully answered.

Such methods of indirection, however, were the exception rather than the rule. Generally the Klan would hold its meetings, pass its judgments and execute its sentences within the active body of its membership, following a systematic order of procedure. The Grand Cyclops of the Den would send out word by the Night Hawks when a meeting was to be held, naming the place, all communications being oral to prevent the existence of any incriminating documentary evidence; and the members would, one by one, gather at the prescribed rendezvous.

It was customary for the local Dens to have more than one place of meeting, and they would rotate their gatherings between these places so as to avoid attracting attention by too frequently getting together in the same place. In Nashville, for example, the Den commanded by Captain John W. Morton met sometimes in the Maxwell House, sometimes in a room over Smith's drugstore on the corner of Church and Vine Streets, sometimes in a room on the top floor of the Masonic Temple, and many times over the storeroom of the N.C. & St. L. Railway. Another rendezvous of this Den was the old powder magazine in the abandoned Fort Negley. In the rural sections meetings were generally held in the open air, mostly in the woods, the place of one meeting being decided upon at the previous gathering. In Memphis a favorite meeting place was in the woods east of town which is now comprised in Overton Park.

At these regular meetings, generally held about once a week, the conduct of any offensive characters would be discussed; and, if the majority voted to punish them, it would be done on a prescribed night. Sometimes it was deemed necessary only to post notices of warning which, in many cases, were sufficient to induce the offenders to mend their ways and avoid the necessity for further treatment in their cases.

The hailing signs, passwords and so forth in use in various parts of the Invisible Empire differed in some minor ways; but they all showed plainly their common origin, the variations doubtless being due to the natural errors incident to oral transmission.

William K. Owens, who confessed that he was a member of Rufus McLain's Den in Yorkville, South Carolina, known as 'The Black Panthers,' stated in his confession that the sign of recognition was three strokes with the left hand against the left ear, the reply or response being the right hand struck on the pocket or put in the pocket, 'done as careless as possible.' The grip, as he described it, was 'the forefinger on the muscle of the arm or wrist, and the little fingers interlaced.' The password, according to Owens, was not pronounced but syllabled.

'If you meet a man at night and think he belongs to the order, and you wish to find out, you spell out the word S–A–Y. If he belongs he will reply N–O–T–H–I–N–G, spelling it.' The word of distress, he said, was 'Avalanche.'

In one county of North Carolina the following colloquy was employed in challenging and answering the challenge:

'Who comes there?'

'A friend.'

'A friend of what?'

'My country.'

'What country?'

'I S–A–Y.'

'N–O–T–H–I–N–G'

'The word?'

'Retribution.'

John R. Taliaferro, who testified that he was a member of a Den in Noxubee County, Mississippi, gave 'Avalanche' as the word of distress. Taliaferro said that the sign of recognition at night, when two parties were going in opposite directions, was for one of them to exclaim: 'Hail.' The other party answered: 'Hail who?' The first party said, 'Mount'; the other replied: 'Nebo' — Mount Nebo being the countersign at night. This password, according to Taliaferro, was used not only in Noxubee County, but also in Winston, Lauderdale, Kemper, Lowndes and Oktibbeha, and Pickens County, Alabama. The symbol of recognition, he said, was for one party to draw his right hand across his chin, the other responding, if a member, by taking hold of the left lapel of his coat and shaking it.

G. Wiley Wells, United States district attorney for the northern district of Mississippi, testified that the word 'Avalanche' was used in Tishomingo County, sometimes alternated with 'Blucher' or 'Star.' 'Who comes there?' was the challenge, to which the reply was 'You know who.' The response to this was 'I know what?' Then, upon coming together, they would extend their hands and give the grip, rubbing the forefinger twice across the wrist. 'In wishing to recognize a party in the daytime,' he said, 'it was done by taking hold of the lapel of the coat, with the thumb of the hand extended to the front partly, and in the air. The response was to place the closed hand on the right hip, with the thumb extended straight out. Another sign of recognition used was to stroke the beard once or twice. If the party recognized this sign, he responded by placing his thumbs in the waistband of his pants, with his forefingers extended.'

Another confessed Ku Klux told that the hailing sign in use by his Den was in three parts: The hailing party would, first, stroke the fingers of his right hand briskly over his hair, beginning at the right forehead and bringing the hand around back of the ear — a natural gesture, as though he were merely stroking his hair back. The answer was the same sign made with the left hand over the left ear. Second, the hailing party would stick the fingers of his right hand into his trousers pocket, with the thumb left outside the pocket, at the same time bringing the right heel into the hollow of the left foot. The answer was the same hand-sign with the left hand, and the left heel brought into the hollow of the right foot. Where a further precaution was needed, the first man would finger the right lapel of his coat with his right hand 'as though searching for a pin,' the answer being the same gesture with the left hand. The grip, this man testified, 'was very simple, being given simply by placing the forefinger of the right hand on the pulse of the person whose hand was being gripped.' (Incidentally, it is interesting to relate, these signs were recognized and confirmed as authentic by a surviving Ku Klux in Tennessee.) The favored password in this Den, as in many others, was 'Avalanche' — and it may be more than a coincidence that this was the name of the leading Democratic paper in Memphis, the home of Grand Wizard Forrest.

A sign of recognition used in Georgia was thus described by a member there: 'Supposing we were in a crowd or in a house where there were a great many people together, and he wanted to know whether I belonged to the organization or not, he would put his foot on top of mine and press it and say: "I ask your pardon." If I belonged to the order I would remark: "It is granted." Then, if I met with a gentleman and shook hands with him, or anything of that sort, and asked him how he was, if he belonged to the organization he would say: "I am *well*, how are you?" "Well" was the word.'

In South Carolina a system of warnings, to be used in public and in the daytime, consisted of taps. 'If you are on the street and you see a man standing about and you are not close to him, if you give the three taps — first one, and after that two together — if he belongs to the Ku Klux he will respond. Sometimes it is used as a caution. If you come up in a crowd of men and see a man in it talking too much and about to divulge something, you can make the taps with your foot on the ground. It wouldn't be noticed by the others unless they were members; and he would understand the meaning of it — to be careful of the crowd.'

In the testimony adduced before the Congressional Committee there were quoted several variants from the official oath as proscribed in the Original Prescript, which was:

'I, ——————, of my own free will and accord, and in the presence of Almighty God, do solemnly swear or affirm that I will never reveal to any one, not a member of the * * by any intimation, sign, symbol, word or act, or in any other manner whatever, any of the secrets, signs, grips, pass-words, mysteries or purposes of the * *, or that I am a member of the same or that I know any one who *is* a member, and that I will abide by the Prescript and Edicts of the * *. So help me God.'

This oath, with one or two unimportant verbal changes, was also prescribed by the Revised and Amended Prescript; but it is interesting to observe the variations between this and the several different but similar obligations reported by some of the witnesses. In North Carolina, for example, there were three entirely different versions introduced into the record. What came to be known as 'the Shotwell oath,' it having been testified that Captain R. A. Shotwell, as chief of the Klan in Rutherford County, had administered it, was as follows:

'I, ——————, before the great immaculate God of heaven and earth, do take and subscribe to the following sacred and binding oath and obligation: I promise and swear that I will uphold and defend the Constitution of the United States as handed down by our forefathers, in its original purity. I promise and swear that I will reject and oppose the principles of the Radical party in all its forms, and forever maintain and contend that intelligent white men shall govern this country. I promise and pledge myself to assist, according to my pecuniary circumstances, all brothers in distress. Females, widows and their households shall ever be specially in my care and protection. I promise and swear that I will obey all instructions given me by my chief; and should I ever divulge, or cause to be divulged, any secrets, signs or passwords of the Invisible Empire, I must meet with the fearful and just penalty of the traitor, which is death — death — death, at the hands of the brethren.'

This seems to have been beyond question the oath used in North Carolina, as it was repeated from memory by J. R. De Priest, who admitted that he was the Cyclops of Den No. 3 in Rutherford County. In examining the North Carolina recusants it was the practice of the examining attorneys to read this oath to them and ask them if they recognized it or if it was the oath they took, all of them giving generally affirmative answers.

David Schenck, who was accused of being the Ku Klux chieftain in Lincoln County, but who denied that honor and vehemently insisted that he was not even a member of the Ku Klux Klan, admitted that in 1868 he had joined a secret or-

ganization 'for mutual protection and benefit' which he said
was called the Invisible Empire. The oath he took, he said,
did not give any intimation of violence or obligate the swearer
to obey his superior's orders, but was 'substantially the obligation published by the military authorities at Yorkville, South
Carolina.' This oath, obtained from a confessed Ku Klux at
Yorkville, was as follows:

'I, —————————, before the Immaculate Judge of heaven and
earth, and upon the Holy Evangelists of Almighty God, do,
of my own free will and accord, subscribe to the following
sacredly binding obligations:

'First. We are on the side of justice, humanity and constitutional liberty, as bequeathed to us in its purity by our forefathers.

'Second. We oppose and reject the principles of the Radical
party.

'Third. We pledge mutual aid to each other in sickness,
distress and pecuniary embarrassment.

'Fourth. Females, friends, widows and their households shall
ever be special objects of our regard and protection.

'Fifth. Any member divulging or causing to be divulged
any of the foregoing obligations shall meet the fearful penalty
and traitor's doom, which is death, death, death!'

In addition to these, there was also quoted in the North
Carolina testimony the text of what was described as 'the Leach
oath,' it being attributed to Governor Leach. It was much
more discursive and verbose than the Shotwell or Yorkville
oaths, but was substantially the same in import. The oaths
were generally memorized and transmitted orally, and it is
not surprising that differences in verbiage should have crept in,
reflecting the vocabular fluency of the votaries.

Similar evidences of individualism and initiative are to be
seen in other occasional departures from the formula laid down
in the Prescript. For instance, some witnesses speak of seeing
bands of Ku Klux carrying a flag with the letters 'K K K' on it.

Such flags were carried by some bands, and one such made of rawhide is preserved in a museum at Florence, Alabama, but they were entirely unauthorized and unofficial. The Original Prescript's Article X was headed 'Ensign' and provided:

'The Grand Banner of this * shall be in the form of an isosceles triangle, five feet long and three feet wide at the staff. The material shall be Yellow, with a Red scalloped border, about three inches in width. There shall be painted upon it, in black, a Dracovolans,† or Flying Dragon, with the following motto inscribed above the Dragon,

'QUOD SEMPER, QUOD UBIQUE, QUOD AD OMNIBUS.'‡

The first footnote says, 'See Webster's Unabridged Pictorial'; and the second obligingly gives the translation of the Latin phrase: 'What always, what everywhere, what by all is held to be true.'

For some unknown reason this Article was omitted from the Revised and Amended Prescript; and from the list of officers was also omitted the 'Grand Ensign,' whose duties in the Original Prescript were thus described: 'It shall be the duty of the Grand Ensign to take charge of the Grand Banner of the *, to preserve it sacredly, and protect it carefully, and to bear it on all occasions of parade or ceremony, and on such other occasions as the Grand Cyclops may direct it to be flung to the night breeze.' This reference to flinging the ensign 'to the night breeze,' by the way, was made much of in the report of the majority of the Congressional Committee, being advanced as evidence of the Ku Klux's operation under cover of darkness.

At least two of the official banners made in accordance with the specifications of the Original Prescript are now known to exist — one in the Confederate Museum at Richmond and one in the private collection of Mr. Lucius E. Burch, Jr., of Memphis — but apparently the banner was considered a

superfluous elaboration, since it was omitted from the provisions
of the Revised Prescript and most Klans were not provided
with them.

In attending regular meetings of a Den, members usually
wore their ordinary clothing, the disguises being donned only
on the occasion of raids, demonstrations or other group appearances in public. On such occasions they were generally
carried in the saddle-bags until the time arrived to put them
on; and, the demonstration over, they were doffed and replaced
in the saddle-bags for concealment. Between times, they were
kept hidden in some place — smokehouses, corn-cribs, hollow
logs and the box tombs of cemeteries being favored repositories
for the incriminating regalia.

Since it was to the weird appearance of their disguises that
the Ku Klux owed so much of the terror they created among
the negroes, it is worth while to pay more than passing attention
to this phase of their operations. In its official investigation the
Government apparently started out with the idea of trying to
establish the fact of a single, central authority somewhere in the
Invisible Empire which supplied the members with their robes,
and the question was asked of all the early witnesses whether the
disguises they may have seen seemed to have been made by
tailors or other skilled hands, and if the Ku Klux were all
dressed alike. It soon became apparent, however, that there
was actually little uniformity about the uniforms, paradoxical
as that may sound; and they were obviously home-made and
not supplied by any central quartermaster like the uniforms
worn by an army.

One of the most romantic features of the whole Ku Klux
movement was the method pursued by the Klansmen in supplying themselves with the disguises in which they appeared.
No man was willing to incriminate his wife, his mother, his
sister or his sweetheart; but it was these women-folks who sat
up till the late hours of the night to ply their needles and threads

to furnish the disguises needed. Here again the indirect method was used; for, whatever they might suspect, the ladies must be able to say that they did not know anything about the Ku Klux. A Southern woman seated by her lamp at night was not startled if a package was tossed into an open window which, upon examination, was found to contain a piece of cloth with directions as to how to make it into a robe of the desired size and style, and also directions as to where to leave it when it was finished. Or a group of robed Ku Klux would ride up to a house in broad daylight, with a supply of material, and openly negotiate with the women of the house for the making of the desired robes, meanwhile cracking jokes with the wide-eyed but unafraid children. The women, of course, never knew the identity of any men involved in such dealings, and they were particular not to try to find out anything definite about it. A young country girl in Tennessee found a package on the front gallery containing calico, buttons and thread, with a note: 'Dear Missy: Please make this into two robes and two masks for Two Ku Klux.' The young woman had no idea of the authors of the note; but she made the two suits of a size to fit her two elder brothers, and left them on a stump by the front fence as directed — and there was never any complaint as to the fit. A man who worked in a small-town general store at the time said: 'I never saw as many big, two-fisted men as suddenly began to sidle up to the dry-goods counter in the store and buy quantities of black or white or red calico. Generally they would buy just about enough to make a full-sized robe for a man — but of course it was none of my business what a man did with a piece of dry goods after he had bought it, and I couldn't swear that any of my customers were Ku Klux.'

There was printed in a Nashville paper a copy of a letter received by two young ladies of the city, requesting them to make two robes, this letter reading:

Misses *X* and *Y:*

Knowing you to be friends of the Ku Klux Klan, the Grand Cyclops takes the privilege of requesting you to make a couple of robes for some of his poor, needy followers, and if you will be so kind as to make them the protecting eye of the Great Grand Cyclops will ever rest upon you. Thinking that you will make them, the following are the directions:

Make two robes reaching to the ground, open in front, bordered with white three inches wide, white cuffs and collars, half moons on the left breast with stars in the center of each moon, and caps of a conical shape twelve inches high with a tassel, with white cloth hanging over the face so as to conceal it, and behind so as to hide the back of the head.

Make the first of the caps red, the second and third white, and the rest red.

By Order of G. G. Cyclops.

ABEL HAASSAANAN, G. Scribe

The Grand Turk will be after them on the night of the 15th, at 10 o'clock.

You are requested to burn this after reading.

Although the Ku Klux in fiction and newspaper stories are invariably described as 'white-robed' figures, the fact seems to be that the matter of color and style was left largely to the individual's personal taste, although all were of a grotesque nature calculated to impress and terrify the ignorant and superstitious. White robes were originally used by the Pulaski organizers of the Klan, and were generally favored by other Klans at first. 'The impression sought to be made,' said Ryland Randolph, Grand Cyclops of the Den at Tuscaloosa, Alabama, 'was that these white-robed night prowlers were the ghosts of the Confederate dead who had arisen from their graves in

order to work vengeance on an undesirable class of both white
and black men. Their robes used in their nocturnal campaigns
consisted simply of sheets wrapped around the bodies and
belted around the waist. The lower portion reached to the
heels, whilst the upper had eye-holes through which to see
and a mouth-hole through which to breathe.'

There was, however, an early departure from the popularity
of the white robes, and black or red with white trimmings
seemed to be favored. Various schemes of ornamentation were
adopted in different sections, governed chiefly by the individual's personal taste and whim, and some of them went in
for ingeniously terrifying appurtenances like the horns popular
in some states.

Accurate information as to the appearance of the Ku Klux
disguises is fortunately not lacking. Aside from the detailed
descriptions given by eye-witnesses, some of the uniforms have
been preserved in the South (although at the time of disbandment it was specifically ordered that they be burned), and also
there was an occasional instance of a captured uniform, although
such instances were rare. One such captured disguise is now
on display in the museum of the Buffalo Historical Society in
Buffalo, New York; and in 1868 a Yankee schoolma'am in
Mississippi wrote home telling of such a capture by the soldiers
there, describing the uniform as 'a suit of black, the yoke
striped with white, the pants of black muslin with a stripe of
white down the side, the mask of white for the head, of the same
material as the sack, holes for the mouth and eyes trimmed
with black. The disguise for the horse was of the same material
as the man's, with a large white star in the forehead.'

One Southern writer who, if not himself a member of the
Klan, seemed to possess a surprisingly great store of first-hand
information, gives this description of the men seen conducting
one raid:

'The horses' bodies were completely enveloped in curtains of black cloth, worn under the saddle, and fastened at the neck to a corselet of the same material, the skirts of the former extending below their knees. Over their heads were masks, of much the same description as those worn by their riders, the material being of a dark color and openings of suitable width having been contrived for the eyes and nostrils. Each steed was decorated also with a white plume, carried vertically above the head; and on the right and left of the housings of black cloth which enveloped their bodies appeared the mystical letters "K K K." Their trappings otherwise were army saddles of uniform pattern, and bridles supplied with the regulation bit used in both armies at the close of the war.

'The riders who bestrode these steeds were even more fantastically arrayed; and in the uniform which they wore the same sacrifice of taste to picturesqueness was to be observed. The most prominent feature of their ghostly toilet was a long black robe, extending from the head to the feet and decorated with innumerable tin buttons an inch and a half in diameter, which under the influence of the starlight shone like miniature moons. These robes were slit in front and rear, in order that they might not impede the movement of the rider, and were secured about the waist with scarfs of red silk. Over their faces they wore masks of some heavy material; the appertures for the eyes, nose and mouth (which were ample for these purposes) being lined with red cloth. The head-dress was even more unique, and consisted of tall black caps, helmet-shaped, and provided with havelocks, resembling those used by the military in the late war. These also were decorated with the regulation buttons, and when worn by officers of commissioned rank, supplemented by gorgeous plumes, white, red or blue, according to rank. Each individual wore about his waist, in addition to the scarf, a belt supporting two large army pistols in scabbards; and on the flaps of the latter, embroidered in white characters, appeared the devices of the order — skull and crossbones, and the mystical K K K.'

After making due allowance for the romantic exaggeration of this Sir Walter Scott style of narration, this may be accepted as an approximately accurate picture of the disguises used in one section of the Invisible Empire. The uniform worn in North Carolina is thus described in graphic detail by Joseph W. Holden, son of Governor W. W. Holden of that state:

'The costume is a long red gown with loose flowing sleeves, with a hood in which the appertures for the eyes, nose and mouth are trimmed with some red material. The hood has three horns, made out of some common cotton-stuff, in shape something like candy bags stuffed, and wrapped with red strings, the horns standing out on the front and sides of the hood. It is a large, loose gown, covering the whole person quite closely, buttoned close around and reaching from the head clear down to the floor, covering the feet and dragging on the ground. It is made of bleached linen, starched and ironed, and in the night by moonlight it glitters and rattles. Then there is a hood with holes cut in for eyes, and a nose six or eight inches long made of cotton cloth stuffed with cotton and lapped with red braid half an inch wide. The eyes are lined with the braid, and the eyebrows are made of the same. The cloth is lined with red flannel. Then there is a long tongue sticking out about six inches and so fixed that it can be moved about by the man's tongue. Then in the mouth are large teeth, which are very frightful. Then under the tongue is a leather bag placed inside so that when the man calls for water he pours it inside the bag and not into his mouth at all.'

James Justice of Rutherfordton, North Carolina, who was taken out and whipped by the Ku Klux, managed to maintain his composure sufficiently to give the following description of the costumes worn by the men who assailed him: 'Some had disguises and some had strange fixings over their bodies. The greatest number had nothing to disguise them except a mask over their heads and faces, with a large crown-piece and with

a very large face. The places where the eye-holes and the
mouth were cut was bound around with some reddish stuff,
and there was either a white strip sewn on or something painted
for a nose. Some had very long white beards. Some had horns
which were erect; others had horns that lopped over like a
mule's ears; and their caps came to a point with tassels. One
had on a red suit out and out — a great deal like those I have
seen on clowns in circuses. There were a number of stripes
on each arm; something bright like silver lace, like stripes on a
sergeant's sleeves. There was something on the breast of one of
them, something round — of a circular form.'

These descriptions give a good idea of the type of costumes
affected in the Carolinas, in which states the horns were especially popular. Everywhere there was evident a tendency,
as time wore on, to depart from the simplicity of the early
costumes and add ornamentation of one kind or another.
In Arkansas it was said: 'The horses and the men were concealed by masks; gowns and trappings made of black calico
bespangled with glittering, metallic cabalistic signs.' A head-
dress used by a Tennessee Cyclops was heavily ornamented
with gold braid, with black lace over the orifices for the eyes and
nose. Some went in for hirsute adornment, a Mississippi negro
thus describing those who visited him: 'They wore just loose
gowns, very much like a study gown; a loose gown put on over
the neck, hanging down nearly to the feet, made out of cheap
calico. On the face there were some whiskers, made of hair
taken from a cow's tail probably.' A similar fancy was reported by a man who saw some Ku Klux in Huntsville, Alabama: 'The disguises were calico robes loosely worn, and then
a disguise over the face. There was long hair on the face, about
a foot long, coming out as if it were mustaches, hanging down
at least a foot.' Another Huntsville man who saw some of the
Ku Klux there in 1869 drew a distinction between them and the
first Ku Klux he had seen in Tennessee: 'What I call our home-

made Ku Klux have rather a cheap rig on by the side of our ordinary Ku Klux. This gown I found was just a loose gown with big long sleeves to it, and then they have a piece of the long gown thrown up over the head if they want to; but it has eye-holes and all Christendom could not tell who was in it just by seeing the eyes. What I call the Tennessee Ku Klux had a very good rig. They look pretty well, with a red coat trimmed off with black, and when they threw the piece up over it was lined with different color from the rest. They had a sort of rubber capes with fixings to come all over them in a rain storm.'

Georgia witnesses described the Ku Klux they had seen in such phrases as these: 'They are always dressed in such a kind of uniform that you can not tell who they are. They have on false faces and some with long beards, some with long hats, and some with no hats at all, some with long ears, some with big eyes, and some with long noses.' 'They had on some sort of a dress with some rings around their eyes and a coat with a star on each shoulder — at least the captain had — with a representation of the moon on his back, under the stars, and something fixed to his hair and hanging down so that it looked like great whiskers.' 'Their uniforms previous to that had been white robes, and their horses were always dressed in white when they turned out. That night when they came to my house they had on black masks and were dressed in black.'

From all this it will be seen that there was a vast difference in the vestments used in various parts of the Invisible Empire; difference, in fact, between the uniforms of closely neighboring Dens. This difference in the color of the disguises worn was the means of impeaching the testimony of a government witness in the trial of the accused Ku Klux in Oxford, Mississippi, in 1870. Joe Davis, a negro, swore that he had been forced to accompany a band of white men who, in the Ku Klux disguise, went to the home of a negro named Jack Dupree and took him out and whipped him. Davis said that he held the horses while Dupree was taken off and whipped; and that when the white men came back to the horses, unaccompanied by Dupree, they said that they had not only whipped him but 'had cut his damned guts out.' At any rate, Dupree disappeared that night and was never seen again.

Davis was a willing, eager witness for the government and glibly identified all the accused participants by name. He over-reached himself, however, when he attempted to tell about the disguise worn by the Ku Klux party he claimed to have ac-companied on their murderous raid. It was a red and black disguise, Joe testified, describing it in detail. Shortly prior to this time a Ku Klux uniform had been captured in Pontotoc, Mississippi, and had been stuffed and hung up to the limb of a tree in the main street of the town as an exhibit. Joe had evidently seen this disguise and studied it closely, for his de-scription fitted it very accurately. It happened, however, that all the witnesses who had actually seen the party that Ku Kluxed Jack Dupree were unanimous in their testimony that the members of the party wore white disguises. This led to the strong suspicion that Davis had not really seen the raiding party at all, much less been a member of it; and it was eventually shown that he had admitted that he did not know anybody connected with the Ku Klux organization.

It was a general rule that members of a Ku Klux raiding party should refrain from all unnecessary conversation. In fact, generally they did not speak at all except to exchange snatches of meaningless gibberish or to groan loudly and dismally in simulation of the sufferings of a departed spirit. It was a part of the Ku Klux regulations that every member should be sup-plied with a whistle — which made 'a shrill, gurgling noise' — and blasts of the whistle instead of spoken commands were used in giving orders when on a raid. If the Cyclops sounded his whistle when they were at rest it was equivalent to the order

'March.' Three blasts served as a warning of danger; and four blasts as a call for aid. Members of a Ku Klux party were never called by their names, but by numbers. These numbers varied from time to time, as they had different methods of numbering. Sometimes they would start with one, the Cyclops being Number One, and assume numbers in regular rotation. Sometimes they would start numbering at one hundred, or perhaps five hundred, use of the larger numbers being effective in creating an exaggerated idea of the size of a Ku Klux band.

The procedure followed on a raid depended on a great many factors — the offense of the victim and the temperament and inclinations of the leader of the raiding party. During the earlier, orderly days, the Klansmen rarely did anything more than warn the negroes to 'behave themselves' or notify some especially obnoxious carpetbagger that he would have to leave town. These warnings were accompanied by the most horrendous threats of what would happen to them if their commands were not obeyed, but the warnings were frequently repeated several times before any drastic action was really taken. The principal desire was to scare the negroes into a submissive spirit by means of gruesome threats — 'We boil niggers' heads and make soup'; 'We'll skin you alive'; 'We'll take you for a trip over the moon'; 'We live off of fried nigger meat'; and so on, depending on the imagination of the threatener.

In a great number of instances this was all that was necessary. The carpetbagger would leave town or the negro would steer his course down the strait and narrow path, and all would be well. But some carpetbaggers refused to be stampeded into departure; some negroes did not believe in ghosts and were not terrified by browbeating. This created a serious problem of procedure. Obviously the Ku Klux would quickly lose power if it began to appear that their orders could be disobeyed with impunity and that their threats were never backed up by action. Action seemed imperatively indicated in these instances, and it is not surprising that this action should have slipped into bloodshed and homicide, all conditions being considered.

The principal basis for criticism of the Ku Klux was this violence which they sometimes employed and which eventually became synonymous with their name. By our advanced standards of today it is difficult to justify, or even to understand how its apologists could justify, the corporal punishment of a fellowman. It seems a brutal and sadistic mode of punishment, however serious may have been the offense for which the recipient of the whipping was punished. But, in justice to the Ku Klux and their apparent lack of all milk of human kindness, it must be remembered that they should be judged by the standards of their time; and by those standards the flogging of a recalcitrant negro was nothing more unusual or inhumane than the punishment of a disobedient child by its parents.

True enough, the more enlightened and advanced slave owners resorted to such whippings only as a matter of last resort, and then only in extreme cases of repeated disobedience or insubordination, or petty offenses against the law. Under the slave code the master was expected to regulate all such matters by his own authority without appealing to the constituted courts; so the whipping of negroes, although by no means so common as represented by the abolitionists, was at least a recognized method of punishing negroes' offenses.

Further precedent for the Ku Klux method of regulation was to be seen in the patrol system which prevailed in the slave states before emancipation. The law provided that every slave must be in his quarters before nine o'clock at night unless he had a pass from his master; and, to enforce this law, the justices of the peace had authority to maintain a regular system of patrols who rode through their precincts at regular intervals — once a week or once a month — to see that all negroes were at home after the curfew hour. White men of military age were subject to this duty as a public service, the same as they were

subject to militia duty, and they served by assignment and
without pay. When they found a negro prowling about after
nine o'clock without a pass they were empowered by the law to
give him a whipping of not to exceed thirty-nine lashes (in some
places the maximum was fifteen lashes); and this system of
patrol and punishment was accepted as a regular and proper
thing by both blacks and whites. The negroes' comic song:
'Run, Nigger, Run; the Patterrole'll Catch You,' was based on
their well-established anxiety about being caught out by
these patrols — there was no question of the patrols' right to
administer punishment.

When the white people after the war were confronted with
the problem of the growing irresponsibility and disorderliness
of the recently freed negroes, with no adequate restraint available through the then existing law courts, it was not entirely
unnatural for them to turn for relief to an extra-legal imitation
of that patrol system which had been a legal and recognized
part of the system of government before the war. It was, of
course, illegal for them thus to take the law into their own
hands in this way; but the methods they pursued, cruel as
they may now appear, were by no means a radical innovation
or necessarily an evidence of innate brutality.

When the Ku Klux first started to operating as regulators
they were apparently as reluctant to resort to the lash as were
the pre-war slave owners. When they did administer a whipping
they generally minimized it in their own discussion of it.
'We gave him a light whipping'; 'We decided to give him a
little brushing'; 'We straightened him out with a hickory' —
such euphemisms were commonly employed. But as the
character of the Klan's personnel began to degenerate, these
whippings increased in frequency and severity; and the brutal
excesses of this period of the Klan's degeneration find no
apologist anywhere. They were as severely condemned by
the Klan's leaders at the time as they are today.

That the Ku Klux resorted to homicide in extreme cases is beyond question; but it is also a fact that the number of killings attributed to them was very greatly exaggerated. It became the fashion during those days to attribute every murder and every rumored murder to the Ku Klux, and in the Northern press these were magnified for political purposes. Some of these murders probably were committed by assassins who used the familiar disguise of the Ku Klux as a cloak; but the genuine Ku Klux resorted to the death penalty only in the most extreme cases where, by their code, such a penalty was justified by the enormity of the offense or by self-defense. By way of palliation it has been pointed out that most of the Ku Klux were ex-soldiers and that this was during a period following four years of bloody war when life had become cheap. It is not an excuse for murder to say that men under these circumstances could not be expected to have the same regard for the sanctity of human life as those who had not been subjected to the brutalities of war, but it is at least an explanation of the frame of mind which made it possible for a group of men to assume the powers of executioners without a feeling of utter revulsion at their own presumption.

In normal times such a course of procedure would have been universally execrated; but these were not normal times, and the report of the hearings before the Congressional Committee is full of such expressions as: 'It is a desperate remedy, but there is no denying that it has done a lot of good'; and 'It was the only manner of punishing criminals in this country, and they think they did exactly right'; and 'It is a terrible thing for such a thing as this to occur, but ultimate good will follow from it,' and so on.

'We are a rough lot of boys,' cried one of a band of Ku Klux as they galloped into a little Alabama town one night. And rough boys they were, indeed.

PART II

The Realms of the Empire

IV.   TENNESSEE

TENNESSEE WAS THE CRADLE of the Ku Klux, and it was in this state that it enjoyed its most widespread and most powerful influence. Violence and bloodshed were rare in this state; but the Klan wielded its mysterious influence in practically all the counties outside of East Tennessee, and in some of these counties it was for a while, in effect, the governing power.

The Reconstruction troubles in Tennessee find their root as far back as 1862, while the war was still raging. In that year the Union army succeeded in getting possession of Middle and West Tennessee, which sections of the state were strongly pro-Confederate in sentiment. The Confederates, on the other hand, were able to cling to East Tennessee, in which section the sentiment was predominantly pro-Union. All sections of the state, therefore, found themselves forced to live temporarily under civil governments which were antagonistic to the popular majorities; and this antagonism, along with the friction already existing between the Unionists of East Tennessee and the other residents of the state, contributed to a topsy-turvy political situation whose complexities vexed the state for more than ten years.

As soon as the Union military forces took possession of Middle Tennessee, including Nashville, the state capital, civil law was suspended in the state by General Grant, who proclaimed martial law, and Andrew Johnson was appointed military governor by President Lincoln. Johnson's régime was very oppressive on the Confederate sympathizers, whom he sharply denounced as traitors, and his hard-handed administration of the law greatly embittered this class of the population. Among other distasteful measures, he prescribed and enforced an 'iron-clad' oath, which few of the native citizens could honestly and conscientiously take. It was officially called an amnesty oath; but the people called it the 'damnasty' oath.

The Federal troops finally conquered East Tennessee late in 1863, but civil government was not restored until March, 1865, when the notorious William G. Brownlow, better known as 'Parson' Brownlow, was elevated to the governorship in a farcical election.

When the new Radical legislature assembled in Nashville in April, 1865, under Governor Brownlow, Tennessee's era of trial and tribulation began. A law was promptly enacted providing for the limitation of the elective franchise, the effect of which was to take the vote away from all ex-Confederates and Confederate sympathizers, along with all white men who were not strictly pro-Radical in their views. Brownlow, by reason of his legalized authority over the registration of voters, really held the power to say who could and who could not vote. In Davidson County in July, 1867, the total registration was 6000, of which 1600 were whites and 4400 negroes; whereas before the war the total all-white registration was 6500.

A special law was passed denying to ex-Confederates the right to possess arms, but conferring this right on 'loyal' men — almost the entire body of so-called loyal men in Middle and West Tennessee at this time being negroes. Also, a state guard was authorized, this also to be composed of 'loyal' men; this in addition to the United States troops who were quartered in the state. The system of law enforcement broke down almost completely, and convictions for such common offenses as murder, rape and arson were hard to obtain. Furthermore, even when criminals were convicted they seldom served their time, as Governor Brownlow was liberal and prompt with pardons for Radical offenders.

To quote the Congressional Committee's minority report: 'The great mass of the people of Tennessee felt that they were outlawed and denied the protection of government. They felt that they had no right of person or of property respected by the ruling powers. They believed that they were purposely disarmed and that, being so, whatever they loved or prized was at the mercy of an ignorant race, whose ignorance and whose passions were being played upon by corrupt parties, with sinister purposes, and an internecine warfare was painfully apprehended. Under these circumstances, and at such a time, produced by this most unhappy legislation and rule, many impulsive men felt that their only means of personal safety and protection to themselves, their wives, their daughters, their mothers, their sisters and their helpless ones, was in secret organization. While all history attests their mistake, all history attests that it is the resort of the oppressed against the oppressor. And while we may and do condemn secret political organizations, we condemn with equal severity the tyranny of the oppressor out of which they have their birth.'

While Brownlow was exercising his peculiar talent for creating discord and cooking up his hell's broth of misgovernment, the organizers of the Loyal League had also been busy and soon had the League thoroughly established throughout the state. Wherever a League blossomed trouble was sure to follow, and in 1867 this trouble was intensified by the approaching election, in which campaign the Radical orators inflamed the negroes against the whites and provoked them to deeds of violence. In Franklin, for example, the members of the League kept the citizens in a constant state of alarm by marching through the town, night after night, making noisy demonstrations with fife and drum and boisterous shouts, and flourishing their weapons. The explosion came when a Conservative negro had the temerity to attempt to make a political speech, and the armed League members broke up the meeting and marched away firing their guns into the air. That night there was a fatal clash between a parade of the exulting negroes of the League and an armed party of Conservatives, black and white, who attempted to prevent their demonstrating on the Public Square. When the gunfire subsided and the smoke cleared away one white Conservative was dead and six white and seven negro members of that party were wounded, along with twenty-seven wounded Leaguers.

As a result of this riot, and similar clashes in other parts of the state, fears were expressed that there would be serious trouble on election day, and leaders of both parties worked together to prevent bloodshed. In Memphis, General Forrest organized a body of volunteer police who co-operated with the city police department on election day to prevent outbreaks; and in the other cities of the state similar efforts were made to insure peace, with the result that the casualties on election day were held to a minimum. But the atmosphere still crackled with the electricity of restrained hostility.

Friction between the native white people and the freed negroes had been growing steadily in all sections of Tennessee ever since the war. Even in the eastern part of the state, the pro-Union and Abolition stronghold, Brownlow's own newspaper, the Knoxville *Whig*, reported rapidly increasing bitterness between the races. White people, the paper said, were being wantonly insulted by negroes who 'frequently elbow unprotected white women off our narrow pavements, and curse white men passing them, just to show their authority.' The Republican *Banner* in Nashville reported many murders by negroes throughout the state; and in Memphis acts of violence by the negro troops garrisoned there became so frequent that the presiding judge of the county, Judge Thomas Leonard, asked that two regiments of white Federal troops be stationed in Memphis to protect the white citizens against the negro soldiers' robberies, assaults and murders. The negro soldiers not only committed these offenses themselves, but they crowded the saloons of the city and constituted a serious disturbing influence on the civilian negroes. This bad feeling grew so intense that in May, 1866, there was precipitated a sanguinary race riot which lasted for three days and resulted in the killing of forty-six negroes and two white men, the wounding of seventy-five others and the destruction of property to the value of $130,000, including the burning of ninety-one negro dwellings, four negro churches and twelve negro schools.

This was the only major outbreak in the state, but it kept the fires of apprehension fanned; and detachments of Brownlow's militia stationed at various points in the state served to irritate the citizens and keep them reminded of the oppressive Brownlow régime. In some localities the white citizens began to organize informal local groups for self-protection. Even in East Tennessee there was talk of forming a 'White Man's Party' to prevent the negroes from gaining control of the state. There was a general feeling of uneasiness and alarm. The citizens felt that their well-being was menaced, but they did not know exactly what to do about it.

It was just about this time that the madcap young men of Pulaski organized their skylarking local club which they called the Ku Klux Klan, little dreaming of the dread portent which that name was to come to have. As the trouble with the negroes grew, and as the alarm of the people was intensified in proportion to the secret and apparently hostile organizations of the former slaves, there was a natural gravitation to the idea of forming some sort of counter-organization of a defensive nature; and the local success of the Ku Klux Klan in Giles County caused it to be seized upon as a new and effective method of procedure which might be used to advantage elsewhere in the state.

The early growth of the Klan was slow, and it was not until about the first of 1868 that it began to be publicly recognized as a force to be reckoned with in Tennessee. There had been occasional references to the Ku Klux in the newspapers from time to time in 1867, but they were mostly of a facetious nature, and there was a general inclination to minimize the matter and laugh it off as a manifestation of boyish exuberance of trivial importance. The papers carried such items as 'The Ku Klux paraded in Murfreesboro last night, 5000 to 7000 strong. Some of them were so tall that they took the slates off the roof of the new church as they rode by.' The term 'Ku Klux' in those days carried the connotation of some sort of an elaborate practical joke. The average person laughed about it, then thought no more about it.

But early in 1868 it began to dawn on the citizens, and on the newspaper editors, that the Ku Klux movement was something much more serious than they had thought — that it had some serious, possibly sinister, purpose. In its issue of February 1 the Nashville *Union and Dispatch* had an item entitled 'The Ku Klux Klan — a Wonderful and Mysterious Order,' in which it said:

'The secret brotherhood known as the Ku Klux Klan is probably the most extraordinary association that the present century has known. A member of the organization, when clad in the trappings of the order, is certainly a strange object. His robe of scarlet, or of somber black, as the case may be, loose-flowing from the waist to the feet, is rather an Oriental affair and would do for the heroes of the Arabian Nights. . . . He gets over the ground with a gliding motion, as if fearful that the horrible cowl which hides his face, and from which a pair of glittering eyes almost pierce the beholder, might by some untoward accident be thrown aside or lose its power of concealment. . . . When first organized it was generally understood that the society was a benevolent association, its design the relief of the widows and orphans of Confederate soldiers. . . . If what is alleged of them now can be anywhere near the truth, it can not be doubted that the unprecedented conduct of armed Leagues organized to terrify Conservatism has led to the retaliation.'

News items reporting operations of the Ku Klux in various parts of Tennessee were plentiful in the papers throughout 1868. A warning was received by a man in Livingston; masked bands were seen in Van Buren County; the tax collector of Sumner County received a terrifying warning letter couched in the studiously bad grammar and worse spelling which so frequently characterized the Ku Klux missives. On May 12 a Nashville paper carried a report of a Ku Klux parade in Murfreesboro the preceding Saturday night: 'They were all dressed in uniforms and their horses caparisoned in the usual style. They commenced to parade about nine o'clock and kept it up until after midnight.' The Ku Klux were so bold and so well established in Murfreesboro that they drilled regularly in one of the open lots near town, like a military company, in full panoply and without any attempt at concealment. 'A Desperate Affray at Fayetteville' was the heading over a story of a 'general fight' there between a number of Union men and 'a party of Conservatives, supposed to be members of the Ku Klux Klan.' A negro named Robert Hogg in Marshall County was reported killed by a white man described as 'an ex-Rebel soldier' and also as 'a desperate and reckless character to be feared and dreaded.' No attempt had been made to arrest him, it was stated in a Radical paper in Nashville, and 'the presence of the Ku Klux Klan gives to the desperado, unless extraordinary means are used, almost certain immunity from arrest.' From Lincoln County came the report that a negro named Dave Walker had received a note signed 'Ku Klux' which said: 'We, the Ku Klux Company, notify you to leave the county within ten days or we will take the matter in hand and we will raise you as high as Haman.'

There was an ominous stir of Ku Klux activity all over the state in the latter part of 1868 and first of 1869. 'The Klan seems to be more insatiate and rampant since the election than before,' said one newspaper comment; and the papers every day carried such headlines as 'Ku Klux Rampant in Coffee County'; 'Negroes of Bedford and Coffee County Whipped'; 'Ku Klux in Gibson County'; 'Ku Klux Seen at Brentwood,' and so on.

In January, 1869, the Nashville papers carried headlines: 'Trouble in Overton County — The Ku Klux Rampant and Threatening — The Town of Livingston in a State of Siege — A Civil War Imminent.' Nor was this alarming summary of events very much of an exaggeration. A few nights previously a band of Ku Klux had galloped into Livingston, where they were met by a doughty band of armed negroes who fired into the raiders from ambush. The Ku Klux retreated, leaving five horses and as many of their 'shrouds' in the hands of the jubilant negroes. The Klansmen, however, were not satisfied with this inglorious end to their foray; and the following week they returned in larger numbers and demanded of a prominent Union man that their property be returned to them, awaiting which they boldly pitched their camp on the edge of the town. The Collector of Internal Revenue at Livingston, a Mr. Stroheimer, was so terrified by the presence of the besieging Ku Klux that he bought the horses back from the negroes with his own money and took them out to the Klansmen's camp as a peace offering, whereupon they retired and left Livingston in peace.

From Maury County it was reported that 'not less than 400 guns and pistols have been taken from the freedmen of this county by the Ku Klux during the last month'; and Ku Klux news of some kind from Maury County was almost a daily affair, as this county was completely under the domination of the

Ku Klux for a period of about two years or more. Nearly all the able-bodied young men were active members, while the disabled veterans of the war and the elderly citizens were advisers and supporters and helpers. Army and militia officers railed and fumed; Freedmen's Bureau agents wrote frequent and eloquent letters of protest to their superiors; but so long as the Grand Wizard's reign continued, Maury County was a loyal province of the Invisible Empire.

One of the earliest and most dramatic public manifestations of the power and the serious purposes of the Ku Klux in Tennessee took place in this county early in 1868. John Bicknell, a highly regarded young dentist of Columbia, while riding along the highway in the direction of Lawrenceburg on February 28, was murdered and robbed by a wayfaring man whom he had befriended by permitting him to ride behind him on his horse. The stranger (who gave several different names — Walker, Watts and Pitts) was later seen making his escape, mounted on Bicknell's horse; and he was pursued and captured by an undisguised band of Columbia members of the Ku Klux, who took him to the jail in Columbia and turned him over to the sheriff. Bicknell had apparently been a member of the Klan, for when his funeral was held a group of twenty Klansmen, mounted and dressed in their white robes, 'with their horses appropriately caparisoned,' followed the procession to the cemetery and remained there in silence while the ceremonies were proceeding at the grave.

That night the murderer, who had meanwhile confessed, was taken from the jail by a band of Ku Klux who rode into town from a southerly direction and was conducted to the near-by bank of Duck River to be hanged. He asked for the privilege of saying a prayer before the noose was placed about his neck, which request was granted; but when the Ku Klux knelt with him to pray he unceremoniously jumped into the river, swam across and made his escape. Stopping at a farmhouse to dry

himself and get warm, he was recognized and taken back to
the jail and lodged in his cell again. Not to be thwarted by this
interruption in their plans, the Ku Klux rode into town again
that night, removed him from jail and took him to a thicket a
mile from town on the Pulaski pike, where he was hanged
without ceremony.

A local newspaper account of the affair stated that 'None of
the strange horsemen were known to the citizens of Columbia,
and the young men of that place who were members of the Ku
Klux Klan, it is said, took no part in the proceedings.' This was
in conformity with the standard Ku Klux custom of having such
work done by squads of Klansmen from a near-by town or
community, so that the local boys could have air-tight alibis.
In this instance the executioners, it will be observed, rode into
town from 'a southerly direction'; and it seems a reasonable
assumption that they came from Pulaski. Pulaski, being the
point of origin of the order, was a conspicuously active center
of Ku Klux activity so long as the organization lived.

Pulaski was the scene of one of the Klan's earliest public
demonstrations when, on June 4, 1867, they held an elaborate
parade, declared to be in honor of their 'first anniversary.' On
the preceding morning there were found posted all over town
printed handbills saying:

To the Chapters of the Central Division:

The pale moon changes. Soon the skies will be bright. All is
well. The Grand Turks will make full reports. Each chapter
will march promptly to the Hall of Banners, and the grand
ceremonies will commence precisely at 12 o'clock midnight,
on Wednesday next. The Chapter will take up the march at
precisely 9 o'clock. They will parade the principal streets and
thence to the Hall of Banners. All Chapters will be prompt.
Let all hope for success to our first anniversary.

By order of the G. G. S.

G. G. C.

An interesting account of the demonstration is taken from the next issue of the Pulaski *Citizen*, which was in position to have all the best inside information:

'On Tuesday morning these notices were found posted conspicuously all over town. All wondered and many expressed the belief that it was all a hoax, and that there was no such thing as a Kuklux Klan. Believing that there was some reality in it, we, with many others, were on the look-out at an early hour Wednesday night. About 10 o'clock we discovered the head of the column as it came over the hill west of the square. The crowd waited impatiently for their approach. A closer view discovered their banners and transparencies, with all manner of mottoes and devices, spears, sabres, &c. The column was led by what we supposed to be the Grand Cyclops, who had on a flowing white robe and a white hat about eighteen inches high. He had a very venerable and benevolent looking face, and long silvery locks. He had an escort on each side of him bearing brilliant transparencies. The master of the ceremonies was gorgeously caparisoned, and his "toot, toot, toot," on a very graveyard-ish looking instrument, seemed to be perfectly understood by every Ku Kluxer. Next to the G. C. there followed two of the tallest men out of jail. One of them had on a robe of many colors, with a hideous mask, and a transparent hat, in which he carried a brilliant gas lamp, a box of matches and several other articles. It is said that he was discovered taking a bottle from a shelf in his hat, and that he and his companion took several social drinks together. The other one had on a blood-red hat which was so tall that we never did see the top of it. They conversed in Dutch, Hebrew, or some other language which we couldn't comprehend. No two of them were dressed alike, all having on masks and some of them fanciful costumes. One fellow out-Falstaffed Falstaff in appearance. There seemed to be about seventy-five in the procession, with several darting about occasionally over town.

'When the procession reached Third Street the master of the ceremonies with a "toot, toot," turned the head of the column up that street towards the depot. On reaching the first cross street, "toot, toot" went the horn, and they filed to the left up to Second Street, up which they marched towards the bridge. A single "toot" now threw the procession into single file, and they marched over to First Street, and Ku Kluxed up and down that street for some time. A long, twisted "t-o-ot" gave the order to counter-march, and they slowly marched to the square. Here the scene was truly imposing, and the "toot, toot's" more frequent. After going around the square several times, a succession of loud and rapid "toots" rallied the whole squad around the grand old Cy, who seemed to impart some important information to them, when they rapidly marched off the square towards the Methodist church. Here they turned down towards the town spring, and the hundreds of astonished and admiring spectators, composed of ladies and gentlemen, children and dogs, waited patiently for their return. But they never came back. Gradually their lights went out, and nothing more was heard from them except an occasional faint "toot" as they slowly continued their pilgrimage over East Hill.'

The Pulaski Ku Klux appeared to enjoy appearing in public. Later in the summer a small group of them, on foot, went to the Tennessee House at midnight, aroused the landlord and told him that they wished to arrange for accommodations for the night for sixty-five of their band who 'had traveled on foot 175 miles since breakfast and were a little fatigued.' The landlord protested that he could care for only twenty, and the Cyclops said he would send that many 'and you see that they lack for nothing' — but they never came. Sometimes small bands of a half-dozen or more would ride through the streets at night, chattering in a meaningless gibberish, and galloping their horses up and down the streets.

In August, 1867, they made a sensational appearance at a

well-attended 'evening picnic,' riding up to the picnic grove out of the darkness in all their sepulchral whiteness. 'The ladies for a few minutes were a little frightened at their hideous faces and fancy costumes,' wrote an eye-witness, 'but they were assured by the one calling himself the Grand Cyclops that their mission was one of peace and protection, especially so far as the ladies were concerned, and that the powerful right arm of each of the numerous brothers of the Kuklux Klan then within the sound of the grand bugler would be raised to strike down the coward who would dare insult the modesty and dignity of any lady present. Thus assured, the ladies crowded around them, and in a few minutes they were the toasts of the evening.... They stayed until the party commenced dispersing and then disappeared as mysteriously as they came.'

Another active center of Ku Klux work in Middle Tennessee for a while was Clarksville, in Montgomery County. One of the meeting places of the Klan there was in the basement of the old Stewart's College; and one old Ku Klux relates that he was initiated into the order in this room by Captain John W. Morton, when Morton went to Clarksville to get the Klan organized there. Another place of meeting was Dunbar's Cave, a cavern near Clarksville which was a popular resort for picnics and outings — but a place carefully avoided by the negroes after dark. On March 17, 1868, there was found on a tree near Clarksville a broadside which read:

> Dunbar's Sepulchre, Bloody Month
> Cloudy Moon, Muddy Hour.

Shrouded Brothers of Fort Donelson, Division No. 51 of the
    Great Circle:

Burst your cerements asunder! Meet at the Den! 'The glow worm shows the motion to be near.' Silence! Watchfulness!! Patience!!! Faithfulness!!!! *The guilty shall be punished!!!!!*

                    By order of the Senior Grand Cyclops
HERNDON, GS

Further evidence of the Klan in Clarksville was given by
the following order found posted in town a short while afterward:

                              Dunbar's Sepulchre, Bloody Month
                              Cloudy Moon, Last Hour.

Special Order No. 2.
Shrouded Brothers of Fort Donelson, Division No. 51.

The Great Past Grand Giant commands you. The dark and
dismal hour draws nigh. Some live to-day, to-morrow die.
The Whetted Sword, the Blade, the Bullet red and the Right
are ours. Be Vigilant to-day. Mark well our friends. Let the
guilty beware.

By order of the Great Grand Cyclops

                                          G C T

HERNDON, GS

According to a newspaper comment, the appearance of this
poster in Clarksville 'created more excitement in the city than
anything since Lee's surrender.'

On account of the strong Union sentiment in East Tennessee,
the Ku Klux Klan did not become established in that part of
the state; but from Middle Tennessee it spread rapidly to the
western portion and soon became a powerful factor in West
Tennessee, not only in Memphis but in the other counties west
of the Tennessee River as well.

An indication of their power in that section was provided by
an episode in Obion County early in 1868 when a party of Ku
Klux visited an old man, a scalawag, in the southern part of the
county who had been encouraging the negroes to thoughts of
social equality and gave him what one of them later described
as 'a little licking.' He promptly went to Union City and swore
out warrants against thirteen citizens, charging them with being
his assailants; and the next day they were brought to trial. The
news of the arrest spread quickly throughout the county, and

early in the morning of the day of the trial an extraordinarily large number of armed horsemen were seen on the roads going in the direction of Union City. There was a dense woods close to the town at that time, and by the time of the trials there were fifteen hundred men gathered in this forest, a few hundred yards from the center of the town; and there they rested at ease, in complete silence, while the trials were proceeding. The accused Ku Klux were able to prove an alibi to the satisfaction of the magistrates before whom they were arraigned, and were discharged. A horseman rode out to the woods with the news, and the Ku Klux force investing the city melted away as silently and mysteriously as it had assembled, and all was peaceful again.

One of the centers of great Ku Klux activity in Tennessee was in Wayne County; and an episode occurring there in August, 1868, furnished one of the most remarkable manifestations of the extraordinary boldness with which the Klan conducted its work and the extent to which it had come to be accepted as a normal feature of current life.

This trouble, like so many others, had its beginning in the root of all evil. A party of Ohio capitalists had come to this county after the war and opened an iron furnace, known as Boyd's Furnace, where they employed something like one hundred negroes in mining the ore. The white men of the vicinity were jealous of the negroes, due to the black men's willingness to work for low wages, and wanted to drive them away. The Northern superintendent of the operation, on the other hand, pointed out that he was getting the ore out of the mines for a dollar and a half a ton with the negroes, whereas it would cost six dollars if he had to employ white labor. Naturally he was slow to see the advisability of making a change.

The jealous white natives undertook to play on the fears of the negroes by telling them fearsome stories of what the dread Ku Klux Klan would do to them unless they gave up their jobs

and went away, and some of the negroes by this means were
scared off. A majority of the bolder ones, however, organized
themselves into a militia company, procured muskets and every
night held drills on the public highway. Genuinely alarmed by
this manifestation, the white men of the community sent word
to the foreman of the furnace that if the drilling was not stopped
they would 'take the matter in hand and disband them by
force.' This served only to increase the alarm of the negroes,
who, supported by the Radical whites, redoubled their martial
preparations.

The Ku Klux construed the negroes' activities as threatening
and loaded with potential danger; and on the fifteenth of
August, in the morning about nine o'clock, a band of about
sixty of the Klan, mounted in full panoply, marched from
Clifton through Waynesboro to the furnace. What transpired
upon their arrival there is best told in the words of the official
report of the United States Army officer who later investigated
the affair:

'They molested no one and no one molested them while
passing through Waynesboro; and when they got to the furnace
the leader inquired for the foreman, who came out to meet them,
while all the colored men took to the woods in the greatest
fright. As soon as the foreman spoke, the leader of the Ku Klux
threw up his mask and told the foreman that their object was a
peaceful one, that they did not want to injure anyone, but would
like to talk with the negroes. The foreman told the leader of the
Ku Klux that it was impossible to induce a negro on his place
to speak to him unless he pledged himself upon honor not to use
any violence. This the 'Cyclops' did, and after a little trouble
the foreman induced the most intelligent of the negroes to come
out of their hiding places and appear before the leader of the
masked party, who talked to them kindly and told them that
the Ku Klux were not their enemies, but that they would insist
upon the negroes ceasing to drill and making the place insecure

for travelers, etc. By his advice, and the influence of the foreman, the negroes were induced to give up their arms to the
foreman, agreeing not to take them out of the store unless permission was granted to do so by the Superintendent of the
works. With this understanding, which appeared satisfactory
to all parties, the masked party left the furnace and for Clifton, via Waynesboro.'

The sheriff of the county, E. F. Turman, had seen the Ku
Klux when they rode through Waynesboro that morning, and
such an audacious demonstration in broad daylight he considered an unbearable affront to his official dignity. Something
had to be done, so, taking two deputies with him, he rode out
from Waynesboro in the direction of the furnace in belated pursuit of them. About a half mile from town they met the masked
party trotting leisurely down the road, returning from their
mission at the furnace. Sheriff Turman and his deputies, undismayed by the superior numbers, drew up in the middle of the
road and the sheriff demanded their surrender. The Ku Klux
leader contemptuously replied to this suggestion: 'Go to hell,'
and kept coming; whereupon the sheriff and his deputies fired
wildly and ineffectually into the body of Klansmen and then
rapidly retreated to Waynesboro, hotly pursued by the masked
band.

The sheriff and his men took refuge in the jail at Waynesboro,
which was surrounded by a stockade; and from behind this
stockade a party of eight or ten of the sheriff's henchmen
exchanged shots with the Ku Klux — all this in broad daylight,
just about high noon. After one or two fusillades, the Klansmen
withdrew, leaving behind three wounded mules and some of
their regalia. The terrified sheriff, fearful that the attack would
be renewed, hastily gathered a posse of fifty-three men whom
he posted in the stockade, with pickets on the pikes leading into
town.

As soon as news of this brush reached Nashville, General

Carlin, who was in command there, sent Lieutenant-Colonel
Joseph W. Gelray of the 45th United States Infantry to Waynesboro to investigate the matter and make a complete report.
Colonel Gelray appears to have been a man of rare diplomacy,
impartiality and coolness; and as soon as he had arrived in
Waynesboro and learned all the facts in the case he proposed
that a committee of four citizens — two Republicans and two
Democrats — accompany him to Clifton, the Ku Klux stronghold in the county, and there confer with the leaders of the
Klan, learn their grievances and objects and see what could be
done towards making peace.

About nine o'clock the next morning a party of citizens called

Arrived in Clifton, Colonel Gelray promptly called a meeting
of the citizens of that little town to discuss the state of affairs.
Gelray made them a tactful talk, pointing out that such disturbances were ruining their material prosperity 'as well as
their character as men and citizens.' The mention of material
prosperity was an especially moving appeal, as all agreed that it
would bankrupt the county to maintain for very long the posse
then gathered in Waynesboro. Before adjourning the meeting,
Gelray stated that he would be at the hotel until ten o'clock the
following morning, and invited a conference with anybody
who had any suggestions to make as to what might be done.

About nine o'clock the next morning a party of citizens called
on Colonel Gelray, headed by a Mr. R. A. Allisson, who
calmly introduced himself as the Cyclops of the Ku Klux there
and stated that he was empowered to enter into a 'treaty of
peace.' Gelray indicated that he thought this a reasonable proceeding in the circumstances, whereupon Cyclops Allisson dic-
tated the following remarkable document:

'I, R. A. Allisson, of the County of Wayne and State of
Tennessee, do hereby pledge my personal and official influence
hereafter to obey and support the laws of Wayne County and
the state of Tennessee, as they are now on the statute books of
Wayne County and state aforesaid; and to aid the legally con-

stituted authorities to the extent of my power and influence in supporting and enforcing the same. I also do pledge that the organization of which I am the official head, known as the Ku Klux Klan, will lay aside their masks and disguises and will raid no more in the county; and that in case the above named organization or Klan, or any member of the same, should raid or attempt to raid, I will aid to the extent of my ability in arresting the party or parties, and turn them over to the county authorities whence they came; and I do further pledge that I have authority vested in me to give the above pledge on the following conditions, to-wit: That the Sheriff of Wayne County proceed to disband the posse under his control, in the manner prescribed by law; give up the stock captured by the posse or Sheriff, provided it be illegal for them or him to hold the same; and providing also that I be not held responsible for any act done by any party or parties under my control, prior to the date of this. If, however, the grand jury find true bills against me or any of the party under my control, I will not forcibly resist the law in my or their behalf.'

Colonel Gelray, after getting Cyclops Allisson's signature to this unique peace treaty, rode back to Waynesboro, where he laid it before the sheriff and citizens, who at once agreed to it, and the sheriff wrote at the bottom of the document: 'I agree to the above; E. F. Turman, Sheriff of Wayne County.' The sheriff then disbanded his posse, and within a half hour there was not an armed man on the streets of Waynesboro.

A curious effort at indirect intimidation of the Radicals was a letter published in the Hartsville *Vidette* of March 27, 1868, which the editor, Captain Frank McDuffy, said he had received from an anonymous correspondent in Lafayette, a small town in the same county. 'A raid will be made on your town from the northern part of the county,' this letter said, 'with intent to break up the organization called the Ku Klux Klan, and to commit other depredations with that as an excuse. The raid

will probably be made within the coming week. Please give the
K K K's warning.' The letter then went on to say, significantly:
'Every negro and white man absent from home between this
time and Saturday night will be counted as a member of the
invading clan and treated accordingly. Radicals, white and
black, are notified to govern themselves accordingly.' This
was commonly regarded as a device to scare the Radicals into
staying at home during the time specified, as there was an
election to be held on the following Saturday. At any rate,
there was no such raid as was threatened — but the Radical
vote was very appreciably reduced.

The beginning of the Ku Klux activities in Memphis was
signalized by a good deal of newspaper publicity, the Ku Klux
organizers, wherever it appeared, seeming to have an excellent
appreciation of the value of advertising and a genius for getting
plenty of it. On March 1, 1868, there appeared in the Memphis
Public Ledger an editorial headed 'The Ku Klux Klan — What
Is It?' which said:

'Those who in many instances have suffered from depredations at the hands of active members of the Loyal Leagues have,
as we are advised, organized an antagonistic society solely for
the purpose of protecting persons and property.... There
will be no violation of law by the Ku Klux, and others who do
attempt wrongful acts may find a power interposing its authority
which is terrible only to thieves and wrong-doers. It is said
(with what degree of truthfulness others must determine) that
the "Ku Klux" constitute already a strong organization in this
county. If no other harm be done than that ascribed to the
association in Middle Tennessee, there surely can be little
reason for condemnation of a society which at worst is but a
counterpart of the Loyal Leagues; with the recommendation
added that while Leagues are composed of the most dangerous
(because the most ignorant) people on the continent, members
of the mystic association (the Ku Klux) are citizens of Tennes-

see and are permanently bound to the soil. These last are interested in the maintenance of order and good government,
while Loyal Leagues have everything to gain by public wrongs
and disorders.' In a news item in the same issue the statement
was made: 'The Ku Klux Klan is spreading all over the state.'

That the 'mystic association' was already established in
Memphis was indicated by the following item which appeared
in the *Public Ledger* on March 11, 1868:

FOUND, on Front Street last night, the folowing document of
weird and significant import:

K K K

Wolf Hole, Bloody Month
Fair Moon, First Hour

General Orders No. 1
Shrouded Brothers of Memphis, Div. No. 60:

In Hoc Signo      12

The Great Grand Past Giant Commands You. The dark and
dismal hour draws nigh. SOME LIVE TO–DAY — TO–
MORROW DIE.
The Bullet Red and the Right are Ours
To-day, the 11th of the mortal's month of March, you will begin
to scatter the clouds of the grave.

On the next day, March 12, the *Public Ledger* carried this
news item:

K K K

Mysterious Discharge of Firearms in Chelsea

Is the Kuklux in Memphis

Has the Great Grand Past Cyclops really emerged from
'Wolf Hole,' marshalled his 'Shrouded Legions' to 'scatter the

clouds of the grave'? That's the question. [And more to that effect.]

Then, after describing a report of the mysterious discharge of firearms in Chelsea (a suburb of Memphis), the news item continued: 'That the shots were actually heard we have from a gentleman residing in the above named vicinity who is in every way reliable, but further than this he was unable to inform us. Who can?'

That the *Public Ledger* might be suspected of being a sort of official mouthpiece of the Ku Klux in Memphis was indicated by the following which appeared in the issue of March 17:

TO WHOM IT MAY CONCERN: The following was found under our office door at an early hour this morning, where it was probably deposited by the storm of last night:

K K K

Wolf's Hole. Dark Moon, Fatal Hour

The Grand Cyclops Commands you to assemble.
The graves are opening, our brothers cry:
    'Traitors tried and traitors die
    'The hole is filling fast and deep
    'Which *tried* ones know, and ever keep.'

On March 20 there was an editorial in the *Ledger* entitled ' "Kuklux" Associations' which said that 'Whether there are such organizations in existence is more than we know. . . . When outrages cease, resistance will cease with them.'

On the twenty-first the *Ledger* said: 'Let the government put down the thefts by negroes, and the crimes on the highways, and the abounded outrages which have been encouraged by Radical leaders, and we'll answer for it that all "Ku Klux Klans" (if such a thing exists at all) will cease at once.'

Such news stories and editorials as these continued to appear almost daily for months. The Ku Klux Klan could not have had more abundant and favorable free advertising in the columns of this Memphis paper if the Grand Wizard of the Invisible Empire himself had been its editor; and there were those in Memphis at the time who understood that there was indeed a close affinity between the editor of the paper and General Forrest — although the editor was always careful to make it clear that he did not know whether such a thing as the Ku Klux was actually in existence. But, at any rate, with the Grand Wizard resident in the city, backed up by such a favorable press as it was able to command, Memphis became a stronghold of Ku Klux activity. The newspaper notices of the Klan's work in Memphis soon began to attract nation-wide attention, and in the New York *Evening Mail* on March 12, 1868, there appeared a story of the Klan's appearance in Memphis, which concluded: 'This is a local political folly, we presume, corresponding to the more general and far more dangerous political follies known as "Grand Army of the Republic," "Boys in Blue," "Constitutional Alliance," and various other politico-military mysteries. . . . General Logan as head of the so-called "Grand Army" holds a position which is not honorable to him as a statesman or as a soldier.'

An interesting inside story of the operations of the Klan in Memphis was told in an article in the *Confederate Veteran* of November, 1930, by George W. Libby, a member of the prominent family of that name in Richmond, Virginia, who went to Memphis after the war and went to work for the firm of Taylor, Cook & Company on Front Street.

'Being a pretty good mixer,' said Mr. Libby, 'I made friends among the young fellows and, gaining an insight of the aims and purposes of the Ku Klux Klan, I expressed a desire to join. A friend took me to one side and said: "If you will see me to-night at the Pat Cleburne saloon, at eight o'clock, I think I can

put you in the way of having your desire gratified." I met him
and was blindfolded, took him by the arm, and was led in many
and various directions until we reached a door upon which we
knocked. Presently I was ushered in and was asked innumerable questions relative to my army record and if I was willing
to jeopardize my life for the South for the protection of our
mothers, wives and daughters. I was given the oath and became a Ku Klux.

'The order had nothing in writing, all communications being
oral, as Governor Brownlow had offered a reward of one
thousand dollars for the capture of an individual member, and
anything in writing would be incriminating. We always went
singly to our meetings. N. B. Forrest of Confederate fame was
at our head, and was known as the Grand Wizard. I heard him
make a speech in one of our Dens in which he said: "Brownlow
says he will bring his militia down here and get us. I say, let
him fetch 'em, and you boys be ready to receive 'em."

'Soon after this the Ku Klux rode into town one night, forty
strong, horses and men disguised, under the command of Major
DuBose, a prominent lawyer and gallant officer of the Confederacy. He marched his company down in front of Police
Headquarters, where the police were drawn up with guns in
their hands. The Major fronted the column with a pistol in
each hand, saluted the chief and said: "Here are the genuine Ku
Klux for whose arrest your Governor has offered a reward.
Take us." The chief, wishing to avoid bloodshed, replied: "You
can go on."

'For several months no colored face was seen on the streets
after dark. Soon Tennessee was free of this disgrace and under
control of its rightful rulers; then the organization was disbanded, having accomplished its purpose.'

Although the Ku Klux organization in Tennessee profited by
the plentiful favorable publicity accorded by the sympathetic
press, the Radical newspapers in the state extended themselves

to the utmost in violent denunciation of it and all its works; but it is obvious that, despite their bluster, they were distinctly jittery.

Nashville was the seat of the Brownlow state government and was swarming with his satellites and henchmen; and a general feeling of vague uneasiness pervaded the Radical portion of the city's population, which included the officials of the city as well as the state. The local Ku Klux fed this uneasiness by launching numerous frightening rumors of impending activities of some mysterious and portentous nature, hinting at a possible invasion of the city by an armed force of Klansmen.

Apprehension of such an invasion of the city came to be so keenly felt and feared that early in March, 1868, the chief of police called on the local garrison of United States troops for aid. Accordingly the commandant of Ash Barracks arranged to maintain a force of ten cavalry and fifty infantry in readiness to move at a moment's notice against any advance by the hooded horsemen. 'It is thought,' said a local newspaper, 'that if the Ku Klux organization can be squelched here, it may eventually lead to a suppression of the order throughout the state.'

The garrison was in a highly nervous state, having convinced themselves that a Ku Klux attack was really impending; and a mild panic was precipitated one night about ten o'clock when the sleeping troopers were aroused by the sounds of shots fired by the sentries, followed by the beating of the long roll and frantic cries of 'Turn out! Turn out!' The whole force rushed to arms to beat off the Ku Klux attacking force; but, to their chagrin, they found it was a false alarm, originating in the imagination of a tipsy trooper who had seen a group of negroes walking in the shadows near the stables and multiplied and transformed them into a mighty host of Ku Klux. The report was widely circulated through Nashville the next day that Ash Barracks had been attacked by a band of forty mounted Ku Klux and that the attacking party had been valiantly repelled by the alert and valiant garrison. The carpetbaggers in town felt a glow of pride and relief when they learned how efficiently they were defended, and the garrison came in for a full measure of praise.

The terror created by this purely imaginary raid was so pleasing to the Ku Klux that they decided to give the Nash-villians a taste of the real thing. On the morning of March 5 there appeared posted in a prominent place in Nashville the following mysterious summons:

Attention, I. O. V.!

Den No. 1, March 4, 1868.

Special Order No. 14

You are hereby summoned to meet in secret conclave to-morrow night (5th) at twelve o'clock. The cock shall crow thrice. The serpent's head shall be crushed. So say you all.
By order of the

MOST WORSHIPFUL GRAND TURK.

The appearance of this notice created a sensation in Nashville, and the city was agog all day with discussion as to what might be impending. Shortly after midnight the watchful citizens were rewarded by the sight of a troop of thirty horsemen 'wearing the masks and dressed in the sombre habiliments of the Ku Klux,' riding slowly and silently into town by way of Church Street, making no hostile gesture and giving no sign of anything but peaceful intentions. A Nashville paper the next morning re-ported the affair, commenting that 'They were at first believed to be a party of young men out on a nocturnal frolic, but a closer inspection led to a different conclusion. Disappearing shortly after their appearance, they were next seen about two o'clock this morning, moving down North Summer Street towards the Sulphur Spring, and are supposed to have left town by that route.' Strangely enough, in view of all the apprehension manifested and the preparations made, the soldiers and the police do not appear to have made any effort to do anything about the Ku Klux parade, although the newspaper account concluded: 'We understand the police are to take steps looking to the prevention of another display of the kind, and serious trouble is anticipated between the Metropolitan Police and the mysterious horsemen. There is a corporation law against the wearing of masks, and by authority of this the Metropolitans will act.'

In the next contact between the Nashville Ku Klux and the Metropolitan Police, however, the Klansmen won a complete victory by sheer moral force, without a shot being fired. This was on the occasion of the dispersal of the Klan when the members of Captain Morton's Den, as a last act of flaunting bravado, staged a parade through the town. The members of the Den who were to make the ride met at their rendezvous in the underground powder magazine of abandoned Fort Negley. Other members of the Den had been stationed at strategic points on the streets of Nashville, dressed in plain clothes but fully armed with pistols. Those who were to make the parade donned their robes in the seclusion of the Magazine, listened to a short speech of instructions from Captain Morton, and mounted their horses. First they paid a visit of admonition to a disorderly negro boarding house in South Nashville, then crossed over and entered the city by way of the Harding Pike, parading through the principal streets and stopping in front of the offices of the *Union and American* and the *Banner*. (There were seventeen in the party, but the newspaper accounts next morning estimated their strength at from two hundred to fifteen hundred.) Following these calls of courtesy they started back in the direction of Fort Negley, the only threat of opposition developing when they reached the corner of Broad and Spruce (now Eighth Avenue). By this time the streets of Nashville were thronged with citizens, and the Metropolitan Police had also been assembled and were drawn up in a line across the street at this corner as the Ku Klux band approached. The plain-clothes Ku Klux had the police individually covered, man for man, each of the Ku Klux carrying his cocked pistol in his pocket ready to shoot his man if the police made a hostile move. The mounted Klansmen never hesitated as they approached the solid line of police ranged before them — and their bluff was effective. The police could not stand the pressure, and as the riders reached them they opened their ranks and let them ride through without a word of protest or opposition.

That was the last appearance of the Ku Klux in Nashville. That night they proceeded to Fort Negley, were formally disbanded, and burned their robes and rituals; and the other Dens in Nashville were disbanded at the same time, without public demonstration or ceremony.

Thomas Dixon in his article in the *Metropolitan Magazine* in 1905 has made a pretty story of this disbandment: 'Outside the city they entered the shadows of a forest. Down its dim cathedral aisles, lit by trembling threads of moonbeams, the white horsemen slowly wound their way to their appointed place. For the last time the chaplain led in prayer, the men disrobed, drew from each horse his white mantle, opened a grave, and solemnly buried their regalia, sprinkling the folds with the ashes of the copy of their burned ritual. This weird ceremony thus ended the most remarkable revolution of history.' As a matter of fact, this weird ceremony ended nothing more than the affairs of that particular Den. Not even the other Dens in Nashville followed any such formal procedure in disbanding, and at least one of them, being of a practical turn of mind, instead of destroying its robes had them laundered and donated them to a local orphans' asylum, where they were used to make summer underwear for the orphans.

But before the Klan reached the disbandment stage in Tennessee it had passed through some tempestuous days. The de-

velopment of the Ku Klux organization right in his own baili-
wick was peculiarly irritating to Governor Brownlow, the fire-
eating arch-Unionist and anti-secessionist who had toured the
North during the war, breathing out the most blood-curdling
imprecations against the rebels and telling of the terrific things
he would do to them if he had the power. But now he was
sitting in the Governor's chair, with all the power of the state
at his command; and the erstwhile rebels had established the
headquarters of their Invisible Empire in his state, probably in
the capital city itself, right under his nose. His political cohorts
were angrily asking him why he didn't do anything about it, and
his enemies were twitting him and mocking him. An impudent
citizen of Concord, Missouri, named W. W. McFarlane, wrote
to him a letter enclosing a ten-cent shinplaster, asking that he
be sent a ritual of the Ku Klux Klan so he could get it started in
Missouri. 'I think it's a good thing, don't you?' innocently inquired Mr. McFarlane.

Brownlow, with his controlled and pliant legislature, had
already had laws enacted authorizing the formation of a state
militia force which should operate at the command of the
Governor, and also had a law passed empowering sheriffs to
recruit county guard units by the employment of any 'loyal'
citizens of the state. In spite of all this concentrated power,
however, the Governor still professed to feel incapable of coping
with the mysterious power of the Ku Klux Klan; and in June,
1868, when Congressman S. M. Arnell telegraphed Brownlow
that the Ku Klux the night before had searched the train for
him, 'pistols and rope in hand,' the Governor telegraphed to
General Thomas at Louisville asking him to send more United
States troops to Tennessee to quell the incipient revolution being
fomented by the masked organization. The level-headed
Thomas refused to be stampeded into sending any more troops,
so Brownlow called an extra session of the legislature to convene
in Nashville on July 27, 1868.

In his message, Governor Brownlow reminded the legislators that when the matter had been previously discussed 'you were assured by leading Conservatives in their respective counties, and doubly assured by the leading rebel journals of the state, that there would be no necessity for any troops whatever, and that law and order would be strictly observed. It turns out that the rebellious elements of the state were at that time secretly arming themselves and perfecting a military organization known as the Ku Klux Klan, composed of ex-Rebel soldiers and those who were in sympathy with them, thus violating their paroles at the time of their surrender, and violating the laws of the state, and plotting and planning mischief in every respect. These men have been arming and organizing for a year past, with an eye to the overthrow of the state government.' Referring further to the Ku Klux in his message, he said: 'This dangerous organization of ex-Rebels now ramifies almost every part of the eleven states that once constituted the Southern Confederacy, and has already grown into a political engine of oppression so powerful and aggressive as to call forth in opposition several notable military orders.' As a means of meeting the threat in Tennessee he said: 'I recommend most emphatically that these organized bands of assassins and robbers be declared outlaws by special legislation, and punished with death wherever found.'

The highly inflammatory nature of the Governor's message created a sensation in the state. A few of the Conservative papers were inclined to oppose the Governor by force. The Gallatin *Examiner* excitedly said: 'We have but one reply to make to the atrocious message of Brownlow. If he wishes war, he will find our entire population ready for it. If peace, he can have it. The fearful responsibility rests with him and his Legislature. If war is the decision, we can promise to make it short and sharp.'

On the other hand, most of the Conservatives, while genuinely alarmed at Brownlow's ferocity, were inclined to make an effort to placate him. A conspicuous and significant event at this time was the 'Council of Peace' called to assemble at Nashville by three prominent Tennesseans who had been generals in the Confederate army: B. F. Cheatham, George Maney and Bushrod R. Johnson. The legislature when it convened had appointed a Special Joint Committee on Military Affairs to investigate the Ku Klux situation, and these three ex-generals had a conference on May 31 with the members of this committee. The next day there was a meeting in Nashville of thirteen of the leading citizens of the state, all of whom had been general officers in the Confederate army, and this council of ex-Confederate leaders adopted a formal memorial to be presented to the legislature in which they expressed a protest against Brownlow's charge of organized enmity to the state government. They denied the need of armed force such as was suggested by the Governor. 'Inasmuch as the supposed danger to the peace of the state,' they said, 'is apprehended from that class of the community with which we are considered identified, as inducement and reason to your honorable body not to organize such military force, we pledge ourselves to maintain the order and peace of the state with whatever of influence we possess, to uphold and support the laws.' This memorial was signed with an imposing roster of names: B. F. Cheatham, W. B. Bate, Tom B. Smith, Wm. A. Quarles, Jos. B. Palmer, George W. Gordon, N. B. Forrest, John C. Brown, Gideon J. Pillow, S. R. Anderson, G. G. Dibrell, Bushrod R. Johnson and George Maney — all former Confederate generals, and at least four of them high officials in the Ku Klux Klan.

There was a good deal of talk at the meeting of the generals with the committee, and nearly everybody made a speech. Forrest was recognized as a sort of spokesman for the petitioners and he was definitely conciliatory, saying that if the disfranchised citizens were given the vote there would be peace.

In conclusion he urged: 'Abolish the Loyal League and the Ku
Klux Klan; let us come together and stand together.' The
members of the committee were courteous and apparently
friendly, but evasive and non-committal. The Radical press of
the state was inclined to sneer at the generals' proffer of the
olive branch. 'If they are able to do that and have not done it,'
said the Nashville *Press and Times*, 'then they appear to be
guilty of all the murders and other outrages perpetrated by the
Ku Klux since that vile body was organized.'

Meanwhile, while the committee was holding its hearings and
making its investigation, the legislature was marking time; and
some of the ultra-Radicals began to get impatient for action.
A group of the more impulsive of the fire-eating Governor's
supporters got together and adopted a resolution demanding
that some immediate steps be taken to protect the loyal people
of the state against 'a set of murderous outlaws . . . known as the
Ku Klux Klan.' The refusal of the Federal Government to send
more troops into the state in response to Brownlow's plea was
ascribed to President Johnson's alleged sympathy with the Ku
Klux movement; and they demanded that something be done
to liquidate the Klan without further delay.

The very next day, however, the Special Joint Committee
made its report, and it was all that the most violent Brownlow
supporter could desire. This committee, strongly partisan and
biased in its make-up, had examined a large number of witnesses (most of them victims or alleged victims of Ku Klux outrages), and they reported that their investigation convinced
them that there existed in the state 'an organization of armed
men going abroad, disguised, robbing poor negroes of their
fire-arms; taking them out of their homes at night, hanging,
shooting and whipping them in the most cruel manner, and
driving them from their homes.' White people also, they
reported, had been subjected to 'the torture of the lash,' these
depredations having been committed all over Middle and

West Tennessee. Particular attention was given to conditions in Maury, Lincoln, Giles, Marshall, Obion, Hardeman, Fayette and Gibson Counties. 'A perfect reign of terror' existed in Maury, Marshall, Rutherford and Giles, they reported; and the clerk of the county court in Gibson was quoted as saying that 'It has gotten to be such a common thing that people think but little about it.'

The committee mentioned scores of cases of alleged offenses committed by the Ku Klux Klan, although it stated that 'to enumerate all the outrages committed by this organization of outlaws would take more time than can be spared.' The testimony of most of the witnesses was of the most alarming nature. A. H. Eastman, the agent of the Freedmen's Bureau at Murfreesboro, stated that for months he had been sleeping with a revolver under his pillow, 'a double-barreled shot-gun, heavily charged with buck-shot at one hand and a hatchet at the other, with an inclination to sell the little piece of mortality with which I am entrusted as dearly as possible.' He stated that the Klan in Rutherford County numbered about eight hundred or a thousand members at that time and had 'the sympathy and encouragement of nearly all the white people' — giving the names of a number of citizens he suspected of being active members. William Green, the Bureau agent at Winchester, reported that 'The Ku Klux have committed so many gross outrages that it is impossible to enumerate them all' and that 'the villains seem determined to over-awe the country.'

The testimony of the witnesses before the committee was replete with accounts of threats, personal abuse and actual assaults and whippings. It is significant, however, that although the report expressed the belief that during the preceding six months the murders would average one a day, in the report itself there were only four killings specifically mentioned with names: a negro man killed by a raiding party; a negro woman said by her husband to have been killed by a raiding party during his absence from home; and a negro and a white man named Bierfield who had been killed in Franklin.

The killing of Bierfield was the result of a complex difficulty growing out of the rape of a little white girl by a negro. The black rapist was promptly hunted down and killed by the child's brother, who was in turn waylaid and killed by a group of the negro's friends who hid behind a low rock wall along the roadside. As this group of assassins galloped off it was seen that their leader was a white man mounted on a white horse; and Bierfield's white horse, the only one in town, was found in his stable later that night covered with sweat. Bierfield was a carpetbagger storekeeper who encouraged the negroes to loaf around his store, and had been heard to tell them that they ought to arm themselves and fight the Ku Klux, offering to furnish them with powder and balls for such a purpose. An intercepted letter confirmed his connection with the white man's murder, and he was visited by a band of Ku Klux who took him from his store and killed him at the corner of Main and Indigo Streets, where the body was found the next morning by Franklin's church-goers. The negro, who was eating a watermelon with Bierfield in his store when the Ku Klux called, was killed accidentally in the mêlée, for which the Ku Klux expressed regret.

It appeared from the committee's report that, aside from their actual deeds of violence, the raiding Ku Klux had evidently indulged in the most unbridled form of threats as to what they were going to do — all this being a part of the standard Ku Klux formula of getting results by intimidation — but apparently those who heard these threats generally accepted them at full face value, and they repeated them breathlessly to the committee: 'They called for a halter and threatened to hang him'; 'They pointed a pistol at me and said they would kill me'; 'They openly declare that they will run off all the Republicans in the county'; 'They told me that they were

going to kill all who had been in the Union Army or belonged
to Union Leagues now'; 'They told my wife that they were
going to commence work and kill all over fourteen years old';
'They threaten to kill every colored man in the county'; 'The
Ku Klux have threatened to kill all colored men who vote for
Brownlow' — the committee's report bristled with such threatening phrases.

The report concluded with the recommendation that the
Governor be invested with full power to call out 'such military
force as may be required to secure obedience to the laws.'

This committee report was all the rubber-stamp legislators
had been waiting for. Disregarding all opposition and all protests,
they rushed through the legislature two laws which probably
served to bring down more obloquy on Brownlow's head than
all the other misdeeds of this stormy petrel. One of these laws
placed the full power of the state militia in the Governor's hand,
and authorized him to declare martial law in any counties of
the state at his discretion. Acting under his new authority,
Brownlow assembled at Nashville a force of sixteen hundred
state troops — black and white; and as soon as he had this
military force organized he declared martial law in the counties
of Overton, Jackson, Maury, Giles, Marshall, Lawrence,
Gibson, Madison and Haywood, sending militia troops into
these counties, where they immediately became embroiled in
trouble with the native white people.

Accompanying this militia law there was also the notorious
anti-Ku Klux law, innocently entitled 'An act to preserve the
public peace' and passed, as one sarcastic Democratic editor
expressed it, 'by the low Senate and the lower House.' This act
provided that any association or connection with the Ku Klux
should be punishable by a fine of five hundred dollars and
imprisonment in the state prison for not less than five years,
with the same punishment fixed for anyone who should 'feed,
lodge, entertain or conceal' a Ku Klux; every inhabitant of the

state was constituted an officer with power to arrest without process anyone 'known to be or suspected of being' a Ku Klux; and informers were to be rewarded with half the fines.

A sympathetic newspaper in Alabama, in an editorial entitled 'Poor Tennessee,' spoke of this law's having been passed by 'the Tennessee bogus Legislature under the vile manipulation of the arch-fiend incarnate, Brownlow,' and went on to say: 'What a time the negroes will have informing falsely on white men and making snug sums thereby; and what a time such negroes will have at the hands of un-caught Ku Kluxes! Fine times ahead in Tennessee!'

As a part of his campaign of extermination against the Ku Klux, Governor Brownlow engaged the services of Captain Seymour Barmore of Cincinnati, who modestly described himself as 'the greatest detective in the world' and who, being a plain-clothes man, dressed in a velvet coat and plum-colored pantaloons, with a flashing diamond pin in his shirt-front. There had been a series of daring and mysterious burglaries in Nashville at about that time, and it was given out to the public that Captain Barmore was in Nashville for the purpose of solving the mystery of the burglaries, and he ostentatiously busied himself in that direction.

Captain Barmore's real purpose was immediately suspected by the watchful Ku Klux, however, and one of their number who took his meals at the St. Cloud Hotel, where Barmore stayed, succeeded in worming his way into the confidence of one of the great detective's confidants. 'He is going to break up this Ku Klux business,' this dupe innocently told his Ku Klux friend one day soon after Barmore's arrival. 'He leaves this afternoon for Pulaski, where the Ku Klux headquarters are, and he will be a member of the Klan before you know it and have all their secrets.' Within a few minutes this information was in the hands of one of the Nashville Dens, and when Captain Barmore's train left Nashville that afternoon it carried also a

Ku Klux shadow, and the news of his coming had been flashed ahead of him to Franklin, between Nashville and Pulaski. Just exactly what happened was never told; but Barmore got off the train at Franklin and turned back. 'I deemed it best to return to Nashville,' he explained mysteriously to his Nashville friend; but he was a bold and determined man, and he declared his intention to expose the Ku Klux Klan if it cost him his life. Also, although he did not publicize that phase of the matter, he had the incentive of a huge reward promised by Brownlow if he was successful.

The very next day Barmore started to Pulaski again; but at Carter's Creek Station near Columbia the train was stopped and boarded by members of the Klan who took him into the woods and formally arraigned him before the assembled Klan for trial as an enemy. They pointed out to him that it was within their power to kill him then and there if they so desired, but told him that they did not resort to such extreme measures except as a matter of last resort. They explained to him the causes that had led them to organize the Klan, and impressed on him its great power and their determination not to be deterred in their purpose. It was later reported that they administered to him what was known as 'the padlock degree,' a painful and embarrassing ceremony employed by them as a warning in extreme cases; but he was not otherwise molested or punished. He was held a prisoner all night, and the next morning was put on the northbound train and sent back to Nashville. Their last word to him was to tell him that if he persisted in his efforts and again fell into their hands he would die.

Barmore would not be warned, however, and two nights later he set out again for Pulaski. He did not leave on the regular four o'clock afternoon train this time, but made the trip to Pulaski on a freight train at night, thereby outwitting the Nashville Ku Klux. The next thing known of him, he had secretly arrived at Pulaski, had attended a meeting of the Klan there and had presumably obtained a full list of its members.

The Pulaski Ku Klux, when they saw Barmore preparing to board the train for Nashville, realized to their horror that the fate of the whole organization was in his hands, and they acted promptly. The candy butcher on the train sent a cryptic message to the agent at Columbia: 'Apples all out. Have two dozen at the station.' The message was properly translated by the Columbia operator, a member of the Klan, and he had 'two dozen at the station' when the train arrived at 1.30 A.M. — but it was two dozen masked and mounted Klansmen and not two dozen apples.

The Ku Klux worked with machine-like precision when the train stopped at the Columbia station. Two of them went to the engine and took charge of the engineer. A pair of them took their places on the platform of each car, and a cordon of pickets was thrown around the station to ward off any possibility of prying intruders, although at 1.30 A.M. there were not many people stirring in Columbia.

Barmore was asleep in his seat, and was awakened by being punched in the ribs with a pistol by a forbidding figure in the dread Ku Klux apparel. Most of the other passengers were asleep; but those who were awake looked on in terrified inaction as the armed Klansman quietly commanded Barmore to come with him. Barmore surrendered without protest or struggle, and after he had been removed from the train the leader of the party blew a shrill blast on his whistle and the two Ku Klux in charge of the engineer permitted him to go ahead. Barmore's captors rode off with him without noise or disturbance; and so quietly was the whole thing done that the people of Columbia knew nothing about it until they read an account of it in the Nashville papers the next day.

There was a great deal of speculation concerning what was generally referred to as Captain Barmore's 'disappearance.' There were some who claimed to believe that Barmore had

merely 'skipped out' and had chosen this dramatic way of
making his exit. Others suggested that it was a hoax conceived
by him for professional advertising. The most obvious explanation, of course, was that he had been made away with by the Ku
Klux; but as no trace of his body was found the mystery deep-
ened. After a few weeks his personal effects were administered
on by a Nashville justice of the peace, and when his carpetbag
was opened it was found to contain a full Ku Klux disguise —
'a black calico gown, bordered with half-diamond linen trimmings, and a black cambric mask tipped off with white cambric
and running down into a narrow twist of about eight inches in
length. The apertures for the eyes and mouth are trimmed with
red cloth, while two small white linen figures representing faces
are pasted on each cheek.' This was the type of disguise then in
use in Pulaski, and it was through its use that the detective had
been able to penetrate the Pulaski Den.

Barmore's mysterious disappearance was the talk of the
country for six weeks; but on February 20 the mystery was
solved when a body was fished out of the swollen waters of Duck
River at Booker's Ferry Bridge about two miles below the city,
and when it was carried to Columbia it was identified as
Barmore's. His body had evidently been weighted with a rock
or other heavy weight which had slipped off, as there was a rope
around his neck with a noose at the end of it. His arms were tied
behind him with a linen handkerchief, and there was a single
bullet-hole in his head. It was obvious that revenge rather
than robbery had been the cause of his death. His two gold
rings were still on the fingers of his left hand, and in his shirt
front was the diamond-studded cross pin which he habitually
wore. His wallet was in his pocket, his money undisturbed —
but there was no list of Ku Klux members there when his body
was found.

The tragic solution of the Barmore mystery attracted attention all over the country, and it was featured in the newspapers

for several days. The Louisville *Courier Journal*, in discussing
the matter, said: 'Barmore was a loose, eccentric dare-devil.
He had no friends among his own class, speaking politically,
for personally he had no class. He led an isolated, wayward,
freakish, mysterious, crooked and vicious life, a detective by
nature.... It is believed by many that he was a spy for both
parties during the war. Assuredly he could not be suspected of
patriotism.... He was brave and enterprising, being a cross
between the bandit and the peddler, with a dash of the gipsy.

'They put him out of the way. Who did the deed we know
not; but, we dare say, had the scene been translated to New
England, and the Radical editors who have denounced it
formed a part of the danger-threatened community, they would
have joined the posse. Rob a people of the law, drive them out
of the courts, proscribe them en masse — all of which Brownlow
has done — and they are bound to protect themselves. If the
people of the North want peace at the South, they must give
peace and protection to the people of the South. They must not
send a lot of vagrants down there to be Governors and Senators
and Judges, backed up by negroes and bayonets, if they expect
good fellowship. Ku Kluxism in Tennessee has been the natural
reaction to Radical ruffianism. Stop the ruffians on the one
side, and the people will have no reason nor inclination to
defend their firesides by acts of ruffianly but justifiable defense.'

Brownlow resigned from the office of governor of Tennessee
on February 25, 1869, to take the seat in the United States
Senate to which he had had himself elected by his legislature;
and he was succeeded as governor by D. C. Senter. Senter
was a Republican, but not of the violently Radical type, and
he immediately gave evidence of his determination to restore
the right of suffrage to the disfranchised native citizens of
Tennessee and otherwise undo the wrongs of the Brownlow
administration. The official order for the dissolution of the Ku
Klux Klan followed closely; and although the Ku Klux tag was

attached to every deed of violence occurring in the South for the next three years, the genuine Ku Klux Klan in Tennessee did not long survive the end of Brownlow's reign as governor.

Tennessee was the only Realm of the Invisible Empire concerning which there remains any vestige of documentary records. The Grand Exchequer of the Silver Creek and Globe Greek Klan, which had its Den at Old Shiloh Church in Marshall County, neglected to destroy his exchequer list of members; and it has recently been brought to light. Also, the Grand Cyclops of another Tennessee Den preserved his copy of the Prescript, upon the yellowed pages of which there remains his penciled memorandum of the officers of the Klan: 'G. Wizzard of Empire, Forrest; G. Dragon of Realm, Gen. Geo. W. Gordon; G. Titan of Dominion, Joe Fussell; G. Giant of Province, E. D. Thompson; G. Cyclops of Den, ? ?' In the place of the coy interrogation marks left by the original Grand Cyclops, there is written in a later handwriting the name of Henry Mann.

General George W. Gordon was the youngest brigadier in the Confederate army at the close of the war in 1865; and, although a young man, he had the natural spark of leadership. He took up the practice of law in Pulaski after the war, and when the Ku Klux Klan was organized there he became one of its earliest members and soon assumed a place of leadership in its councils. He assisted in the propagation of the order, and when the Invisible Empire was formally organized in 1867 he was the natural choice for Grand Dragon of the Realm of Tennessee. In General Gordon's family is preserved a unique Ku Klux badge which he wore, a five-pointed star wrought from a five-dollar gold piece, bearing the three small stars used in the Prescript to indicate the words 'Ku Klux Klan,' and carrying the Latin inscription '*In hoc Signa Spes mea*' (In this sign is my hope). So far as is known, the Grand Dragon of the Realm of Tennessee was the only Ku Klux official who ever wore a badge of office.

The town of Pulaski, where the Ku Klux Klan originated, is located in the southern part of Tennessee, only twenty miles from the Alabama state line. As the fame of the Klan began to spread, therefore, it naturally attracted the attention of the people of northern Alabama; and pretty soon local Dens began to spring up throughout that part of the state, with focal points at Huntsville, Athens and Tuscaloosa.

When the counties in which the Ku Klux were active are blocked out on a map of the state of Alabama, it will be observed that the organization's activities were confined very largely to the northern part of the state, being practically unknown south of Montgomery. In that part of the state where it was established, however, it operated with great energy and potency; and among its reputed leaders it included some of the foremost men of the state. Aside from Tennessee, there were probably more Ku Klux Dens in Alabama than in any other state in the Invisible Empire.

Alabama had strong provocation for resorting to the Ku Klux idea as a defensive device, as that state was at an early date subjected to a highly oppressive carpetbagger government, operating under a constitution which was not only very objectionable to the people but which had been drafted and adopted by dubious political methods. In speaking of the convention which drew up the constitution, Samuel A. Hale, a staunch Union man before, during and after the war, stated that the men who composed the convention were a lot of 'worthless vagabonds, homeless, houseless drunken knaves,' who had been elected in an election which was 'as shameless a fraud as was ever perpetrated upon the face of the earth.' He gave it as his opinion that one of the predominating causes for the organization of the Ku Klux Klan was 'the appointment of these worthless vagabonds to office.' Mr. Hale was a native of New Hampshire who had lived in Alabama the better part of his life and had always been an intensely loyal Union man; but the enormities of the Reconstruction sickened him.

The people of Alabama chafed under the galling of the government which had been imposed on them, and resented particularly the rising spirit of truculent independence on the part of the newly freed negroes. As the negroes were organized into secret societies like the Loyal League, and spent a large part of their time in marching to the beat of drums and drilling in public with a conspicuous flourish of arms, the apprehension of the people increased. Spontaneously bands of regulators began to spring up locally. For instance, a man in Tallapoosa County named John T. Wright organized a regulatory body, composed mostly of returned Confederate soldiers, called 'The Black Cavalry.' This never amounted to much; but Wright became one of the Alabama organizers of the Ku Klux Klan when the influence of the new secret society began to spread into that state. Wright, and many others like him, already had the germ of a similar idea; the Ku Klux Klan offered an organized mechanism for carrying it out.

The exact date of the birth of the Ku Klux Klan in Alabama cannot be accurately and definitely determined, but it is a matter of record that the ubiquitous General Forrest was in northern Alabama in the spring of 1868; and it was soon after that time that the people of Alabama began to see the Ku Klux bands riding about at night. Colonel William M. Lowe, a

lawyer of Huntsville, recalled that General Forrest called to
see him about some insurance business at that time and that,
the insurance matter disposed of, the general told him something about the blossoming of the Ku Klux in Tennessee.
Colonel Lowe hastened to add, however, that he assured General
Forrest that he was not interested in any such movement and
would not have anything to do with it.

One of the earliest converts in Alabama was Ryland Randolph
of Tuscaloosa, editor of the *Independent Monitor* published in that
city, which carried at its masthead the trenchant motto: 'White
man — right or wrong — still the white man.' He rendered
yeoman service to the Klan during the period of its activity;
and his gift for searing invective and violent verbal pyrotechnics
soon brought him into national notoriety. Randolph was a
firebrand whose antipathy for the carpetbaggers and Radicals
kept him in constant hot water even before he became active in
the Ku Klux Klan. As early as 1867 his life was threatened on
account of some of his sulphuric utterances, and he applied to
H. S. Whitfield, a Radical then in charge of the town's affairs,
for a pass. Whitfield, who cordially detested Randolph, obliged
with a document saying: 'To all whom it may concern: Let
this damned rebel pass whenever he pleases. If he never comes
back, so much the better.' This insulting document was construed by Randolph as a mortal insult, and he promptly chal-
lenged Whitfield to a duel, but the matter was eventually
patched up without bloodshed.

In a letter written thirty years later to Doctor W. L. Fleming,
Mr. Randolph related how he joined the Ku Klux organization
as soon as he heard of it, going on to say: 'It originated with
returned soldiers, for the purpose of punishing those negroes
who had become notoriously and offensively insolent to white
people; and, in some cases, to chastise those white-skinned
men who, at that particular time, were showing an inclination
to socially affiliate with negroes. The impression sought to be

made upon the latter was that these white-robed night prowlers were the ghosts of the Confederate dead who had arisen from their graves in order to work vengeance on an undesirable class of both white and black men. Their robes used in these nocturnal campaigns consisted simply of sheets wrapped around the bodies and belted around the waist. The lower portion reached to the heels, whilst the upper had eyeholes through which to see and mouthpiece through which to breathe. Of course, every man so caparisoned had one or more pistols in holsters buckled to his waist. The Ku Klux organization flourished principally in middle and northern Alabama, notably in Montgomery, Greene, Tuscaloosa and Pickens counties. ... In some instances organizers were sent to towns to establish the Klans. These latter were formed into companies, officered somewhat in military style. In 1868 I was honored by being chosen leader of the Tuscaloosa Klan and I am gratified to be able to say that my Klan did much good service in Tuscaloosa county.'

As soon as Randolph became Cyclops of the Tuscaloosa Den he began to use his paper in behalf of the organization's work. He began by reprinting items from newspapers in other Southern cities telling of the Klan's activities, and then on April 1, 1868, printed an article entitled 'The Ku Klux Phylarchy' in which he said: 'Early on last Friday morning our attention was directed to crowds, both black and white, who were collected around Spiller's, Glascock's and the old Washington Hall corners. Upon visiting these triple precincts we found large posters pasted on the walls, headed with large letters of blood. During the day we received an anonymous note, also indited in blood, of which the following is a true copy:' The anonymous note, 'indited in blood,' was an alleged order from the Ku Klux Cyclops directing him to reprint the posters in his paper, the order ending with this couplet:

'Cyclops warns it — print it well
'Or glide instanter down to hell.'

Editor Randolph, acting under the orders of Cyclops Randolph, then proceeded to print the text of the Ku Klux posters which had been composed and printed the night before by Ryland Randolph the job printer, in all their blood-and-thunder nonsense. Each of the posters was headed 'Ku Klux' in big black letters, and a specimen one of them read:

> Hollow Hell, Devil's Den, Horrible
> Shadows. Ghostly Sepulchre.
> Head Quarters of the Immortal Ate
> of the K. K. K. Gloomy Month. Bloody
> Moon. Black Night, Last Hour.

General Orders No. 3.

Shrouded Brotherhood! Murdered Heroes!

Fling the bloody dirt that covers you to the four winds! Erect the Goddess on the banks of the Avernus. Mark well your foes! Strike with the red hot spear! Prepare Charon for his task!

Enemies reform! The skies shall be blackened! A single Star shall look down upon horrible deeds! The night owl shall hoot a requiem o'er Ghostly Corpses!

Beware! Beware! Beware!

The Great Cyclops is angry! Hobgoblins report! Shears and lash! Tar and Feathers! Hell and Fury!

Revenge! Revenge! Revenge!

Bad men, white, black, yellow, repent!

The hour is at hand! Be ye ready! Life is short. J.H.S.Y.W.!!!

Ghosts! Ghosts! Ghosts!

Drink thy tea made of distilled hell, stirred with the lightning of heaven, and sweetened with the gall of thine enemies!

All will be well!!!

By order of the Great

BLUFUSTIN

G.S.   K.K.K.

A true copy,
   Peterloo.
P.S.   K. K. K.

It might be remarked right here, incidentally, that in spite of this pointed reference to 'tar and feathers' in the poster, there was in fact no single instance of the use of tar and feathers ever attributed to the Ku Klux. They committed various forms of violence, but this particular form of punishment was never used by them.

Randolph lost no time in getting to work as an operating Ku Klux, and within a few days had attracted attention to himself by becoming embroiled in a street fight in Tuscaloosa, in the course of which he drew his knife and slashed a negro named Balus, who was assaulting a white man who happened to be a member of Randolph's Klan. In his issue of the next day he referred to this episode in an editorial entitled 'Niggers — Radicals — Ghosts,' in which he said: 'The cutting and beating of the insolent fellow Balus on the 28th ult., in presence of crowds of his fellow niggers, has had a salutary influence over the whole of niggerdom hereabout. They now feel their inferiority, in every particular, to the white man.' He then proceeded to say that 'It is reported that the Ku Klux Klan is preparing to visit North Port' [a town across the river], boldly giving the names of probable victims of the Klan's vengeance: 'D. M. Harless, the fellow who piloted Croxton's forces thither, is trembling in his shoes. We are afraid the Ghosts will *hang* him.... W. T. Hammer, the meanest, mangiest hound in Christendom, is good for a suspension from a good, high limb till his disgraced life abandons its carrion habitation,' etc. Then, as a spur to the superstitious fears of the negroes, he wrote: 'A couple of friends who were passing through the cemetery the other night overheard mutterings against the men specified, which leads us to believe that they are "spotted" and can not live in this county,' etc., etc.

About this time General Shepherd, the military commandant of the state of Alabama, from his office in Montgomery on April 4 issued his famous 'General Order No. 11.' This order started off: 'The outrage against life, the peace and good order of the community, in this sub-District, perpetrated by a band disguised with masks and styling itself the Ku Klux Klan, constitutes a public evil. It is therefore ordered that the various sheriffs, majors, marshalls, magistrates, constables, chiefs of police and police shall be held accountable by the Post Commanders over their respective districts for the suppression of the iniquitous organization, and the apprehension of its members wherever found'; and then went on to decree that 'All placards and newspaper cards of the Ku Klux Klan are prohibited,' etc.

This order was derided by the *Monitor*, which spoke of its 'resemblance to the Pope's famous bull against the comet,' and also compared General Shepherd with 'Xerxes, madly lashing the waves of the Hellespont in his impotent wrath at their destruction of his bridge of boats, and Canute coolly commanding the tide to retire from his approach.'

The Montgomery *Sentinel* in its issue of the eighth defiantly noted: 'The Ku Klux Klan met, it is said, at their usual place last night, in spite of Gen. Shepherd's order'; and the *Monitor* on April 21 said: 'Rumor says that Gen. Shepherd's order gave rise to an acrimonious debate in the recent council of the Ku Klux Klan about 12 o'clock last Saturday night at the old graveyard. The Grand Cyclops was rather of the opinion that it was unconstitutional and consequently of no force or effect with the Klan.'

Eutaw in Greene County was another hotbed of Ku Klux activity throughout Reconstruction times. As early as 1867 a preacher named Hill (described by a local paper as 'an infamous old scalawag') was set upon and whipped by a group of native young men who were incensed at his tendency to inflame the negroes. For this offense they were arrested by United States troops, and after being held in prison at Mobile and Selma for several weeks were tried and convicted by a

military commission. Seven of them were sentenced to serve
terms of imprisonment on the Dry Tortugas; and they were
actually transported there and started serving their sentences,
but were soon pardoned. They were received as returned
heroes when they got back to Eutaw; and one of them, John
Cullen, opened a saloon which he called 'The Dry Tortugas'
and which became a favorite rendezvous of patriotic and
thirsty natives.

Later there was an affray on the public square in Eutaw in
connection with a public speaking, in the course of which several
negroes were wounded, but nobody killed. Efforts were made
to identify this as a 'Ku Klux outrage'; and although it was
never possible to connect the Ku Klux organization with the
trouble, it added to the tense feeling in the town and county.

There was no question, however, regarding the connection
of the Ku Klux Klan with the killing of Alexander Boyd, the
county solicitor or prosecuting attorney, who signed his own
death warrant by talking too much. Boyd's killing grew in-
directly out of the murder of a white man by two negroes on
the public highway in Greene County late in 1869. The victim,
Sam Snoddy, was last seen talking to a negro man named Sam
Caldwell, who was observed the next day washing some bloody
clothes. Caldwell was accordingly arrested along with two
other negroes accused of being accomplices — Henry Miller
and Caldwell's father, who went by the name of Sam Colwin.
Caldwell and Miller escaped from jail, and Miller was later
found dead; Caldwell's body was never found. Colwin's body,
perforated with sixteen bullet-holes, was also later found hung
to a tree, after he had been released from jail by the Radical
authorities. The Ku Klux were immediately suspected of being
responsible for the deaths of all three of the negroes, although
there seemed to be no direct evidence connecting them with
the matter.

Alexander Boyd, aside from being a Radical office-holder,

did not enjoy any great measure of popularity in Greene
County. Fifteen years before this time he had killed a young
man named Brown, for which he was sentenced to serve ten
years in prison. A friendly governor, however, commuted his
sentence to one year in jail, and when he had served that time
he moved off to Arkansas, leaving behind him a large number
of the friends and relatives of the deceased Brown who felt that
Boyd had not paid a sufficiently heavy penalty for his crime.
After the war he came back to Eutaw, espoused the Republican
cause and was appointed county solicitor; and this did not add
anything to his popularity. He was 'a very disagreeable man
to do business with,' testified some of the people; and others
went further, saying that he was a man who 'sold the administration of the law' — that he would 'let a man off when he
would pay for it, and prosecute him for vengeance when disposed
to do so.'

Even so, Boyd's personal unpopularity might have had no
fatal consequences had he not made the mistake of boasting
publicly that he knew who killed Sam Colwin and the other
negroes and that he was going to bring them to justice at the
next term of court. That was a tragic error on his part. At
eleven o'clock on the night following this injudicious threat, a
band of Ku Klux in customary disguise rode into Eutaw and
in a methodical and businesslike manner went about the work
of liquidating Mr. Boyd. Some said there were thirty-five in
the Ku Klux band; some said there were seventy-five. At any
rate, there were enough to post pickets on the corners of the
public square, the main body riding directly to Clearfield's
Tavern where Mr. Boyd lived. Leaving guards outside, the
Ku Klux entered the hotel and forced the clerk to lead them
to Rooms Nos. 4 and 5, which were the rooms occupied by
Boyd.

It did not take them long to transact their bloody business.
Immediately after their entry into the room there were sounds

of scuffling. Men on the street heard a terrified voice cry out: 'Murder! Murder! Murder!' This outcry was followed by a volley of pistol shots. The executioners came down to the street without any evidence of haste or alarm, gathered up the guards and pickets with a few blasts from the leader's whistle and mounted their horses. Riding once around the public square as a final gesture of nonchalant defiance, the Ku Klux rode out of town unpursued. Witnesses of the affair testified to the methodical form of procedure: 'There was scarcely a word spoken by them. The sentinels were sent out and brought in by a mere wave of the hand.'

After the Ku Klux had gone, Mr. Clearfield, the tavern-keeper (who had been playing billiards in a bar-room across the street), went up to Mr. Boyd's room and there found the body of the unfortunate solicitor riddled with bullets, two being squarely through the forehead.

The killing created great excitement in Eutaw, and the Republicans and negroes were in a fury of indignation. The next day a body of armed negroes marched into the town from the surrounding country and staged a warlike demonstration, threatening to burn down the hotel where the assassination took place. Cooler Republicans persuaded them to disperse and go home; but they departed heaping imprecations on the Ku Klux Klan, and threatening future vengeance.

The Circuit Court judge, a Republican, at the next term of court gave the grand jury a vigorous charge on the subject and appointed an energetic and competent Republican attorney in Mr. Boyd's place. The grand jury, a mixed jury of blacks and whites, remained in session two weeks and examined more than five hundred witnesses, including men summoned from the vicinity of every bridge and ferry in the county. The witnesses were examined and cross-examined; but the grand jury's final report was that they were not able to get the slightest hint or clew pointing to any man. The Ku Klux had ridden out of town in the direction of Springfield, and the jury reported its conclusion that they were all from Pickens County, which was adjoining. The grand jury of Pickens County, however, reported that the masked men seen that night rode right on through that county. The theory was expressed that perhaps they had come from Tennessee — which was about three hundred miles away. That was as near as anybody ever came to solving the identity of the masked executioners.

Mr. Boyd's remains were interred in a Eutaw cemetery, with a tombstone upon which his uncle had chiseled the pregnant epitaph: 'Murdered by the Ku Klux!!'

Early in the fall of 1869 there was an outburst of disorder in Tuscumbia, when a group of negroes set fire to the female academy there and burned it to the ground, fortunately with no loss of life as it was just before the school sessions were to begin.

This act of arson was the work of eight negro members of the Loyal League in Tuscumbia who had been aroused to action by a negro agitator from Memphis who was a porter on the sleeping-car of the Memphis & Charleston Railroad. This porter, as was developed by the later confessions of the participants, told the Tuscumbia negroes that they were at war with the white race and should use the torch on them. Thus goaded, the eight Loyal Leaguers started out to burn the town; but, characteristically, they ran into difficulty in deciding whose house to set afire first. They were favorable to the idea of burning the town as a general proposition, but whenever it came to the point of actually applying the torch to any particular house there was always one of the negroes who would speak up and say: 'No, let's not burn his house; he's a good man,' or 'He's been good to me,' until the leaders despaired of finding any place to start and finally hit upon the idea of burning the academy, as it was devoid of personal defenders.

For this wanton and criminal act the three ringleaders were

taken out by the Ku Klux and hung to the railroad bridge at
Tuscumbia. The other five, who were merely following the
leaders, were indicted for arson and tried in the courts, several
of the leading attorneys of Tuscumbia volunteering for their
defense. While their conviction was being appealed they escaped
from jail and fled to Kentucky; but the current report in
Tuscumbia was that they also had been taken out of the jail
and executed by the Ku Klux and their bodies mysteriously
disposed of.

The congressional committee devoted more attention to
Alabama than to any other Realm of the Invisible Empire,
and they took so much testimony and examined so many witnesses that the transcript of the evidence fills three big volumes.

One of the most eager and voluble witnesses who testified
before the committee was the Reverend A. S. Lakin, a minister
of the Northern Methodist Church, who had come to the state
in the interest of that church after the war. He told the most
hair-raising stories concerning his personal adventures with
the Ku Klux and his many miraculous escapes from death at
their hands; but he overplayed his hand to such an extent as to
destroy the effect of his testimony. As one of the committee
said of him at the time: 'He came to Washington brimful of gall,
bitterness and falsehood, which he poured out before us in such
a way that it was hardly possible to determine which of the
ingredients predominated. There was hardly a statement
made by him which was not either wholly false or grossly exaggerated. The man seemed to be incapable of speaking the
truth in a plain, unvarnished way; and his neighbors spoke of
him as a man utterly unreliable in his statements. The kindest
thing said was that he was a man of fertile imagination, upon
which he drew freely.'

Parson Lakin was a man of pious and unctuous manner,
always insisting that he was just a plain minister of the gospel,
going about trying to do good, and that he had no interest in

politics or political affairs. From the testimony of the native
Alabamians, however, it appeared that he was too modest in
recounting his own activities along political lines, particularly
the work he had done in organizing the negroes into Loyal
Leagues, influencing them to vote the Radical ticket and influencing them to hate their former masters.

Nicholas Davis, an Alabama Republican, testifying as to
Lakin's character, particularly with reference to his statement
that he was merely a minister of the gospel and took no part in
politics, said: 'If he said that he told a lie. I heard him make a
political speech; he is an old ruffian. He was a candidate for
United States Senator. Was not that politics? Besides, was he
not trying to make himself president of the Alabama University,
and didn't he afterwards run for Superintendent of Education? Didn't he electioneer with me, the old Heathen Chinee?
He ought to be run out of this community; that old fellow is a
hell of an old rascal. I told him to his face: "Mr. Lakin, didn't
you try to be president of the Alabama University?" He said
he did. I said: "It would have been a disgrace to the state.
You don't know an adjective from an adverb, nor nothing else."
He is a humbug, a liar and a slanderer; that's what he is, and
he ain't nothing else.'

An excellent example of the fertility of Parson Lakin's imagination and his talent for tales of horror is provided by the story
he gravely told of the birth of a 'Ku Klux baby.' Accounts of
this horrid and unnatural thing were printed all over the
country, backed up by the Reverend Lakin's deliberate statement that he had 'examined the child very carefully and
minutely' and that the baby was 'a perfect representation and
facsimile of a disguised Ku Klux,' even to the extent of having
horns on its head. This, the Parson charged, was the result of
sinister prenatal influence, the unfortunate mother having been
scared, he said, by a visitation of Ku Klux before the baby was
born. People all over the country shuddered at the thought of

such a thing. There seemed to be no end to the depravity of the Ku Klux.

The attending physician, however, Doctor Garlington Coker, testified before the investigating committee that the baby's alleged resemblance to a Ku Klux was entirely a figment of the imagination. The baby, he testified, was a stillbirth, being born 'not only dead, but slightly putrefied, so much so that at the slightest touch the skin would slip from the flesh. The skin of the forehead had slipped down over the face in part, so as to make an unsightly appearance. After the child was laid out, some ladies suggested that it was a Ku Klux child. I examined the child again, told them that it did not resemble any Ku Klux that I had ever seen, and asked the mother if she had been frightened by a Ku Klux. She told me that she had never seen a Ku Klux in her life. The unsightly appearance of the child did not resemble Ku Klux, and was but the result of partial decomposition.'

This was too good a story, however, for the imaginative Parson Lakin to have it ruined by the interposition of facts; so he took up the cry of 'Ku Klux baby' and succeeded in persuading the husband of the poor woman, one Benjamin Horton, that there was such a resemblance. He also prevailed on Horton to permit the baby's body to be exhibited at a near-by camp-meeting before it was buried, and here the morbid and gullible gathered to look at the pitiful and unsightly spectacle. Lakin, who had an incredible capacity for making mountains of mole-hills, gradually built this up into an example of a new and marrow-chilling form of Ku Klux outrage, and it was widely accepted as such.

The Ku Klux themselves, however, did not seem to relish all this unfavorable publicity, and as a means of displaying their displeasure they decided to flog the unfortunate father of the child. About three o'clock in the morning they rode up to Horton's house and battered on his door. Peeping through the chinking he ascertained the nature of his visitors and attempted to parley with them, but they would brook no delay. 'Get up!' they commanded sternly. 'Arise, Horton, and put on your breeches and come out.' Thus commanded, Horton arose, put on his breeches and went out; with the result that he was given a whipping of eighteen lashes with a hickory switch. Before the Ku Klux departed they told him that he talked too much, and that if they ever again heard him say anything at all about the Ku Klux — either for them or against them — they would come back and give him two hundred lashes on his naked back twice a week.

Horton, when asked why he took no steps to prosecute the Ku Klux who had visited him, said: 'A man might as well go and dig his grave as to go to Blountsville and apply against a Ku Klux or try to warrant him. He wouldn't live long. I was too sharp to do that. I like my life as well as anything else.' His father, Samuel Horton, testified that he also was warned by the Ku Klux, and that he then went off to Georgia.

'Did you run off?' a committeeman asked him.

'No, sir; I never run.'

'You made pretty fast walking?'

'I drove pretty peart.'

'You made the horses run?'

'If you had known that two or three men were after you dressed in scarlet, you wouldn't have stayed there.'

The 'Ku Klux baby,' however, was merely one of the many lurid tales told by Parson Lakin; and it was indicative of the times that a man of this stripe, publicly accused of every form of misbehavior and crime ranging from chronic prevarication to seduction, was actually appointed president of the University of Alabama, located at Tuscaloosa. This did such violence to the sensibilities of the people of Alabama, who were accustomed to seeing a man of scholarly attainments at the head of the state university, that there was a perfect uproar of protest.

Editor Randolph of the *Independent Monitor* was almost beside himself at the very thought of living in the same town with Lakin and the other carpetbaggers and scalawags appointed to the university faculty, and he exploded in his issue of August 11, 1868: 'If these scoundrels expect to live quietly here and draw their salaries, extorted from the sweating brows of the toiling taxpayers of Alabama, *we tell them they are mistaken.* This community will be too disagreeable for them, and the sooner they resign the better.'

Undismayed, President-Elect Lakin, accompanied by Doctor N. B. Cloud, State Superintendent of Public Instruction, went to Tuscaloosa to take over the university preparatory to opening up the school for the fall term; and there they were greeted with a crude woodcut cartoon in the *Monitor* showing two grotesque figures (one carrying a carpetbag) hanging to the limb of a tree, headed 'A Prospective Scene in the City of Oake, March 4th, 1869.' The reading matter accompanying the cartoon stated that 'The above cut represents the fate in store for those great pests of Southern society — the carpetbagger and scalawag — if found in Dixie's land after the break of day on the 4th of March next .... The contract for hanging will be given to the negro who, having mounted the carpetbagger and the scalawag on the mule that he *didn't* draw at the elections, will tie them to a limb and, leading the said mule from under them, over the *forty acres of ground* that he also didn't get, will leave the vagabonds high in mid-air, a feast for anthropophagous vermin.'

In an adjacent column was a news item which stated: 'Scallawag Cloud of Montgomery and Carpetbagger Lakin of Nowhere arrived here Thursday — Cloud the Radical jockey comes as the trainer of Lakin, the negro-loving jackass .... Both would make first-rate hemp stretchers.' Then: 'Later — On Friday afternoon Lakin incontinently departed, by way of the Huntsville road. On Saturday morning Cloud also "made tracks" in direction of Montgomery.... Every fellow they met on the street appeared, to their alarmed fancies and guilty consciences, to be Ku Kluxes in disguise.'

This highly incendiary cartoon and editorial were seized upon with great avidity by the Northern press and reprinted by the Cincinnati *Commercial* and other papers as a sample of the bloodthirsty spirit prevailing in the South. At the same time, Southern Democratic organizations formally denounced Randolph as a rabid extremist whose truculence was doing the South more harm than good. So much of a furor was aroused that Randolph wrote a lame letter of explanation to the Cincinnati *Enquirer* in which he said: ' ... The sketch was understood by everyone here to be a piece of pleasantry, gotten up in a spirit of fun by the devils of the *Monitor* office, as a scarecrow for an incendiary carpetbagger from Ohio, one A. S. Lakin, and an Alabama scalawag, N. B. Cloud, who were in this locality on a short visit with exaggerated ideas of their own personal danger. Had it been intended seriously I would never have allowed it to go in the columns of the *Monitor*, nor as such would it have met the approbation of one man in the county, outside the walls of the lunatic asylum. In this wood-cut the mythical Ku Klux were represented as a retreating jackass, which of itself should have been sufficiently suggestive to the Commercial man that a grim joke was attempted to be perpetrated at the expense of those whose ears like his own seem too long and heavy to be susceptible of anything but the most malicious falsehoods,' etc., etc.

Despite this experience, however — or, perhaps, because of it — Editor-Cyclops Randolph continued to regard himself as the custodian of the sanctity of the university's prestige, and when announcement was made a few months later of the appointment of a new faculty who planned to come to Tuscaloosa and open up the school for the spring term, he carried this item, dripping with sinister suggestion: 'In reply to a communication from Sipsey Swamp signed "K.K.K.," we have to inform the writer that the new nigger faculty will be here on or about the 1st of March next.' R. D. Harper was the man who had been selected to serve as president of the school, and of him Mr. Randolph said: 'Lakin's chances of security would have been infinitely better.' To maintain the atmosphere of lurking danger, the *Monitor* in its next issue reported: 'Quite a large body of sinister looking creatures are reported to us as having been seen at the University grounds on Saturday night last. All appeared dressed in white and hovered about the president's mansion for some time. Thence they went to the house of each professor. The negroes who saw them were so alarmed that they took to their heels without making close scrutiny of the strange figures. It is supposed that the ghosts of the Confederate dead are making themselves familiar with the premises in order to visit Harper et als in March next. Alas! We are very much afraid they will not let the new faculty sleep there.'

The outcome of this campaign was summed up in the brief announcement in the *Monitor* of March 23: 'R. D. Harper has wisely resigned his office of president of the State University,' etc.

Such systematic intimidation was a regular part of the standard Ku Klux technique in dealing with individual cases. For creating the proper psychological effect on whole communities and large groups, however, the favored Ku Klux device was the mass parade in full uniform. One of the most spectacular appearances of the Ku Klux in Alabama was in Huntsville on a Saturday night late in October, 1868. This was the date of a big political rally of negroes in Huntsville, and during the course of the morning a very inflammatory speech had been made by a white Republican orator from Decatur named C. C. Sheets — a man who was later appointed by President Grant as United States Consul to Elsinore in Denmark.

Mr. Sheets told his audience that he had been rudely interrupted by the Ku Klux a few days before while making a speech at Florence and that he had been intimidated into promising them then that he would not make any more such abusive and incendiary speeches as he had been making. 'But,' he said, 'now that I have got up here in Huntsville, where there are so many colored people, I'm not afraid to say what I please.' So he proceeded to tell them that if they would do what it became them as men to do, they would arm themselves and shoot down their enemies wherever they found them; that the reason the Ku Klux paraded the country was because the negroes had shown themselves weak-kneed and afraid to assert themselves; and more to that effect. The passions of the negroes were very much aroused by this speech, and there were open avowals by them that the next time they saw any of the Ku Klux they would shoot them on sight, that the Ku Klux were afraid to show themselves in Huntsville, and so on. The more they talked the braver they got.

The example set by Mr. Sheets was contagious, and similarly provocative speeches were made by others in the meeting. A white blacksmith, described as 'a carpetbagger and a drunken, dissipated fellow,' was particularly bitter in haranguing the negroes and urging them to deeds of violence. A rumor circulated throughout the town that afternoon that the Ku Klux planned to accept the challenge and would ride into Huntsville that very night, and this aroused the oratorical blacksmith to greater flights. 'If they come into town, shoot them down,' he excitedly urged the negroes. 'Fire on them; kill them! Don't wait for them to come into town. Go out and meet them and waylay them. That's the way to handle them.'

Inspired by this advice, one party of excited negroes did go out to the Pinhook bridge to ambush the Ku Klux if they came in that way; and another party went out on the Meridianville pike for a similar purpose. During the course of the afternoon, however, their enthusiasm died down, their ardor weakened, and both of the ambushing parties drifted back into town to listen to the round of speeches and take part in the excitement on the public square.

Meanwhile someone had indeed carried word to the Ku Klux of the challenging statements made by the orators at the rally, and during the course of the evening a band of about one hundred and fifty hooded men rode into town in ghostly silence. In a flourish of bravado they rode slowly and deliberately around the public square, completely encircling the court-house where the Radical meeting was still in progress. Then, having completed the circuit, they withdrew to the neighborhood of the market-house on one of the streets approaching the square and stood there at ease in military formation, making no sound and making no threatening gesture, but obviously on the alert.

General Ruger, in charge of the United States troops in Huntsville, viewed the parade from the balcony of his hotel, in company with some of his staff; and, as military men, they commented favorably on the admirable manner in which the men were deployed into line and their general bearing and movement. Somebody asked him what he was going to do about it, and he replied: 'What can I do about it? It is very absurd, of course; but there is no law, federal or state, forbidding men to masquerade on horseback at night'; and the complacent general went back to his dinner.

But the appearance of the Ku Klux on the scene, even though they gave no sign of intended violence, had created an electric charge of excitement which swept through the crowd congregated on the square and communicated itself to those gathered on the inside listening to the speaking. 'The Ku Klux have come!' rang out on every side; and the crowds outside the court room churned around in a frenzy of excitement as the ghostly troopers rode by. Those inside quickly lost interest in the speaking and wanted to see what was going on outside. They boiled out of the courthouse door on the north side, and added to the general confusion by their excited outcries.

As was perhaps inevitable in such a milling mob of excited, armed men, somebody fired a gun, the testimony showing that the first shot came from among those in the courthouse yard around the door and was directed at the crowd of negroes and whites in the street. Thereupon there was a general round of firing, wholly on the part of the crowd gathered about the courthouse, as a result of which there were two killed and five wounded. One of those killed was Judge Silas Thurlow, a Republican, who was struck in the head by a stray ball. The Ku Klux, marshaled in regular formation near the market-house, were under the observation of a number of witnesses during the entire affray, and according to the testimony of all these witnesses, including General Ruger, the Ku Klux took no part in the firing. After the rioting was over the whistle of the Cyclops sounded and they rode out of town as quietly as they had come, not having fired a shot or committed an overt act during their stay.

This affair was written up in the Northern newspapers in the most exaggerated style, with representations that as a result of a deep-laid political conspiracy a peaceable meeting of Republicans had been raided and forcibly broken up by the Ku Klux Klan and that a large number of Republicans had been killed. There was a prompt and thorough investigation by the Federal authorities, more than seventy witnesses being examined, and it was the universal evidence that the Ku Klux took no part in the riot, although one Republican lawyer expressed the view that they were 'the proximate cause' of the disturbance inasmuch as their appearance threw the negroes into a frenzy of fear which caused them to start shooting each other. After the affair was over and the Ku Klux were dispersed, three men on foot were arrested who had Ku Klux disguises in their saddle-bags which they were carrying. They were held in jail during the night but released the next day, as they were guilty of no offense against the laws then in force; but the disguises were confiscated and pictures of them were widely circulated in the North.

The parade at Huntsville was characteristic of the boldness with which the Ku Klux operated in Alabama, their audacity reaching a peak when they coolly defied a detachment of United States troops in Athens in 1870. Fearing the possibility of trouble in connection with the election in November of that year, the sheriff of Limestone County sent to the military commander at Huntsville and asked for a detachment of troops to be sent to Athens to preserve order on election day. The squad of twenty bluecoats, commanded by a Lieutenant Lynch, arrived in Athens two days before the election and went into camp near the public square.

On the morning of election day, about eight o'clock, a squad of twelve Ku Klux calmly rode into Athens, all in full disguise and their horses disguised. They rode straight to the place where the Federal troops were camped, and their leader saluted Lieutenant Lynch and courteously announced: 'We have come to ask why you are here — what your instructions are.' Lynch considered this an impertinent question and, with all the dignity of a young army officer, replied that he could not hold any intercourse with them, asking them to leave. The Ku Klux, however, showed no disposition to leave; so Lieutenant Lynch hurried to the office of the Freedmen's Bureau and asked its agent, John H. Wager, to go back with him and lend his moral support in parleying with the unwelcome visitors. When Lynch and Wager got back to the street the band of Ku Klux rode up to meet them and the Cyclops said: 'We have been to see the mayor and he tells us that you are here to prevent disorder. That is what we want to do, so there is no use in our staying; but, Lieutenant, if they don't behave themselves, just scratch on the ground and we'll be with you.' Then, with a courtly bow from the Cyclops, the Klansmen wheeled and galloped out of town, leaving a spluttering lieutenant and a flabbergasted Freedmen's Bureau agent.

This sortie into Athens was a much more audacious and dangerous enterprise than the earlier Huntsville parade, for by this time the severe Alabama Ku Klux law was in effect. This law, passed on December 26, 1868, pronounced every man found in disguise an outlaw and a felon and gave any man the right to shoot him down, and also authorized any person injured by any disguised parties to sue the county for damages and indemnification to the amount of five thousand dollars. There were arrests and prosecutions under this law; but, despite a hostile government and judicial system, the men accused of being Ku Klux seemed somehow always to slip between the fingers of the avenging courts.

In some sections of the state, however, the Ku Klux activities did not go unchallenged, and their sway was by no means undisputed. In Fayette County there had been a very strong Union sentiment before the war, and a large number of soldiers for the Federal army had been recruited in this county. When the Ku Klux began their depredations there, the Federal veterans organized a counter-group called the Mossbacks; and the Mossbacks and the Ku Klux carried on a violent conflict in this county for several months, creating something bordering on a state of terrorism. Encounters were not infrequent; some were killed and many were wounded; but no effective steps were ever taken by the civil or military authorities to quell this intra-county civil war.

In spite of this opposition, the Ku Klux seemed to be particularly bold and audacious in Fayette County. There were four companies of them in the county, numbering two hundred members. Not only did they stage demonstrations on the public square while court was in session, but on one occasion

they had the impudence to ride into town, arrayed in their
disguises, and participate in a political meeting held in the
courthouse at night for the nomination of a county officer.
Emboldened by this, they came into town on another occasion
at night, obtained the keys to the courthouse and held one of
their meetings in the courtroom, with a Lictor at the door to
refuse admission to any who did not have the countersign.
Later, when the judge charged the grand jury to be especially
active in an effort to suppress the Ku Klux, the Klan staged a
parade of nearly a hundred mounted men in the square, and
left in the courthouse yard a note which was ornamented with
the picture of a coffin and which read simply: 'Go slow. K. K. K.'

Radicals were not safe from the attention of the Ku Klux,
even when they were not in politics. If they fraternized with
the negroes or had the reputation of talking to them in a way to
excite them, the long arm of the Ku Klux reached out after
them; nobody was immune from their attention. John Tayloe
Coleman, who had drifted out to Alabama from Virginia just
before the war, espoused the Radical party and taught a negro
school. Later he was appointed, through the political influence
of Congressman Hays, as mail-route agent on the railroad
running from Selma to Meridian. During February, 1871, as
the train had stopped at Kewaunee Wood-Pile in Mississippi to
take on wood, Coleman was standing in his mail-car making
up the mail, with his back to the door leading into the passenger
cars, when, he related:

'I felt a pressure on my shoulder as if someone had come in
and laid his hand on me. I turned around and there stood a
man disguised from head to foot in a white gown that was drawn
together at the top, just like a common tobacco bag, and it
just fell over him and nearly touched his feet, and was bound
around with red — around the mouth and around the eyes.
He stood in this position with a pistol in each hand, with his
arms extended toward me, and as I turned around I came
right upon these two pistols.

'Of course I was very much frightened and I hollered to him not to shoot. The man remarked to me: "Do you know where this is?" and I said: "Yes, sir; Kewaunee Wood-Pile." He said: "You are perhaps aware that there was a mail agent killed here, shot right here at this place." I told him I was aware of the fact, knowing that he referred to the murder of Frank Diggs, a negro mail agent who was killed there several months previously. "You, in your actions," warned the Ku Klux, "will govern yourself in such a way that you will attend to your own business and nobody else's; or else you may look for the same fate." He said further: "It is not worth while for you to try to do anything. I could have a thousand men in fifteen minutes; they are all out here in the woods." As a matter of fact, the train was full of men that night, strangers to me, who were going down to Meridian. It was said that trouble was expected at Meridian, and they were going down there to help out. After flourishing his pistols around several times, the disguised man walked back through the door leading in the direction of the passenger cars, and that was the last I saw of him. About a week after that, I was informed by the watchman at York station, as well as the telegraph operator, the train conductor and the baggage master, that there had been a party of eighteen disguised men at York waiting for the train; but it was running behind time and they got impatient and left, after waiting until nearly daylight, leaving the message: "Tell Coleman to stay on the east side of the Bigbee river; and if he does not he can decide to leave his shoe-string with us." '

Mr. Coleman very prudently took this pointed hint and arranged for a transfer to the railroad line running from Montgomery to Calera. The Ku Klux, however, kept their eye on him; and as late as October, 1871, he received a message, illustrated with a number of threatening symbols such as daggers, coffins, skulls and crossbones, saying:

'Dam Your Soul. The Horrible *Sepulchre* and Bloody Moon

has at last arrived. Some live to-day to-morrow "*Die.*" We the undersigned understand through our Grand "*Cyclops*" that you have recommended a big Black Nigger for male agent on our nu rode; wel, sir, Jest you understand in time that if he gets on the rode you can make up your mind to pull roape. If you have anything to say in regard to the matter, meet the Grand Cyclops and Conclave at Den No. 4 at 12 o'clock midnight, Oct. 1st, 1871.

'When you are in Calera we warn you to hold your tongue and not speak so much with your mouth or otherwise you will be taken on supprise and led out by the Klan and learnt to stretch hemp. Beware! Beware! Beware! Beware!'

Coleman discreetly held his tongue, as suggested, and refrained from speaking too much with his mouth, and so was fortunate enough to escape the necessity for pulling 'roape.'

There seems to be considerable room for doubt as to the authenticity of this Ku Klux warning, as it is extremely doubtful whether there was a legitimate organization of Ku Klux in Alabama as late as October, 1871. Steps looking to the dissolution of the order in this state had been taken more than two years previously; and, although the dissolution orders then issued probably did not reach all the Dens in the state, the leaders had by that time decided that it was time to break it up. The character of the Klan's membership had declined; it was getting out of the control of its officers; and its responsible heads had come to recognize that, uncontrolled and in bad hands, the Ku Klux Klan was an extremely dangerous instrumentality.

This change of sentiment developed gradually. As late as April 6, 1869, for example, Ryland Randolph in his Tuscaloosa paper was indulging in very thinly veiled recommendations of Ku Klux violence. In speaking of Professor J. F. D. Richards, one of the members of the carpetbagger faculty of the state university, he said: 'He is the best subject for Ku Klux treatment we have ever seen. If boys were anything like as mischievous as formerly, he would be driven off the street with well-aimed rotten eggs.'

Within two weeks, however, even the fire-eating Randolph had cooled down considerably and was saying plaintively: 'Everything that is now perpetrated is erroneously attributed to Ku Kluxers, and we are sick of hearing of these mythical personages. If one man beats another, it is a Ku Klux outrage,' etc. That very day a white man named Murchison Findley was killed by a negro, and in his issue of April 27 Randolph warned the people not to take this as a provocation for punishing negroes indiscriminately, thereby probably bringing on martial law. 'We want no Tennessee form of government among us,' he said.

On June 22 he crossed the Rubicon with an editorial entitled 'Let Murders Cease,' in which the erstwhile roaring Cyclops waved the olive branch. 'We regret to chronicle the murder of a man named Miller which occurred near New Lexington several days ago, owing, it is supposed, to political considerations, though this is not certain. . . . It is now time, we are free to announce, for murders and assassinations to cease. . . . We now have a sheriff of our own choice, and we must sustain him by making arrests whenever the offending parties shall be identified. . . . Again we repeat, let us have quiet. *Let these murders cease.*'

This was just about the time of the official disbandment of the Ku Klux Klan in northern Alabama, and an editorial of this tenor in Randolph's paper at this time is especially significant. By September he had become aggressively pacific, and in his edition of the twenty-first of that month he fulminated: 'Carpetbag incendiaries are roaming through the northern counties of the state claiming to be Ku Klux, so as to make capital for their party as well as to rob negroes and have the deeds laid on respectable whites. None of the outrages that are now committed are the work of so-called Ku Kluxes.

Those clans have long since ceased to exist; and whenever a radical sheet attributes dark deeds to any such organization it knowingly falsifies the facts.'

This was a prejudiced but fairly accurate statement of the condition of affairs in Alabama at that time. Since the familiar Ku Klux disguise offered such a convenient and serviceable cloak to deeds of violence, it was beginning to be used by anybody who wanted to commit some crime or wished to wreak some private vengeance without the danger of disclosing his identity.

Negroes were Ku Kluxing one another, common outlaws and robbers were donning white robes and masks and infesting the highways. Volunteer groups of regulators, without claim to any sort of formal organization, were dressing up in Ku Klux suits and flogging or otherwise maltreating those who had incurred their displeasure.

One of the efforts at social regulation undertaken by the latter-day band of regulators, operating in the disguise of the Ku Klux, was the punishment of a negro named Bill Washington who lived near Tuscaloosa. Washington, as a manifestation of his freedom and his new social status, had taken unto himself a white wife, described as 'a low woman.' This so greatly outraged the moral dignity of the community that a group of hotheaded young men decided to swoop down on him and Ku Klux him. In approaching Washington, however, they caught a Tartar, as he refused to submit tamely despite their superior numbers. When they knocked on his door he refused to open it; and when they broke it down he greeted them with a blast from his shotgun which fatally wounded one of the young men. Washington, of course, was immediately killed by the raiders, who then made off carrying their wounded comrade with them. He had received the full load of the shotgun in his breast and died within a few days, much to the distress of his father and mother, who were most estimable people, and also to the sorrow of the mulatto girl with whom he had been living in adultery.

The extent to which the Ku Klux name and uniform were being used for deeds of out-and-out outlawry was testified to by Daniel Coleman of Limestone County. He testified that in 1871 there was operating in that part of the state an organized body of counterfeit Ku Klux who were banded together 'for the purpose of horse-thieving — stealing and thieving generally.' He said that they had assumed the disguise formerly used by the old Ku Klux Klan with the idea of palming themselves off as Ku Klux; and testified further that this gang was part of an organization which had connections extending into Kentucky and clear up into Ohio, with arrangements made for running off the stolen horses to points in the latter states. Incidentally, to keep themselves occupied in their spare time, these horse thieves engaged in illicit distilling on a rather elaborate scale. In posting their notices, *à la* Ku Klux, these desperadoes had the ironic audacity to sign themselves 'Men of Justice' — but their neighbors' horses kept disappearing during the night-time.

Meanwhile the original Ku Klux had been officially disbanded, and a notice to that effect had appeared in some of the Alabama newspapers during the summer of 1869 signed by the 'Grand Cyclops.' After this the activities of the authentic Klan were officially discontinued; but the machinery they had set up was too effective to be abandoned entirely by evilly inclined people, and there were still sporadic reports of acts of violence committed by small squads of disguised men — all, naturally enough, attributed to the Ku Klux.

Things reached a climax when a gang of masked men kidnapped a justice of the peace in Limestone County named Leonard L. Weir and subjected him to the most brutal punishment and abuse. Weir recognized a number of them and had them indicted, after a posse of the native white men of Athens (many of them former Ku Klux) had been organized for his rescue. After his assailants were indicted, the commissioners'

court of the county met and made an appropriation of money
to employ the best available counsel for their prosecution.

On September 25, 1871, the citizens of Limestone County
held a mass meeting in the courthouse to protest against the
outrages that had been committed by these lawless bands, and
adopted resolutions expressing a determination to devise 'ways
and means for the suppression of lawlessness and crime, to express our indignation at the recent outrages in the county, and
to unite our efforts for the maintenance of the supremacy of
the law.' A concluding paragraph of the resolution stated that
'We are in dead earnest, and we mean what we say when we
declare that we intend by every means known to the law, "let
it fall on whom it may," to put down the lawlessness that now
curses and blights the county.'

This meeting was attended by a number of the leading
citizens who were known to have been affiliated with the
original Ku Klux Klan in the county, and their names were
signed to the resolutions which were ordered published in the
local newspapers; this action being taken as a sort of public
notification that the genuine Ku Klux were actively up in
arms against the deviltries of the spurious Klan then operating.
To add emphasis to this public pronouncement there also appeared in the Athens newspapers a public notice headed 'Important Order' and signed 'Ex-Cyclops,' which said:

'Whereas, Once it was proper and necessary that steps should
be taken to put down and destroy the dangerous power and
influence of the Union Leagues and evil bands of men; and
whereas, law-abiding responsible and prudent men united
themselves together under the name of Ku Klux, met and
restored peace and safety to the citizens of the county; accomplished the object of their combination, and in obedience
to an act of our Legislature disbanded, and ceased to exist as
an organization; and whereas, it has come to the knowledge of
those who were once genuine Ku Klux that some of its members

and others claiming to be Ku Klux, and disguised, are constantly seen in the Northern portion of this county, and are robbing and plundering the weak and defenseless negroes and whites, and are greatly disturbing the peace and quiet of that locality,

'Now we, the once genuine Ku Klux, in council for that purpose do solemnly declare, that those men are known, and can be named and located, and are thieves and robbers; and that unless they cease these outrages and pull off their disguises, we will have them published and turn them over to the civil authorities to be dealt with under the severe penalty of the law. The power that created and supported this laudable Klan until its disbandment is and will be invoked to crush out and destroy its spurious and bogus off-springs. We here give assurance to the people that it is none of the good elements of the deceased organization that are either seen in disguise or that commit these outrages, and request them to resist to the extent of the law upon the subject, and their rights to defend their property, homes and lives.'

This was just about the death knell of the Ku Klux Klan in Alabama. As long as the original, formally organized Klan was operating, supported by the sympathies of most of the responsible population of the state, it was impossible for the organized powers of the government to cope with it. But when the good people deserted the Klan, and it lost the support of public sentiment, it was impossible for it to survive and be countenanced as a symbol of violence in disguise.

VI.   MISSISSIPPI

T HE KU KLUX MOVEMENT IN MISSISSIPPI seems to have passed through two entirely different and fairly well-defined stages of existence, although it is not entirely clear whether the latter stage was directly connected with the first. There appears to be general agreement that the Ku Klux were active in a number of the counties of the state during 1867 and 1868; and this activity seems to have been, beyond any question, tied in closely with the Ku Klux organization then operating in various sections of the South. According to several people, however, both Democrats and Republicans, this movement died out in Mississippi some time in 1868 or early in 1869; and one of the most prominent and active carpetbaggers in Mississippi testified that 'I never saw a more quiet election in the North than that of 1869 in Mississippi.'

Some time during 1870, however, there was another Ku Klux irruption; and the second manifestation was just as violent as the first, if not more so. That this latter activity was not an entirely irregular and informal affair is indicated by the statement made relative to the organization in Lee County, for example. In this county, according to the statement of a former member of the order, 'The Ku Klux Klan was organized by an Irishman named John Cole who lived near Saltillo. Mr. Cole was sent to Memphis in the spring of 1870 to take the required oath and get a commission to organize a Klan in Lee County. ... The entire membership was made up of men prominent in both church and state, and exercised great power for good throughout the country in keeping down the vicious negroes.' There was evidently at that time a recognized Ku Klux headquarters in Memphis; and the Mississippians, it will be observed, were careful to obtain authority from headquarters before proceeding to organize.

Speaking of the cause of the 1870–71 revival of activities of the Klan, a writer in the *Publications* of the Mississippi Historical Society has said, by way of explanation: 'First, there was a comparative failure of the cotton crop in 1870, which added to the unrest. The excitement of the Alabama election in August, 1870, in which the Ku Klux were active in some of the border counties, was felt to an extent in the East Mississippi counties. Then there came on the time for paying the exorbitant tax; in some of the counties amounting to as much as 4% of an extravagant valuation of properties. Under the operation of an act of the Legislature of 1870 changing the time for collecting the taxes, two annual collections fell in one year. By far the largest item of taxation was the school system, newly installed. The main immediate precipitant and provocation of the disorders, it is indisputable, was a school system primarily designed for negro education. To this the hostility was general. It is quite easy to moralize against such a sentiment as unpatriotic and unwise. But was there not a cause, deep-rooted in racial instinct and training, and fed on bad government? Be this as it may, where discontent ripened into lawlessness, the nearest objects for it to be vented on were school houses and school teachers, some of the school houses being burned and a number of the more obnoxious teachers being ordered out of their counties. Some, on refusing to obey the order, were whipped. This was outrageous, and would have been punished by law had the citizens controlled the machinery of the law.... Dissatisfaction with the establishment of negro schools and the heavy and arbitrary taxation levied by the county boards, under authority of the school law of 1870, was the soil in which the Ku Klux seed sprouted.... The law itself was the least of it. Every teacher of a negro school, supported at the expense of the white people, was a Radical tool and emissary to excite race hatred among the negroes.... All over the state robbery under the school system was especially rank.'

Aside from this duplex appearance of the Ku Klux, the Reconstruction of Mississippi had proceeded along lines approximately parallel to those in other Southern States. In June, 1865, William A. Sharkey was appointed provisional governor of the state by President Johnson; but in the election held in the fall of that year, despite the disfranchisement of most of the native whites, a Conservative, Benjamin G. Humphreys, was elected governor. It was charged that the white people had intimidated the negroes and prevented them from voting; but, whether that was so or not, Governor Humphreys served as governor until he was in 1868 removed from office by General Grant, at which time General Adelbert Ames of Massachusetts was appointed provisional governor of the state.

Meanwhile the new problems created by friction between the whites and the newly freed blacks were rising in Mississippi as elsewhere throughout the South, intensified by the pernicious activities of the Freedmen's Bureau and the Loyal Leagues. So provocative did the Loyal Leagues become that the Central Democratic Association of the state of Mississippi early in 1868 adopted resolutions denouncing the League as being 'not only mischievous but well calculated to disturb the peace and good order of society.' These resolutions pledged protection to those negroes who did not join the League, threatened not to 'employ, countenance or support in any manner any man, white or black,' who belonged to the organization; and declared that 'Our respect for a colored man is far above that which we enter-

tain for any Northern man or renegade Southern man who
avows doctrines favorable to, or in encouragement of, the Loyal
League, which society we know to be in direct violation of the
laws of the state.'

This opposition to the Loyal League was intense and bitter
throughout the state, and in the Vicksburg *Times* in June, 1868,
there was published a blacklist of merchants and hotels employ-
ing negroes who belonged to the League, together with lists of
draymen, barbers and other negro laborers who were members.
'The Southern Democrat who feeds a Radical, black or white,'
said this newspaper, 'is false to his country, false to God and false
to himself. He who supports them in any shape is a coward who
disgraces the name of man.'

Flare-ups were of regular occurrence; and the possibility of
some sort of desperate action by the irresponsible and uncontrolled negroes kept the white population in a state of subdued
terror. So serious and genuine were the apprehensions of
trouble from the negroes during these times that General Ord,
then in charge of that military district, became alarmed and in
1867 asked Governor Humphreys to issue an official proclamation on the subject, which the governor did.

In this proclamation Humphreys referred to the reports
reaching him and General Ord that 'combinations and conspiracies are being formed among the blacks to seize the lands
and establish farms, expecting and hoping that Congress will
arrange a plan of division and distribution, but unless this is
done by January next they will proceed to help themselves, and
are determined to go to war and are confident that they will be
victors in any conflict with the whites.' The proclamation went
on to admonish the negroes that if they entertained any such
expectations of a division of the land they had been deceived,
and that 'the first outbreak against the quiet and peace of
society that assumes the form of insurrection will signalize the
destruction of your cherished hopes and the ruin of your race.'

General Ord backed up the governor, and the immediate threat of insurrection was quelled; but the fear remained in the white men's — and women's — hearts.

In such circumstances as these, with the fear of a negro insurrection constantly before them and with no adequate protection in the courts, the residents of the different localities instinctively began to organize informal bands of young men to patrol the country at night for the purpose of keeping order. In one county a group of ex-Confederate soldiers effected a more or less formal organization known as Heggie's Scouts, in the formation of which General Forrest was said to have been instrumental. Forrest was making his headquarters at Aberdeen, in Monroe County, at this time in connection with his railroad promotion work; and on the week-ends he spent in his quarters at Aberdeen he was frequently consulted by the native white people as to what they might do to protect themselves. In their state of mind, it did not take much persuasion to win them over to the Ku Klux idea; and in that part of Mississippi subject to Forrest's influence the Ku Klux Klan soon began to make itself felt as an active force in the community.

In no other state than Mississippi did the matter of negro schools seem to occupy the Klan's attention to such a great degree, and in our present state of enlightenment it seems strange that opposition to a state school system should have been at the root of any Ku Klux trouble; but it must be remembered that prior to the war there had been no thought of public education of the negroes, and very little thought of any public-school system at all. The opening of public schools for negroes not only raised the issue of having the taxpayers' money used for a strange new purpose, but there was also the fear that the ultimate object of the system was to establish mixed schools where white and negro children would be brought together as a first entering wedge in some enforced system of social equality of the races.

However unwarranted and unworthy such opposition may now appear to be, it was apparently one of the principal objects of some of the men who composed the Mississippi Ku Klux in 1870 and 1871; and directly as a result of their violently manifested protest the collection of the excessive school taxes was halted in Monroe, Lowndes, and other counties. Furthermore, members of the school boards were frequently the recipients of Ku Klux notices ordering them to resign (which they generally did); and teachers of negro schools received warnings to cease their pedagogical work and depart.

A particularly obnoxious cog in the machinery of the school system was A. P. Huggins, who lived in Aberdeen and who was superintendent of the public schools of that county and also assistant assessor of internal revenue. He was an Ohio-born carpetbagger who had served in the Union army and who had taken up his residence in Mississippi immediately following the conclusion of the war. Holding the two offices of tax collector and school superintendent, Huggins was a dual object of the local Klan's animosity; and it was inevitable that he should feel the weight of their hand.

His fate overtook him one night in March, 1868, while he was spending the night with a Mr. George R. Ross. Mr. Huggins retired early, and at about ten o'clock was awakened by the calls of a band of Ku Klux who had surrounded the house. He went outside at their command and held considerable parley with them, Huggins later expressing surprise at the character of the men comprising the group. 'They were a much different class of men than I ever supposed I would meet in a Ku Klux gang,' he later said, describing them as 'genteel persons, men of cultivation.'

The leader of the Ku Klux told Huggins that his case had been considered by the local Den and that it had been decided that he must leave the state within ten days. The Cyclops told him, Huggins said, that 'the Ku Klux rule was, first, to give the

warning; second, to enforce obedience to their laws by whipping; third, to kill by the Klan operating as a group; and, fourth,
if that was not done and if the one who was warned still failed to
obey, then they were sworn to kill him privately by assassination.'

Despite this dread threat, the spunky Huggins told them
flatly that he intended to pay no attention to their warning and
that he would stay there as long as he chose. They, in the most
polite and civil manner, urged upon him the wisdom of obeying
their decree, but he was obstinate in his refusal. Thereupon they
proceeded to disarm him, stripped him of his coat, and in a
calm and deliberate manner administered to him the punishment to which he had been sentenced, a whipping of seventy-five
lashes. At intervals they would withhold the lash and ask him if
he was ready to agree to leave the state, but he steadfastly refused. ('He was a gritty chap,' one of the Ku Klux later said
admiringly.) So the flogging continued until Huggins fainted
away. They then revived him and, after warning him that the
next form of punishment would be death, rode away and left
him.

Bad enough in itself, the whipping of Mr. Huggins developed
into a matter of more than personal and local interest. A Lieutenant Pickett of the United States Army who was then stationed
in Mississippi obtained from Huggins the blood-stained nightshirt which he wore on the night of the flogging, and took it to
Washington with him and presented it to Ben Butler. Butler,
gleeful at such a splendid chance to make a sensational anti-
Southern speech, appeared on the floor of the Senate with the
gory garment in his hands and made a typically denunciatory
address to that august body, waving the ensanguined nightshirt
above his head as he talked. It was from this that the 'bloody
shirt' expression originated; and thus the humble nightdress of
that forgotten carpetbagger has become immortalized in the
vernacular of the nation.

Another sensational and tragic affair growing out of the Ku Klux Klan's antagonism for the negro school system was what was known as 'The Pontotoc Raid,' which took place in May, 1871. Several schoolhouses had been burned in the county, and Colonel Robert W. Flournoy, who was county superintendent of schools and also editor of the Pontotoc *Equal Rights* (aside from being assistant postmaster and a practicing attorney), boldly charged the acts of arson to the Ku Klux and vigorously denounced them for it. He admitted himself that he wrote 'some very bitter articles' in which he denounced them as 'a body of midnight prowlers, robbers and assassins.' These editorial attacks continued for two or three weeks; and Flournoy was then warned that the Ku Klux were threatening to visit him in retaliation.

Sure enough, on the night of May 12 the Ku Klux came galloping into town, 'riding two and two, like cavalry'; but there were widely differing stories as to the purposes of their visit and just what happened after they got there. According to friends and apologists of the raiders, their purposes were entirely innocent and pacific. They were not Ku Klux at all, merely a bunch of frivolous young men who went on the trip to Pontotoc from a distant corner of the county 'for fun and frolic.' They carried with them horns and dinner-bells and tin pans, along with a home-made noise-making device which they called a 'dumb-bell,' described as 'a raw-hide stretched over a hollow drum, with a string in it waxed over; and pulling it by the string, as the fingers slip over the string it makes a shrieking noise. They carried that to Pontotoc to scare Mr. Flournoy and break up the paper he was editing. They did nothing in the world, no harm at all, and were going off when they were fired on and a man killed.'

A somewhat different version of the affair was given by Judge Austin Pollard, who was chancellor of the district embracing Pontotoc and three other counties. Judge Pollard and his friends

had taken heed of the warning that the Ku Klux were planning
to visit Pontotoc, and they were not caught napping. As he
related it, 'I had been on a hunting expedition with some
friends of mine, and afterward we met at the court-house in the
town of Pontotoc, and four of us sat playing a game of euchre.'
John L. Gorman, a printer employed on Flournoy's paper,
acted as a sort of picket for Pollard and his friends; and shortly
before midnight he rushed into the room and exclaimed
excitedly: 'Gentlemen, the Ku Klux are here!'

This broke up the euchre game in short order, and Judge
Pollard and his friends quickly grabbed up their guns and proceeded to a nearby blacksmith shop, where they hid themselves
to await the coming of the Klansmen. Pollard related that
someone suggested that they should fire on the Ku Klux without parley, but that he demurred, as he wanted no bloodshed.
Then somebody suggested that he, being chancellor of the district, should advance to meet them and demand their surrender, which he agreed to do. 'Gentlemen,' he said when he
met them, according to his story, 'If your mission is one of
peace and pleasantry you will not be molested; if, on the other
hand, you are for bloodshed, in the name of and by virtue of
the laws of the state of Mississippi, I demand that you surrender.' Perhaps the Ku Klux were panic-stricken by this
ponderous challenge. At any rate, as Judge Pollard told it:
'Instantly a pistol shot was fired from the crowd of men in disguise; very soon afterward another pistol shot was fired; and I
heard a voice from another street commanding them to "Halt,"
and then another pistol was fired from the Ku Klux band, and
then the firing became general on both sides.'

Some witnesses to the affray said that there was no formal
challenge of the Ku Klux party, but that they were ambushed
by Judge Pollard and his party secreted in the blacksmith shop.
But, however it started, there was a lot of shooting and the Ku
Klux party fled precipitately, without pursuit. Judge Pollard

and his party patrolled the streets of Pontotoc the rest of the night, but there was no further disturbance or confusion.

When daylight came a man was found lying in the street, dressed in full Ku Klux regalia. He was severely wounded and bleeding profusely, but he was not dead, and after his mask had been cut from his face he rallied and talked a little. He gave his name as George F. Dillard, but it later developed that this was the name of his brother who had been killed at the battle of Shiloh. His name was found to be Richard Dillard, and he lived in a distant part of the county. Nobody in Pontotoc knew him. After lingering a short while he died; and his mother, notified of his death, sent a wagon for his body and took it home and buried it.

A version of the affair somewhat different from Judge Pollard's came from another source. A dentist in Pontotoc, Doctor H. H. Porter, owned a printing press and a small font of type, and he set to work and printed a broadside account of the embroglio on a single sheet of paper headed 'The Pontotoc Times. Published in Pontotoc, Miss., by Dr. H. H. Porter. Free. Vol. 1. No. 1,' explaining his volunteer one-time newspaper by the statement that 'there being no paper published here which is generally read by the white people, I propose publishing a brief account of what transpired on last Friday night.'

Doctor Porter's account of the affray is dramatic and thrilling, if not entirely impartial and unbiased. 'It was about eleven o'clock,' he relates. 'A company of masked serenaders made its appearance on the square with horns, bells, tin pans — in fact, all sorts of things that would make a racket — with which they were amusing themselves and all whom they could attract. From a consciousness of their own deserts, it appears that some persons imagined them to be "sure enough Ku Klux" and right after themselves. Accordingly, a company of men, ten or twelve, that had been keeping late hours over on the east side of the square (this needs no explanation) were paraded, armed

with double-barrel shotguns loaded with buckshot, and ambushed in Ren. Grant's wood shop. As the company approached, starting out of town... the ambushing party discharged a raking fire of upwards of twenty guns at short distance, killing one of the boys (Richard Dillard) and wounding
many horses, several of which were collected up and returned
to their rightful owners.'

The retreating band of Ku Klux lost their bearings in trying
to get out of the unfamiliar town and got on the wrong road.
By the time they got on the road leading to Fosterville in the
northwestern part of the county, which was where they had
come from, it was so near day that most of them discarded their
disguises, and the next day there were twenty-seven Ku Klux
disguises picked up in the roads near Pontotoc.

Dillard, after his death, was denounced by a carpetbagger in
Pontotoc as 'one of the most desperate characters who has ever
inhabited this part of the country.' Among the natives, however, he was looked upon as a sort of hero and martyr; and a
Pontotoc man named Pitts who started a movement to erect a
monument to Dillard obtained sixty signatures to his subscription list.

It was openly asserted in Pontotoc that the leader of the Ku
Klux raiding party was Tom Sadler, who was sheriff of the
county. His father came to Pontotoc and claimed as his own
one of the impounded wounded horses; but the elder Sadler
decried the suggestion that his son had any part in the raid. He
surmised that some mischievous young men had broken into his
barn and taken out his horse unbeknownst to him; he knew Tom
didn't do it. Tom Sadler went off to Texas the day after the
raid; but the timing of his wanderlust was probably only a
coincidence.

In 1870 the Mississippi state legislature passed the anti-Ku
Klux law, proscribing all members of the order, and Governor
Alcorn offered a reward of five thousand dollars for the arrest

and conviction of any person found guilty of committing crimes
of violence in disguise. It was a curious circumstance, and an
ironic one, that the first claim for this reward and the first indictments under the act grew out of the Ku Kluxing of a
Democratic negro named Adam Kennard by a group of hostile
negroes in Ku Klux disguise, led by a notorious white Radical.
Out of the Kennard incident there developed an affair which
provides an excellent example of the seething and complex state
of affairs in Mississippi (and, in fact, in the entire South) at
this time. This was known as 'The Meridian Riot,' which took
place in June, 1871, and which was generally described in the
North as 'another Ku Klux outrage.'

Meridian is in Lauderdale County, Mississippi, fifteen miles
from the Alabama state line, Lauderdale County immediately
adjoining Sumter County in Alabama, of which Livingston is
the county seat. In March, 1871, Adam Kennard came to
Meridian from Livingston, representing himself as a deputy
sheriff, and seeking to arrest three negroes who were accused of
having fled to Meridian from Sumter County after breaking
their labor contracts with their employers there. Kennard was
able to show no warrant or requisition, and his authority was
resisted to such an extent that he was unable to make the arrests. He persisted, however, and as a result of his persistence
he was visited one night by a band of disguised men who took
him out and robbed him of his clothing and money, whipped
him very severely, and shot and wounded him as he ran away
from his assailants. It developed that the assault was committed by a band of negroes, led by a white man whom Kennard
identified, despite his disguise, as a scalawag named Daniel
Price; and he had Price and the negroes arrested and prosecuted
under the new Ku Klux law. Kennard asserted that there could
be no mistake about his identification of Price, that he knew him
intimately, they having been political cronies previously in
Livingston when both were active in Republican affairs.

Price, who seems to have had an unusual gift for provoking trouble, had left Alabama under something of a cloud. In Livingston he had offended the white natives by his undue familiarity with the negroes, associating with them entirely to the exclusion of the white race and constantly agitating them to assert their new-found social and political rights. It was also stated that while a resident of Livingston he 'took up with a yellow girl' and 'stayed with her like a wife.' It being suggested by some tolerant person that perhaps this flaw in Mr. Price's moral armor was not exactly unique in those times, a native of Livingston explained the public's disapproval of his conduct by saying: 'It's just like old Judge Pickens said — "lying by the thing don't do so well"; that's different from "taking a little and running." But he was a very daring, bold man, and stayed by her against all opposition.'

Aside from this affront to the public morals, it was also stated that Price was a pardoned convict out of the penitentiary, where he had been imprisoned for grand larceny; and that he was afterward a member of the Confederate army, from which he deserted to join the Union troops. After the surrender he went to Livingston and taught a negro school, threw in his lot with the Radical party and was elected circuit-court clerk in 1868. He was described as 'an unprincipled man' and 'an instrument of difficulty and bitterness on the part of the colored people.' The statement was made that 'he had such control over the negroes that, if he had desired it, at any moment a torch could have been put to every house in town and a knife to every throat; and the people did not believe that he was too good to do it.'

Price reached the pinnacle of his bad eminence in Livingston when he did actually advise the negroes of the county to arm themselves and march on the town and lay it in ashes. Fortunately for Livingston, some of the cooler heads among the white advisers of the negroes got word of the mad plan and persuaded the excited negroes to go home and put up their guns. Feeling ran high against Price; and he wisely decided that this was a propitious time to leave Livingston and take up his residence in Meridian.

Arrived in Meridian, Price slipped right into the smooth-working Radical machinery there and had little difficulty in having himself made county superintendent of schools, in addition to teaching a negro school himself. His incendiary oratory made him popular with the negroes and the Radical whites; and, when he was arrested for Ku Kluxing Adam Kennard, he was released on two hundred dollars bail bond and his Meridian friends rallied enthusiastically to his defense.

Kennard also had some loyal white friends in Livingston, and when the day set for Price's trial arrived Kennard appeared on the scene in Meridian accompanied by a large crowd of armed white men from Sumter County, Alabama, who announced that they had come to see that Kennard had a fair showing in the court and was allowed to testify and to introduce the evidence that he claimed to be able to produce. They all carried double-barreled shotguns, and their number was variously estimated at from one hundred and fifty to three hundred — probably nearer the smaller figure.

The Alabamians were not disguised, but the people of Meridian referred to them as 'the Ku Klux from Alabama' — an example of the current inclination to attach the Ku Klux label to all extra-legal activities — and the charge was not denied. Upon their arrival in Meridian these undisguised Ku Klux immediately proceeded to round up the three negroes whom Kennard had vainly sought to arrest, tied them and sent them back to Livingston on the next train. They then boldly stacked their arms in the street and went into the hotels of the city and ate breakfast. Breakfast finished, they cavalierly told the intimidated hotelkeepers: 'We are for the good of the city; charge it to the city' and walked out.

With this miniature army of occupation on their hands, the court authorities at Meridian prudently continued the trial for a week. The next week the Alabamians were again in town, and the case was again continued. Price, apparently emboldened by the delay in bringing him to trial, openly threatened that if his trial resulted in his being sent to jail he 'would then and there commence shooting,' stating further that he had arranged for thirty armed negroes to be in the courtroom and 'see him out.' Fearing riot and bloodshed if Price's trial should be held under such hair-trigger conditions, his lawyer and the prosecuting attorney agreed that it would be better for everybody concerned, and certainly conducive to the peace of the community, if Price should forfeit his bond and silently steal away, to which suggestion he discreetly acceded.

So far as Price himself was concerned, that ended the case; but it was just the setting of the scenery for the really serious aftermath. The Meridian negroes were greatly inflamed by Price's secret and ignominious flight. They felt that he should have remained there with them and fought the matter to a finish. They also keenly resented the forcible arrest of the three negroes by the Alabama Ku Klux. As a result of this seething feeling of discontent, a call was issued for a negro meeting to be held on the following Saturday in the courthouse. A white man who presumed to inquire as to the purpose of the proposed meeting was told that it was strictly a negro affair and that 'you rebs' had better stay away from there.

The meeting attracted a large crowd of blacks, and throughout the afternoon they were subjected to a terrific flow of oratory from three negro leaders of violently radical sentiments — Warren Tyler, William Clopton and Aaron Moore, the latter a member of Congress. Clopton told the negroes that they ought to arm themselves and take action to resist the Ku Klux. 'Ku Kluxing has got to be stopped!' he shouted, amid a salvo of applause, going on to tell them that every white man was a Ku

Klux and that the negroes ought to take matters into their own
hands and fight for their rights. Tyler said that they ought to
follow the example of the Indians in the way of vengeance.
'When one of an Indian tribe was killed by a white man,' he
said, 'they always took revenge by killing a white man, whether
they killed the right white man or not.' Moore referred his
hearers to the Biblical story of the destruction of Sodom and
Gomorrah, and made the dark prediction that before many days
Meridian 'might be laid in dust and ashes.' Other speakers
continued along the same inflammatory lines, working the
negroes up to a point of frenzy, and the meeting adjourned in
disorder after pledging its allegiance to the Loyal League.

Reports of the militant and hostile nature of the negro meeting
spread around Meridian, and the white citizens became very
much alarmed for their safety. Nor was their anxiety allayed
when the negroes, after the meeting adjourned, marched
through the streets beating drums and indulging in noisy
demonstrations and open threats of violence. Meridian, it will
be recalled, had been put to the torch by General Sherman in
1863 and totally destroyed; and in 1870 it was a ramshackle sort
of town, made up mostly of buildings of flimsy construction.
The citizens of Meridian were therefore at this time peculiarly
sensitive to any threatened danger from fire, and all the negroes'
talk about laying the town in ashes created particularly uneasy
forebodings. So, when immediately after nightfall it was discovered that one of the largest storehouses of the town was on
fire, a shudder of terror ran through the whole populace, and
everybody excitedly turned out to try to prevent the spread of
the flames and the complete destruction of the city. The fire
following so closely on the negroes' meeting, it was generally
suspected and openly charged that they had set fire to the building as the opening gun in a warfare of arson, and this belief was
intensified when the negroes not only refused to help put out the
blaze but gathered on the street in large groups abusing those

who were working at the job of fire-fighting, meanwhile firing their guns in loud volleys in an apparent effort to intimidate them and add to the confusion.

'Damn old Meridian; she has give us a lot of trouble; let's burn her all up tonight!' cried Bill Clopton, who made himself especially conspicuous, loudly telling the negroes: 'This is a white man's fire. Don't you help them put it out. God damn the white people!' and further: 'Why in the hell don't you go home and get your guns, something to shoot with? What in the hell are you standing here for?' He was also heard to say, in answer to another negro's question: 'Yes, kill all of them — women and children too.' He punctuated his remarks by indiscriminately firing his pistol into the air; and finally became so insufferably obnoxious that somebody knocked him in the head with the butt of a pistol and temporarily quieted him.

As a consequence of the fire, Clopton, Tyler and Moore were arrested, charged with arson and disorderly conduct. When they were arraigned for preliminary examination on Monday, Tyler (who was a shrewd and intelligent negro) undertook to conduct his own case. The atmosphere of the courtroom was surcharged with suppressed excitement as the examination proceeded, and the explosion came at the conclusion of the testimony of a white witness named James Brantley who testified against Tyler. As Brantley rose to leave the witness chair, Tyler said: 'Just wait right there a minute; I want to introduce two or three witnesses to impeach your veracity.' Brantley, incensed at this, grabbed up a hickory walking stick and raised it as though to threaten Tyler. Tyler fled precipitately; but as he passed through the door of the courtroom he turned and, pulling a pistol from his pocket, fired wildly into the room. The bullet struck the judge on the bench, Judge Bramlette, killing him instantly; and immediately the whole courtroom was in an uproar which rapidly spread throughout the entire town. A perfect fusillade of pistol fire crashed out in the courtroom and several were wounded — among them Tyler, who, despite his wounds, made his escape from the building and hid in a friendly negro's shop. Also among the wounded was the firebrand Clopton, who, when it was found that he was not dead, was taken to the second-floor balcony and thrown into the street. He survived this maltreatment also, and he was then carried back into the courthouse and his throat cut, which finished him.

Within fifteen minutes there were three hundred armed men in the streets of Meridian — citizens of the town, attracted by the firing, reinforced by some of the so-called Alabama Ku Klux. Tyler was finally discovered in his hiding place and killed. Moore was also sought, but managed to make his escape, although he was pursued for fifty miles down the railroad by a posse in a special train. The armed white men offered themselves to the sheriff to act under his orders, but the sheriff seems to have lost control of the situation completely, and the citizens voluntarily divided themselves into groups and patrolled the streets throughout the afternoon and succeeding night. Three negroes who were arrested during the afternoon were taken from the custody of a deputy sheriff during the night and killed; and there was the wildest sort of disorder all night, with both whites and blacks in a state of the utmost alarm and fury.

This particular 'Ku Klux outrage' was promptly investigated by the circuit judge of the district, Robert Leachman; and six white men were ordered held to answer before the grand jury at its next term and placed under bond. The grand jury, however, failed to find indictments against any of them; and that was the last of that. No white men, Ku Klux or otherwise, were punished — and Adam Kennard did not collect the five thousand dollars reward for the arrest and conviction of a Ku Klux.

The climax of the Ku Klux troubles in Mississippi came with the famous trial in Oxford in 1871 under the Federal Ku Klux Act of 1871. When Congress passed this law there was a temporary lull in the activities of the Klan in Mississippi, there being apparently more fear of the Federal Government's power to suppress the organization than there was of the state. A prominent lawyer of Iuka, however, published an article in the Iuka *Gazette*, expressing the legal view that it would be very difficult to punish anybody under the Ku Klux law enacted by Congress, that it was a very defective act and would not reach the offenses it sought to correct. The opinion was also expressed in this article that the United States Government was exceeding its jurisdiction, and that it had no business interfering in the affairs of Mississippi or any other state. The effect of this article was to inspire the Ku Klux with new courage, and they began to operate again with renewed vigor.

The Oxford trial was officially styled 'The United States of America vs. W. D. Walton et al.' It was the first trial held in Mississippi under the Federal law, and was regarded as a test of the constitutionality of the act. It was also regarded as a test of the ability of the United States Government to cope with the Invisible Empire. There was a formidable array of legal talent on both sides, and a tremendous amount of interest developed throughout the whole country in the outcome of this battle in the little Mississippi courthouse.

The prosecution of Walton et al. grew out of the mysterious murder of a negro named Aleck Page who lived in Monroe County. On the night of March 29, 1871, Page was taken from his home by a group of men dressed in the familiar garb of the Ku Klux Klan, was whipped and then hanged, and his body buried in a shallow grave, where it was later found by searchers.

As a result of this outrage the Federal grand jury of the northern district of Mississippi indicted W. D. Walton and twenty-seven other citizens of Monroe County, including four negroes — Michael Forshee, Ben Lumpkin, Burrill Willis and Jefferson Willis — and they were carried to Oxford to stand trial in the Federal Court there.

From the outset there were difficulties and complications in
the conduct of the case. That Aleck Page was taken out and
killed and that the deed was done in the night-time by masked
men were indisputable facts, but beyond those facts there was
an immediate divergence of opinion, and the evidence introduced was amazingly conflicting. The government's chief
dependence was on the testimony of three negroes, Joe Davis,
Henry Hatch and Fanny Page, the last of whom was the wife of
the victim of the outrage and in the house when Aleck was taken
out to his death. All the witnesses, however, had the fatal fault
of knowing too much.

Fanny Page testified that during the mêlée in the house,
although the men were disguised, she not only recognized the
six negroes (Davis and Hatch in addition to those indicted),
but also recognized six white men whose names she gave.
When asked to identify these white men when the prisoners
were arraigned in court she was unable to do so, in her confusion pointing out the prosecuting attorney as one of the culprits.
Testimony was introduced to show that at one time she had said
she did not recognize any of those who Ku Kluxed her husband,
and that at another time she said that all of those engaged in the
affair were negroes. (Another negro who saw the body of
marauders that night also stated that 'It was niggers done it.')
Fanny, immediately following the event, when asked if she
recognized any of those engaged in it had said: 'La, no; you
never see such things as they had on their heads! You couldn't
tell whether they was women or men, and couldn't recognize
nobody.'

Joe Davis also proved to be an unsatisfactory witness. He
testified that he and Henry Hatch, the other negro who turned
state's evidence, had been forced to join the Ku Klux by duress;
but he testified further that the other negroes, among the
defendants, had joined the Klan voluntarily and were regular
members of the organization in good standing. Other witnesses

later swore that Joe had been heard to tell Mike Forshee that he had better tell lies, as he had done, and he would get clear; and also that he had told the other negro defendants that unless they swore they were Ku Klux they would never get home.

Henry Hatch testified that he was with the raiding party and that he helped bury the body. His description of the disguises used, however, was entirely different from that given by Joe Davis. It was also testified that he had repeatedly stated in public that he had no idea of who killed Aleck Page and that he never saw a Ku Klux in his life. Hatch also had difficulty in identifying the prisoners whom he claimed to have seen taking part in the outrage on Page.

The testimony of all three witnesses was full of contradictions and incongruities, not the least of which was their insistence that the white Ku Klux had solicited the membership of the negroes in their organization and had entrusted them with their bloody secrets.

A particularly peculiar feature of the case was that there was never any satisfactory theory advanced as to just why Aleck Page should have been killed at all. The prosecution attempted to show that it was done because he was a Republican; but evidence was introduced to prove that he was in fact a Democrat and had frequently made Democratic political speeches. The defense undertook to charge that Joe Davis himself had a motive for the crime, due to some personal animosity for Page. Davis admitted that Page had 'spoke some blackguard words' about his wife; but he protested that despite those blackguard words they had remained very close friends. It was also mentioned that Page had insulted a white woman in the neighborhood, and that his punishment might have been on that account. But none of these theories was very strongly supported.

The prisoners were defended by some of the most prominent attorneys of Mississippi, including General Samuel J. Gholson, who was reputed to be the Grand Giant of the Ku Klux in Monroe County, but who denied that distinction. The defense of the accused was the old reliable alibi. One was sick in bed with the asthma, and had two witnesses who swore they sat up with him all night; one succeeded in proving that he was so dead drunk on the night of the outrage that he was in a comatose condition from which he did not recover until the next day; another was sitting up with his sick sister. W. D. Walton was at home in bed, to which fact his wife testified. Incidentally, the wife of this defendant must have been a remarkably personable woman, as into the dry-as-dust record of the trial the official reporter interjected this strangely incongruous comment: 'The witness, who was really handsome and most elegantly attired, made the court and counsel a most profound curtsey, tapped her husband on the head with her fan as she passed out of court, saying in a cheerful, laughing, good-humored tone: "Good-bye, Billy," and left the court amid a round of applause.'

The court heard all the testimony, pondered it judicially and admitted the prisoners to bail. This was the first step in the collapse of the government's case. Eventually everybody went scot free. Aleck Page was dead; everybody agreed to that. But all efforts to pierce the veil behind which the Invisible Empire operated were fruitless.

An enterprising printer in Memphis published a stenographic report of the trial in pamphlet form. These pamphlets were sold for the purpose of raising funds for the defendants' attorneys' fees, and a considerable sum was collected in this way.

The Oxford trial was a fiasco from the government's standpoint. One significant fact, however, was that before the trial the Ku Klux rode the country regularly two or three nights a week; after the Oxford trial, whether the defendants there arraigned were innocent or guilty, the Ku Klux rode no more in that section.

By this time, however, the need for the corrective influence of the Ku Klux had about ended anyhow; and when the Congres-

sional Investigating Committee came to look into Mississippi
affairs it was hard to find any 'Ku Klux outrages' of recent
vintage. It was, in fact, hard for them to obtain any very
reliable information of any kind. The Ku Klux Klan had died
its natural death in Mississippi before the Congressional Committee got there; and all that ensued was a threshing of old
straw, a rattling of dry bones.

Of all the more than six hundred arrests and indictments in
Mississippi under both state and Federal Ku Klux laws, there
was not a single jury conviction and no valid claim of the
five thousand dollars reward dangled before the people by
Governor Alcorn as a temptation to assist in the arrest and
conviction of a Ku Klux.

VII.   GEORGIA

THREE MONTHS AFTER LEE SURRENDERED at Appomattox President Andrew Johnson appointed James Johnson, a highly respected Columbus lawyer, as governor of Georgia; and, assisted by the state's wartime chief executive, Joseph E. Brown, now turned Republican, the new appointee conscientiously took up the task of restoring Georgia to the Union. He promptly issued a call for a state convention, which met in October and repealed the ordinance of secession, abolished slavery and took other steps looking to the readmission of the state. Governor Johnson, however, served for only a few months, and at the regular election held in November, 1865, he was succeeded by Charles J. Jenkins, an old-line Whig.

Jenkins, although a staunch Union man, had equally firm convictions about the rights of the states; and in March, 1867, when Congress passed the Reconstruction Act over the President's veto, Governor Jenkins applied to the Supreme Court of the United States for an injunction to prevent Secretary Stanton and Generals Grant and Pope from putting the act into effect in Georgia. This heroic gesture was fruitless, as the Court denied its jurisdiction; but Jenkins seemed sincerely determined to give the state an honest administration. In December, 1867, he refused to pay out forty thousand dollars of the state's money to cover the expenses of the rump constitutional convention

being held in Atlanta; and for this flagrant act of defiant
honesty he was removed from office in January by General
Meade, who had succeeded Pope as commander of the Third
Military District. The Secretary of State and the Comptroller
were removed at the same time, Meade appointing army officers
to their places; and thus, by a stroke of the pen, Georgia was
reduced to a military government.

There ensued the usual train of troubles and disorder common
to the Southern States at that time. The carpetbaggers were
swarming in and, together with the scalawags, soon were in control of the state government, including the judiciary. The Loyal
Leagues began to blossom in all their menacing, militant
mystery; and unrest among the negroes rapidly increased.
Mrs. Frances Butler Leigh in her *Ten Years on a Georgia Planta-
tion* tells of the ominous change in the demeanor of the negro
servants after they began to fall under the influence of the
League's teachings. They assumed, she said, an obnoxiously
familiar air with their employers, treated the women with dis-
respect, worked only when they felt so inclined and threw fear
into the white people's hearts by their marching about with guns
on their shoulders. Mrs. Leigh wrote that in those times she never
slept without a pistol under her pillow, as did women on isolated plantations throughout the South.

As a natural corollary of the growing terror, the Ku Klux
Klan soon appeared in Georgia, as it had in other states. The
native white citizens saw these menacing organizations led by
unscrupulous white agitators, and in their helpless political
condition they felt the futility of ordinary, lawful defensive
measures. John B. Gordon, late general in the Confederate
army, reflected the prevailing sentiment of the native population of his state — and of the South — when he told the Congressional Committee:

'We, in Georgia, do not believe that we have been given
proper credit for our honesty of purpose. We believe that if our

people had been trusted, as we thought they ought to have been trusted — if we had been treated in the same spirit which, as we thought, was manifested on the Federal side at Appomattox Court House — a spirit which implied that there had been a conflict of theories, an honest difference of opinion as to our rights under the general government — a difference upon which the South had adopted one construction and the North another, both parties having vindicated their sincerity upon the field in a contest which, now that it had been fought out, was to be forgotten — if this had been the spirit in which we had been treated, the alienation would have been cured. But to say to our people: "You are unworthy to vote; you can not hold office; we are unwilling to trust you; you are not honest men; your former slaves are better fitted to administer the laws than you are" — this sort of dealing with us has definitely alienated our people. The burning of Atlanta and all the devastation through Georgia never created a tithe of the animosity that has been created by this sort of treatment of our people.'

General Gordon was commonly reputed to be the Grand Dragon of the Ku Klux in the state of Georgia, and there is every reason to believe that he was. When he was called upon to testify about the matter, however, he stated: 'I do not know anything about any Ku Klux organization, as the papers talk about it. I have never heard of anything of that sort except in the papers and by general report; but I do know that an organization did exist in Georgia at one time. I know that in 1868 I was approached and asked to attach myself to a secret organization in Georgia; I was approached by some of the best citizens of the state, some of the most peaceable, law-abiding men.' He joined this unnamed organization, he said, but he went on: 'We never called it Ku Klux, and therefore I do not know anything about Ku Klux.'

In making this equivocal statement, General Gordon apparently was merely using the protective device generally adopted by members of the organization, and it by no means follows that he was not in fact the leader of the Ku Klux movement in Georgia. Despite his equivocation, his further statement regarding the conditions rendering such a protective organization necessary (whether they called it the Ku Klux or not) is illuminating as representing the feeling of the people at that time:

'The organization was simply a brotherhood of the property-holders, the peaceable, law-abiding citizens of the state, for self-protection. The instinct of self-protection prompted the organization — the sense of insecurity and danger, particularly in those neighborhoods where the negro population largely predominated. The reasons which prompted this organization were three or four. The first and main reason was the organization of the Union League, as they called it, about which we knew nothing more than this: That the negroes would desert the plantations and go off at night in large numbers, and on being asked where they had been would reply: "We have been to the muster," or "We have been to the lodge," or "We have been to the meeting." Those things were observed for a great length of time. We knew that the carpetbaggers, as the people of Georgia called those men who came from a distance and had no interest at all with us, who were unknown to us entirely, who from all that we could learn of them did not have any very exalted position at home — these men were organizing the colored people. We knew that, beyond all question. We knew of certain instances where great crimes had been committed; where overseers had been driven from plantations and the negroes had asserted their right to hold the property for their own benefit. Apprehension took possession of the entire public mind of the state. Men in many instances were afraid to go away from their homes and leave their wives and children, for fear of outrage. Rapes were already being committed in the country.

'There was this general organization of the black race on the

one hand, and the entire disorganization of the white race on
the other hand. We were afraid to have a public organization
because we were afraid it would be construed at once, by the
authorities at Washington, as an organization antagonistic to
the government of the United States. It was therefore necessary, in order to protect our families from outrage and preserve
our own lives, to have something that we could regard as a
brotherhood — a combination of the best men of the country
to act purely in self-defense, to repel the attack in case we should
be attacked by these people. . . . You must remember that we
were in a state of anarchy there for a long time. We had no law
but drum-head courts-martial.'

Describing the operations of his organization, General
Gordon testified that the members did not wear disguises or
ride about the country at night, and further stated that he did
not believe that any crime had ever been committed by the
organization, that 'it was purely a peace police.' Denying that
it had any political purpose, he said: 'While I am not going to
state what my position was in that organization, I will say that
I certainly would have known if there had been any such purpose' — a boast which might well be made by the Grand
Dragon of the Realm of Georgia.

The first public newspaper reference to the Ku Klux in
Georgia was in an Atlanta paper in March, 1868, at which
time, by a notable coincidence, one of the prominent people
visiting in town was General Nathan Bedford Forrest. He, it
was reported, was there for a few days attending to some insurance matters. It seems safe to assume that the Ku Klux
movement was launched in Georgia at about this time, and
certainly the Ku Klux were in existence and took an active part
in the state election that year in which General Gordon was the
Democratic candidate for governor against a New York carpetbagger named Rufus B. Bullock. Newspaper references to the
Ku Klux began to appear with increasing frequency. Also,

about this time, there began to appear in Georgia papers the gruesome Ku Klux notices with all their fearful threats; and objectionable carpetbaggers and scalawags began to receive threatening letters.

The threats of violence, however, were not all on one side. On April 2 there appeared in the Savannah papers a sinister, anonymous notice (generally attributed to Aaron Alpeoria Bradley, a notorious negro jail-bird from New York) which read:

> KKK and all BAD MEN of the city of Savannah who now threaten the lives of all the Leaders and Nominees of the Republican Party, and the President and Members of the Union League of America: If you Strike a Blow, the Man or Men will be followed, and the house in which he or they take shelter will be burned to the ground.

> TAKE HEED!   MARK WELL!
>
> Members of the Union League
>
> For God, Life and Liberty!!!

The state election in 1868 was bitterly contested and marked by all sorts of violence, oral and physical. An affair at this time which created a tremendous sensation in the North was the so-called 'Camilla riot.' This bloody affray grew out of a march of three hundred negroes from Albany to Camilla, with two Republican leaders at their head who were candidates in the election. The sheriff at Camilla was alarmed when he received word of the threatened visitation, and he mounted his horse and galloped out to meet the party of negroes a few miles from town. There he parleyed with the leaders, urging them to disband and disarm; but this effort was fruitless. The sheriff then rode back to Camilla post-haste and quickly gathered a posse which went out to meet the advancing negroes. When the two groups met there was a spontaneous burst of firing on both sides; and when the smoke finally cleared away there were eight dead negroes on the ground and three times that many wounded. Only two of the whites were wounded, and none killed. This affair was pictured in the North as 'a shocking massacre'; but a legislative committee investigated and reported that the white office-seekers who led the marching negroes were responsible for the whole trouble.

It was under such turbulent conditions that the election was held, and when the votes were finally counted it was announced that Mr. Bullock had been elected, and he was sworn into office by General Meade. The Democrats raised a loud and anguished cry of protest, claiming that Gordon had been shamelessly counted out; but their protest was disregarded, and Bullock took his seat and started out on a career of unblushing corruption and misrule, which was to end in his disgrace and flight from the state three years later.

A controlling factor in piling up the Bullock vote was the well-oiled machinery of the Loyal League organization, by means of which the ignorant negroes were herded to the polls and voted in droves — all, of course, for the Republican ticket. A typical Loyal League leader was Thomas M. Allen, a negro preacher in Marietta, who combined politics with his religion as a profession and was the head of the League there. 'In my county,' he testified pompously, 'the colored people come to me for instruction, and I give them the best instructions I could. I took the New York *Tribune* and other papers, and in that way I found out a good deal, and I told them whatever I thought was right' — including instructions as to how to vote.

Following the election a Methodist minister from Vermont, disgusted at the sheep-like behavior of the newly enfranchised negroes, told Allen that in future elections 'You ought to count the negro voters and then take a bundle of tickets and throw them into the ballot box, and let the colored people stay at home and work.' Allen innocently asked why, and the white preacher said: 'Because they just vote as you tell them,' going on to say bitterly: 'You have just as much right to vote as that horse.' Allen was a simple, literal-minded fellow and he protested at this: 'I don't think you tell the truth when you say that horse has as much right to vote as a man.' The Vermont man insisted: 'I can make that horse take a ticket and carry it up to the box and drop it there.' But Allen obstinately protested: 'You can't do it; you might make a circus horse do it, but you can't make that horse do it.'

With the Republican victory, the negroes became more unmanageable than ever, seeming to feel that there was no sort of restraint on their excesses. The conviction that the election had been stolen from their favorite son and illegally bestowed on an alien carpetbagger did not operate to soothe the already outraged feelings of the native Georgians. It was a crowning blow, following three years of indignity. They had no respect for the state government forced on them; they resented the treatment accorded them; and, feeling a complete lack of confidence in the courts as a means of redressing their wrongs, they turned to the Ku Klux Klan as a means of taking care of themselves.

The Klan now grew in numbers and in potency in Georgia; and at first, when it was under the control of men like Gordon, it was an effective check on unrestrained violence. Years after the Reconstruction was ended, John Calvin Reed wrote an article in Joel Chandler Harris's *Uncle Remus Magazine* in which he admitted that he was the Grand Giant of the Ku Klux in Oglethorpe County, and that the chief of its operations in that part of the state was Dudley M. Du Bose, son-in-law of Robert Toombs. Mr. Reed described the Klan as 'an underground and nocturnal constabulary — detective, interclusive, interceptive, repressive, preventive and, in the main, punitive only now and then.' So the work of the 'underground and nocturnal constabulary' went on. Its punitive measures, even 'now and then,'

attracted the attention of General Howard, and in his report
for the year 1868 he mentioned that 'Numerous outrages have
been perpetrated upon freed people in this state, some of them
remarkable for atrocity,' but nothing was done about it at that
time.

In June, 1869, a complaint of outrages in Georgia was referred to General A. H. Terry, in command of the Department
of the South, and in his report made August 14, 1869, General
Terry said: 'In many parts of the state there is practically no
government. The worst of crimes are committed and no
attempt is made to punish those who commit them. Murders
have been and are frequent; the abuse in various ways of the
blacks is too common to excite notice. There can be no doubt of
the existence of numerous insurrectionary organizations known
as Ku Klux Klans who, shielded by their disguises, by the
secrecy of their movements, and by the terror which they inspire, perpetrate crime with impunity.'

Then, being a military man and a firm believer in the supreme
potency of martial law, he went on adroitly to say: 'There is
great reason to believe that in some cases local magistrates are
in sympathy with the members of this organization. In many
places they are over-awed by them and dare not attempt to
punish them. To punish such offenders by civil proceedings
would be a difficult task, even were magistrates in all cases
disposed and had they the courage to do their duty, for the same
influences which govern them equally affect juries and witnesses.'

It took some time for this leaven to work, but General Terry
finally was successful in achieving the substitution of military
for civil law in Georgia, even though it was not until several
months after he first suggested it. Georgia's stout fight in the
state election in 1868 had already put her under suspicion, and
it was the last straw when in November of that year she had the
effrontery to cast a big popular majority vote for the presi-

dential electors who favored the Democratic nominees, Seymour and Blair. This was an unpardonable offense, and when
the House and Senate convened in Washington to count the
electoral votes in February, 1869, Senator Wade brazenly
announced that he was instructed by his party to receive the
vote of Georgia if it did not change the result but to reject it if
it did.

President Grant in his message to Congress in December,
1869, suggested that something ought to be done in regard to
Georgia; and Congress obediently passed an act immediately
which gave the military officers, under Grant, authority to
remodel the Georgia legislature and authorized the President
to give aid to the governor of the state 'to prevent disturbances.'
Promptly following the passage of this act, the state legislature
was manipulated and remolded nearer to the Radicals' desire
by the most high-handed and arbitrary exclusion of Democrats
who had been elected and the substitution in their places of
negroes and carpetbaggers who had been defeated. Comfortable Radical majorities having been assured by this shameless
procedure, the legislature lost no time in launching on an orgy
of partisan legislation, featured by bribery and corruption,
which soon reduced the state to the verge of bankruptcy.

Worst of all, a program of virtual military rule was put into
effect without any formal declaration of martial law; and,
without any previous warning, the soldiers began to arrest
citizens and throw them into prison without warrant and without disclosing any charge. The only authority for such a seizure
of power by the military forces was embodied in a telegram sent
to General Terry on January 12, 1870, by General W. T.
Sherman, in response to Terry's appeal for more power. Sherman's message said: 'I will sustain you in the exercise of any
authority that will maintain substantial good order until the
state of Georgia is recognized by the Executive and by Congress.
Even then some lawful means will be found whereby we can

defend our own friends from the Ku Klux.... You, personally, are vested with executive authority over governor and legislature until the state is fully admitted.' This was all the authority Terry required, and he proceeded to crack down on the citizens of Georgia with all the zeal of a military despot. This arbitrary imposition of military rule on a sovereign state so outraged Representative Beck of Kentucky that he declared that President Grant and General Terry were 'the original Ku Klux in Georgia,' going on to say that it was apparently the popular inclination in the North at that time to feel 'that whatever the President and General Terry did was right and that whoever opposed them were Ku Klux and scoundrels.' But, Mr. Beck continued: 'I hold that whoever in time of peace arrests a citizen in violation of the Constitution, without any charge against him, and puts him in jail is himself a violator of the law.'

In at least one instance, however, the Ku Klux were able to give General Terry a Roland for his Oliver. It had been announced that whenever his forces made an arrest a writ of habeas corpus would not be recognized; but sometimes the Ku Klux had a way of enforcing their own habeas corpus proceedings — they would find a way to 'have the body,' even though they could not get a legal writ. A detachment of United States troops under command of a lieutenant went to Rome in January, 1870; and there, without warrant and without revealing to the victim the charge against him, they went in the night to the home of a man named Ethridge, took him from his bed and lodged him in the county jail as a military prisoner. Habeas corpus proceedings were denied, and all that Ethridge could learn was that in due season he would be apprised of the charge against him and given a military trial.

The next night a large body of masked Ku Klux rode up to the home in Rome of the judge of the circuit court, Judge Kirby, and told him that he must go to the jail and persuade the commander of the troops to release Ethridge, that they had two hundred and fifty men in their party and would kill him if he refused to do as they demanded. Judge Kirby protested, but they insisted, so at last Kirby and the Ku Klux leader went to the jail and woke up the lieutenant, and the judge urged him to release the prisoner to the Ku Klux. The lieutenant voiced his objection to such an irregular proceeding, but Kirby told him that his little detachment of soldiers was hopelessly out-numbered by the Ku Klux and that they would take Ethridge out of the jail by force if he were not surrendered peacefully. The lieutenant admitted the cogency of this argument, but suggested that he be permitted to go out and inspect the as-sembled Ku Klux forces for himself to make sure that he really was outnumbered. This request was accepted as a reasonable one, and he was courteously escorted out to the woods where the Ku Klux band was waiting at ease. After looking them over, he was convinced and went back to the jail and unlocked Ethridge's cell, the Ku Klux leader assuring the lieutenant that the man would be available to answer any civil proceeding.

Floyd County, of which Rome was the county seat, was immediately adjacent to the Alabama line, and was a center of Ku Klux activity from the time of the first appearance of the order in Georgia. When the superior court of the county met in Rome in January, 1871, the grand jury for the first week made a report in which it deplored the activities of 'secret, dis-guised parties of men, going about over the county at night for the supposed purpose of correcting existing evils in the commu-nity.' After pointing out the dangerous nature of such activities, the report went on: 'Even supposing their intentions to be good, their secrecy and disguise open the way for wicked and malicious persons to band themselves together for purposes of theft, plunder, violence and bloodshed, and thus the harm growing out of their organization outweighs the good they propose to accomplish. . . . We feel it our duty as grand jurors to condemn in unqualified terms all such organizations, and urgently call upon all good citizens to discourage, discountenance and frown down all such, and use their influence to banish them from among us. And we even go so far as to recommend any person or persons, if any there be in our county, who may belong to such secret bands to abandon them at once and throw their influence in favor of vindicating and enforcing the laws.'

This report was denounced by the newspapers of Rome as an unjust indictment of the whole county which would place the citizens of the county in a false light, and one of the papers predicted that it would probably be used by Governor Bullock 'in his manipulation of the affairs of the state' and by the Radical element of Congress to the detriment of Georgia. The two succeeding grand juries, perhaps influenced by the newspapers' protests, made reports denying the existence in the county of any organized forces for law-breaking; but meanwhile Governor Bullock had indeed acted as was predicted by the Rome editor, and on February 15, 1871, he issued a proclamation calling attention to the misdeeds of 'a band of disguised men' in Floyd County, and offering rewards aggregating sixteen thousand dollars for the arrest and conviction of the persons engaged in the alleged outrages enumerated.

This offering of such an excessive reward for supposititious offenses was denounced by the Floyd County press as an offense 'as outrageous as are the acts of any Ku Klux that ever plied the lash or sounded a whistle,' and the Governor was urged to withdraw his proclamation. But Bullock paid no attention to that suggestion. By that time he and his political associates, carpetbaggers and scalawags, were getting into hot water at every turn.

A typical office-holder of the period was the sheriff of Warren County, an ignorant scalawag of lowly origin named 'Chap' Norris, who had been a shoemaker before the war. Through one subterfuge or another he had managed to stay out of the

Confederate army; and after the end of the war took up politics
as a profession, embraced the Radical cause and soon found
himself sheriff of the county, which proved to be much more
pleasant and lucrative employment than he had found at the
cobbler's bench.

The Ku Klux were well organized in Warren County; and,
although the results of their work were plain to be seen, they
managed to escape detection. The editor of the local paper, the
Warrenton *Clipper*, was Charles Wallace, who was also generally
understood to be the Cyclops of the Warrenton Den of the Klan.
Mr. Wallace became involved in a personal controversy with
another resident of Warrenton, Doctor G. W. Darden, growing
out of Wallace's belief that Darden had blackballed him when
he applied for membership in the Masonic lodge. Wallace
published a card in his paper denouncing Doctor Darden in the
most violent terms; and Darden, his honor offended, waylaid
Wallace on the street in Warrenton and murdered him with a
blast from a double-barreled shotgun.

This murder created the most intense indignation among
Wallace's friends; but no move to arrest Darden was made by
the terrified sheriff. Later in the day, however, as murmurs of
possible retaliation spread through the town, Darden's wife
accompanied him to the jail and persuaded the sheriff to lock
him up for his own protection, having done which Sheriff
Norris hastily left town to avoid having any part in the trouble
he feared was impending.

As was related in the *Clipper's* subsequent account of the
affair, 'By nine or ten o'clock of that night a number of mysterious beings entered the town from different directions and sought
for the keys to the jail. The Radical sheriff of the county
having left that night for parts unknown, carrying the keys
with him, they commenced breaking down the doors of the jail.
About two o'clock in the morning Dr. Darden was taken out
and, after giving him time to write to his family, he was taken

near the railroad and shot. Who the avengers were, where they
came from, or how they left, nobody knows.'

The coroner's jury found that Doctor Darden had come to
his death by gunshot wounds at the hands of persons unknown
to the jury — and, while they may have been unknown to the
jury, there was pretty general understanding among the citizens
of Warrenton that the act was one of vengeance on the part of
Wallace's fellow-Klansmen.

Sheriff Norris's flight carried him to Atlanta, whence he returned to Warrenton with a squad of soldiers who arrested
five men whom the sheriff charged with being members of the
Ku Klux band who took Darden out of the jail and killed him.
These men were released under bail at length; but meanwhile,
according to Norris's story later, representatives of the arrested
men approached him and proposed to him that he refrain from
pushing the matter, as it would cause trouble in the whole community. The Governor had offered a reward of five thousand
dollars for each convicted Ku Klux, and Norris was anxious to
collect the twenty-five thousand dollars if possible; but he finally
accepted, by way of compromise, a promissory note for five
thousand dollars signed by some responsible local men, in return for which he promised to stop the prosecutions and leave
town — which he did not do. Norris was subsequently indicted for accepting a bribe and was also prosecuted by all the
arrested Ku Klux on the charge of false imprisonment; so he
was eventually glad to drop the whole matter, although his
political crony, Governor Bullock, had considerately provided
him in advance with a pardon to be used in the remote con-
tingency of his conviction. Sheriff Norris was very much
upset by the suggestion of moral turpitude in connection with
his acceptance of the five thousand dollars note. He had a
duplex defense: In the first place it wasn't a bribe; and, anyhow, some of the army officers at Warrenton had taken bigger
bribes than he did.

Bullock thoroughly and effectively capitalized the killing of Darden, and all other Ku Klux manifestations, and flooded the North with all sorts of exaggerated stories of the reign of terror alleged to prevail in Georgia. This use of reports of so-called 'Ku Klux outrages' for the purpose of alarming and inflaming the North, thereby providing sentiment to back up the Radical regulatory laws, became so flagrant that during the 1870 campaign the Atlanta *Constitution,* in sarcastic vein, printed this card:

WANTED — KU KLUX OUTRAGES

Wanted, a liberal supply of Ku Klux outrages in Georgia. They may be as ferocious and bloodthirsty as possible. No regard need be paid to the truth. Parties furnishing must be precise and circumstantial. They must be supplied during the next ten days, to influence the Georgia bill in the House. Accounts of Democrats giving the devil to Republicans are preferred. A hash of negroes murdered by the Ku Klux will be acceptable. A deuce of bobbery is necessary. Raw head and bloody bones, in every style, can be served up to profit.

The highest price paid. Apply to R. B. Bullock, or the Slander Mill, Atlanta, Ga., and to Forney's *Chronicle,* Benjamin F. Butler, or to the Reconstruction Committee, Washington, D.C.

Georgia Railroad Bonds traded for this commodity.

The 'Slander Mill' was used as a synonym for the State Capitol. The reference to the Georgia railroad bonds was an allusion to the current rumor that a large issue of such bonds was being used in a corrupt effort to influence votes.

To a great extent this great flood of outrage propaganda was designed by Bullock as a smoke screen to obscure the visibility of the corruption of his own administration, and also to bolster up the Republican cause in the 1870 elections for members of Congress and the state legislature; but, despite the most that Bullock could do, the Democrats carried this election overwhelmingly. Under Georgia's laws, however, the new Conservative legislature would not convene until November, 1871. This left Bullock nearly an entire year for the pursuit of plunder, which he improved to the greatest possible extent; and then, the day before the legislature was to convene, he resigned his office and fled the state in time to prevent his impeachment by the incoming legislators.

Meanwhile Congress had passed the Ku Klux Law, and the Congressional Committee had launched its investigation of Ku Klux affairs in Georgia. Henry W. Grady, who was later to achieve some degree of eminence in Georgia and throughout the nation for his oratory, was at that time the youthful editor of the Rome *Southerner and Commercial*, and was openly suspected of active connection with the Ku Klux Klan. When the Committee began its investigation in Georgia, Grady did not hesitate to pronounce it a political maneuver, and offered the following advice in an editorial headed 'The Ku Klux Klan':

'The *Commercial*, as a guardian of the good of the public, appeals to those of its friends who have any connection whatever with secret organizations to remain perfectly quiet and orderly, for the present at any rate. Let there be no suspicion of disorder or lawlessness; let there be no parading of disguised men, no stopping of innocent men and forcing them to dance; this is all child's play and foolishness.' And, further: 'The eyes of the continent are on us. . . . Then let us be quiet and bide our time; a passion chained down is a more fearsome and a nobler thing than a passion gratified. . . . Remember, brothers, that the strength and power of any secret organization rests in the attribute of mystery and hidden force, and in the fact that upon the thousand hills of our country a legion of brave hearts that are throbbing quietly can be called together by a tiny signal, and when the work is done can melt away into shadowy nothing. Every time you act you weaken your strength; then be quiet.'

Although this outburst of rhetoric seemed to indicate that Mr. Grady knew something about Ku Klux affairs he was not, strangely enough, called before the committee. B. F. Sawyer, the editor of the other Rome paper, the *Courier*, however, was summoned to Atlanta to testify; and when he received his summons he published an item in his paper in which he derided the Committee, stating that 'the Spanish Inquisition was not more disgraceful and dangerous than this rotten concern.' Referring to his own pending appearance before the Committee, he said in sarcastic tone: 'They will be very apt to worm all the secrets of the Ku Klux out of him.' The august Committee had its dignity offended by this derisive item, and when Sawyer appeared they demanded to know what he meant by his reference to their worming the secrets of the order out of him. He apologetically explained that it was merely a 'pleasantry,' and that 'the idea intended to be conveyed was that if your committee was to trouble themselves to shear a pig they would get but little wool.'

Apparently the Committee members did shear a great number of pigs; certainly their expedition resulted in a very small production of wool. There was a stream of witnesses hailed before them in Washington and in Atlanta, most of them Radicals and a very large proportion of them illiterate negroes of the lowest mentality. While they were holding their sessions in Atlanta in November the state senate of Georgia was also meeting there, and they adopted resolutions stating that 'it has been alleged by certain politicians, North and South, who esteem the success of the party to which they belong and the accomplishment of their political purposes more highly than the peace, happiness and prosperity of the country, that there exists in this state and other Southern States certain lawless bands of persons commonly called Ku Klux who are banded together for political purposes and are in the habit of committing great outrages upon the peaceable and law-abiding citizens of the country and that the state courts fail and refuse to afford sufficient redress,' but that they were satisfied that no such political organization existed in Georgia. The resolution sharply attacked the credibility of a number of the witnesses then being examined, and urged that all the judges of the superior courts of Georgia be summoned before the committee as a more effective means of arriving at the facts regarded law-breaking in the state. The Congressional Committee paid no attention to this suggestion. It continued to shear its pigs, and eventually wound up its hearings and went back to Washington. Meanwhile the Ku Klux Klan, which was being so industriously investigated, was quietly dissolving, in Georgia and elsewhere, and fading out of existence.

When General Gordon testified before the Committee in 1871 he stated that at that time he did not believe that any such organization existed or had existed for a long time, that he had not heard of it for two years. As to the reason for its passing away, he explained: 'Well, sir, it just dissolved, because the courts became generally established; and though the courts were in the hands of the opposition party our people believed they were trying to do justice, that a general protection was extended over us. Our people thought that we could get justice at the hands of these judges. Though they were of the opposing party and though negroes were on the juries, we were satisfied that in the existing condition of things we were safe.' Lieutenant George S. Hoyt of the United States Army, who was stationed in Georgia with the army of occupation, stated that although there had been a general, state organization of the Ku Klux in 1868, it was his understanding that later the state organization was broken up and that the later disturbances were attributable to 'a sort of local organization, not connected together.'

Certainly by the end of 1871 the better element of people in Georgia seemed to be convinced that the Ku Klux were degenerating into an instrumentality of outlawry which was bringing odium on the whole section, and there began to be demands for its stamping out. The Augusta *Constitutionalist* published a strong editorial in which it was urged that steps be taken to bring to an end the Ku Klux activities in the state.

'Exceptional cases have arisen,' they said, 'and may arise again, in the Southern States since the close of the war, under the despotic rule of the bayonet and under the corrupt government of carpetbaggers' where it became 'almost a virtue to meet despotism and connivance with crime with swift retribution. If there was any mistake made in such Ku Kluxism it was in not striking high enough.' But it went on to show how mob law soon exceeds all restraint, and concluded: 'It is about time that the communities in which the operation of the Ku Kluxers have taken place should speak out and call on these secret champions of society to unmask. It is time their faces should be scrutinized and their credentials examined. . . . It is time the community should in public meetings and through the public press declare its true sentiments. There has been too long a reprehensible silence on this subject. In the absence of the voice of protest it has been assumed that these secret organizations possessed the sympathy and approbation of society. . . . If the citizens of Georgia do not through their own grand juries and through their own courts of justice take cognizance of the infractions of its laws and the violations of the rights of property, persons and life of its own citizens, white and black, they can with but poor grace raise a clamor against the unconstitutional Ku Kluxism of the Congress of the United States, which has authorized the President to suspend the writ of habeas corpus and to send Federal troops to preserve order. . . . There is but one way to escape such results. It is for the people of Georgia in the several counties which have reason to fear Federal interference to rise up and by their conduct show that they are capable of protecting the lives of their own citizens and to bring to punishment those who defy the laws of the state. The legislature should speak out, by joint resolutions, condemning in the strongest language secret organizations and midnight mobs, and exhort the people to bring to bear every legal and moral influence for the vindication of the peace, good order and dignity of the state. We have no longer an executive who will indiscriminately pardon criminals, and there is good reason now to hope that the decrees of our tribunals of criminal justice will be respected and enforced.'

This editorial was reproduced in the Savannah *News* and other Georgia papers, and fairly represented the feelings of the people at that time. Particularly significant was the reference to the change in the state government which promised greater security. This was the kernel of the whole thing. The government of the state was now back in the hands of the people; there was no longer any necessity for a secret band of regulators; and the Ku Klux Klan quickly withered away in the light of the changed conditions.

The story of the development and decline of the Klan in Georgia was authoritatively epitomized by John C. Reed in his 'The Brothers' War,' published in 1905, when he said: 'It is high time that the Ku Klux be understood. When in 1867 it was strenuously attempted to give rule to scalawags and negroes, the very best of the South led the unanimous revolt. Their first taste of political power incited the negroes to license and riot, imperiling every condition of decent life. In the twinkling of an eye the Ku Klux organized. It mustered, not assassins, thugs, and cut-throats, as has been often alleged, but the choicest Southern manhood. Every good woman knew that the order was now the solitary defense of her purity, and she consecrated it with all-availing prayers. In Georgia we won the election of December, 1870, in the teeth of gigantic odds.

This decisive deliverance from the most monstrous and horrible misrule recorded among Anglo-Saxons was the achievement of the Ku Klux. Its high mission performed, the Klan, burning its disguises, rituals, and other belongings, disbanded two or three months later. Its reputation is not to be sullied by what masked men — bogus Ku Klux as we, the genuine, called them — did afterwards.' And, to leave no possible misunderstanding as to how he felt about it, Mr. Reed concluded his passing reference to the Klan by saying: 'I shall always remember with pride my service in the famous 8th Georgia Volunteers. . . . But I am prouder of my career in the Ku Klux Klan.'

Possibly on account of its geographical nearness to Washington, the activities of the Ku Klux in North Carolina appear to have attracted more attention at the seat of the Federal Government than those in any other Realm of the Invisible Empire; and it was, in fact, directly as a result of the terrifying reports of depredations and bloody disorders in North Carolina that President Grant in 1871 launched the general congressional investigation into conditions 'in the late insurrectionary states.'

Up to that time, affairs in the Old North State had followed the usual pattern of the period. One of the first steps in the reconstruction of the state immediately after the war was the forcible ousting of Zebulon B. Vance from the Governor's office to which he had been elected, and the appointment in his place as provisional Governor of W. W. Holden. Holden, a native North Carolinian, was a man of considerable native ability; but he was an opportunist in politics, apparently devoid of fixed principles. Before the war he had been originally a Whig, but flopped more or less gracefully to the Democrats when given a job as editor of a Democratic paper. For years he was an avowed apostle of secession, then suddenly switched in 1858 to the pro-Union side; but he opposed Lincoln's call for troops to hold the Union together and voted for the secession ordinance. During the course of the war he broke out in an attack on the Confederate Government in 1863 and urged an immediate peace. After the close of the war he first espoused Andrew Johnson's principles, then turned against Johnson and became head of the Loyal League in North Carolina, the League reaching a membership of eighty thousand in the state under his guidance.

In the gubernatorial election held in 1866 Holden was defeated by Jonathan Worth, an old-time Whig and staunch Union man of conservative traits. With the aid of his eighty thousand enfranchised Loyal Leaguers, however, and backed by military force, Holden was elected governor on the Radical ticket in 1868; and he subjected the state to three years of misrule and oppression until he was impeached in 1871.

The circumstances leading up to the organization of the Ku Klux movement in North Carolina were parallel with those in other Southern States at the time. The negroes were organizing in their Loyal Leagues and drilling at night, stationing their sentinels on the highways, halting white people on the roads and causing them to pass around the meeting places. There was no explanation of all this martial activity on the part of the recent slaves, and the white population was mystified and alarmed. The general air of uneasiness was accentuated by the unscrupulous white agitators who were, for political purposes, telling the negroes that the white people were their enemies and were planning to put them back into slavery. In League meetings the negroes were repeatedly told the pleasant myth that the white men's farms were to be seized and divided up among the freedmen and each negro given his forty acres and a horse or mule; but, worse than that, the inflaming addresses they heard at these meetings frequently provoked them to a rage which led to riot and bloodshed.

During the session of the state legislature in 1868 an address was issued by that deliberative body to the native people of

North Carolina, written by Senator Pool and signed by ninety Radical members, in which the white citizens were sharply harangued as to their duty to the freedmen and threatened with broad suggestions of what the negroes might do to them.

'Did it ever occur to you, ye gentlemen of property,' this incendiary document said, 'To you, ye men — and especially ye women — who never received anything from these colored people but services, kindness and protection; did it ever occur to you that these same people, who are so very bad, will not be willing to sleep in the cold when your houses are denied them, merely because they will not vote as you do; that they may not be willing to starve while they are willing to work for bread? Did it never occur to you that revenge, which is so sweet to you, may be as sweet to them? Hear us, if nothing else you will hear, did it never occur to you that if you kill their children with hunger they will kill your children with fear? Did it never occur to you that if you, good people, maliciously determine that they shall not have shelter, they may determine that you shall have no shelter?' And so on.

The result of a succession of things like this was to create a feeling of genuine terror on the part of the white people, which was intensified as the negroes and Radicals gained power. Even as late as the spring of 1871 the citizens of the counties of Gaston, Rutherford and Cleveland, on the southern border of the state, were living in fear of a raid from the negroes of South Carolina, where there had been fatal clashes between the races; and the North Carolinians for several days and nights maintained an armed guard over their towns, making ready to defend themselves if necessary.

Just exactly when the Ku Klux Klan was first introduced into North Carolina is not entirely clear, but it seems not to have been noticeably active there until some time in 1868; and there was testimony to the effect that it was introduced into the state from some of the adjoining counties in South

Carolina rather than directly from Tennessee. On the other hand, General Forrest was in North Carolina in the early part of 1868; and in those days when General Forrest appeared it was generally found that he had sowed the dragon's teeth of Ku Kluxism. Further testimony regarding Forrest's connection with the North Carolina Ku Klux is provided by General Homer Atkinson, still living in Virginia, who states that he was living in New York in 1868 and that he there received a letter from General Forrest requesting him to go to North Carolina and help organize the Klan there, which he did. Certain it is that the Ku Klux organization was an authentic offshoot of the original mother Klan, for the terminology was the same and, furthermore, the flag of the Ku Klux of Cabarrus County, now preserved in a Richmond museum, is exactly as described in the Original Prescript of the order.

Early in 1868 there had spontaneously sprung into existence in North Carolina organizations known as the White Brotherhood and the Constitutional Union Guards, not to mention local groups of regulators without formal organization or title. These appear to have been merged into the Ku Klux Klan during the latter part of 1868, and after that date all disorders charged to disguised groups of men were generally tagged 'Ku Klux.' It appears that 'The Invisible Empire' was a name generally used in North Carolina at that time as being synonymous with the Ku Klux Klan. Judge Tourgee was of the opinion that 'The Invisible Empire' was some sort of a higher degree of the Ku Klux; and at the time there seemed to be no popular understanding of the fact that 'The Invisible Empire' was merely the term used within the Ku Klux organization itself in referring to the entire territory covered by its operations. John B. Harrill, a confessed member of the organization in North Carolina, testified that the name 'Invisible Empire' was used so that if they were ever called on to testify in court they could swear that they 'never belonged to the Ku Klux, that they never knew a Ku Klux, or anything in that way.' A similar statement was made by an Arkansas member regarding the use of names.

David Schenck, an admitted member of the Invisible Empire, although stoutly denying any connection with or knowledge of the Ku Klux Klan, gave a description of the signs, passwords and oath of the Invisible Empire, which corresponded exactly with the signs testified to by members of the Ku Klux Klan in North Carolina and elsewhere. It is also significant that the sign of distress, the word 'Avalanche,' was the same as was used by admitted Ku Klux elsewhere in North Carolina and in other parts of the South.

There seems to be no doubt that the Ku Klux Klan when it was originally formed in North Carolina was in the hands of men of the very highest standing in the state. Ex-Governor Zebulon B. Vance was generally supposed to be the Grand Dragon of the Realm; and the testimony of some of the confessed Ku Klux was to the effect that within the Klan Vance was generally looked upon as the chief of the state. Hamilton C. Jones of Raleigh, a prominent and highly regarded man of that time, was also understood to be high in the Klan's affairs, probably second only to Vance. Among others known to be prominent in the Ku Klux work in the state was Colonel LeRoy McAfee, who served as a Grand Titan in western North Carolina, and who was among the first to take steps to disband the Klan when it began to drift into excesses. Colonel McAfee was the uncle of Thomas Dixon, Jr., whose best-seller novel *The Clansman* was dedicated to him, Mr. Dixon stating that the book was founded largely on information supplied him by the ex-Titan.

The Clansman told the story of the Ku Klux in a sympathetic and powerfully appealing manner which thrilled hundreds of thousands of readers, not to mention the millions who saw it on the screen as *The Birth of a Nation*. An earlier, highly colored account of the Ku Klux times in North Carolina, from the opposite viewpoint, is contained in a book entitled *A Fool's Errand — by One of the Fools,* written by Albion W. Tourgee in the early eighties. Tourgee was a carpetbagger, an ex-officer in Sherman's army, who settled in Alamance County after the war. He fraternized freely with the negroes, made speeches at their meetings, and on the rising tide of Radicalism (assisted by a bit of special legislation) he was swept into a position as a judge of the circuit court, although at the time he did not even pretend to be a lawyer and had no license to practice law. Judge Tourgee's book, along with two or three others of similar nature, enjoyed wide popularity at the time. This was the first widely circulated account of the purported acts of the notorious and mysterious Ku Klux Klan, and Tourgee had sufficient literary skill to make his story a readable one, even if all the members of the Loyal League were dusky models of nobility and uprightness and all the Ku Klux and their friends perfect examples of unadulterated wickedness and debasement. The hero, a wise and noble resident of North Carolina recently removed there from a Northern state, was generally supposed to be a thinly disguised autobiographical picture of the author.

Despite its great popularity at the time, however, the modern reader who accepts Judge Tourgee's book as telling an unbiased story of Reconstruction days in North Carolina will get a highly distorted picture of those times. In North Carolina, as elsewhere, the Loyal Leagues were generally regarded by the whites as dangerous hotbeds of hostility, and there was plenty of evidence to support this theory. During 1869 there was an epidemic of barn-burnings in several of the counties of the state, with evidence to show that these burnings were part of a systematic plan on the part of organizations of negroes who met and planned such programs of arson. In one county they burned eight in one night; and the native white farmers were in a state bordering on terror, aside from the pecuniary losses involved. Some of the offenders in Gaston County were detected and arrested, and they confessed not only that the Loyal League in that county was sponsoring the incendiarism there but that they were acting on orders received from the head of the League in Raleigh.

In Wake County they burned all the barns along the Cape Fear River in a systematic manner; and when a farmer named Mimms ran out and tried to extinguish his burning barn he was shot by the incendiaries. It was the understanding of the citizens that the negroes were meeting and planning these burnings at a rendezvous in a country schoolhouse, and a party of Ku Klux raided the schoolhouse one night while a meeting was in progress. The negroes had warning of their coming and fled in time to escape; but the raiders caught a white man named Dicken, who was accused of aiding and abetting the negroes, and as an act of poetic justice he was compelled to apply the torch to the schoolhouse where the meetings had been held.

It is significant of the turbulence of the times and the distorted standards prevailing that one witness, after testifying to a series of barn-burnings by an organization of negroes, was asked the point-blank question: 'What has been the conduct generally of the colored people in your country?' He replied seriously: 'Very good, with the exception of rapes, murders and thefts, and things of that kind.' But the victims of these rapes, murders, thefts and things of that kind found it difficult to consider such conduct as 'very good.' Their protests at their helpless plight were loud and bitter; and as protests proved unavailing, more and more Ku Klux dens began to spring up throughout the state. The judiciary system of the state at this time was a farce, a large proportion of the judges being incompetent, many of them corrupt and all of them of the Radical persuasion. If the courts did happen to convict a negro or a carpetbagger of arson or burglary or assault, he was generally let off with a nominal fine; or, if sentenced to prison, was often pardoned by the Governor immediately. In such revolutionary circumstances the citizens' only avenue of relief seemed to be through the medium of self-constituted organizations of regulators like the Ku Klux Klan.

Ku Klux affairs reached a climax in North Carolina early in 1870, with outbursts of notable violence in Alamance, Orange, Chatham and neighboring counties. In Alamance the order was supposed to have been disbanded late in 1869, at which time the Ku Klux staged a public parade at Graham as a final demonstration. A negro, later identified as Wyatt Outlaw, the head of the Loyal League in that county, fired into this parade; and one morning in February, 1870, his body was found hanging to a tree in the courthouse yard. On the other hand, a group of members of the Constitutional Union Guard in Alamance saved the life of State Senator Shoffner, author of the hated state Ku Klux law, when they heard that a band of Ku Klux were coming from Orange County to hang the senator. The visiting band was turned back at the county line and Shoffner was hustled off to safety in Greensboro.

Governor Holden adopted different methods to handle these outbreaks. In Orange County he hired a prominent citizen of Hillsboro, Doctor Pride Jones, giving him a captain's commission, for the purpose of suppressing the Ku Klux activities in that county. Doctor (or Captain) Jones moved in a mysterious way but he got results. He was very emphatic in pointing out at the beginning that he was not a member of the Ku Klux; but he seemed to know the identity of the proper persons to approach; and within four weeks he reported that the order in that county had been disbanded, Holden having authorized him to assure the Orange County Ku Klux that if they would go and sin no more they would not be prosecuted for past offenses. Doctor Pride in his report to the Governor said plainly that the organization resulted from the fact that barns were being burned and that women were in mortal terror of assault,

and that in the absence of effective courts the citizens had
taken the law into their own hands. He did not seem to be
entirely lacking in sympathy for their motives.

In other counties Governor Holden was not quite so diplomatic or lenient. Caswell County was generally looked upon
as a Ku Klux stronghold, and Holden sent one of his political
henchmen, State Senator John W. Stephens, there in the capacity of a detective. Stephens was a typical scalawag politician,
popularly known as 'Chicken' Stephens in commemoration
of his having been convicted of chicken-stealing before the war.
It was a current joke that, having stolen a chicken and been
elected to the state senate, he was considering stealing a turkey
gobbler so he could run for Congress. Stephens had hardly arrived in Yanceyville before he started making speeches to the
negroes at their League meetings; and on one occasion, it was
charged, gave every negro a box of matches with the suggestion
that they would be useful in burning the white people's houses
and barns. There ensued a perfect orgy of arson. Nine barns
were burned in one night; the hotel in Yanceyville was burned,
along with a row of brick houses, and the tobacco crops of
several of the leading citizens were destroyed. Stephens was
held responsible for this by the local Ku Klux, and a few days
later, on July 2, while he was attending a mass meeting of
citizens in the courthouse at Yanceyville he was called out of
the room, and nothing more was seen of him until his dead
body was found the next day in a little room on the ground
floor used for storing firewood. The Radicals howled that he
had been killed by the Ku Klux; the Ku Klux started the
usual counter-cry that he had been murdered by his own party
for the purpose of throwing suspicion on the Klan.

Despite the most vigorous investigation, the affair remained
an unsolved mystery until October, 1935, when Captain John
G. Lea died at the home of his son, Weldon Lea, in South
Boston, Virginia. There was then revealed an affidavit which

Captain Lea had made on July 2, 1919, and which had lain sealed in the files of the North Carolina Historical Commission at Raleigh since then, in which he told how Stephens had been killed 'by appointed executioners of the Ku Klux Klan' after he had had 'a fair trial before a jury of twelve men.' There were a dozen who took part in the assassination, he said, and they all swore never to tell anything about it until the last one died. Captain Lea was the last, and he made his affidavit on the anniversary of the event, depositing it with the Historical Commission with the proviso that it should not be opened until his death. According to his story, the actual executioners of Stephens were Captain J. Thomas Mitchell and Thomas Oliver, Mitchell strangling Stephens with a rope as Oliver plunged a knife into his breast and his throat.

Captain Lea in his affidavit revealed that he was the organizer of the Klan in Caswell County; and that when the mass meeting was called to be held in Yanceyville he summoned the Caswell Klansmen to assemble there that afternoon with their robes under their saddles. While the meeting was in full blast, ex-Sheriff Wiley, by prearrangement, beckoned to Stephens and asked him to step down to the corridor on the lower floor. There he was quickly surrounded by a dozen robed Klansmen, one of whom quickly muffled his cries, the others pushing him into the little room, where he was quickly killed, Wiley meanwhile having passed on out in the street to establish his alibi. Their work done, the avenging Ku Klux removed their robes and rolled them into small bundles which they secreted under their coats, left the room, closed the door and locked it on the outside, and threw the key into County Line Creek.

The killing of Stephens gave Holden just the excuse he needed for taking a daring and drastic step. The state legislature in January, 1870, acting at Holden's direction, had enacted what was known as the Shoffner Bill or Ku Klux Law, which permitted the Governor to declare any county in the state in in-

surrection and to raise militia and send them there. Backed
up by this power, and sensing the rising tide of Democratic
voting strength in the state which threatened the success of
the Radical ticket in the next election, Holden now boldly
declared that the state was overrun with Ku Klux to such an
extent that it was impossible for the civil authorities to cope
with them, and he proceeded to raise two companies of militia
with which he planned to terrorize the counties where the
Ku Klux had been reported most active.

One of these militia companies was commanded by Colonel
George W. Kirk, who was popularly known as 'Bloody' Kirk
or 'Cut-Throat' Kirk, both appellations having been well earned
during the wartime days when Kirk commanded a band of
pro-Union guerrillas in the mountains of East Tennessee.
He recruited his new militia force of six hundred and seventy
very largely from these wartime outlaws, fortified with other
vagabonds and desperadoes, some black and some white,
four hundred of them being under age and two hundred not
citizens of the state. After mobilizing them at Morganton, he
marched his motley and irresponsible little army eastward,
his troops signalizing their passage through the country with
a series of crimes and misdemeanors which the New York
World denounced as 'a disgrace to the Nineteenth Century.'
As Kirk's 'Angels,' so-called, approached Caswell and Alamance
Counties, Governor Holden officially declared those counties
in a state of insurrection, and proclaimed martial law in them.
Kirk pounced down and made wholesale arrests of suspected
members of the Ku Klux Klan; and when some of them obtained habeas corpus writs ordering their release he defied the
state's supreme court by ignoring the writs, insolently declaring
that 'those things have played out now.'

To back up Holden's claim that the state was in a condition
bordering on insurrection, Judge Tourgee wrote a letter to
Senator Abbott of North Carolina, another carpetbagger, which

was widely published during the 1870 campaign. This letter, as published, declared that the Ku Klux had broken into 4000 or 5000 houses, that they had burned fourteen houses in his immediate district and that he knew of thirteen murders in the district. This letter was used with telling effect, without comment from Judge Tourgee; but after the Radicals had gained the full benefit of its contents and the election was over, he blandly stated that it had been misquoted. 'I wrote four arsons instead of fourteen,' he said. 'Instead of 4000 or 5000 houses opened, I wrote 400 or 500. I said thirteen murders in the state, not in the district.' Incidentally, it was later found that three of the men reported murdered were still alive; and it was also stated that some of the house-burnings and other acts of violence were perpetrated by Holden's supporters to provoke resistance to the exaggerated Ku Klux menace. After the election Kirk's Ku Klux prisoners were brought before Judge Brooks of the United States district court and all were released.

When the Congressional Committee completed its investigation of affairs in the state, the majority reported that 'The Ku Klux organization does exist' and that it had political purposes which it sought to carry out by 'murders, whippings, intimidation and violence.' On the other hand, the minority report said that the outrages had been 'grossly and wilfully exaggerated' and that no act of lawlessness at all had been proven 'except in six, perhaps eight, of the eighty-seven North Carolina counties.'

Granting that both the majority and minority reports were colored by political feeling, it is interesting to read the official report of the United States Army officer, Colonel Hunt of Fort Adams, who commanded the affected district and who wrote on January 2, 1871: 'Evidence of the existence of such organizations was produced. Nearly all the cases inquired into, however, proved that other than political purposes were effected through the organization, whose machinery was used to punish thefts, burglaries, insults to women, and other offenses in no way connected with politics. In fine, their principal work seemed to be the work of regulators, or vigilance committees. Bad enough in themselves, these crimes were in the bitterness of party feeling exaggerated and misrepresented. To what extent murders and outrages were for political purposes I am not in position to state. For when the legislature passed laws to punish members of secret organizations they were to a great extent if not wholly dissolved.'

The Democrats carried the election in 1870, but not before there had been wholesale indictments of suspected Ku Klux scattered through a number of North Carolina counties. These prosecutions under the Shoffner Law and the Federal Ku Klux Law continued until in 1871 there had been a total of 61 bills of indictment found, embracing no less than 763 defendants. A large part of these indictments were found in Rutherford County, and provide a striking example of the extensive results that can ensue from small causes. Almost all the Ku Klux trouble in Rutherford County originated in a remarkably venomous politico-family feud in that county between two half-brothers, Aaron and Samuel Biggerstaff.

The origin of the Biggerstaff feud is more or less obscure, but dated back to the days of the Civil War. Aaron Biggerstaff was a Republican and Samuel a Democrat. Aaron had been a Union sympathizer during the war, and had been active in helping escaped Union prisoners to make their way through the mountains. He was a member of the secret society called 'The Red Strings' or 'Heroes of America,' which was later merged into the Loyal League; and during the latter days of the war acted as a guide to a body of Federal cavalry who were visiting the farms in that vicinity taking up the farmers' horses, among the places visited being that of Samuel Biggerstaff.

In February, 1870, there was some internal strife in Rutherford County, involving some illicit distilling operations, and an obscure citizen named McGahey was accused of informing on the moonshiners. Soon afterward his house was visited by a masked band of men at night; and, although he was not at home, the raiders vented their spleen by abusing and threatening his wife. McGahey was a man of some spirit and mettle, and when he got home and was informed of the raid he called together some of his neighbors, including Aaron Biggerstaff, to go with him in pursuit of the raiders, there being a light snow on the ground which made the footprints plainly visible. The footprints led in the direction of Samuel Biggerstaff's home; and when the avenging party got there they fired into the house, narrowly missing killing Samuel and some of his family.

McGahey's wife the next morning told him that she had recognized one of the masked visitors as a young man of the neighborhood named Decatur DePriest; whereupon McGahey took his shotgun and went to DePriest's home, called him to the front door and without parley killed him. McGahey then left the country and was heard of no more. Samuel Biggerstaff, incensed at the attack on his home, had Aaron Biggerstaff and some of the other members of the party arrested. They were duly convicted of having committed the assault, but a friendly Radical judge let them off with a nominal fine of twenty-five dollars.

Decatur DePriest, it later developed, was the Cyclops of the local Den of Ku Klux; and following his murder there were no Ku Klux activities in that vicinity for several months. Animosity against Aaron Biggerstaff continued to smolder, however; and when the barn of one of his neighbors, William P. Carson, was burned, he was accused of the arson. The members of the local Ku Klux Den meanwhile had been pulling themselves together following the shock of Decatur DePriest's death; and, with the burning of Carson's barn as an immediate provocation, Aaron Biggerstaff was taken from his home by the Ku Klux one night and severely whipped.

Promptly next day Biggerstaff had warrants sworn out for about forty of his neighbors, including his brother Samuel, whom he accused of being members of the whipping party. These men were released on bail; and several weeks later, as Biggerstaff and some of the members of his family were on their way to court to testify against the defendants, they were way-laid by another raiding party — some masked and some un-masked — and frightened to such an extent that they did not go to court.

The various Biggerstaff raids and the prosecutions growing out of them culminated in a spectacular Ku Klux raid on the town of Rutherfordton on a Sunday night, June 11, 1870. This well-organized foray had for its principal purpose the destruction of the plant of the *Star*, a Republican newspaper edited by T. B. Carpenter, and the punishment of Aaron Bigger-staff, James M. Justice and George W. Logan, the latter the scalawag circuit judge.

The party making the Rutherfordton raid, according to the later confessions of participants, was under the direction and leadership of Randolph A. Shotwell, the Grand Giant of Rutherford County — and, incidentally, the editor of the Rutherfordton *Vindicator*. The raiding party, however, was composed of some ninety members, made up of groups from four different Dens. There were detachments from the Cherry Mountain Den, the Bald Rock Den and the Burnt Chimney Den in the immediate county, and about forty men from the Horse Creek Den in the near-by Spartanburg district of South Carolina. The different detachments were handled with military efficiency, effecting a junction at an appointed rendezvous at Cox's blacksmith shop, and thence marching into the town and proceeding about their appointed and prearranged duties. Some were assigned to the demolition of the *Star* plant; some searched for Logan and Biggerstaff; some were posted as sentinels about the town and on the roads leading into it; and one group went to Justice's house after him.

Judge Logan was a prime example of the genus scalawag. He was a native Southerner, and had served as a member of the Confederate Congress. With the failure of the Confederate cause, however, he hastily left the sinking ship and proclaimed that when he took the oath to support the Confederate Constitution he did so with the deliberate intention of violating it. Like most new converts, he became a fire-eating Radical, and when he was elevated to the Federal bench and started dispensing justice there was an immediate uproar of complaint about the partisanship he manifested in his decisions. Aside from his partisanship, he was so generally incompetent that in June, 1871, a meeting of the bar in his district was held and resolutions of condemnation were adopted stating that he was 'not qualified either by learning or capacity to discharge the duties of the office,' and that by reason of his incompetent administration of his duties 'public confidence in the efficiency of the government and the laws has been impaired, and crimes have been multiplied.' This resolution was signed by all the practicing attorneys in the district, Democrats and Republicans alike. Justice was a scalawag lawyer who had been active in the prosecution of Aaron Biggerstaff's assailants, and had procured the indictment of other alleged members of the Ku Klux. He had made himself obnoxious to the members of the Klan by his violent and vociferous denunciations of them and all their works, declaring that all the Ku Klux leaders ought to be killed. Carpenter was not only offensive as the editor of a Radical newspaper; he had boasted that he had a list of the names of two hundred Ku Klux in the county and that he was going to have them all arrested.

Fortunately for Logan, he was out of town the night the Ku Klux raiders swept into Rutherfordton and deployed for action. Biggerstaff was in town, but he so skilfully hid himself that he could not be found. Carpenter was also out of town, but his newspaper plant was raided and wrecked, the press

broken and the cases of type overturned and pied. Failing to
find the other objects of their search, Justice had to bear the
brunt of the Ku Klux fury, and they gave him a very unpleasant
evening.

Justice later stated that he was not entirely surprised by the
raid, as before retiring to his bed that evening he had heard two
pistol shots on the outskirts of the town, which was generally
understood to be the signal given when the Ku Klux were to
assemble. Despite this alarum, he went peacefully to sleep; but
during the night he was awakened by shots fired outside his
house, closely followed by a rush on his front door which broke
it down, and before he could make any defensive move his bed
was surrounded by a crowd of disguised men, looking, he said,
'more like a man would imagine that devils would look than
you would ever suppose human beings would fix themselves
up to look.'

'Don't say a word; your time has come,' they gruffly told
him; and, after considerable manhandling, he was dragged
out in his nightclothes, and, through the pouring rain, was
marched barefooted to the edge of town. He complained that
it hurt his feet, but they told him that made no difference, he
wouldn't need his feet very long as they were going to kill him.
He attempted to argue this point with them, but they told him:
'You have been making some very strong speeches lately; you
are in favor of hanging our leaders. Our party proposes to rid
this country of this damned, infamous nigger government, and
you propose to defeat us by hanging our leaders, you damned
rascal.'

Eventually Justice was taken to the leader of this detachment
of the band, a man whom he later described as 'sensible and
fair-minded,' by whom he was subjected to a long grilling regarding the steps which he and the others had taken against
the Ku Klux. At length the leader told Justice that if he would
lead a party of the raiders back to town and help them find

Biggerstaff they would spare his life. Justice was in such terror that he eagerly accepted the suggestion that he betray Biggerstaff in return for their sparing him, but some of the Ku Klux objected very strongly to such an arrangement. One of them said: 'Don't you turn this damn rascal loose. He says he don't know any of us, but if you turn him loose he will go right off and swear to every one of us. He will go to Washington in less than a week and have the troops here and play hell with us. Damn him, kill him now that we have got him.'

The leader responded sternly: 'Remember our oath: "Justice and humanity,"' repeating this three or four times. They were loud and clamorous, however, in their insistence that he must be killed; and the leader finally placed a bodyguard of four armed men around Justice to protect him from any too impetuous individual, while he continued to parley with him. All this time, however, the clamor continued: 'Kill him; kill him'; and some of the raiders came up and poked their pistols in Justice's face, reaching across the guard, threatening to shoot him then and there.

The chief was irritated by this and cried out: 'Where is the chief of the Horse Creek Camp?' And, when told that the chief of that Den had gone up the road, he said petulantly: 'Is there no officer here?' A voice replied that he was second in command, whereupon the leader said: 'Well, damn you, take charge of your men and command them if you have any control over them. I was given this command, and I will be respected. You are the worst men I ever saw.'

This display of authority served to still the clamor, and the men of the rank and file withdrew to a respectful distance; whereupon the leader told Justice that he had no personal feeling in the matter, that he was from South Carolina and had come there to lead the raid at the request of the local dens. 'These men want to kill you very badly,' he said, 'but I want to save you if I can. I have an absolute order to take your life tonight; but we have a rule that if a man behaves so as to justify it we may spare him. I think you ought to be spared; and if you will stop supporting the damned Radical party I think you will be all right, and I should like to know you in our order.' Justice, according to his own account of the affair, was ready to promise anything to save his life, and he responded eagerly, 'Yes, yes.'

The leader finally said: 'Let's have this all understood. Do you promise here now to be a true friend to the Southern cause?' Justice, in his later recital of the events of that stormy night, said: 'I made an evasive answer. I said: "Yes, sir, I will here-after be a true friend of Southern men." He said "Southern cause" but I said "Southern men," which he accepted as an answer to his proposition.' Overlooking this equivocation, the leader then told Justice that he must promise to meet them at a Ku Klux rendezvous at Cowpens battleground — which, Mr. Justice carefully explained in telling his story, was 'where a battle was fought, near King's Mountain, in the old Revolu-tionary War.' Justice raised the objection that they might kill him if he attended the meeting, saying he was afraid to go that far away from home after dark. They pointed out to him, however, that if they wanted to kill him they could do it right then; and, as a compromise, suggested that he meet them at Cox's Blacksmith Shop, which was nearer town. Justice agreed to this, and then asked them to tell him how to approach the meeting — to give him some password by which he might make himself known — and, his account continues:

'He said, "When a voice calls out to you 'Halt,' you will say 'Number One'; then you will be asked 'Who are you?' and you will reply 'A friend'; and you will then be asked 'A friend to what?' The answer you will give will be 'A friend to my country.' You will then be asked 'How can you prove that?' and you will say 'I s-a-y.' That is not our password, I want you to understand that, but you will get through with that.

I assure you that you will be treated all right that night." After
we had some more words in a friendly way I expressed my
gratitude not only to him but to the men who stood around me,
for discharging me. I shook hands with each of them in a
friendly way, and told them "Good-bye," and they let me go
and I ran home as rapidly as possible.'

Needless to say, Justice did not keep his appointment with
his new Ku Klux chums, but, on the contrary, went immediately
to Raleigh and appeared before the Federal grand jury there,
as a result of which bills of indictment were found against a
large number of residents of Rutherford County whom Justice
claimed to have recognized the night of the raid. A United
States marshal went to Rutherfordton, accompanied by a
troop of mounted infantry, to serve the warrants; and as a
result of this show of force and the indictment of some of the
leaders of the Ku Klux movement in that locality, a sort of
panic ensued among the members of the organization. The
reputed leaders of several of the Dens hastily left the country.
On the other hand, some of the weaker members were frightened
into confessing, and this precipitated an epidemic of confessions which did not end until 763 residents of that and adjoining
counties had been indicted under the Federal Ku Klux Act.

It was charged that Judge Logan had offered 'base and
dishonorable inducements' to extort these confessions out of
some of the prisoners; but, even admitting that some of the
confessions bear internal evidence of proving what the prose-
cutors wanted to prove, it seems apparent that they were in a
general way pretty close to the facts. At any rate, eight of the
defendants were finally convicted and sentenced to serve terms
in prison, among them being the reputed leader of the Klan
in the county. The conduct of the trial was subjected to sharp
criticism, not only in the South but in other parts of the country,
even by papers which were militantly hostile to the Ku Klux.
For example, the New York *Sun* said: 'With violent partisans

as prosecuting officers, a packed jury, and a hostile court against them, it is no wonder that these men were convicted. They may all have received only their just deserts in the end; but no one can pretend that the manner of their conviction was anything but a mockery of justice and an outrage on judicial propriety.'

The opinion was expressed by conservative residents of Rutherford County that the whole reign of terror in that county grew out of the court's leniency with the original assailants of Samuel Biggerstaff. 'If,' said one of them, 'Aaron Biggerstaff had been punished for his assault upon his brother with deliberate purpose to kill, these troubles would not have arisen'; pointing out that Aaron Biggerstaff had been dismissed with a slap on the wrist in the shape of a twenty-five-dollar fine, whereas the men accused of whipping him were arrested on bench warrants the next day and held in bail in the state courts, and also arrested under Federal warrants and carried off to Raleigh, two hundred and fifty miles from their homes, and lodged in jail among strangers, where they were held until released under five hundred dollars bail.

The Rutherfordton raid was the last outstanding, big-scale Ku Klux demonstration in North Carolina. Not only did the wholesale indictments tend to discourage membership in the proscribed organization; but, even before that, the more level-headed leaders had begun to take steps looking to its disbandment. David Schenck, reputedly the Grand Giant of Lincoln County, testified that he left the order early in 1870 when it began to get out of hand and deeds of violence were committed. He said that when he severed his connection with it he caused at least three Dens to be disbanded and also caused his personal and political friends to use their influence in the same direction, with the result that 'nine-tenths of the respectable men who had ever had any connection with it left it.' Afterward, he said, 'men of violent character reorganized it, and it was not the original society. It degenerated into a band of robbers, rioters and lynch-law men who deserve the severest punishment. I think it has been very grossly perverted to improper purposes.'

In the spring of 1870, when cooler heads in the organization began to recognize the fact that violently inclined individuals in the order were committing excesses which were not only wrong in themselves but were bringing disrepute on the conservative people of the state, ex-Governor Bragg wrote to some of the more prominent men in various sections of the state where the Ku Klux were active, urging them to take whatever steps they could to have the organization disbanded. Among others, this letter was addressed to Mr. Schenck and also to Plato Durham of Shelby, who was generally understood to be the chief of the Klan in Cleveland County. Mr. Schenck replied that he was already doing all he could in a quiet way, having already effected the disbandment of three Dens, but that he was afraid to come out publicly and denounce the excesses, as he feared that the lawless men then in control of the Ku Klux affairs would take personal vengeance on him.

Mr. Durham, in a conscientious effort to do something, made a mistake which caused him a great deal of trouble. Hearing of the suggested raid on Aaron Biggerstaff, he attended the preliminary meeting of the Cherry Mountain Den at which the raid was discussed and made them a speech urging them to refrain from the project. He took the precaution to carry along with him nine unmasked friends who could serve as witnesses of the purpose of his attendance at the Klan meeting; but when the wholesale confessions started to pouring in, Mr. Durham's nine friends were all indicted (thus stilling their voices as witnesses in his defense), while by promising immunity to some of the actual parties to the raid it was possible to get them to testify that Durham had talked to them for the purpose of advising and urging the raid, and he was consequently indicted.

The authorities were very liberal in the granting of immunity to recusants who would make the right kind of confessions. In this way they were able to indict a large number of suspected Ku Klux; although the price paid for the necessary evidence was frequently the liberation of known criminals. For instance, in 1871 Anderson Davis and six or seven others were arrested, charged with Ku Kluxing under the Federal law; and when the district court met they all confessed their guilt. They were, however, released from custody, it being charged that Judge Bond made a deal with them whereby he promised to set them free if they would implicate others as members of the organization. They delivered handsomely, and upon their testimony some eighty or ninety citizens of Lincolnton and its vicinity were indicted.

The community was very much incensed at this, seeing seven confessedly guilty men escape punishment as a reward for implicating a number of others, many of whom were popularly regarded as being innocent of any wrongdoing. Davis himself had a most unsavory reputation and record. David Schenck said that Davis, 'who had committed more offenses than any of them, had been for a long time a member of the Union League, and afterwards joined the Ku Klux in 1870 and 1871, after it had degenerated into a mob of rioters. He joined them and was a common robber. He had committed burglary and robbery and every other crime known to the catalogue. He had formerly been a leader among the negroes, and he is now still a very loud-mouthed Republican.'

Davis was fairly typical of the class of irresponsible people who used the Ku Klux regalia as a cloak for their misdeeds during its declining days and thereby brought discredit on the organization. By 1871 the real Ku Klux were rapidly disappearing from the scene. They had served their purpose, socially and politically. The carpetbaggers and scalawags were on the way out. The native Democrats were regaining control of the state's political machinery, and Holden was facing impeachment proceedings which left him permanently bereft of his citizenship.

Among other reform measures taken by the new Democratic legislature in 1871 was the enactment of a law providing for the disbanding of all secret political organizations. This was aimed directly at the Loyal Leagues, and was immediately successful in their extinguishment. The Ku Klux Klan disappeared from sight at about the same time — whether because its members regarded it as coming within the provisions of the new law or because they felt that, with the Loyal League disbanded, there was no further need for the Klan's existence in North Carolina.

IX.   SOUTH CAROLINA

Probably more than any other Southern State, South Carolina had provocation for a resort to Ku Kluxism or any other desperate expedient for the preservation of its rights, for post-war South Carolina was the victim of the most outrageous debauchery of a state government ever witnessed in this country. Immediately following the war, there was no intimation that South Carolina's period of travail would be any more painful or more extended than that of any other Southern state. In his original program of reconstruction, President Johnson had appointed Benjamin Franklin Perry governor. Perry was not appointed until June, 1865; and to hasten the work of getting the state government reorganized, he, although a strong pro-Union man, resorted to the simple and practical expedient of restoring to office all those who held public positions in 1861 and who were therefore familiar with their duties and best fitted to step in and get the governmental machinery to functioning smoothly again. Perry, however, served only until the first election was held in October, 1865, at which time James L. Orr was elected governor in a makeshift election in which only 18,885 votes were cast in the whole state.

Orr had a long record of public service. Before the war he had represented South Carolina in Congress, having been elected Speaker of the House of Representatives; and he also served a term in the Confederate Senate during the war. He was elected governor in 1865 as a Conservative, and seemed genuinely anxious to serve his state well; but he soon came to the conclusion that it was futile to resist the dominant Republican Party, and he slowly drifted into its ranks. He said he deplored the disfranchisement of many of the best citizens of the state, and he deprecated the enfranchisement of the colored race without regard to their education and their fitness to exercise the right of suffrage; but when Congress passed the Reconstruction Act in 1867 he advised acquiescence in the measures of Congress, even though they were objectionable.

At the election held in 1867 the moderate but wishy-washy Orr was succeeded as governor by Richard K. Scott, who was inaugurated in July, 1868. Scott was a carpetbagger from Ohio, an officer in the Freedmen's Bureau who had popularized himself with the negroes by posing as their aggressive champion; and his subordinate state officers were a choice lot of carpetbaggers and scalawags — black, white and mulatto — at least one of them a fugitive from criminal prosecution at home. An element of honesty and respectability was introduced in the person of Daniel H. Chamberlain, who filled the office of attorney-general, an ex-officer of the Union army who had settled in South Carolina at the close of the war and gained the respect of a great many of the native people there, even though they differed politically. He was an exception to the rule, however, most of the state officials being of similar stripe to the degenerate Franklin J. Moses, who was denounced by one of his own colleagues as being 'as infamous a character as ever in any age disgraced and prostituted public position.' Of the 124 members of the state's House of Representatives, 76 were negroes and, of course, Republicans; and of the 48 white men in the House only 14 were Democrats. Of the 33 members of the Senate 9 were negroes, and only 7 of the total membership were Democrats.

Scott's administration of affairs in South Carolina was so corrupt and so oppressive that even a Northern observer like S. S. Cox of New York declared that since the world began no parallel could be found for its unblushing knavery. 'If the entire body of penitentiary convicts,' he said, 'could be invested with supreme power in a state, they could not present a more revolting mockery of all that is honorable and respectable in the conduct of human affairs. The knaves and their sympathizers, North and South, complain that the taxpayers forcibly overthrew, by unfair and by violent means, the reign of scoundrelism, enthroned by ignorance. If ever revolutionary methods were justifiable for the overthrow of tyranny and robbery, assuredly the carpetbag domination of South Carolina called for it. Only scoundrels and hypocrites will pretend to deplore the result.'

It was the outrageous excesses of the Scott administration that finally aroused the people of South Carolina to the fighting point, but the seeds of trouble were sown during the early post-war days during the mild administrations of Perry and Orr. While these men successively were trying to reconstruct and re-establish the state, the agents of the Union League were descending on it like a plague of locusts, organizing the new-freed negroes into this militant secret society, swearing them to oppose and hate the white people, arming them and maliciously inciting them to active violence. The easily influenced negroes, here as elsewhere, were led into excesses, and these immediately developed a tendency on the part of the outraged whites to resort to direct retaliatory and defensive action.

Some of these volunteer regulators called themselves Ku Klux as early as 1867, but there was no regular organization of the real Ku Klux Klan in South Carolina until the summer of 1868. In July of that year the excesses of the so-called Ku Klux in this state attracted the attention of General George W. Gordon, who was the Grand Dragon of Tennessee and also a sort of assistant Grand Wizard of the Empire, and he sent

R. J. Brunson of Pulaski, Tennessee, to Rock Hill, South Carolina, with a supply of the printed rituals of the Klan, with orders to organize the genuine Ku Klux Klan in a formal manner in that state. Brunson has related that he remained in South Carolina for three months engaged in this work, organized several Dens and then returned home.

The Ku Klux operations in South Carolina were principally in what was locally known as the 'up country' — nine counties lying north and west of Columbia: York, Spartanburg, Newberry, Union, Laurens, Chester, Lancaster, Fairfield and Chesterfield. The Ku Klux seemed to be most active and numerous in York County and in the neighborhood of Spartanburg; and they were hardly known at all in the low country.

As was true in Mississippi, the Ku Klux movement in South Carolina appears to have experienced two separate manifestations — one in 1868 and a revival in 1870, the latter having been the more violent and sensational. During 1868 the Klan seems to have indulged in nothing more serious than the distribution of the customary warnings to obnoxious characters, backed up with occasional floggings; at that time they had not gone to the extremity of homicide.

A typical Ku Klux 'outrage' of the 1868 period occurred in Newberry just prior to the election of that year. In order to control the ignorant negro vote, the Radical leaders in the various precincts had been supplied with pre-marked Republican ballots which were to be given to the individual negro voters when they appeared at the polls. The Ku Klux heard of this, and the night before the election they donned their vestments and visited the negro leaders and took the marked ballots away from them. As the negro voters could neither read nor write, they were unable to mark their own ballots the next day and consequently the Republican candidates got few votes in those precincts.

Such more or less harmless hazing was about the extent of

the Ku Klux work at first, and it would probably have dwindled
away to nothing if there had not been a strong provocation for
its revival and extension early in the turbulent reign of Governor
Scott. The foundation for serious trouble was laid in March,
1869, when the legislature passed an act authorizing the governor to raise a militia force to be known as the National Guard;
it being specified that no military organization could be formed
in the state without the permission and approval of the governor.
On its face the act seemed innocent enough. Nobody paid
much attention to it at the time, and the governor did not avail
himself of the power conferred on him by it until more than a
year later, during the state election campaign in 1870.

At that time the corruption of Scott's administration had so
aroused the people that there had been organized an effort to
encompass the defeat of him and his corrupt cohorts by the
formation of what was known as the Union Reform Party, a
coalition of Conservatives and those Republicans who gagged
at Scott's excesses. To emphasize the non-partisan nature of
the movement, the nominee of this party for governor was
Judge Richard B. Carpenter, a Republican; and the campaign
was pitched solely on the desirability of replacing the corrupt
Radical administration with decently honest officials regardless
of party. Scott, fearful of the outcome of this spontaneous
movement if it were left to develop unchecked, bethought himself of the militia law and secretly proceeded to organize fourteen
full regiments of negro troops, and armed them with a new
supply of ten thousand Winchester rifles and a million car-
tridges bought for that special purpose, at a cost of over four
hundred thousand dollars to the state. Emissaries of the governor were sent through the state organizing these forces in
every county; and before the white citizens knew what was
happening they woke up and found that they were under the
surveillance of a large force of armed negroes, intoxicated
with their new power.

With arms in their hands the 'hep men,' as they were called by the civilian negroes, became unbearably insolent and aggressive. A favorite pastime was swaggering in groups along the sidewalks, pushing the unarmed white people out of their way into the streets. They would march along the roads, wantonly killing dogs and livestock with their new toys, the militia guns, and firing volleys above dwelling houses and churches where services were being held. After their drills and parades, which were frequent, they would generally be exhorted by orators, black and white, who dwelt with unction on the miseries of their previous servitude and inculcated mistrust of their old masters. The land and all the property in the state, they were told, really belonged to them, since their labor had created it; and the orators declared that the Radicals would bring about a redistribution of the property among its rightful owners the negroes, repeating the alluring fiction of 'forty acres and a mule.' The idea that their former masters were their friends was ridiculed by these speakers. A mulatto spellbinder, a member of Congress, told an audience of negro voters in Columbia: 'I am an illustration of the only love they had for the negro race — the tid-bits of sexual intercourse.' Joe Crews, a scalawag member of the legislature from Laurens, in his speeches pointedly mentioned that matches were for sale at five cents a box and that they provided a cheap and easy means of vengeance.

The most violent outburst of Ku Kluxism in South Carolina was contemporaneous with the arming of this new-made black militia. There had been Loyal Leagues since 1867, and there had been Ku Klux Dens since 1868; but the spark generated by the friction between these two organizations was not fanned into full flame until the white people of South Carolina found themselves under the dominance of the armed and totally irresponsible negro militia and felt that some form of defensive action was immediately essential.

The campaign and election in the fall of 1870 was featured by a number of fatal clashes between the blacks and the whites; and the news of these 'riots,' generally very much magnified and distorted, was flashed all over the country as an evidence of the fact that South Carolina was on the brink of insurrection.

The most notorious and widely advertised of these affrays was the 'Laurens riot,' which occurred on the day after the election. Laurens was the home of Joe Crews, a particularly active and offensive scalawag trouble-maker, who had harangued the negro militia stationed there into a state of nervous truculence which had reached the boiling point. The white people, alarmed by the militia's hostile manifestations, were also on edge. It was freely predicted that a clash between the two races was inevitable, and the white people had privately armed themselves in preparation for the outbreak they felt was sure to come. The whole situation was like the traditional open powder keg, just waiting for a spark to set it off.

The fatal spark was provided by the accidental discharge of a pistol which was dropped by an onlooker at a fight on the courthouse square between a citizen and one of the constabulary. The fight was entirely non-political in character, but when the report of the pistol was heard everybody in Laurens concluded that the expected clash had at last come. The negroes rushed to Joe Crews's barn where their rifles were stored and, after arming themselves, rallied at their armory and started firing promiscuously from within the building. The white people also gathered together in a body and took part in the firing; and word was sent into the surrounding country for reinforcements. By nightfall Laurens was occupied by a force of armed white men estimated to number as high as twenty-five hundred; but the sheriff raised a posse of a hundred men and took charge of all the arms held by Crews and the negroes, and eventually things quieted down — but not until several negroes had been killed. All of the white men engaged in this affray were undisguised; but there was a general rumor, never confirmed, that the Ku Klux organization of the county did take part in the affair and provided a large number of the reinforcements arriving in town after the shooting started.

There was a clash or 'riot' on a smaller scale at Newberry, one at Camden and another at Clinton, but no casualties at either place and no Ku Klux involved. At a political speaking in Chester, just prior to the election, there was a brawl involving two or three hundred men of both colors; but it was all in the open, with no suggestion of Ku Klux being implicated. But although the Ku Klux as such did not directly participate in these riots, their organization in the nine up-country counties had been growing steadily during the summer and it was soon apparent that they would be a factor which must be dealt with.

A perfect hotbed of Ku Kluxism at this time was York County, and the Klan's activities in York may be taken as fairly characteristic of all that section of South Carolina in which the Ku Klux were active. There had been a good deal of trouble with the negroes in this county, with frequent clashes and some bloodshed. A blustering negro agitator named Tom Roundtree (also known as Tom Black) was killed on December 3, 1870, by a band of disguised men supposed to be Ku Klux, although some of the white people of the town advanced the theory that he had been killed by negroes who wanted to rob him of the money he had just received for his cotton crop. It was beyond question the Ku Klux, however, who killed a negro named Jim Williams (also known as Jim Rainey), who was captain of one of the militia companies and who made himself especially objectionable by his threatening behavior. He went a step too far in his bluster, however, when he was heard to threaten a raid on the town in which all the white people would be killed 'from the cradle to the grave.' This proved to be his death warrant, and on the night of March 6, 1871, the local Den of Ku Klux, known as the Rattlesnake

Den, met at their customary rendezvous, the Briar Patch, put on their disguises and went to Williams's house, where they took him into the road and hung him to a convenient tree.

As a result of these killings the negro militia in York County grew more truculent, but there was no open clash until one day when one of the militiamen, with fixed bayonet, attacked a Doctor Thomason of the town, who promptly knocked him down and stunned him. News that one of their number had been murdered was carried to the militia, and they got their arms and gathered together in a threatening manner. The white men also armed themselves and assembled, but they were hopelessly in the minority and word went out into the surrounding country for reinforcements. Among others who appeared in Yorkville in response to this call for help was a band of mounted strangers who were later identified as having come from Cleveland County, North Carolina, and who boldly rode into Yorkville shouting gaily: 'Here's your Ku Klux!' They stayed in Yorkville for two or three days, until the trouble blew over. They camped on the property of Major J. W. Avery (suspected of being the Ku Klux chief in Yorkville), and were fed by Major Avery and some of the other suspected Ku Klux. The militia seemed impressed by this display of force and quieted down, and the North Carolina Ku Klux at length went home without firing a shot or striking a blow.

The negroes continued resentful and antagonistic, but hardly bold enough to stage an open attack on the whites. They did, however, institute a system of patrolling the town and picketing the roads at night; and there was some fear expressed that the Ku Klux might stage a raid on the town in retaliation. Edward M. Rose, the scalawag county treasurer, was an active and prolific source of bad advice to the negroes; and, in this emergency, he was overheard telling a group of them that if the Ku Klux did make a raid and the white people did not turn out to repel them the negroes should burn the town. That the negroes were inclined to take this advice seriously was indicated by the fact that a series of mysterious fires began about this time, and a number of barns, stables and gin-houses were burned.

One night there were six such fires burning in sight of the courthouse at Yorkville, their incendiary origin being evidenced by the fact that they all started at one time. Just before the fires were sighted, Rose had fired a volley of thirty-two shots from two sixteen-shot repeating rifles, and the people of the town jumped to the conclusion that this was an agreed signal for the negroes to set fire to the barns and gins. Rose was already in distinctly bad odor with the people, and this was the last straw. A meeting of the Ku Klux was held on the night of February 26, 1871, and it was decided to go to Rose's office, where he had sleeping quarters, take him before the Klan for trial, and, if he was found guilty, to execute him. Rose was on the alert and escaped the raiding Ku Klux by jumping out of the back window of his office, and the raiders had to take their satisfaction out of breaking up his furniture.

William K. Owens of Yorkville, who later confessed his membership in the Ku Klux, testified that most of those who took part in the Rose raid were not from Yorkville but from the outlying parts of the county. The raid was managed, he said, by John M. Tomlinson of Yorkville, who led a small party of the town Klansmen out to a point about a mile from town, 'just above Uncle Ben Kerr's,' where the entire party assembled a little after midnight, to the number of forty or fifty. Owens testified that the intendant of Yorkville, Frank C. Harris, was a member of the Ku Klux, and that both the town's two constables, Rufus McLain and William Snyder, were also members. In such circumstances, it is hardly necessary to add, the town authorities' investigation of the raid was fruitless.

The day prior to the raid on Rose's office it was reported in Yorkville that a company of United States troops were coming to the town from Chester. That night several rails were removed from the track of the King's Mountain Railroad — presumably by the Ku Klux — and the troops did not reach Yorkville until Monday, the day after the raid. As soon as the soldiers established themselves in the town, Rose came back and took refuge in their camp and stayed four or five days. One night, however, the camp was fired into by unknown parties, and Captain Christopher, suspecting Rose of being the object of the shooting, ordered his departure. Rose disguised himself in a soldier's uniform and left town on the night train, and the next time he was heard from he was in Canada, his flight to that faraway refuge being explained when the state auditor examined his books and reported that he was twelve thousand dollars short in his accounts.

The presence of the troops in Yorkville temporarily dampened the enthusiasm of the Ku Klux there, but pretty soon they became active again; and when the probate judge received a shipment of ammunition for the negro militia and stored it in his office, the Ku Klux broke into his office at night, confiscated the ammunition and threw it into a well.

The first open outburst of Ku Klux activity in Union County was in connection with a white Radical named A. B. Owens, who made a habit of assembling the negroes around his house and urging them to violence. His wife objected to this, whereupon he proceeded to give her a good beating. The climax in his case came when a notice was stuck up in the street stating that the house of Doctor Wade Fowler ought to be burned. This notice was said to be in the handwriting of Owens, and when Fowler's home was burned by an incendiary, the Ku Klux called on Owens. Their purpose, presumably, was to whip him; but he saw them coming and fired on them, and they returned his fire, killing him.

This killing of one of their white advisers incensed the negro militia and intensified their belligerence. This culminated in a murder and a subsequent Ku Klux raid which brought on reverberations reaching all over the country. A one-armed ex-Confederate soldier named Matthew Stevens who lived in Unionville, unable to do other manual labor, had got a horse and wagon and was engaged in the hauling business. On December 31, 1870, while hauling a barrel of whisky into Unionville from a rural distillery, he was met on the road by a squad of forty negro militia, under the command of one of their regular officers, who stopped him and demanded that he turn the barrel of whisky over to them. He declined to do so, explaining that it was not his property, but in an effort to placate them he did give them a bottle of whisky he had in the wagon. This did not appease them, however; and, enraged by his refusal to comply with their demand, they fired several shots into his wagon. Stevens, terrified, jumped to the ground and ran into a negro cabin by the side of the road. The militiamen dragged him from this refuge; and, upon the orders of the officer in command, three of the negroes took him into the near-by woods and killed him, firing a number of shots into his head and body.

It was the testimony of everybody that Stevens was a peaceable and well-behaved man, and there seemed to have been no reason for killing him except that he was a white man and the negro militia had been taught to believe that all white men were their enemies. In fact, one negro testified that they had started out from their camp that day with the deliberate purpose of killing the first white man they encountered, no matter who he was.

This unprovoked murder of an inoffensive and helpless man aroused the people of Unionville. Ten members of the militia were identified by a witness as being members of the party of killers, and they were arrested and lodged in the county jail at Unionville — but not until one of them, resisting arrest, had mortally wounded a white deputy sheriff. On the night of

January 4 a party of Ku Klux rode into town, surrounded the jail and demanded entrance. The jailer had locked the door and thrown the key away; but the Ku Klux forced the door, made their way to the cells where the prisoners were confined and selected five of them, including the captain of the company, who had been identified as the ones directly involved in the killing of Stevens.

One of the Klansmen, dressed all in ghostly white, was stationed on the steps just outside the jail door; and as the quaking prisoners were led out, one by one, their captors would stop and inquire of the white-clad sentinel: 'Is this one of the men who killed you, Stevens?' The pseudo-Stevens would answer yes; and, on the strength of this ghostly identification, the five were led away for execution. This stage of the proceedings seems to have been bungled, however, as three of the men escaped, and only two were shot and killed.

Following the raid a strong guard of white men was maintained at the jail for some time; but eventually, the excitement having apparently subsided, this guard was removed. Meanwhile the Radical friends of the negro militia were seeking the discovery of some device whereby the remaining prisoners might escape punishment, and succeeded in getting from Judge Thomas, the Federal judge at Columbia, a sort of informal order that the prisoners be removed from Unionville and placed in his custody there. This was not an actual habeas corpus writ, and was generally regarded in Unionville as an irregular procedure whereby the negroes were to be spirited away to Columbia, released on some sort of straw bail and permitted to escape. The bearer of the order for the removal of the negroes had been enjoined to secrecy, but the news of the proposed transfer quickly leaked out and was the talk of the town.

On the night of February 12 about midnight another squad of Ku Klux rode into town, surrounded the jail and placed pickets about the square. Entrance to the jail was more easily effected on this occasion (the jailer later being accused of being a member of the Ku Klux and also a brother-in-law of Stevens). The raiding party of Ku Klux were evidently well organized and trained. They rode into town in regular cavalry formation, and while they were raiding the jail they posted sentinels and kept up communications by couriers riding every few minutes, just like a military operation. Estimates as to the size of the body of men varied from three hundred to eight hundred, and the party was said to have been made up of groups from Laurens, Spartanburg, Newberry and York Counties, summoned by couriers sent out during the day. A Unionville physician, Doctor Thompson, returning from a late call, encountered the Ku Klux on the public square, and when he discovered their mission he volunteered to tell them that one of the negroes held in jail, Jim Hardy, was said to have made an effort to have Stevens's life spared, and on this account Doctor Thompson thought Hardy should not be executed. The Ku Klux leader thanked him for this information, and when entrance to the jail was effected, Jim Hardy's name was called and he was left behind when the other eight were taken out and killed — two hung and six shot.

In order that there might be no misunderstanding of the cause of this second raid on the jail, the Ku Klux before they left Unionville posted the following notice on the courthouse bulletin board:

TO THE PUBLIC

K K K

TAKEN BY HABEAS CORPUS

In silence and secrecy, thought has been working, and the benignant efficacies of concealment speak for themselves. Once again we have been forced by force to use *Force*. Justice was lame, and she had to lean on us. Information being received that a 'doubting Thomas,' the inferior of nothing, the superior of nothing, and of consequence the equal of nothing, who has neither eyes to see the scars of oppression nor ears to hear the cause of humanity, even though he wears the Judicial silk, had ordered some guilty prisoners from Union to the City of Columbia and of Injustice and Prejudice, for an *unfair trial of life,* thus clutching at the wheel-spokes of Destiny — then this thing was created and projected; otherwise it would never have been. We yield to the inevitable and inexorable, and account this the *best.* 'Let not thy right hand know what thy left hand doeth' is our motto.

We want peace, but this cannot be until Justice returns. We want and will have Justice, but this cannot be until the bleeding fight of freedom is fought. Until then this Molock of Iniquity will have his victims, even if the Michael of Justice must have his martyrs.

K.K.K.

Following the two raids on the Unionville jail the Ku Klux continued to make themselves felt in Union County for several months, although there were no more killings. On March 9, 1871, they posted a notice on the courthouse door, headed 'Special Order No. 3 — K.K.K.,' calling on the members of the state legislature from Union County, the school commissioner and the county commissioners to resign within fifteen days, and also demanding that the clerk of the county commission 'renounce and relinquish' his position by public notice. The clerk immediately complied with the demand, publishing a notice in the *Times* stating that he was resigning his office and renouncing his connection with the Radical Party, 'in obedience to Ku Klux Order No. 3.'

The Ku Klux Klan was definitely in the saddle in Union and in several other of the up-country counties, but such high-handed actions could not continue unchallenged. Early in 1870 the state legislature took official cognizance of the Ku Klux disturbances in the state and appointed investigating committees in the various congressional districts. The majority reports of these committees were strongly condemnatory, as expected; but Doctor Javan Bryant, a Republican member of the committee investigating the Third District, surprised everybody by bringing in a minority report in which he said, in the florid rhetoric of the period:

'No one can fail to be struck, upon reading the evidence taken by the committee, with the many vague, incoherent and ludicrous accounts given by these poor colored people, many of whom were so ignorant as not even to know their own names, of the herculean size, hideous proportions and diabolical features of what they called Ku Klux. And it affords me great pleasure to be able to report that, after having thoroughly investigated the matter, I am of opinion that the ghosts, hobgoblins, jack-o'-the-lanterns and Ku Klux of the Third Congressional District are but allotropic conditions of the witches of New England, whose larvae, having long lain dormant until imported hither in the carpetbags of some pious political priests, germinated in the too credulous minds of their poor proselytes, and loomed into luxuriance in the fertile fields of their own imaginations.'

Doctor Bryant, however, was himself the victim of self-delusion if he really believed that the Ku Klux were the mythical products of a fevered carpetbagger imagination. That they existed in the flesh was amply and grimly demonstrated during the summer and fall of 1870, preceding the state election; but if the purpose of the Klan was political its work was not signally effective, as the Republican ticket swept the field over the wreckage of the hybrid Reform Party. The outcome of the election was, of course, highly unsatisfactory and disappointing to the Democrats, and the result was no more disconcerting than the methods by which it was accomplished. The armed

negroes had been insolent and overbearing at the polls, and
their victory increased their feeling of importance and power.
On the other hand, the native whites were not only chagrined
by defeat, but were increasingly fearful of the danger of a
really sanguinary clash with the armed negroes.

The day after the election the riot at Laurens took place,
and when the news of this reached Columbia the two companies
of negro militia there were immediately mustered and appeared
on the streets in full uniform, armed and equipped with wagons
loaded with provisions, ready to start for Laurens. The negroes
boasted openly that if Governor Scott would give them marching orders they would move through the country and not leave
a house standing, and that they would 'sweep even the cradles.'
They gathered at the Columbia armory and stayed there all
night, firing occasional volleys down the streets, to the terror
of the populace. Governor Scott was finally prevailed upon
to order them to disperse, but the people of Columbia were so
alarmed that they held a meeting there in a few days, attended
by about thirty of the leading Democrats of the state, to see
what could be done. At this meeting it was decided to make
plans for the organization of local 'Councils of Safety' throughout the state, and a proposed constitution for the guidance of
such councils was adopted, printed and distributed to the
different counties.

The constitution stated that 'The objects of this organization
are, first, to preserve the peace, enforce the laws and protect
and defend the persons and property of the good people of
this state; and, second, to labor for the restoration of constitutional liberty, as taught by our forefathers, and to reform abuses
in the government, state and national.' It further specified,
somewhat cryptically, that 'Its operations shall be two-fold:
1. Political, social and moral, under the forms of established
laws. 2. Physical, according to the recognized principles of
the law of self-defense.' Membership was limited to 'approved

white men' above the age of eighteen years; members were to
be required to take an oath of secrecy and loyalty to the order;
and further mystery was provided by the specification that
members were to be designated by letters of the alphabet.
Copies of the constitution were distributed promiscuously,
and some of the edge of its secrecy was taken off by the publication of the constitution in the Columbia *Republican*. Only two
or three scattered councils were ever established, and after they
were established they did not know exactly what to do, so
the Council of Safety soon came to nothing.

Some of the imaginative Republicans professed to believe
that this was the framework around which the Ku Klux organization in South Carolina was built, but there is no foundation
whatever for this belief. The Ku Klux Klan was organized
in South Carolina two years before the abortive Council of
Safety movement; furthermore, the latter group did not con-
template any secrecy as to its existence or the personnel of its
membership. On the whole, its plan appeared to be immeasur-
ably more moderate than the current Ku Klux practice.

The Council of Safety movement was significant as a symptom
of the prevailing feeling of tension in South Carolina, tension
existing on both sides. Alarmed by the growing friction and
disorder, Governor Scott in the latter part of 1870, when a
resolution was introduced into the legislature authorizing him
to declare martial law and send troops to Spartanburg, Laurens
and Union Counties, called into counsel at Columbia a number
of the leading Democrats of the state to advise him. This group
included General Kershaw, General McGowan, Gabriel
Cannon, T. Y. Simmons, editor of the Charleston *Courier*, and
other leaders. They were unanimously of the opinion that
things were drifting dangerously in the direction of a war of the
races, and that the only preventive would be for the governor
to disarm and disperse the negro militia and replace some of
the grossly incompetent public officials with able and honest

men. If these measures were taken, the governor was assured, the Democratic leaders would go home and use their exertions to preserve the peace, stop violence and put down Ku Klux interference with anyone. They all made it clear that they did not have any personal knowledge of the Ku Klux; but they thought they might be able to help to stop it if the cause were removed.

There was, as a matter of fact, a growing feeling that the excesses committed in the name of the Ku Klux — whether bogus or genuine — were making it difficult to compose the existing difficulties. Public meetings were held in York, Union and Spartanburg Counties deploring the disorders, and prominent in these meetings were men who had been previously suspected of direct or indirect affiliation with the Ku Klux. Whether through prudence or fear, Governor Scott soon took action to dissolve his malodorous militia and constabulary. Simultaneously the Ku Klux disorders ceased, and there were no complaints of Ku Klux in South Carolina after May, 1871.

Meanwhile, however, the outbreaks there had attracted the attention of the government at Washington, and on March 24, 1871, President Grant issued his proclamation addressed to the people of South Carolina denouncing 'combinations of armed men, unauthorized by law,' and calling on them to disperse within twenty days. On April 20 Grant affixed his signature to the Ku Klux bill just passed by Congress, and on May 3 he issued another proclamation calling special attention to it.

In July the special sub-committee of the Congressional Investigating Committee went to South Carolina and began to take testimony there. This sub-committee, consisting of Senator Scott and Representatives Stevenson and Van Trump, spent almost the entire month of July in examining witnesses at Columbia, Spartanburg, Union and Yorkville. Of the witnesses examined, fifty-three were negroes, described by Mr. Van

Trump as being 'of the very lowest grade of intelligence belonging to human beings.' No less than thirty-six negroes
testified at Spartanburg, and while they were in town in attendance at the hearing they were herded together at the
post-office under the shepherding of the carpetbagger postmaster. There was a remarkable uniformity about their testimony as to what the Ku Klux said and did, all of them being
careful to express the view that the organization's objects were
political; and although Mr. Van Trump carefully and courteously refrained from charging that there had been any coach-
ing or drilling of the witnesses by his Republican colleagues,
he did go so far as to say that these ignorant negroes 'were just
the kind of material to be molded at the will and command of
any unscrupulous white man who had a common purpose with
them in establishing any given state of facts.'

While the committee was holding its hearings in Spartanburg, a committee of local citizens was appointed for the purpose
of suggesting to Mr. Van Trump questions to be asked the
witnesses when they appeared. The chairman of this committee was L. M. Gentry, proprietor of the town's leading
livery stable and a prominent Democratic leader in the county.
Some of the witnesses openly charged that Mr. Gentry was a
member of the Ku Klux and that on the night of big Ku Klux
raids all the horses in his stable were always mysteriously absent.
Mr. Gentry, however, not only indignantly denied the accusation, but made the countercharge that C. L. Casey, the local
United States deputy marshal, had been out in the country
drumming up negro witnesses, telling them that if they would
go to Spartanburg and testify that they had been outraged
they would be paid two dollars a day and ten cents a mile for
mileage — fabulous pay for those days.

When the sub-committee finished its hearings and returned
to Washington, Chairman Scott on July 29 wrote a letter to
President Grant setting forth the revolutionary conditions

alleged to exist in South Carolina and urging the President to take prompt action. Mr. Van Trump in a minority report expressed the firm conviction that the disorders in South Carolina were 'the clearest natural offspring of as corrupt and oppressive a system of local state government as ever disgraced humanity, and utterly unparalleled in the history of civilization.'

'No modern instance of wrong and oppression, of robbery and usurpation,' he said, 'can approach it in wickedness and infamy nor can any people on the face of the globe, not even the unhappy Poles in their darkest days of suffering, rival the great body of the best citizens of South Carolina for the patient (we had almost said abject) forbearance with which they have submitted to the infernal persecution of their rulers.' He further declared that 'No fair-minded man, we care not what may be his prejudices or his party ties, can go down to South Carolina and see the practical workings of the system there without being driven to the admission that the policy which has made a San Domingo of one of the states of the Union is one of the most terrible blunders ever committed, one of the most reckless and unwise political movements ever inaugurated in a government of fixed laws and constitutions.'

President Grant, in response to Senator Scott's suggestion, ignoring Van Trump's fervent protest, sent Amos T. Akerman, the Attorney-General of the United States, to Yorkville to confer with Major Lewis Merrill, commander of the United States troops stationed there; and Akerman's report, following his conference with Major Merrill, fully substantiated all Scott's charges.

Meanwhile the grand jury of York County met at its regular term in September to investigate the disordered affairs of the county, and Major Merrill, who had boasted that he knew the names of a number of active Ku Klux, was urged to appear before them and give the evidence he had. Merrill declined, basing his declination on some legal technicality; but the real and more material reason for his unwillingness to co-operate with the state courts was to be divulged later. Despite his refusal to co-operate, the Grand Jury did find indictments against two men charged with having participated in the raid on the county treasurer's office; but no presentment was found in the killing of Jim Williams or Tom Roundtree.

The Radicals in Washington, meanwhile, were continuing their pressure on President Grant, and on October 12, 1871, he issued a proclamation declaring that 'unlawful combinations and conspiracies' existed in the counties of Spartanburg, York, Marion, Chester, Laurens, Newberry, Fairfield, Lancaster and Chesterfield, and calling on all persons composing these unlawful combinations and conspiracies to disperse within five days and to surrender to the United States marshals 'all arms, ammunition, uniforms, disguises and other means and implements used.' (It was called to Grant's attention that Marion County must have been mentioned by error, as no Ku Klux activities had been reported there; so Union County was later quietly substituted for Marion.) It soon became apparent that none of the Ku Klux had any idea of responding to the invitation to surrender any arms, ammunition, uniforms or other implements; so on October 17 the President issued another pronunciamento suspending the writ of habeas corpus in the counties named, and the Federal authorities took over an active investigation of Ku Klux affairs in the state.

President Grant's proclamation focussed the attention of the country on South Carolina, and the leading metropolitan newspapers sent staff representatives to the state to investigate and report. Most of these correspondents sent back the lurid and partisan stories expected of them, but some of them gave evidence of a sincere effort to make an unbiased study of conditions and report them as they found them. The correspondent of the New York *Herald*, in particular, seemed inclined to analyze the situation and paint a true picture of it in his dispatches. There were, he pointed out, three distinct classes of people in the piedmont region of South Carolina where the Ku Klux flourished — 'a class of respectable, intelligent men, of limited education; a class of honest, ignorant, independent white farmers, owning a little land; and a class of low, degraded white men, many of whom are engaged in illicit distilling.' A large proportion of the Ku Klux outrages, he said, were attributable to this latter class, although he said that many members of the first two classes joined the order for self-preservation, as the only means of protecting themselves from barn-burning and the other terrors to which they were subjected under the vicious state government. A good many of the illicit distillers, he thought, used the Ku Klux as a cloak for their private crimes and misdemeanors; but he expressed the further view that it should have been easily possible for the state authorities to arrest and convict these criminals without suspending the writ of habeas corpus, 'stigmatizing entire communities as lawless, and paralyzing the industry of the state.'

Following the testimony taken by the congressional subcommittee at Spartanburg, a large number of those accused by the negro witnesses had been arrested, and it was announced that several of them had confessed that they were or had been members of the Ku Klux. The *Herald* correspondent had the traditional newspaper man's curiosity for getting at the bottom of things, and he immediately applied to the United States Commissioner for permission to examine these confessions. One of them was selected and shown to him, in which the confessor stated that his Den had voted the infliction of punishment on five different persons, for offenses as assigned: a negro whipped who had assaulted his former master and beaten him almost to death; a negro whipped who had asserted his new-found equality by shoving a white man out of his way at an election, and had further offended by giving information to a revenue officer; two men whipped who were charged with robbing a smokehouse; one negro whipped who had boasted that when the Yankees came he would go to all the quiltings with the white folks and sit beside the white girls, and would have him a white wife; another man was charged with having stabbed an officer who had a warrant for his arrest, and the Ku Klux ordered him whipped, but he could not be found.

It had been persistently claimed in the North that the Ku Klux was purely a political organization; and as this confession did not seem to bear out that theory, the *Herald* man asked the Commissioner to let him examine all of them and make a list of the causes assigned for the punishments inflicted. This the Commissioner declined, which naturally aroused the newspaper man's suspicions as to what was in the confessions, and he wrote an article in the *Herald* so stating.

This New York correspondent, after completing his investigation of conditions in Spartanburg County, published the following summary of his findings:

'First. That for four months past no Ku Klux outrages have been committed in Spartanburg County, which the Federal officials admit.

'Second. That the Ku Klux organization was originally formed for the self-protection of its members, and not for any special political purpose.

'Third. That men of infamous character entered the Ku Klux organization and perpetrated a series of gross outrages upon individuals.

'Fourth. That in many instances white and black Radicals borrowed the disguise of the Ku Klux and outraged their neighbors, knowing that the blame would not be laid upon them.

'Fifth. That if the state government of South Carolina had

not been, as it still is, in the hands of corrupt and infamous political adventurers, and had the laws of the state been fairly and impartially administered, public sentiment would have crushed the Ku Klux organization in its incipiency.

'Sixth. That there was not any necessity for the suspension of the writ of habeas corpus, because there was not at any time any disposition on the part of the citizens to resist the warrants of arrest. Every white man in Spartanburg County could have been arrested by a deputy marshal's posse.

'Seventh. That the Ku Klux, while formidable in numbers, perhaps, never entertained the idea of resisting the United States Government. If its designs were treasonable it could, in a single night, have overpowered and annihilated the entire military force in this county.

'Eighth. That the effect of the present movement is dangerous to the future of the Union. It has revived old animosities, re-awakened slumbering sentiments, and embittered the whites, not only in the nine counties, but throughout South Carolina and the South generally.'

After the passage of nearly seventy years, and in the light of all the knowledge subsequently available, it is hard to improve on this as a restrained and lucid statement of Ku Klux conditions in South Carolina at that time.

With martial law in effect, the military forces had been busily engaged in drag-netting the up-country counties for Ku Klux suspects. Squads of cavalry were sent out to arrest them, generally at night and without warrants and without observance of the prisoners' right to know the cause of their arrest. The total of those arrested mounted into large numbers — more than fifteen hundred. There were one hundred and ninety-five in Yorkville alone, who were taken to Columbia and there released under heavy bail. In Union County some two hundred were arrested; there were several hundred in Spartanburg; some in Chester and some in Newberry and other counties.

Most of those released on bail were never brought to trial. For instance, forty citizens of Laurens were arrested on account of the riot there, and all of them were bailed and never tried.

The wholesale arrests terrified a number of those who were really members of the Ku Klux, and several of them precipitately fled from the state. Among the refugees was Doctor J. Rufus Bratton, a leading physician of York County, who had been active among those protesting against the disorders of the negro militia and who was very strongly suspected of being a member of the Ku Klux — which he probably was. At any rate, when the soldiers took possession of Yorkville, Doctor Bratton quietly departed for London, Ontario, and took up the practice of medicine there; and out of this there almost developed an international incident. The Radicals were particularly eager for Doctor Bratton's scalp; and in the summer of 1872 he was seized in the night-time by two Canadian private detectives in the pay of the United States Government officers. They gagged and blindfolded Doctor Bratton and took him across the boundary line onto American soil, where he was delivered into the custody of two United States marshals who hustled him back to Yorkville, where he was placed under a ten-thousand-dollar bail bond. The officials of the Canadian Government were indignant at this high-handed kidnapping of a resident of their country, and the British Government made formal protest to Washington. The justice of the British protest was recognized, and Doctor Bratton was released from his bond and permitted to return to Ontario, where he continued the practice of his profession until 1876, when the Federal troops were withdrawn from South Carolina. He then went back to Yorkville and spent the rest of his life there, and no case was ever brought against him in any court. In the meantime, incidentally, the mills of Canadian justice had been grinding fine, and the two detectives who had kidnapped Doctor Bratton were arrested, tried and sent to prison.

The Ku Klux trials in South Carolina attracted widespread attention all over the country. The first batch of defendants were arraigned in Columbia at the winter term of the Circuit Court of the United States on November 28, 1871, with the Honorable Hugh L. Bond of Baltimore, circuit judge, and the Honorable George S. Bryan of Charleston, district judge, jointly presiding. The government was represented by District Attorney D. T. Corbin of Vermont, assisted by D. H. Chamberlain, the attorney-general of South Carolina. Judge Bond's handling of the Ku Klux trials in North Carolina had not contributed anything to his reputation for fairness and impartiality, and a fund of ten thousand dollars was raised by popular subscription (with some help from Ku Klux in other states) to pay additional legal talent to assist the local lawyers retained by such of the defendants as were able to hire lawyers. Accordingly two distinguished attorneys appeared in court in behalf of the Ku Klux: the Honorable Reverdy Johnson of Maryland and the Honorable Henry Stanbery of Ohio, who had respectively filled the office of Attorney-General in the cabinets of Presidents Taylor and Johnson. On the grand jury which returned the indictments there were six whites and twenty-one negroes, the foreman being a carpetbagger Methodist preacher. Of the panel summoned for the trial jury one, C. H. Bankhead, later turned up as a spy and witness for the government; but he and eleven negroes constituted the jury by which one of the defendants, John S. Millar, was tried. The first case tried, which was typical of all of them, was that of Robert Hayes Mitchell. His jury consisted of eleven negroes and one white Republican.

The government's case against all these defendants rested largely on the testimony of confessed members of the Ku Klux, foremost among whom were Kirkland L. Gunn and Charles

W. Foster. Gunn and Foster, along with some of the other recusants, were given immunity as a reward for their testimony; and it was also charged that they had been paid for their services in sums ranging from two hundred to thirty-five hundred dollars, but this was denied. The government also introduced in its evidence an alleged copy of the constitution of the order supplied Major Merrill by Samuel G. Brown, who confessed that he was a member of the Klan. When placed on the stand, however, Brown refused to implicate other members of the order, and he was consequently fined one thousand dollars and sentenced to five years in prison.

The whole number of persons convicted in the South Carolina trials was fifty-five, of whom only five were actually placed on trial — Robert Hayes Mitchell, John W. Mitchell, Doctor Thomas B. Whitesides, Samuel G. Brown and Doctor Edward T. Avery. The last-named defendant, incidentally, escaped punishment by the simple procedure of coolly walking out of the courthouse and disappearing during a recess in his trial. A large number of those pleading guilty and throwing themselves on the mercy of the court were immature, ignorant young men, and they received prison sentences of from three to eighteen months, along with fines.

At the April, 1872, term of the Federal Court in Charleston there were further trials. Some of the defendants pleaded guilty; and there were twenty-eight sentences in all, with prison terms ranging from three months to ten years and fines from ten to one thousand dollars. At the November, 1872, term of court in Columbia there were still more trials, with nine sentences.

Efforts were made by the defendants' counsel to have four of the South Carolina cases carried to the Supreme Court of the United States to test the constitutionality of the Ku Klux law, but each time the effort failed on account of some technicality, and the ultimate result was that the validity of this law was never officially passed on by the nation's highest court.

In the summer of 1873 President Grant let it be known that he was willing to extend amnesty to all the convicted Ku Klux whose fellow-citizens and neighbors applied for their pardon; and so, one by one, all of the Ku Klux prisoners were eventually released.

A malodorous repercussion of the South Carolina trials developed in 1873 when the state legislature made an appropriation of thirty-five thousand dollars to pay the rewards offered by Governor Scott in the summer of 1871 when he authorized the payment of two hundred dollars for the arrest and conviction of Ku Klux under the Federal law. It then developed that Major Merrill's unwillingness to co-operate with the state authorities and his zeal for prosecution under the Federal law grew out of this prospect of a monetary reward. Major Merrill was a practical man who did not wish to give away his information without remuneration in a local court when it had a cash value in the Federal Court. He collected a total of twenty thousand dollars from the state in the way of Ku Klux rewards; and although there was a considerable raising of eyebrows at the ethics involved in such conduct on the part of a United States Army officer, Major Merrill found the twenty thousand dollars ample salve against the slings and arrows of his ultra-ethical critics.

X.   ARKANSAS

Reconstruction in Arkansas presented some unusual features, growing out of the peculiarly involved political conditions prevailing in that state at the close of the war.

As early as the latter part of 1863 a sufficient portion of Arkansas territory was in the hands of the Federals to justify the Union men in the laying of plans for the establishment of a new pro-Union state government. Accordingly, a state constitutional convention assembled in Little Rock on January 4, 1864; and as a result of this meeting there was set up a wobbly sort of provisional government with Isaac Murphy, a strong Union man, bearing the title of governor. Murphy managed to hold together some semblance of a state government during the closing days of the war, although its legitimacy was vociferously derided by all those loyal to the Southern cause.

After the close of the war, however, the ex-Confederates and other Democrats of Arkansas surprisingly decided that the most expedient political course for them to pursue was to give open espousal to the Murphy government, but to concentrate their energies upon the election of a Democratic majority in both houses of the state legislature which would serve to handcuff the hostile governor. They were successful in carrying out this plan at the biennial election held in 1866, there being at that time in Arkansas no restriction of the right of the ex-Confederates to vote.

As soon as it convened, this newly elected state legislature sent a commission to Washington to confer with the Federal Government regarding the admission of the state's representatives to Congress, as a first step in the readmission of Arkansas to the Union. The Federal authorities were non-committal, but the commission came back home encouraged, and in its report to the legislature sought to impress upon the citizens of Arkansas 'the importance, the absolute necessity, of remaining quiet, of preserving good order, and a quiet submission to and a rigid enforcement of the law everywhere within the limits of the state.'

The commission quoted a newspaper editorial of similar tone which said: 'If there ever was a time in the history of the people when they had everything to gain by being perfectly quiet and impassive under the bluster and threats of a certain class of politicians, that time is at hand in the South. There is no provocation which should induce them to lose their self-possession and make imprudent or passionate remarks. They should allow the Butlers, the Stevenses and the Sumners to do all the bullying. They should listen to the violent harangues of these men with perfect equanimity. They should exhibit no antagonism to these chiefs of crimination against their section.'

In conclusion, the report said: 'If we demonstrate by our conduct, our prudence and our silence, that we are pursuing our private interests without detriment to anyone, and that we are determined not to regard the calumnies of our enemies, the great mass of the people of the North will see that these mischief-makers have deceived them and will change their tone with reference to our people.'

The Butlers and the Stevenses and the Sumners, however, were not to be lulled into tolerant inaction by this program of passive non-resistance. On the contrary, within less than three weeks they had forced through Congress those Reconstruction Acts which showed very clearly their determination to treat the

Southern States as conquered provinces, and which opened the
eyes of the Southern people as to the futility of their hopes for a
quiet and peaceful re-entry into the Union.

Encouraged by the registration and franchise provisions of the
new laws, the Union men of Arkansas — including the carpetbaggers, the scalawags and the newly enfranchised negroes —
speedily set to work to organize the Republican Party in the
state, and at a convention in Little Rock in April, 1867, nomi-
nated a slate of Republican candidates for all the state offices.
With practically all the Democratic voters disfranchised by the
new laws, the Republicans had little trouble in sweeping to
victory. At that time there were 94,500 men of voting age in
Arkansas — 70,000 native whites, 23,000 negroes and 1500
carpetbaggers; but so efficient was the Radical machine that
they were able to elect 82 out of 83 members of the state legislature. On July 2, 1868, there was established a new state
government, overwhelmingly controlled by the Radicals, with
carpetbagger Powell Clayton at its head as governor. Governor
Clayton was a shrewd and determined partisan who was
cordially detested by the native population, and during his
term of office Arkansas experienced an era of tumult and disorder the like of which it had never seen before and has not
seen since.

The enactment of the Reconstruction Acts by Congress was
followed almost immediately by the appearance of the Ku Klux
Klan in Arkansas. The disfranchised people were chagrined at
their mistreatment and apprehensive of trouble; and when
General Forrest came over into Arkansas from Memphis with
the new Ku Klux Klan idea and enlisted the assistance of the
influential Albert Pike in its establishment in the state, he found
willing ears for his story of the new defensive device which had
been developed in Middle Tennessee. A better promoter of
the idea than General Pike could not have been found, and
during the month of April, 1868, there were increasing mani-

festations of the activities of the strange, new order throughout the eastern part of the state. Hooded figures were to be seen riding the highways at night, and notices began to appear — published in the newspapers or tacked on trees and doors — couched in the stilted, grandiloquent and terrifying phraseology which characterized all the official pronouncements of the Klan. As early as April 6 there was published in the Pine Bluff *Republican* the following notice, said to have been found posted in that city:

K K K

Corinth Division
Pine Bluff Retreat

Special Order No. 2.

Spirit Brothers; Shadows of Martyrs; Phantoms from gory fields; Followers of Brutus!!!!! Rally, rally, rally. — When shadows gather, moons grow dim, and stars tremble, glide to the Council Hall and wash your hands in tyrants' blood; and gaze upon the list of condemned traitors. The time has arrived. Blood must flow. The true must be saved.

> Work in Darkness
> Bury in waters
> Make no sound
> Trust not the air
> Strike High and Sure
> Vengeance! Vengeance! Vengeance!

Tried, condemned. Execute well. Fear is dead. Every man is a judge and this executes!!!!!! Fail not!!

Mandate of the

M. G. C.

By D.M.G.C. 12 m p 2.

There was at first an inclination on the part of the Radical newspapers to minimize and ridicule the Ku Klux Klan and its potentialities. The editor of the Pine Bluff *Republican*, which reprinted this warning notice, in an editorial on May 16 sneered: 'This nefarious and despicable so-called organization is nothing but gas; it is heard of a great many times and at different places; but is never seen.... As to the organization being formidable or substantial, it is all stuff. You might take a pair of General Sherman's old boots for a commander and three hundred monkeys armed with cornstalks and run the last one of them out of the country.'

Contrary to this belittling opinion, however, the Ku Klux increased with the greatest rapidity once they got started, and in the course of a few months had spread terror throughout the eastern part of the state. In November, 1868, the alarmed Governor Clayton sent a special message to the state legislature then in session, opening his message with the stark declaration: 'We are in the midst of civil commotion.' He then went on to describe the development of what he called 'a deep-laid conspiracy' to overthrow the lawful authority of the state by means of a 'treasonable organization having its ramifications in many parts of the state,' enumerating a long list of alleged acts of Ku Klux violence in the counties of Ashley, Columbia, Lafayette, Sevier, Little River, Monroe, Crittenden, Woodruff, Craighead, Fulton, Conway, White and Drew. 'In these and other counties,' the Governor said, 'a reign of terror' was being carried on which was tending in the direction of 'anarchy and destruction.'

Commenting later on these alleged acts of the Ku Klux in various parts of the state, Governor Clayton said: 'There were no successful efforts made by the civil authorities to arrest, much less to prosecute, the perpetrators of the crimes referred to. This may be explained, first, by the fact that the Ku Klux terrorized the officers whose duty it was to execute the laws; second, by the ease with which one or more members of the Ku

Klux organization could get themselves summoned to appear on juries; third, by the inactivity of officers who were either inefficient or who themselves belonged to the organization. It proved to be absolutely impossible for the state authorities, in the face of the ingenious Ku Klux means to block their operations, to bring any member of the Klan to justice through ordinary criminal proceedings, no matter what the crime might be with which he was charged. The question resolved itself into a plain proposition: Should the Ku Klux organization rule Arkansas, or should its members be made subservient to the laws of the state? Of course the Ku Klux set up no claim to constitutional authority; but, declaring that the government of Arkansas was "unconstitutional, null and void," and that no man was bound to respect it, the Klan assumed powers that plunged at least thirteen counties of the state into conditions of anarchy. As a last resort, the declaration of martial law and the suspension of the writ of habeas corpus became inevitable.'

Accordingly, proceeding on this recitation of Ku Klux terrorism as a justification, Governor Clayton announced the declaration of martial law in the affected parts of the state; and one of his first acts was to proceed with the organization of a state militia force, composed principally of negroes and irresponsible white men. The state of Arkansas at this time had no supply of arms of its own; and, efforts to obtain arms from the government at Washington being unsuccessful, Clayton arranged to purchase in the North four thousand stands of arms, with corresponding ammunition, to be brought to Little Rock from Detroit.

In some way the guns were misrouted to Memphis; and when Governor Clayton endeavored to have them brought on to Little Rock, via Helena, by some of the packets regularly in the river trade, he found that all of the Southern steamboat captains were unwilling to handle the unholy cargo. So the Governor chartered a steamboat, the *Hesper*, to go to Memphis and get the guns; and on October 15, 1868, the *Hesper* put out from Memphis for Helena with its trouble-making load. It was openly charged in Memphis at the time that a local carpetbagger named Barbour Lewis had negotiated the sale of the guns, purchasing them in Detroit for seventy cents each, they being left-over army rifles, and selling them to Clayton for $27.50 each, thus turning a more or less honest penny for himself while at the same time supplying the negro militia with guns with which to intimidate the white people. This little detail, however, was beside the point. The principal anxiety of the native citizens of Memphis at the time was to do something to prevent the guns from reaching their destination, and there was a buzz of activity among the Memphians suspected of belonging to the Ku Klux Klan. There was a big society ball scheduled to be held in the old Overton Hotel in Memphis that night; and late in the afternoon an astonishingly large number of the young ladies who were preparing to attend received communications from their prospective escorts that on account of a sudden emergency they would be a little late in calling for them that evening.

Before the Ku Klux could get into action, however, the *Hesper* hauled in her gangplank and started down the river; but she was hardly out of sight around the first bend before a hundred masked men descended on the tug *Nettie Jones* under Captain John Ford at the Fort Pickering wharf in Memphis, commandeered the tug and set out in pursuit of the *Hesper*. They came up with her at Cat Island, twenty-five miles down the river, where she was taking on wood; and, without ceremony, they ran alongside her and quickly took possession. Methodically the boarding Ku Klux subdued the captain and crew and then went about the task of breaking open the gun cases and throwing all the guns and ammunition into the muddy water of the Mississippi. A few shots were fired during the course of the proceedings, just to show that they meant business, but nobody was hurt, and as soon as their task was finished the

Ku Klux set the *Hesper* adrift and started back towards Memphis in the *Nettie Jones*.

When the *Nettie Jones* reached President's Island Chute, about eight miles below Memphis, she was hailed by some men on the Tennessee bank of the river and Captain Ford was ordered to land on the island. A masked man in a skiff then pulled out to the island and, three at a time, took all the sea-going Ku Klux ashore. Their horses had been hid in a near-by canebrake, and the young men quickly doffed their disguises, mounted their horses and made their way back to the city.

There were an unusually large number of couples who did not arrive at the ball until a very late hour that night, and some of the usually immaculate young dandies had flecks of mud on their boots. But the Memphians had learned not to ask questions about the mysterious nocturnal excursions of their young men. The ball was a big success, and everybody was mightily surprised when they read in the *Avalanche* next morning the news of the *Hesper's* misadventure.

Governor Clayton exploded in a fulmination of rage and protest when he learned of the fate of his precious rifles. 'It's piracy!' he cried; the Radical newspapers in Memphis re-echoed the cry; and the Northern press joined in the chorus. The New York *Tribune* sent a correspondent to Memphis to investigate the matter, and in its issue of November 2 it presented an extensive summary of the details of the affair, in which it said:

'That General Forrest himself in person commanded the expedition that committed the late piratical destruction of the Arkansas arms is now the general belief of Memphis Republicans. There are several reasons for this: First — He is recognized as the leader of the organization, proof sufficient of which is found in his own admissions in his famous "big talk" some time ago. Second — Of all men believed connected with the organization no man, from his well-known characteristics,

would be so likely to be called upon to lead so desperate a
venture as General N. B. Forrest. Third — It has been reported that the day before the outrage he "wanted to find five
hundred desperate men." Fourth — The description given by
the crew of the Steamer *Hesper* of the Ku Klux leader on the
tug is as follows: "A very large, well-dressed man, very broad
shouldered, a little stooping as he walked, and having a sharp,
quick voice." Now, give this description to any man in Memphis and he will at once select General Forrest. The command
of the land forces on the Tennessee side is ascribed by the knowing ones to no less a personage than Mr. J. J. DuBose, reputed
adjutant general of the organization for West Tennessee. This
gentleman will hardly deny that on the evening of the piracy
he went from his room with two revolvers buckled about his
waist and a revolving carbine wrapped up in a blanket, his
avowed purpose being to go out of town on the midnight train.
He is next heard of riding out of town in the direction of the
scene of the piracy. Returning to his room before day, his
clothes and boots are covered with mud as though he had been
out on a night campaign.'

An attempt to minimize the effect of this accusation was made
by the *Public Ledger* of Memphis next day in an editorial re-
joinder in which it said: 'That General Forrest was at home
during the night on which these arms were destroyed is known
to over fifty persons.' And the Memphis editor then went on
indignantly to vilify Horace Greeley, editor of the *Tribune*, as
'a political demagogue and harlot of the most abandoned order,'
who was 'endeavoring to induce the people of the North to believe that there exists an organization called "the Ku Klux
Klan" whose avowed object is to overturn the government and
divide the Union.'

Granting that General Forrest's alibi must be taken with a
large-sized grain of salt, it is obvious that the expedition against
the *Hesper* was led by someone of ability and experience in

commanding men. There was a strong feeling in Memphis, at that time and for many years afterward, that the actual leader of the boarding party was Luke E. Wright; and though he never actually admitted it, there seems to be strong reason for believing that he was. The War Department took cognizance of the matter and offered a reward of five thousand dollars for the discovery of the identity of the pirates or their leader, but the reward was never claimed. Years later, when General Wright was Secretary of War in President Taft's Cabinet, some slyly humorous person suggested to the Secretary that he, being a Memphis man, might be able to ferret out the *Hesper* mystery and claim the five thousand dollars reward which was still officially outstanding. General Wright, however, is quoted as replying with a question: 'Wouldn't a man be a damned fool to pay out a reward for the arrest of himself?' And that is as near as the mystery came to being solved.

But, although misfortune overtook this effort to arm his motley militia, Governor Clayton finally succeeded in enlisting a force of state troops who were able to supply their own arms; and meanwhile he had been persisting doggedly in his efforts to ferret out the Ku Klux organization and end its depredations in the state. All his efforts in this direction, however, were unsuccessful until fate played into his hands. In September, 1868, there came to the Governor's home one night a man whom he in his reminiscences does not identify by name but guardedly calls 'a mysterious stranger.' The stranger insisted upon seeing Clayton alone upon 'very important business'; and, after being admitted, stated that he was in position to impart very valuable information relative to the Ku Klux organization in Arkansas. His proposal was that, after he had conveyed the information, if the Governor considered it of sufficient value, he would give the informer three hundred dollars to cover the expense of removing himself and his family from the state, also exacting the requirement that the Governor must give his pledge not to divulge his name. The Governor agreed to all this; and then, as he tells it:

'He then informed me that he was the Cyclops of a certain Ku Klux Den in Independence County; that he joined the Klan believing its purpose to be protective against negro aggression and politically a harmless adjunct to the Democratic party in its efforts to carry the forthcoming elections; but its usurpations of power, including those that controlled life and death, and the shocking outrages committed by it throughout the state, had convinced him that the day of exposure was near and that when that day came he intended, with his family, to be safely located beyond the jurisdiction of the state and the reach of the long arm of the avenging Klan.'

The renegade Cyclops then gave Clayton a copy of the printed Ku Klux ritual and explained all its provisions. He also told him of the Klan's operations in neighboring counties, and gave him such information as would enable the Governor's secret agents to gain admittance to Ku Klux Dens throughout the sphere of its activities. Clayton promptly organized a secret-service force of twelve men who were assigned to the duty of capitalizing on the information imparted by the 'mysterious stranger,' and to them was assigned the dangerous duty of gaining access to the Ku Klux Dens in the localities allotted to them. These spies accomplished their work with varying degrees of success; and one of them, Albert H. Parker, met a tragic end which created a tremendous stir.

Parker was a native of New York State who had drifted to the Southwest before the war and had served, with more or less unwillingness, in the Confederate army. Following the war he settled in Kansas, and after Clayton was elected governor he moved to Arkansas and applied to the new governor for a job. It was about this time that Clayton was given the benefit of the revelations of the Klan's inner workings by the turncoat Cyclops, and Parker was given employment as an under-cover man to go to Searcy in White County and uncover the activities of the Ku Klux in that district.

Aided by the information he had been given regarding the Klan's operations and methods, together with his record as a Confederate soldier, Parker soon ingratiated himself sufficiently into the confidence of the Searcy natives to gain a dangerously accurate impression of the personnel of the Ku Klux organization in that section. He wrote to Governor Clayton that he had found that General Forrest was the head of the entire Invisible Empire, and also gave him the names and official positions held by the key men in the local organization — General Dandridge McRae, he said, was the Grand Titan of the Dominion; Colonel Jacob Froelich, editor of the Searcy *Gazette*, the Grand Giant of the Province (White County); James W. Russell, Grand Cyclops of the Searcy Den, with W. N. Brundridge as his Grand Magi and LeRoy L. Burrow as the Grand Monk. He also reported that John M. McCauley was serving as a sort of adjutant to General McRae and was actively engaged in organizing new Dens throughout the Grand Titan's Dominion.

When he first arrived in Searcy, Parker represented himself as being there for the purpose of buying horses and cattle; but when he remained there several weeks without buying any, the natives began to suspect his motives. Accordingly he was subjected to a quiet counter-espionage by the Ku Klux. All his movements were closely watched, and his outgoing mail was intercepted by the local postmaster, who was a member of the Klan. Thus the native Ku Klux discovered to their horror that they had been nurturing a spy in their midst, and that he was on the eve of returning to Little Rock to report the names of all those whose identity as members of the Klan he had discovered.

A meeting of the local Den was promptly called. The members were thoroughly alarmed, and justifiably so. If Parker was permitted to return to Little Rock and make his report to the Governor, and then testify in court against the Ku Klux whose names he had discovered, it probably meant death to them. They decided that there was but one course for them to pursue; it was decreed that Parker's lips must be forever sealed.

The next evening the unsuspecting spy was encountered by one of the members of the Klan, innocently carrying a water bucket on his arm, who invited him to walk with him to the near-by town spring to get a bucket of water. Arrived at the spring, they found four other members of the Ku Klux lounging there; and as Parker walked up they all drew their pistols and one of them placed his hand on his shoulder and told him he was under arrest. After searching him for weapons, which he did not have, and gagging him with a knotted handkerchief, they marched the terrified Parker off to a secluded spot by an old well on an abandoned farm about three quarters of a mile away. Before arriving at the well, the members of the party stopped and assumed their Ku Klux disguises; and then announced to Parker that he was a prisoner of the Ku Klux Klan.

'Did you ever see any Ku Klux before?' they asked him. Parker, in a feeble effort at conciliation, said that he had been looking for some Ku Klux, that he wanted to join them. 'Yes,' said the leader of the party, 'we thought you had been looking for us, judging from the letters you have been writing back to Little Rock.' Parker denied writing any such letters; but they had the documentary evidence, and they cut his parley short by telling him that he had been condemned to die, that he had but a short while to live, and that if he had anything to say he had better be at it. Parker then broke down and confessed that he was a spy, but he begged for his life, saying that if they would spare him he would agree to kill any Radical in White County whom they might designate.

'If you agreed to kill every Radical in Arkansas it wouldn't save you now,' they told him. 'You know too much.' Parker still protested, but his protests were cut short by their telling him that the time for his execution had come. 'If you want to pray before you die you may do so,' he was considerately told. Parker, however, said that he had never prayed in his life and asked that they pray for him. One of them kindly consented to perform this last service for the victim; they all knelt on the ground; and at the conclusion of the courtly Klansman's heavenly petition they all rose to their feet except Parker, who remained kneeling, sunk in abject and trembling terror. Undeterred, however, the Ku Klux went about their deadly work. The Klansmen lined up in the formation of a firing squad, the leader gave the command to fire, and they blazed away in unison. As soon as the breath had left it Parker's body was picked up and thrown into the abandoned well. 'Work in Darkness; Bury in Water,' the edict had said. In Parker's case its fulfillment was literal and complete.

The next day the local hotel-keeper announced that his erstwhile guest had disappeared — had left between suns without paying his board bill, was the way the Searcy Boniface expressed it, going on to say that he was not surprised, as it was not unusual for strangers to treat him that way. Governor Clayton, of course, was alarmed at the disappearance of his agent, and had a strong suspicion as to what had occurred. There was not a shred of evidence, however, to connect the Ku Klux with the spy's disappearance, and as the months wore on it seemed that it would be recorded as another unsolved mystery.

It was not until eighteen months later that the mystery was solved, and then it was the result of the voluntary confession of a youthful member of the party of Ku Klux executioners, John M. McCauley, upon whose conscience the bloody dead lay heavy. Upon learning of his confession, Clayton sent a detail of his Governor's Guard to Searcy, and McCauley, LeRoy Burrow, William L. Edwards and John G. Holland were arrested, charged with the murder. Burrow joined McCauley in turning state's evidence; under oath they told the gruesome story of Parker's execution; and the decomposed body was exhumed from the well.

Edwards and Holland were held in jail in Little Rock without bail. General McRae and Colonel Froelich, alarmed by the disclosure of their connection with the Klan, fled the country — just ahead of Governer Clayton's offer of a reward of five hundred dollars for the arrest of either of them as an accessory to Parker's death. Meanwhile the friends of the imperiled Titan and Giant became active, and a political deal was hatched up between the Democrats and the so-called Brindle-tail Republicans whereby the Democrats agreed not to put out a state ticket in 1872 if the Brindle-tails would consent to the acquittal of the accused Ku Klux. Informed of this deal, McRae and Froelich returned to Arkansas and gave bond for their appearance, and the other prisoners were then released on bail also. When the accused men were finally brought to trial, the prosecuting attorney, as per the arrangement, announced that his witnesses had scattered and asked for a continuance. This was refused, the trial proceeded and, in the absence of sufficient evidence to convict, the prisoners were officially acquitted and set free.

Governor Clayton was furious, naturally enough, and fumed that he should never have entrusted the matter to the doubtful processes of the civil law but should have had the prisoners tried before a military commission, which could have been depended on to convict the accused. The application of martial law was now being pressed more rigorously than ever, and a condition bordering on civil war soon developed in some sections between the state troops on one side and the Ku Klux and their sympathizers on the other. 'Clayton's Militia' became an epithet in the mouths of the people antagonistic to the carpetbagger state government; and the depredations of the militia, white and negro, stirred the Ku Klux to new degrees of boldness in their activities.

When martial law was declared and the militia began assembling at their appointed places of rendezvous in the different
sections of the state, the Ku Klux prepared boldly to meet and
oppose the troops in an organized way. As the militia assembled at Murfreesboro under General Catterson and Major
Denby, the Ku Klux gathered a force of two hundred men at
near-by Center Point, and soon had five hundred more men on
the march headed that way. The military organization of the
state troops, however, proved superior to the loose discipline of
the Ku Klux; and when the soldiers moved on Center Point the
Klan retreated after the exchange of a few volleys. The
militia occupied a building in the upper story of which they
found the Ku Klux uniforms stored, and also captured several
members of the order. So afraid of the dread 'Clayton's Militia'
were the people that most of the citizens abandoned their
homes and camped out during the troops' occupation of the
town. The Klansmen continued their opposition as long as the
militia remained in that section, but their efforts at open,
armed warfare were abandoned.

The militia, however, did not stay their hand. They roamed
the country, destroying property and indiscriminately taking
prisoners, whom they mistreated and tortured. In January,
1869, a news item in a Memphis paper from Selma in Drew
County related that 'On Friday night about twenty of Catterson's thieves entered this place and completely gutted the town,'
stealing merchandise from the stores to the value of six thousand
and eight hundred dollars. Hamburg in Ashley County and
Warren in Bradley County, it was stated, 'have been sacked in
a similar manner by Catterson's cut-throats.' In Selma, it was
said, the militiamen broke down the stores' doors with axes; and
when a frightened storekeeper heard the racket at his door and
called out: 'Who is there?' he was answered: 'The State Guard,
God damn you.' On the same night they also robbed two stores
at Monticello; and the newspaper correspondent concluded his

story by saying: 'Catterson and his thieves are on their way to Little Rock, where they ought to be — in the penitentiary.'

The operations of Clayton's Militia degenerated into such an orgy of bloodshed and disorder that the Governor himself later felt impelled to attempt to explain and make apology for it. 'Some evils have resulted from the occupancy of counties by martial law,' he admitted, but he minimized these evils and said: 'In some cases unauthorized bands of men pretending to be militia forces have committed depredations, robbing and plundering citizens indiscriminately, but this evil was stopped and checked altogether . . . by an order . . . directing the citizens to shoot all men found in such bands acting without authority of the state government.'

Similarly the name and garb of the Ku Klux were used by independent bandits, notably by a desperate character named Cullen Baker who was described by the newspapers as a man 'who has probably caused more excitement and committed more crimes than any man in modern times.' Governor Clayton offered a reward of one thousand dollars for the arrest of Baker; whereupon that desperado impudently posted upon the trees and public places in his vicinity a reward of five thousand dollars for the delivery to him of Governor Clayton, dead or alive. Baker was eventually shot from ambush by his brother-in-law, who was gratefully paid the reward of one thousand dollars, and the newspapers announced that 'the country breathes free once more.'

Another contemporaneous outlaw in Monticello cold-bloodedly killed a deputy sheriff who was attempting to serve a writ; and then, 'to make an impressive tableau,' killed an entirely inoffensive and unoffending negro man and tied the white man and the negro together in the attitude of kissing each other, and left their bodies in the public road for two days. This miscreant was arrested, tried by a military commission and summarily executed. It was the independent crime of a de-

praved outlaw; but it was inevitably given the Ku Klux
tag.

All these excesses served to heighten the bad blood on both
sides, and the unfortunate state passed through a period of
bloody tumult as recriminations, attacks and counter-attacks
destroyed the peace of the people. The Radicals denounced the
Ku Klux and the Rebels; and the native people exhausted the
vocabulary of invective in heaping epithets on the militia.
The commanders of the militia brigades admitted that some of
their members were guilty of offenses ranging from larceny to
rape. They reported further that 'Subordinates at times
doubtless exceeded their orders; also persons not of the forces,
but representing themselves as belonging to them, in some
instances plundered the people. In cases where orders were disobeyed and instructions departed from, the delinquents when
detected were punished according to the military code.' But the
native whites retorted that such punishments had been so rare
as to escape public notice.

Aside from such minor matters as robbery, assault and
torturing victims with thumbscrews, one of the things which
brought the militia into particular disrepute was the singularly
bad luck they experienced in bringing in their Ku Klux prisoners. 'The prisoners were killed while attempting to escape'
became such a familiar phrase in the militia commanders' reports that even Governor Clayton expressed a desire for more
details as to the circumstances surrounding some of these at-
tempts at escape — but there was never forthcoming any explanation which served to convince the people that the phrase
'killed while attempting to escape' was anything more than a
synonym for murder.

But, after so long a time, order was at last restored. The
Governor called in his militia and restored civil law, and the Ku
Klux formally disbanded their organizations. In this connec-
tion, Governor Clayton told an amusing story of his experience

with a delegation of the leading citizens of Woodruff County, composed of Colonel A. C. Pickett, the Honorable C. L. Gauze and John W. Slayton, who called on him in Little Rock and asked to have civil law restored in their county. Governor Clayton in his reminiscences says: 'Colonel Pickett was the spokesman, and commenced by saying: "Governor, I know not how it is in other counties in the state, but we can assure you there are no Ku Klux in Woodruff County."' Pickett, of course, did not know of the inside information gained by the Governor through the operations of his secret-service force. 'At this point,' the Governor continues, 'I interrupted the Colonel and drew from a drawer in my desk a list of the Ku Klux in Woodruff County sent me by General Upham a few days before. Handing it to him I remarked: "Colonel, please look over this list, and I think you will find that your name, like that of Ben Adhem, leads all the rest." The Colonel glanced over it, and before he had time to reply I said: "Now, gentlemen, don't come to me with lies on your lips. If you will go back home and in good faith disband the Ku Klux organizations there and furnish me with conclusive evidence that you have done so, and I have means of knowing whether you do or not, I will revoke martial law and restore the civil authorities there." The Colonel and his associates seemed much crestfallen, and for a time they were speechless. At length they agreed that they would go back and comply with my requirements, which in due time they did. Years afterward, when Colonel Gauze became a member of Congress from that district, he and I frequently laughed over the Pickett episode. He told me that they had made life unbearable for the Colonel on their way back to Woodruff County because of the sudden termination of a speech that he had previously prepared and read to them.'

Possibly this story gained something in the Governor's telling, but it seems to be a fact that the disbandment of the Ku Klux Klan in Arkansas resulted from some such more or less formal agreement with the Governor. At any rate, after so long a time, the orderly processes of the law were restored in Arkansas; and when this happy state of affairs eventuated, the Ku Klux Klan ceased to function there.

XI.   FLORIDA

Florida, described by one venomous New York newspaper as 'the smallest tadpole in the dirty pool of secession,' was not by reason of its contemptible size spared any of the rigors of Reconstruction. William Marvin was appointed provisional governor by President Johnson on July 13, 1865, and served until an election was held in November, at which time David S. Walker was elected governor, taking office on January 17, 1866. The ordinance of secession was repealed, the Thirteenth Amendment was ratified and Florida seemed to be started on the way towards a peaceful and painless restoration to the Union. But in April, 1867, the state became a part of the Third Military District, under the command of General John Pope, and there ensued a year of military rule. In May, 1868, an election was held at which time Harrison Reed, a carpetbagger, was elected governor, and in June of that year the state was admitted to the Union and all the state offices were turned over to the newly constituted state government.

Before Governor Reed had been in office six months he was impeached, charged with various crimes and misdemeanors, including falsehood and lying, embezzlement of securities and money, and with corruption and bribery. Reed, however, successfully resisted this impeachment in the courts, and managed to hold on to his office; and when the state legislature assembled in January he was able to engineer the passage of a resolution stating that there had been nothing in his conduct to justify impeachment. Hardly had this little matter been patched up, however, than he was again impeached in January, 1870, at which time he was charged with 'high crimes and misdemeanors, malfeasance and incompetency in office.' This impeachment also fell through, thanks to Reed's mastery of state politics, although a distinctly unpleasant aroma lingered about the Governor's chair. In February, 1872, a third attempt was made to remove Reed by impeachment, on fourteen charges involving bribery, appropriation of state money to his own use and fraudulent conspiracy; but the Governor slipped through the net again when the impeachment managers applied for a continuance to give them time to collect evidence and summon witnesses, which application was refused and the court adjourned.

While all this sordid drama was dragging across the boards at the state capital in Tallahassee, the usual infestation of carpetbaggers and Loyal Leaguers was sweeping through the state, teaching the negroes to hate their former masters and to vote the Republican ticket. 'Jesus Christ was a Republican,' the credulous blacks were piously told; and the Leagues grew in numbers and strength as their organizers and leaders waxed fat. As the belligerence of the negroes increased, the development of violent defensive measures followed as naturally as cause follows effect. 'The state was cursed with a rising tide of violence,' says Henry's *Story of the Reconstruction,* 'descending in many cases to the depths of barbarity. Much of the violence was the work of bands of white "regulators," whose methods went from warnings to whippings, to banishment, to murder and even to torture and the mutilation of corpses. The disorder was curiously "spotty," with peace and apparent content prevailing in one county while in its neighbor there was violence which, upon a few occasions, amounted to practical anarchy.'

In Leon County, in which Tallahassee is located, the negroes outnumbered the white people seven to one, and during the years immediately following the war they behaved in a most threatening and menacing manner. One witness before the Congressional Committee testified that 'they were very disquiet, and used to go to Tallahassee in crowds of a thousand at a time, armed with guns and clubs and other weapons, and parade the streets,' creating so much disturbance that 'the female portion of the community were very much excited.'

The Union League was organized in Florida as soon as the organizers could get down there after the war, and it soon embraced practically all the negroes in its membership. In 1871 Governor Reed was president of the League, in addition to being governor of the state, and the organization had the additional advantage of the prestige and power afforded by the high political office of its president.

As in other states also, the Freedmen's Bureau became an irritant between the white landowners and the ex-slaves; and it was a common practice for the agents of the Bureau to induce the negroes to break their contracts with their employers. In some instances they were told that contracts made without the sanction of the Bureau were illegal and void — and when new contracts were made the agents collected their fees.

The resentment of the native whites at these mounting abuses soon began to manifest itself; and although it is difficult to discover just exactly when and by whom the Ku Klux idea was introduced into Florida, there seems to be no doubt that the Klan was operative in the northern portion of the state. William Bryson, judge of the third judicial circuit, testified that there was an organization known as the Ku Klux in his district, and that he had been shown some of its signs and secrets by a man named George R. Cook, who was 'originally from Tennessee' — apparently there was always a man from Tennessee on hand when Ku Klux developments began anywhere. Judge Bryson said that this man showed him a star with five points, but went on to say, 'I was so stupid that it took me a long time to know what it meant. After a time he showed me that there were three K's to be made of it.' Having disposed of this matter, the Ku Klux messenger told Judge Bryson not to hold court, that if he did he would be assassinated; but, the judge related, 'I did hold court, and I was not assassinated.' Unfortunately, Judge Bryson did not go into details as to just how the three K's were made from the five-pointed star; and modern readers who happen to be as 'stupid' as he will have to figure it out for themselves. Another prominent citizen who testified to first-hand knowledge of the existence of the Ku Klux in Florida was the Secretary of State, J. C. Gibbs, a negro from Philadelphia. Gibbs testified that a white man named Mark Richardson in Taylor County told him that he was a member of the Klan in that county and knew where their regalia was hidden. He also said that others from Taylor County reported the presence in that county of a band of armed marauders who carried a banner with 'K.K.K.' on it, and that when they first appeared in the county they stated that they were after Mark Richardson. Richardson, however, seems to have thwarted them by joining the organization — at least that is what he later stated.

There existed in Florida at that time an organization which was commonly regarded by the people as being equivalent to the Ku Klux, and it is quite possible that it may have been used as a screen for the Klan. This organization was known as the Young Men's Democratic Club; and that it was operating in other states is indicated by the fact that in the constitution of the club as submitted to the Congressional Committee there was a blank space for the name of the state as well as the county.

In its plan of organization it was prescribed that 'the white voters and disfranchised citizens' of each county should be divided into sections of fifties, each to be numbered individually, with a chief of each fifty. These fifties were to be subdivided into groups of ten, each with a sub-chief; and the chiefs of the tens were required to make a list of 'the names, place of residence, by whom employed, vocation, height, complexion, where registered, and political bias of every white and colored voter in their respective limits.' It is interesting to compare this with the testimony of General Forrest before the Committee, where he said: 'In each voting precinct there is a captain who, in addition to his other duties, is required to make out a list of men in his district, giving all the Radicals and all the Democrats who are positively known, and showing also the doubtful on both sides and of both colors. This list of names is forwarded to the grand commander of the state, who is thus enabled to know who are our friends and who are not.'

Frank Myers, who claimed that he had formerly belonged to the Young Men's Democratic Club in Alachua County, and who produced a written copy of its constitution which he said was provided him for the purpose of organizing local clubs in Hernando County, stated that the real work of the club was done by a 'secret service club' which existed within the other club and to which carefully selected members were invited to belong. Such a 'secret service' group was indeed provided for in the printed constitution of the club, with only a very vague statement of its objects and duties. Myers said that the purpose of this secret-service club was 'in case it became necessary, as they feared it would, to use force or violence to prevent certain parties from exerting too great an influence with the colored population in that county, to be prepared to do it effectually and secretly'; and he further stated that this inner organization was 'commonly and popularly known as the Ku Klux.'

Joseph John Williams of Tallahassee, who freely admitted that he was the central chief of the Young Men's Democratic Club in Leon County, denied emphatically that it had any connection with the Ku Klux, and made the further statement, regarding the club, that 'The same plan now exists in the state of Virginia; I believe that Extra Billy Smith is at the head of exactly the same organization there.' Williams, however, denied any knowledge of any 'secret service committee' within the club.

But whether it was the Ku Klux Klan or the Secret-Service Committee, there was certainly some sort of formal organization in Florida which had for its purpose the regulation of the conduct of the negroes and carpetbaggers, and most people referred to these regulators as Ku Klux. Emanuel Fortune, one-time shoemaker, later carpenter and still later a common laborer, who proudly described himself as being 'a leading man in politics' in Jackson County, left there in May, 1868, because he said he thought his life was in danger. Although an almost totally illiterate negro — he could read 'tolerably well' but could not read writing at all and 'could not write writing very well' — he had been elected to the state legislature after the war and also been elected to the constitutional convention, and was a companion and political crony of the carpetbaggers and white Radicals. There was no doubt in his mind as to the existence of a Ku Klux organization in Jackson County; he knew a man 'who saw two disguised men there about eight feet high, in the moonlight, sitting in a place where they finally killed a man,' and Emanuel avoided that place ever afterward.

Jackson County was indeed a veritable hotbed of Ku Kluxism. One of the first victims of the wrath of the natives of that county was Samuel Fleishman, a carpetbagger who conducted a store in Marianna, the county seat, for Altman and Brother. Fleishman catered especially to the black trade, and was heard to tell a crowd of negroes in his store that whenever a negro was killed they should murder three white men in retaliation. As a result of this, Fleishman was summoned one day in October, 1869, to appear before an assemblage of more than twenty of the citizens of Marianna in J. P. Coker's store, where he was told that it had been decided that it would be safest for him and for the town for him to leave there without delay. He protested, but they told him that they would give him until sundown to get ready to leave; that if he stayed there he would certainly be killed, and if he were killed there would be an outbreak of trouble which would result in others being killed also. At sundown a committee of citizens called for him at his store and, in spite of all his protests, escorted him out of town to the Georgia state line, warning him that if he ever returned to Marianna it would be at the risk of his life. Fleishman went straight to Tallahassee, where he asked for protection; but he was not given much encouragement by the state officials upon whom he called. Nothing daunted, he set out for Marianna alone, protesting that he would be ruined if forced to abandon his business there. On the way to Marianna he met a white man on horseback who knew him and who advised him to turn back, telling him that he would be killed if he showed himself in Marianna; but Fleishman went resolutely ahead. The next morning his body was found in the road on the outskirts of Marianna. His assassins were never apprehended, but the Radicals all said, 'Ku Klux.'

Violent deaths were no novelty in Jackson County at that time. In fact, the mortality rate ran unusually high for a year or two. One of the killings which particularly incensed the Radicals was that of John Q. Dickinson, a carpetbagger from Vermont who had been elected county court clerk, and who was shot down in April, 1871, after having received a number of threatening letters. As usual there were divergent stories as to the manner and cause of his death. His political opponents — and some of the Radicals — circulated the story that he was killed by a negro named Homer Bryant on account of Dickinson's alleged unlawful relations with Bryant's wife. Dickinson's friends, however, expressed the greatest indignation at this charge, insisting that he was 'a high-type gentleman, a good man, a man of pure life.' One enthusiast even went so far as to suggest that his statue be placed in the Hall of Fame as one of Florida's foremost citizens in all its history.

Dickinson in fact appears to have been of ability above that of the average carpetbagger, being a man of good family and a graduate of Harvard. He associated with the negroes, however, on a basis of equality, made himself their guide and counselor and thereby acquired the ill-will of the native population. In a letter written just before his death Dickinson spoke of 'the terrible scenes through which I have passed in Marianna,' and said that 'I blush to say that for nearly three years I have managed to live here only by dexterously compromising the expression of my opinions and by a circumspect walk,' and further, 'I have striven, even to a loss of self-respect and several times by incurring personal danger, to do the best thing under the circumstances.'

To what an extreme extent he was willing to sacrifice his self-respect in the interest of peace is indicated by an incident in Dickinson's office when J. P. Coker, the reputed head of the Ku Klux in Jackson County, called there on business and found the place crowded with negroes, who were being registered by the clerk. Coker impatiently insisted upon being given immediate attention, and when Dickinson showed an inclination to argue the matter with him Coker struck at him, knocking his hat off his head. 'Coker, you keep your hands off me,' Dickinson mildly protested; but Coker, in a rage, replied: 'I have a mind to put your eyes and mouth into one, you God damned nigger-loving son of a bitch.' Dickinson discreetly refrained from any reply, continuing his business with the negroes, whereupon the irate Coker exclaimed: 'You are a God damned liar; and, if you take that you are nothing but a cowardly son of a bitch.' Dickinson did take it, however; and Coker, unable to sustain a one-sided fight, left the office.

But Dickinson's humiliating pacifism could not save him. His fate was sealed. The immediate cause of his death was a dispute with a man named Ely whose land Dickinson advertised to be sold for taxes which Ely said he had paid. Ely was heard to threaten Dickinson with death if he did not take the advertisement out of the paper; but when Dickinson was actually killed Ely disclaimed any knowledge of it and was able to establish an air-tight alibi. The Radicals immediately raised the cry that he had been murdered by the Ku Klux; but nobody was ever officially charged with the crime.

A particularly conspicuous stormy petrel in Jackson County was Major W. J. Purman, a carpetbagger from Pennsylvania, who took up his residence in Marianna after the war, was elected to the state senate from that county, and became an energetic and aggressive leader among the negroes and the Radicals, by whom he was held in high esteem. By the same token he became immensely unpopular with the native whites, and there were frequent mutterings of their ill-will. One night as he was returning, in company with a Doctor Finlayson, from a concert given by the local garrison of soldiers, they were shot from ambush, Dr. Finlayson being killed and Major Purman seriously wounded. As soon as he recovered, in five or six weeks, he found it advisable to leave on 'a business trip' to Alabama, from whence he went to Washington and in September returned to Florida — but not to Marianna. He prudently stopped at Tallahassee to spy out the land, and was there warned not to return to Marianna, as conditions there had grown worse instead of better and it would not be safe for him to show himself.

Affairs in Jackson County had indeed reached the boiling point during Purman's absence. The white and black residents were on the verge of open warfare, and there had been blood spilled on both sides. On September 28, 1869, the negroes were having a picnic near Marianna, and the crowd of them were fired into by an unidentified white man, one man and a little boy being killed. A day or two after that, just at dusk, presumably in retaliation, a negro fired a double-barreled shotgun into a party of people sitting on the piazza of the hotel at Marianna — J. P. Coker, Colonel C. F. McClellan and Colonel McClel-

lan's daughter. Miss McClellan was killed and her father
wounded by the fire, and there ensued the most tremendous
indignation and excitement in Marianna. Scores of mounted,
armed men assembled there and placed the town under a sort
of informal and unofficial martial law; and there were emphatic
and unrestrained avowals that the blood of Miss McClellan
must be avenged.

Colonel McClellan was a leading attorney of Marianna, who
came there originally from Kentucky. He was physically a
man of very large proportions, and called himself a 'Kentucky
war horse.' He was looked upon as a leader by the natives
opposed to the carpetbaggers and Radicals, but his enemies
described him as 'an agitator and instigator' and 'a man of
boisterous, rugged, harsh ways and manners — not a peaceable
man at all.' Mr. Coker was a leading merchant in Marianna, a
man of means and standing, and described by a local carpetbagger as 'the generalissimo of the Ku Klux there' and as 'a
general ring-leader of badness.'

The wanton murder of this entirely innocent and inoffensive
young woman aroused the greatest possible indignation, and
there was an outcry for the apprehension and punishment of her
murderer. Suspicion, based on the testimony of eye-witnesses,
pointed to a local negro constable, Calvin Rogers, who was a
Radical firebrand; and a few nights later Rogers was mysteriously killed, presumably by the Ku Klux. This ended the
McClellan incident on the surface, but the affair left a feeling of
tension which was at fever heat when Purman returned to
Tallahassee from his visit to the North; and he lingered there
for nearly a year, being sustained meanwhile by appointment to
a lucrative Federal job.

In August, 1870, accompanied by Colonel Charles Memorial
Hamilton, carpetbagger member of Congress from Florida,
Purman went back to Marianna, where the presence of the two
hated Radical leaders created an immediate sensation. During

the day there was an ominous sound throughout Marianna and its vicinity — the repeated discharge of firearms, generally interpreted as being incident to the cleaning out of pistols and shotguns preparatory to serious operations. Purman and Hamilton lodged at the home of Thomas M. West, the scalawag sheriff of the county; and during the day they received a secret message that an effort would be made to kill all of them, and that their three watchdogs would be poisoned that night in preparation for the attack on them. The next morning the watchdogs were in fact found dead, and the alarmed sheriff and his guests summoned a number of their negro friends to arm themselves and come to their assistance.

Marianna was in a tumult that day. Men on horseback galloped frantically through the streets, there was a sound of horns blowing and general excitement as armed, mounted men began to gather in the town. About noon a lone scout rode up to the sheriff's house for a brief reconnaissance, and withdrew as soon as he saw the armed negroes at every window. Contrary to the expectation of the beleaguered men, there was no raid on them that night; but the next day there was a noticeable increase in the number of armed men gathering in the town. Some came in buggies, bringing their shotguns; others were on horseback, with their blankets and overcoats strapped behind their saddles — the customary preparation in that county when a man was getting ready to 'go to Texas,' which was the current slang expression for leaving for parts unknown. Also conspicuous in town were a select group of notorious desperadoes from Columbus, Georgia, known by the sinister entitlement of 'twenty-dollar men,' that being, according to current report, the flat fee charged by them for a murder.

Before noon of that day parties of armed men were to be seen riding out of Marianna — one squad on each of the roads leading out of town. Some gave it out that they were going hunting; others carried fishing rods and announced that they

were embarking on an angling expedition. The suspicions of the
besieged Radicals were aroused by all this stir, and they sent
out spies who came back with the report that 'every cross-
road, by-path, dog-path, every possible avenue of escape from
town was blockaded' and that everybody who tried to leave
town was stopped and examined before being allowed to proceed.

The sheriff, dismayed by these alarming reports, called in
several of the prominent men of Marianna, some of the oldest
citizens of high standing and integrity, and complained to them
concerning their state of siege; but these citizens laughed at
their fears and told them that they must be mistaken. Purman
and Hamilton, however, were convinced that if they attempted
to leave town unprotected they would be killed; so after four or
five days of nervous waiting the sheriff issued a summons for a
posse of five hundred men with four days' rations, and announced
his plan to march Purman and Hamilton out of town under the
protection of this body of men. The older citizens immediately
appealed to the sheriff not to do any such provocative thing,
saying that the 'rash young men' of the town (meaning the Ku
Klux) would regard it as an aggressive step and that it might
precipitate a small-scale, local civil war. 'For God's sake, don't
do that,' they begged. 'Ask any means for your safety and you
shall have it.' The sheriff and his thoroughly frightened guests
now conferred, and finally hit upon the plan of asking ten of the
oldest leading citizens of Marianna to act as their escort out of
town, to which the citizens willingly agreed. The ten old
citizens accordingly loaded themselves into three carriages and
escorted the mounted party of fifteen Radicals and negroes to
Bainbridge in Georgia, whence they made their way to the
safety of Tallahassee.

Purman later admitted that although the party of Marianna
citizens regarded themselves merely as an escort to insure the
safe passage of the refugees from the danger zone, the refugees

themselves viewed the citizens in the light of hostages and calmly admitted that it was the plan of himself and the other Radicals to kill these 'hostages' if they were attacked on the way. No such attack occurred, however, and when the party arrived at Bainbridge, Mr. Purman testified, he generously abandoned the idea of killing them and 'treated them gloriously to champagne.'

The fugitives were physically safe when they reached Tallahassee, but there is reason to believe that they did not receive any too warm a welcome there even from their political friends. Governor Reed, fellow-Radical that he was, told Purman and Hamilton frankly to their faces that he considered them very largely responsible for the turbulent state of affairs in Jackson County; and this was one of the Governor's statements to which the native citizens enthusiastically agreed.

Major Purman was very emphatic in the expression of his belief that at this time Florida was ruled by Ku Kluxism, although the Radicals held all the state offices and outnumbered their political opponents in voting strength. The Ku Klux, Major Purman testified, would 'combine to prevent the arrest of any man; they will spirit him away or protect and conceal him and make it dangerous for officers of the law to attempt to arrest him. Or, if they do stand their trial, as they have done in different portions of the state, and any one of these men is on the jury, he will hang the jury and you can not convict any of them.'

It was a peculiarly bloodthirsty type of Ku Klux they had in Jackson County, he testified. Did they whip anybody there? he was asked; to which he replied: 'No, sir, they make clean work of it in Jackson County. They believe there in gun-powder entirely. They do not resort to those trifling things.' Richard Pousser, a negro who succeeded the deceased Calvin Rogers as constable in Marianna, gave similarly impressive testimony when asked if there was an organization of Ku Klux in that county. 'There sure is,' he said. 'I am now toting their bullet right in my shoulder.'

Stories of all the disorders in Florida, bad enough in themselves, were circulated in the North in exaggerated and distorted style; and Florida, despite its status as a 'small tadpole,' gained a reputation in the Northern States as a particularly dangerous place for visitors. Judge T. T. Long, in charge of the fourth judicial circuit in Florida, testified, however, that there had never been any trouble there with people who came there and behaved themselves; and he further stated that he knew of but one killing into which politics entered. 'I think whiskey has more to do with them than anything else,' he said.

Captain C. B. Wilder, a former officer in the Union army and an abolitionist before the war, who came to Florida after Lee's surrender, partly for his health and partly to invest his money, being a man of means, ridiculed the theory that Northern people were not safe in the South because of the activities of the Ku Klux. He went so far as to express the view that the carpetbaggers had circulated these reports with the idea of making capital of the matter in Washington and perpetuating themselves in power, quoting one carpetbagger as saying: 'It is the best thing in the world for our party to have such things occur. We can publish them and create a sensation that will foster the Republican party.' Captain Wilder scathingly denounced the character of the men constituting Florida's state government, stating bluntly that the carpetbaggers by their misrule had brought about a condition 'more ruinous than all the Ku Klux in the state.' He complained bitterly of the squandering of the state's funds by its corrupt officials, stating that taxes had increased one thousand per cent in a year and that he could recall but one honest man in the state government. United States senatorships and Federal appointments were being sold to the highest bidder, he asserted; and he specifically charged that of $2,800,000 of bonds issued to build a railroad, only $308,938 was actually applied to that purpose.

L. G. Dennis, a carpetbagger from Massachusetts, who was a

United States revenue collector and also state senator from Alachua County, related that he had received a number of threatening letters, one of which he produced:

> K.K.K.
> No man e'er felt the halter draw
> With good opinion of the law.
> K.K.K.
> Twice the secret report was heard
> When again you hear his voice
> Your doom is sealed.
> K.K.K.
> Dead men tell no tales.
> K.K.K.
> Dead! dead! under the roses.
> K.K.K.
> Our motto is death to Radicals — Beware!
> K.K.K.

In spite of these sinister threats, followed up by several abortive efforts to take his life, Dennis held on to both his offices.
As a feature of his hazing, a group of ten or twelve alleged Ku
Klux held a sort of mock trial of him in the streets of Gainesville
one night about midnight. Some boxes were carried into the
street from one of the stores, and one of the Ku Klux mounted
the box and acted as the judge. Dennis was charged with the
serious offense of being a Radical, and was convicted and sentenced to be executed. The young men engaging in this horse-
play were described as being members of the first families; but
they were also said to be 'desperate, bad men; men who boast of
having killed two or three negroes apiece.'

All of the Ku Klux activity in Florida was in the northern
counties, principally along the Georgia state line. B. F. Tidwell,
scalawag county judge of Madison County, testified that there
had been 'over twenty' people killed in that county by an organization commonly spoken of as the Ku Klux. David Montgom-

ery, carpetbagger sheriff of the county, stated that he had been informed by a man named R. H. Williard that he had been invited to join the Klan; and another citizen of the county by the name of McClary was quoted as having boasted while in his cups that he 'could just blow his horn and have eighty men at his call at any time.' That this organization was a branch of the veritable Ku Klux Klan was further evidenced by its plan of operation as revealed by William Sapp, a suspected member: 'If there was anything to be done down in our county they sent word across the line into Georgia and the party came from there; and if there was anything to be done over there, a party would go from our county over there.' A negro justice of the peace in Madison County by the name of Hall received a letter signed 'K.K.K.' notifying him that he must resign; and it was stated that numerous such letters were received by obnoxious Radical office-holders in the county.

E. G. Johnson, a scalawag member of the state senate from Lake City, in October, 1871, received a letter purporting to come from the Ku Klux in which his life was threatened unless he resigned his seat in the senate. This letter stated that the organization had four thousand members in Florida and that 'all the Ku Klux laws, all the courts, all the soldiers, all the devils in hell can not stop the resolves of the brotherhood. The destroyers of our rights — that is, unprincipled leaders such as you — if they persist, will fall one by one; it is sworn to by brave men, who are obliged to act in secrecy from the force of circumstances.' Johnson boldly published the letter in the Lake City *Herald*, describing it as a 'Ku Klux letter,' with a statement alleging that he knew the authors and that they would be safe so long as they did not carry their threat into execution. But, he said, 'just so sure as I fall, they will know that I have placed avengers upon their tracks that will never rest until they have visited upon them swift and just retribution.' Johnson, however, did not 'fall'; and nobody ever knew whether his dark threat of 'swift and sure retribution' was just a bluff or if he really had arranged for the post-mortem vengeance as claimed.

R. W. Cone, a scalawag who lived in Palatka in Baker County, had incurred the ill-will of his neighbors in the first place by dodging service in the Confederate army, and after the war he intensified his unpopularity by consorting with the Radicals and the negroes. The climax was reached when he served on a Federal grand jury of mixed white and black personnel, which, according to the local complaint, 'took negroes' testimony in preference to white men's.' Cone shortly thereafter found a notice on his front gate warning him to leave town; and when he arrived at his store he found a similar notice tacked to the door. This notice was not in handwriting, which might be identified, but was cunningly contrived of single words cut out of the pages of newspapers, pasted together, and was signed 'K.K.K.' Cone was inclined to defy the power of the Invisible Empire, and publicly announced that he was ready to defend himself against aggression. Undismayed by this, however, the Ku Klux burst into his house one night soon thereafter, took him out into the woods and whipped him with stirrup-leathers taken from their saddles — whereupon he discreetly moved to Jacksonville. Cone testified before the Congressional Committee that his whipping was no isolated instance of such punishment. 'This Ku Klux business, or regulating business, whatever they call it,' he said, 'has been going on here ever since the war — and even before the war.'

In Florida the negro militia did not come to be such a disturbing factor as it was in most of the other Southern States. The Governor was authorized to enlist such a force, but he never proceeded very far along this line. His first effort failed because of a mishap to the guns which he had bought in New York with which to arm them — an incident reminiscent of the fate of the guns shipped from Memphis to Arkansas on the *Hesper*. The Florida guns reached Jacksonville all right, and there they were loaded into two cars and the cars locked. When the train reached Tallahassee the cars were still locked — but they were empty; the guns had mysteriously disappeared en route. A thorough search finally disclosed a large number of the guns, broken and rendered useless, scattered along the right of way of the railroad; others were later seen in the hands of a Ku Klux raiding party in Madison County; but nobody, including the members of the train crew, could offer any explanation of the mystery. Thirty years later an old man, then living in Texas, in reminiscent mood told gleefully of how the feat was accomplished. 'Every telegraph operator, brakeman, engineer and conductor on the road was a Ku Klux,' he stated. The shipment was watched at every point, and between Lake City and Madison the entire two carloads of guns were thrown from the moving train by a select band of Ku Klux, under the personal command of this narrator, who had quietly boarded the train at its last stop. The Ku Klux left the train at Madison, having accomplished their work of destruction in spite of the fact that there were attached to the train two coaches filled with United States troops sent to guard the precious shipment.

This unfortunate experience seemed to discourage any further efforts to arm the state militia and put it into action; and, besides, the Governor by this time had his time so fully engaged in trying to defend himself from political attack and hold on to his office that he lost some of his zest for persecuting the citizens. Gradually the native white citizens regained control of the state government; and, as the need for their services diminished, the Ku Klux faded out of existence.

XII.   LOUISIANA,
VIRGINIA AND TEXAS

ALTHOUGH THE ORIGINAL PLAN for the Invisible Empire, as outlined in the official Prescript, contemplated an organization extending into all the states which had comprised the Southern Confederacy, its activities were confined almost entirely to those states already mentioned in detail — Tennessee, Alabama, North and South Carolina, Georgia, Florida, Mississippi and Arkansas. In the states of Louisiana, Virginia and Texas it is hard to find any convincing evidence of the existence of the Ku Klux Klan; although in Louisiana and Texas, at least, there were similar organizations carrying on regulatory work on a more or less extensive scale.

In Virginia the Klan does not seem to have been active at all. There was an occasional outburst of violence in some of the south-side counties, along the Carolina border, to which the Ku Klux name was attached; but it is extremely doubtful whether these were attributable to the genuine Ku Klux Klan. The Klan was operating in some of the adjoining counties in North Carolina, and it is possible that some of the Carolina Klansmen occasionally may have made a foray across the line on some special occasion. The report of the Congressional Committee, which was seeking Ku Klux outrages with microscopical care, said that in Virginia 'The Ku Klux, although manifesting themselves in 1868, have not again renewed their

activities'; and such a restrained statement from the committee
is tantamount to an admission that the Ku Klux did not operate
in the state.

The only conspicuous charge of Ku Kluxism in Virginia was
made by Luther C. Tibbets, a carpetbagger who took up his
residence in Fredericksburg after the war and soon became implicated in some complex legal difficulties there involving a
tenant of his named James B. Summons, also a carpetbagger.
As a result of these difficulties, Tibbets returned to the North,
where he published a pamphlet with the resounding title
'Spirit of the South; or Persecution in the Name of the Law as
Administered in Virginia.' In the course of this pamphlet
Tibbets quoted two letters of warning from the Ku Klux Klan
received by Summons. The first of these, addressed to 'J. Summons, the Radical, in care of the other Radical, L. C. Tibbets,'
read as follows:

> Hole in the Wall, No Place, July 29, 1868.
>
> To J. Summons, the Radical:
>
> You are hereby warned and notified to leave the County of
> Spottsylvania within ten (10) days from the receipt of this
> notification, or take the consequences of your remaining and of
> disregarding the third warning which you have received from
> this commandery of our order. There is not Yankee hounds
> enough on the soil of Virginia to turn the bullet from your heart
> if you remain.
>
> Your inveterate enemy, for the order of the K.K.K.
>
> LUCIFER

Mr. Summons apparently showed no signs of taking this
letter seriously, for a week later, they wrote him again:

> The Hole in the Wall, No Place, August 5, 1868.
>
> Summons: — As the time is drawing near when your limit
> will expire, I again caution you to leave the county. It is not

our desire or our object to shed blood, and it is only done in extreme cases when assassination can not be avoided in order to carry out our plans. Therefore this, the fourth warning. Although your enemy, I warn you as a friend.

My other communications were unofficial, being written by myself at the suggestion of some of the Klan. You will observe that this bears our seal, and if you are not entirely bereft of reason you will regard it.

By order of the G. C.

G. L.

In the lower corner of this letter was a skull and crossbones, the 'our seal' referred to, and it was elaborately decorated with vignettes of coffins, death's heads, whips, etc. Apparently this warning got the desired results, for Summons and Tibbets both left town promptly. When Tibbets published his pamphlet, General George Stoneman ordered an investigation of the episode. S. F. Chalfin, A.A.G., in an official report to Stoneman in October minimized the whole affair. 'Statements that Tibbets was forced to leave here to avoid being murdered, I regard as purely sensational,' wrote Chalfin. 'I have no reason to suppose that any "Klan" exists anywhere in this vicinity. It is quite possible that some foolish young men have sent anonymous threats couched in the fantastic language and emblems, well-knowing Mr. Tibbets' highly excitable character.'

Just why it should have been so is not entirely clear, but Virginia appears to have escaped from the searing Reconstruction ordeal with a minimum of damage and distress. The brutalities and excesses practiced by the Radicals in the other Southern States were practically unknown in the Old Dominion, and Virginia was restored to her place in the Union, with an orderly civil government, in a relatively short while after the end of the war. In the absence of oppression and abuse, there was little or no need for retaliatory measures; furthermore the

Virginia negroes were of a naturally orderly and well-behaved type; consequently, there being no crying need for it, the Ku Klux Klan did not become a factor in the reconstruction of Virginia.

Texas, on the other hand, although it suffered all the rigors of the most obnoxious post-war misgovernment, was not so physically situated as to encourage or support any closely knit state organization of regulators. There were, to be sure, local bands of regulators — plenty of them. In San Antonio there was a group known as 'the Confederate Vigilantes,' there were 'Hunters' Clubs' and other groups without names. In his annual report dated November 4, 1868, General Reynolds, the military commander in Texas, said: 'Armed organizations known as "Ku Klux Klans" exist independently or in concert with other armed bands in many parts of Texas, but are most numerous, bold and aggressive east of Trinity River. The precise objects of the organizations can not be readily explained, but seem in this state to be to disarm, rob, and in many cases murder, Union men and negroes, and, as occasion may offer, murder United States officers and soldiers; also to intimidate everyone who knows anything of the organization but will not join it.'

The phraseology used by General Reynolds is worthy of note. The armed organizations of which he speaks may have been, and probably were, known as Ku Klux Klans. That was a popular appellation for any sort of organized regulators in those days; but the fact that people called them Ku Klux did not, of course, make them Ku Klux; and although their objectives and methods may have been similar, there does not seem to be any evidence of connection between these Texas groups and the Ku Klux Klan of which General Forrest was the Grand Wizard.

An example of the conditions which made some sort of protective organization a necessity is to be seen in a news item in the Crockett *Sentinel* of April 24, 1868, which said: 'Saturday night, after the Loyal League had adjourned, about twelve o'clock, a large party of negro fellows entered the yard of our townsman, Mr. W. H. Cundiff, tied their horses to his shade trees, entered his parlor and spent the night. Mr. Cundiff was away from his home at the time, and his house was occupied by Mrs. Cundiff and her little children, who passed a night of horrible torture and suspense, knowing not what fiendish deed the ruffians would attempt. . . . It is an outrage that demands retaliation, one that the law is inadequate to reach, and that will demand the attention of the community. We believe that the peace and safety of our community demand the suppression of this infernal institution.'

This was not an isolated example. Texans were constantly subjected to such indignities after the war; and Texans were never so constituted as to bear indignities passively. That 'attention of the community' suggested by the Crockett editor was soon forthcoming; and the lawless negroes and carpetbaggers of Texas soon found that there was in existence an elusive but powerful defensive mechanism which would not permit abuses to go unpunished. Just how this mechanism operated is thrillingly and artistically told in Laura Krey's *And Tell of Time*, which, though historical fiction, is a faithful picture of conditions as they prevailed in Texas after the war.

Any consideration of post-war conditions in Louisiana is complicated by the confusion in identity between the various protective organizations existing at that time, particularly the popular confusion of the Knights of the White Camelia with the Ku Klux Klan.

'The Joint Committee Upon the Conduct of the Late Election and the Present Condition of Peace and Order in the State' reported in January, 1869, that they were 'in possession of detailed, trustworthy and sworn information of the existence of a secret political and semi-military organization in this state styled "The Knights of the White Camelia". . . . The testimony before the committee shows that this order is the real organization which is known to the public as the Ku Klux . . . that mischievous and unlawful society.' The Committee's report further said that 'Large numbers of respectable Southern law-abiding citizens were, in the political excitement preceding the late election, drawn into this society. Most of such men we believe to have been ignorant of its real character and designs. Such men are rapidly withdrawing from its folds. The time is not far distant when it will be abandoned to the reckless and lawless portions of society, who have everything to gain and nothing to lose by tumult, violence and anarchy.'

This was a fairly accurate prediction of the trend to be taken by the members of such societies in some sections of the state; but the Committee was in error in presuming that the Knights of the White Camelia and the Ku Klux were identical. As a matter of fact, there were many prominent men who were members of the White Camelia and were proud of their membership, making no secret of it; but they all denied any connection between that order and the Ku Klux, generally condemning the excesses attributed to the Klan. The situation was complicated by the fact that in some instances reckless individuals would join the White Camelia and would then disguise themselves in the costumes popularly associated with the Ku Klux and make raids. These were acts of individual initiative; but when it became known that members of the White Camelia were indulging in such excesses, it was not unnatural for the uninitiated to conclude that the two orders were one and the same.

All students of Reconstruction affairs in Louisiana seem agreed, however, that such a view of the matter was erroneous. John Rose Ficklen in his *History of Reconstruction in Louisiana* says: 'The Ku Klux Klan was quite distinct in its methods, if not in its objects, from the Knights of the White Camelia, and the latter generally denied that the Klan existed in Louisiana. It seems true that as an organization it did not exist, but the testimony of many witnesses shows that reckless bands of whites did disguise themselves and, adopting the methods of the order as it existed in other states, did range some of the country parishes at night, intimidating the ignorant, superstitious darkies and endeavoring to frighten away the more extreme of the Radical whites.'

In an article on 'The White League in Louisiana' H. Oscar Lestage, Jr., said: 'The Ku Klux Klan probably never existed in Louisiana, yet various leagues such as the Knights of the White Camelia, Seymour and Blair Societies, Innocents, and other Democratic clubs, were prominent over the entire state. All had "white supremacy" as an ultimate aim. Despite efforts to check radical clubs, many outrageous deeds were committed in some localities. At first only negroes were intimidated, but in a short time even white immigrants from other states were robbed and plundered. It was not long, however, before legitimate organizations put to rout almost all of the clandestine groups.'

The Reconstruction period in Louisiana was punctuated by frequent outbreaks of violence in various parts of the state, and riots and riotous demonstrations were common occurrences in New Orleans and the other cities as well as in the country parishes. As one government report expressed it, 'Predatory bands of colored men rode about, burning houses and threatening murder and outrage, while other bodies of idle white men pursued them or engaged in similar amusements on their own account.' This state of affairs persisted in Louisiana longer probably than in any other Southern state; and it is hardly an exaggeration to say that for ten years following the close of the war Louisiana was in a condition bordering on anarchy.

Disorder was rampant in the state. In Colfax a band of three hundred negroes seized the town and barricaded themselves in the courthouse; and when attacked by the sheriff and a posse of one hundred and fifty white men an engagement ensued in which sixty men were killed on both sides and the courthouse and its contents burned. There was a bloody affray in Opelousas, when bands of armed negroes marched on the town and were met by an armed body of the townspeople, several on each side being killed. In St. Bernard Parish a white family was murdered by some negroes, which brought on retaliatory measures which almost precipitated a race war. A political marching club composed of negroes attacked a white restaurant in New Orleans, resulting in the loss of several lives in the ensuing fracas.

In their spontaneous acts of retaliation and defense the white people frequently resorted to disguises, resembling the Ku Klux costume, and rather encouraged the impression that they were members of a far-flung secret organization. 'Some sixty or seventy armed men, with masks on their faces and white sheets on their horses' seized and destroyed the ballots just prior to the election in Franklinton in Washington Parish. In Franklinton the negroes who voted the Democratic ticket were given written certificates to that effect, without which they were unable to buy goods from the leading stores. These certificates were signed 'R. Babington, Secretary'; and the Radicals jumped to the conclusion that Mr. Babington was secretary of the local Ku Klux Klan. At Trenton in Ouachita Parish a 'party of white men, dressed in black robes and their faces painted black' burned five houses occupied by negroes suspected of organized stealing. A mob twice destroyed the plant of the Radical newspaper published in Alexandria, the *Rapides Tribune*. M. J. Lemmon the agent of the Freedmen's Bureau in Catahoula Parish, found tied to a corncob on his front porch a note signed 'K.K.K.' warning him to leave town. In Union Parish there was a Central Democratic Club, and negroes were induced to join it and vote Democratic by the representation that by so doing they would be protected from the Ku Klux. In Sabine Parish there was an organization, which dressed in white sheets and was locally known as the Ku Klux, which specialized in punishing white

men for stealing hogs. Explaining this unusual chromatic dis-
crimination, a witness said: 'They seemed to think the negroes
had the privilege to steal hogs; but a white man stealing hogs,
they would go for him.' Apparently emboldened by this immunity, a negro took a white man's horse out of his barn and cut
his throat; whereupon the regulators hanged the offending
negro. They also began to notify obnoxious persons to leave
town, whereupon, the witness related: 'We held a meeting and
stopped it. When they were driving out hog thieves we didn't
care about it, but when they tried to drive out good citizens we
stopped it.'

W. A. Moulton, chairman of the Board of Supervisors of
Morehouse Parish, received a notice signed 'K.K.K.' warning
him to leave the parish. This notice said:

Old Graveyard — The Hour of Midnight

W. A. Moulton:

The time has come! Nine (9) days is left you! The time is
yours! Improve it! or suffer the penalty! The pale-faces are
against you! Depart, ye cursed! We *cannot* live together! Nine
days!

K.K.K.

Thomas Hudnall, a strong pro-Union man of Morehouse
Parish, testified that 'While under the influence of liquor, Dr.
Tom Tourdain told me that he belonged to the Ku Klux Klan
and that the order had effected a thorough organization in the
Parish of Morehouse and that they were cooperating with those
of Franklin Parish.'

At Tangipahoa in St. Helen Parish there were reports
of a band of armed men, 'their horses as well as themselves
covered with white sheets, *en masque*,' who went about to negroes'
homes frightening them; and in Claiborne Parish there were 'a
number of reckless men prowling about intimidating negroes.'

In Claiborne such a band killed a carpetbagger agitator named W. R. Meadows who preached social equality to the negroes and brought on his death by making a public speech in which he told them that 'Now is a good time to get white wives.'

An apparently deliberate effort to cow the negroes is to be seen in an article which appeared in the *Planters Banner* of Franklin, early in 1868, in which it was alleged that the Ku Klux were operating in St. Mary, Attakapas and other parishes, with devastating results. 'The negroes of Lafayette parish,' it said, 'were lately nearly all of them preparing to leave, the K.K.K.'s having frightened them every night and carried off a carpetbagger from Illinois. One negro, a big-talking Radical, somewhere in the Parish of St. Martin, was lately carried off by these Confederate ghosts at night and has never been heard of since. A night traveler called at the negro quarters, somewhere in Attakapas, and asked for water. After he had drunk three buckets full of good cistern water, at which the negro was much astonished, he thanked the colored man and told him he was very thirsty, that he had traveled nearly a thousand miles in 24 hours and that was the best drink of water he had had since he was killed at the Battle of Shiloh. The negro dropped the bucket, tumbled over two chairs and a table, escaped through a back window and has not since been heard from. He was a Radical negro. White men on white horses have lately been seen sailing through the air at midnight at Pattersonville, Jeanerette and at various places all over the southern part of the state. If negroes attempt to run away from the K.K.K.'s these spirits always follow them and catch them, and no living man hears from them again. The leader of this new order is said to be perfectly terrible. He is 10 feet high and his horse is 15. He carries a lance and shield like those of Goliath of the Philistines.'

This seems to have been obviously an effort to intimidate the negroes by means of an appeal to their superstitious fears; but, with such propaganda publicly appearing, it is not surprising that the general public should fall into the habit of charging all sorts of violence and disorder to the Ku Klux Slate. The Committee on Contested Elections drew the proper distinction when they reported that 'The evidence of the existence of Ku Klux methods in Louisiana, though not of any organization connected with the parent association, is found abundantly.' The Committee from the House of Representatives which in 1873 investigated conditions in Louisiana, however, attributed all such depredations to the Ku Klux. In its report it stated that more than two thousand persons had been 'killed, wounded and otherwise injured' in the state during the presidential election in 1872, and that 'midnight raids, secret murders and open riot kept the people in constant terror.' In St. Landry Parish, it was stated, occurred 'one of the bloodiest riots on record, in which the Ku Klux killed and wounded over 200 Republicans, hunting and chasing them for two days and nights through fields and swamps.' Aside from the fact that this was undoubtedly a gross exaggeration of the number killed, it is also in error in attributing all this disorder to the Ku Klux — except as the name had come to be applied loosely, if inaccurately, to all violence of this kind. There were certainly no Ku Klux Klans operating in Louisiana (or anywhere else) in 1872, if there had ever been any in the state at all; but the Ku Klux had made their name a synonym for any sort of defensive or punitive violence, and it was the common tag for everything of the kind.

Louisiana's Reconstruction period was a peculiarly turbulent and tumultuous one, featured by riotous factional rivalries which kept public affairs in a constant stir. General W. H. Emory, in charge of the United States troops in New Orleans, described the state government as 'odious beyond expression' and 'distasteful to all parties, Republicans and Democrats, black and white'; but this odious and universally despised set of state officials managed by various devices to continue in office for a painfully long period. Opposition to this misrule being impossible of effective expression in any legal manner, it found its manifestation in armed rebellion almost amounting to revolution; but the organizations which finally ousted the birds of prey from the state were the White League and the Knights of the White Camelia; and the Ku Klux Klan cannot be given the credit for the rescue of Louisiana from the hands of its despoilers.

PART III

The Decline of the Empire

XIII.   THE CONGRESSIONAL INVESTIGATION

THE ATTENTION OF THE COUNTRY AT LARGE was first focussed on the Ku Klux Klan by President Grant's special message to Congress on December 5, 1870, in which he declared that the 'free exercise of franchise has by violence and intimidation been denied to citizens in several of the states lately in rebellion,' he having been moved to this action by the continued outcries from Governor Holden of North Carolina, who was clamorously appealing for the help of the Federal Government, alleging that the Ku Klux had North Carolina in a state of terror by their acts of violence.

Following the President's message, Senator Morton introduced a resolution in the Senate calling on him for information in his possession as to 'disloyal or evil-designed organizations' in North Carolina; and Grant on January 13 submitted a reply in which he listed nearly five thousand alleged disorders, outrages and homicides in North Carolina and elsewhere.

Accordingly a select committee from the Senate was sent down to investigate affairs in North Carolina, and this committee made its report on March 10. The majority declared with emphasis that 'the Ku Klux organization does exist,' and that it was indulging in a carnival of murders, intimidation and violence of all kinds; but the minority report said that the reports had been 'grossly and wilfully exaggerated.' The majority also reported that while engaged in prosecuting their inquiry in North Carolina they had received many complaints of insecurity from Ku Klux outrages in other states, suggesting the possibility that the public interest might be served by the further pursuit of the investigation on a larger, South-wide scale.

Following this committee's report, President Grant on March 23 sent a message to Congress calling on them to take some action which would 'effectively secure life, liberty and property and the enforcement of the laws in all parts of the United States.' The suggestion of a need for further Federal legislation was expressed in these words: 'That the power to correct these evils is beyond the control of state authorities I do not doubt. That the power of the Executive of the United States, acting within the limits of existing laws, is sufficient for present emergencies, is not clear.'

Congress responded to this invitation by enacting the infamous Ku Klux Law, officially designated as 'An act to enforce the provisions of the Fourteenth Amendment to the Constitution of the United States, and for other purposes'; and this 'other purposes' included such outrageous forms of prostitution of popular government as to bring down on the law the execration of fair-minded people of all parties in all sections of the country. Besides passing this law, Congress also adopted a resolution calling for the appointment of a Joint Select Committee of members of the Senate and the House of Representatives whose duty it should be 'to inquire into the condition of the late insurrectionary states.' The resolution was passed on April 7, and the members of the committee were appointed promptly within a few days by both branches.

The committee was composed of the following seven Senators and fourteen Representatives: Senators: John Scott, chairman; Zachariah Chandler, Benjamin F. Rice, T. F. Bayard, Frank P. Blair, John Pool, and Daniel D. Pratt. Representatives: Luke P. Poland, chairman; Horace Maynard, Glenni W

Scofield, Burton C. Cook, John Coburn, Job E. Stevenson, Charles W. Buckley, William E. Lansing, Samuel S. Cox, James B. Beck, Daniel W. Voorhees, Philadelph Van Trump, Alfred M. Waddell, and James C. Robinson. During the course of the hearings Messrs. Buckley, Cook, and Voorhees retired from membership on the committee, and were replaced by John F. Farnsworth, Benjamin F. Butler, and James M. Hanks, the political balance remaining undisturbed — thirteen Republicans and eight Democrats.

The first meeting of the committee was held on April 20, Senator Scott being elected chairman of the joint committee, and a sub-committee was appointed to prepare a plan of procedure. The next meeting was held on May 17, when (after voting to pay themselves eight dollars a day for expenses in addition to mileage at ten cents a mile) they voted to set up a sub-committee of eight which would proceed at once with the investigation by holding hearings in Washington to which witnesses would be called, with authority to take testimony wherever they considered advisable by a sub-committee of their own number. This sub-committee was instructed to report to a meeting of the full committee in Washington on September 20, at which time other sub-committees were to be appointed to visit such localities in the South as the sub-committee should report to be 'in a disturbed condition.' The sub-committee of eight was made up of Messrs. Scott and Poland, as chairmen of their respective Senate and House Committees, together with Messrs. Pool, Blair, Coburn, Stevenson, Beck, and Van Trump.

Before adjournment of the first organization meeting, while plans for the course of procedure were being discussed, Senator Bayard introduced a resolution providing that in the examination of witnesses the investigation should be governed by the legal rules of evidence prevailing in the courts. Mr. Van Trump submitted a proposal that in taking testimony 'mere rumors

and what is known in the courts as hearsay testimony' should
be excluded. Senator Bayard also proposed that witnesses
should be limited in their testimony to facts existing at the
time or which had occurred since the enactment of the law
providing for the investigation.

All these precautionary proposals were rejected, however,
with the result that what purported to be an official fact-finding
investigation degenerated into a clearing-house for the threshing
over of any and all rumors concerning any disorder which may
have been attributed to the Ku Klux since the end of the war.
There was, of course, a great deal of valuable factual information developed by the investigation; but there was also a lot of
obviously idle gossip, and more than a little plain, old-fashioned
lying. Any witnesses who showed any hesitancy about testifying
to matters beyond their personal knowledge were quickly informed that the bars were down and that they might tell about
anything they had heard in the way of rumor or gossip, with
the result that the facts are hopelessly buried in a mass of other
material of very doubtful credibility.

The Committee's value as an effective investigatory and
deliberative body was seriously lessened by the sharp line of
cleavage which immediately developed between the thirteen
Republicans and the eight Democrats constituting its membership; and in the examination of witnesses, both at Washington
and at various points in the South, politics was very clearly
one of the governing factors in the proceedings. The Republican
members diligently sought to establish from the witnesses that
the Ku Klux Klan was a political organization, composed exclusively of Democrats, and designed primarily for the persecution of Republicans, black and white, and especially for the
intimidation of negro voters. The Democrats, on the other
hand, worked just as hard to sustain the theory that the Ku
Klux had no political purposes whatever, that they did not
concern themselves with the politics of their victims, but were

organized and operated entirely as a widespread vigilance committee for the preservation of law and order.

The examination of witnesses was a travesty on the ordinary, established system of legal procedure. Leading questions were the customary thing; that witnesses had been coached and drilled was freely charged, and apparently not without some basis; testimony was easily put into the mouths of ignorant and unsophisticated witnesses; and when some conscientious witness displayed hesitation about testifying to something of which he had no knowledge he was heartily assured that he need feel no qualms about retailing all the loose rumors and gossip he had heard. This resulted in the development of some very sensational and racy testimony; but it is doubtful whether it contributed anything to the legitimate objectives of a fact-finding body.

The sub-committee of eight held its first meeting in Washington on May 20, adjourned until June 1, and really got down to business with the examination of witnesses on June 5. The committee continued diligently with its hearings until July 30, when a sub-committee of three, Messrs. Pool, Blair and Buckley, was appointed to finish up with the examination of all witnesses on hand or on the way to Washington and then adjourn, the last hearing being held on August 4. Meanwhile a sub-sub-committee of three, headed by Senator Scott, had been sent to North and South Carolina to investigate conditions there; and this committee returned and made an oral report on July 31.

The entire personnel of the Joint Select Committee resumed its activities on September 20; and immediately two sub-committees of five each were appointed to go to the South and conduct hearings there. Messrs. Maynard, Scofield, Lansing, Bayard and Voorhees constituted the committee to visit the Carolinas, Georgia and Florida; and Messrs. Pratt, Rice, Buckley, Blair and Robinson were sent to Tennessee, Alabama and Mississippi. Having done this, the Joint Select Committee adjourned to meet on the first day of the next session of Congress.

Accordingly the whole committee met in Washington on December 6, but immediately took an adjournment to December 21. The sub-committees having meanwhile visited the Southern states designated and carried on their local investigations, the reports of these committees were received on December 21, and adjournment was then taken until January 23. Routine business was transacted at this meeting and at subsequent meetings on February 10, 15, 17 and 19, when the committee finally adjourned, after having authorized the printing of forty thousand copies of its report.

The final report as published is a monumental and forbidding affair, constituting thirteen octavo volumes of closely printed small type. One volume contains the majority and minority reports; and the remaining twelve are devoted to a stenographic report of the testimony taken at the hearings held in Washington and throughout the South. Here is preserved a verbatim account of all that was said by the hundreds and hundreds of witnesses examined, ranging from the most ignorant and illiterate negroes to the leading and most cultured white citizens. During the days this committee was sitting there streamed before it an amazingly varied array of humanity. There were governors and senators and representatives, state legislators, mayors, sheriffs, coroners and office-holders of all grades, color and character. There were United States Army officers and ex-Confederate generals, not to mention veteran soldiers of all ranks who had served in the recent war. There were lawyers and doctors and editors and saloonkeepers and butchers, grocerymen, farmers, moonshine distillers, barbers, horse-doctors, millers, tailors, druggists and livery-stable proprietors. There were schoolteachers and preachers in profusion, black and white. There were negroes by the score, a few of them educated but most of them grossly and pitifully illiterate. Some of the negroes did not know what state they lived in; many of them went by two or three different names, as their

fancy guided them. This multiplicity of names was a constant
source of confusion to the investigators from the North, who
never seemed quite able to understand how a witness could
refer severally to Tom Wilson and Ike Harper and Charlie
Johnson and be talking about the same negro all the time.
One negro preacher who called himself Isaac the Apostle was
summoned, and gravely recorded on the record as 'Isaac A.
Postle' and his wife as 'Mrs. Postle.' A negro known as Doc
Huskie was entered as Doctor Huskie, and the examining
Senator politely asked him: 'Are you a physician?' to which
the grinning negro replied: 'I ain't no doctor; they just calls
me doctor.'

Members of the committee were frequently baffled by the
colloquial expressions of the witnesses, particularly the negroes.
'He got a deef and dumb letter,' one of them stated, whereupon
he was interrupted by a bewildered Senator who asked: 'He
got a what?' 'A deef and dumb letter,' the negro repeated.
'You know — a letter without no name signed to it.'

Another source of confusion was the manner in which so
many of the negro witnesses, unfamiliar with the intricacies
of the Gregorian calendar, would set the time of some occurrence. In Georgia a witness told how some event took place
at 'goober digging time.' 'And when do you dig goobers?'
patiently inquired one of the urban committeemen. 'In the
spring or in the fall?' Other witnesses would use such expressions as 'It was along about wheat sowing time'; or 'It was just
after the crops was laid by'; or 'It was along about the time we
plowed corn the second time.' And it took the members of the
committee a long time to understand that when a man in the
South said 'evening' he meant the whole period of time between noon and dark. One negro explained his uncertainty
about the time of an event by saying: 'I can't keep no books —
I can't read nor write my own name, much less keep books;
but it was in April some time.'

The volubility and rambling garrulity of the negro witnesses frequently exhausted the patience of the investigators, but they were seldom successful in their efforts to make a loquacious negro witness come to the point without wandering over a lot of extraneous territory. 'Never mind all those details; get on with your story,' the investigators would wearily interrupt; but the average negro witness valued too highly this one gorgeous opportunity to tell his story to an appreciative audience, and he generally insisted on going into all the most elaborate details of what the Ku Klux said and did to him and what he said and did to them. And, of course, he invariably protested his entire innocence of any offense which might have incurred the Ku Klux displeasure.

'I don't know anything that I had said or done that injured anyone, further than being a radical in that part of the land,' said William Coleman (colored) of Winston County, Mississippi, and then went on with a typically rambling and attenuated story, from which no details were omitted, no matter how irrelevant. 'As for interrupting anyone,' he continued, 'I didn't; for I had plenty of my own of anything that I wanted myself. I had done bought my land and paid for it, and I had a great deal of hogs; I had eighteen head of hogs to kill this fall. I had twelve head of sheep, and one good milk cow, and a yearling, and the cow had a right young calf again, and I had my mule and my filly, and all of it was paid for but my mule, and I had my brother hired to pay for him. It was like I was getting the mule from you, and you wanted a hand to work the value of the mule out in work.'

Here the chairman interrupted him in an effort to get him back on the subject: 'Did any of the Ku Klux come to your house?' And Coleman was off again:

'They did. They come about a half hour or more before day, as nigh as I can recollect, by my brains being frightened at their coming up this kind of way. They were shooting and going on at me through the house, and when they busted the door open, coming in shooting, I was frightened, and I can only tell you as nigh as my recollection will afford at this time that it was about a half hour to day. None of the shot hit me, but they aimed to hit me; but I had one door just like that at the side of the house and the other at this side, and there was the chimney, and there was my bed in that corner opposite, and they came first to that door (illustrating) and hollered "Hallo"; bum, bum, bum on the lock. I jumped up and said "Hallo." Then one at the door said "Raise a light in there." "What for; who is you?" I said. He says, "Raise a light in there, God damn you; or I'll come in there and smoke my pipe in your ear." He said that, just so. I said, "Is that you, Uncle Davy?" Said he, "No, God damn you, it isn't Uncle Davy; open that door." Says I, "I am not going to open my door to turn nobody on me that won't tell who they are before I do it. Who are you?" He says, "God damn you, we didn't come to tell you who we are."

'I was peeping through the little hole in the door. I had bored a gimlet hole about as big as that pen to put a string through, and had a latch inside so that when I had been off at work anywhere and happened to come home at night I could open the door without my wife having to get up, and she would put the string through the door and I would pull it and that was the way I would get in. So I looked through this hole and I saw men standing out there with horns and faces on all of them, and they all had great long cow-tails down the breast. (I said it was a cow-tail; it was hair, and it was right white.) They told me they rode from Shiloh in two hours, and come to kill me.

'They shot right smart into the house before they got in, but how many times I don't know, they shot so fast outside; but when they come in they didn't have but three loads to shoot. I know by the way they tangled about in the house they would have put it in me if they had had it; but they only shot three times in the house. The men behind me had busted through that door; both doors were busted open. By the time the fellows at the back door had got in that door, those fellows at the front door busted in and they all met in the middle of the floor, and I didn't have a thing to fight with, only a little piece of ax-handle; and when I started from the first door to the second, pieces of the door flew and met me. I jumped for a piece of ax-handle and fought them, squandering about, and they were knocking about me with guns and firing balls that cut several holes in my head. The notches is in my head now.

'I dashed about among them, but they knocked me down several times. Every time I would get up they would knock me down again. I saw they were going to kill me, and I turned in and laid there after they had knocked me down so many times. The last time they knocked me down I laid there a good while before I moved, and when I had strength I jumped to split between a man's legs that was standing over me, and as I jumped they struck at me jumping between his legs, and they struck him and he hollered, "Don't hit me, God damn you"; but they done knocked him down then, though they hadn't knocked him so he couldn't talk. They surrounded me on the floor and tore my shirt off. Some had me by the legs and some by the arms and neck and anywhere, just like dogs string out a coon, and they took me out to the big road before my gate and whipped me until I couldn't move or holler or do nothing but just lay there like a log, and every lick they hit me I grunted just like a mule when he is stalled fast and whipped.'

Interrogated as to the reasons assigned for whipping him, Coleman continued: 'They told me, "God damn you, when you meet a white man in the road, lift your hat. I'll learn you, God damn you, that you are a nigger and not to be going about like you thought yourself a white man. You calls yourself like you was a white man, God damn you." But here is what I put it to: Because I had my filly; I had bought her to ride, not to stand in the stable, but to ride when I got ready, like you would do with your property. When I bought her I bought her for $75. She was not nigh grown, a little thing with flaxen mane and tail, and light cream-color, and I would get on my filly on a Saturday evening and ride. I would work until Saturday evening, but I won't work no longer for no man, for my own work or for nobody else, unless it is mighty urgent; then I will go on until night. But if it is nothing but work, straight along, I will work until Saturday at twelve o'clock, and I will strike off then. I believe if a man does it all over the world, he can make an honest living and put his work to good use.'

But at length, worn out by all this tedious and interminable narrative, the chairman interrupted to say:

'Leave out all those little particulars and come to the point.' Whereupon Coleman, in injured dignity, retorted:

'I have to tell it going along straight, and if I do I will tell you the whole truth; but if you push me over as I am going along, I will get out of the way and tell no truth, because I will not go straight through with it.' So the defeated chairman crumpled and said weakly:

'Take your own way and go on.' And Coleman went on, telling of his own troubles until he had wrung the last gory detail out of that, and then continuing to tell of all the other Ku Klux victims he had ever heard about. Sol Triplett, a brother in the church, had been killed — 'by the Ku Klux, so said to be,' although not disguised in any way. He did not know why Sol was killed. 'I lived so far from him, when I got the chance to go down there I had enough to talk about about the church affairs, without raking up those scattering things about what had been done in the neighborhood.' If the church

needed a new roof, or if there was a fish-fry or a basket picnic
to be arranged, how could anybody be expected to have time
to devote to delving into the cause of the demise of Brother
Sol Triplett? Then there was the case of another brother in
the church, Mose Bird. Mose had had the bad judgment to
get himself embroiled in an altercation with a white man
named Jim Boyd Hughes, a reputed member of the Ku Klux.
As Coleman related it, with graphic brevity: 'They had a little
falling out about something. Mose, he knocked Jim Boyd on
the head with a rock and cut his head open. And the first
thing anybody knows, Mose Bird was dead. Nobody heard
hide nor hair of Mose Bird since.' Was he afraid to go back
to Winston County? he was finally asked. And Coleman
climaxed his dramatic if tedious story with the eloquent declaration: 'I wouldn't go back there if I had a gold piece of land
there. My life is better to me than anything there. I would
not go back there if there was gold there higher than one of
these pine trees.'

Some of the negroes made good witnesses and told graphic
and convincing stories which had the ring of truth. Some had
very obviously been coached. Some became hopelessly tangled
in their own lies upon cross-examination. Fairly typical of
this type of testimony was that of an ignorant old negro preacher
named George Roper who was the principal witness called to
appear before the committee in Huntsville, Alabama, to tell
them about conditions there. In the course of his direct testimony, which was of a rambling, self-laudatory nature, he
remarked that he had been offered his hat full of money 'to
vote on the other side.' When cross-examined by Mr. Beck
there ensued the following illuminating exchange of questions
and evasive and non-responsive answers:

'Who was it offered you your hat full of money to vote the
Democratic ticket?'

'Nobody. I told the boys around: "Boys, have good principles;

hold your head up right; for if I was offered today my hat full of money for my principles, I would not sell it." '

'You said: "I wouldn't tell a lie for nothing, for I refused my hat full of money to vote on the other side" ' said Mr. Beck, reading from the stenographic record. 'Why did you make that statement yesterday?' And George, thinking that the gentleman was just quoting what he had said from memory, protested:

'Well, sir, you misunderstood me fairly. I said to the colored people that I wouldn't take my hat full of money. I refused my hat full of money for my principles, that is what I said. You misunderstood me fairly.'

'Can you read or write?' asked Mr. Beck, starting off on another tack.

'No, sir.'

'How do you get your information sufficient to be a political teacher?'

'Well, sir, from going and seeking to God, for what little wisdom I have — mother's wisdom; I have got no learning. I haven't learning as much as a school-boy, but seeking to God night and day for what little I have got, and I wouldn't tell you nor no man a lie, for I have been tried; and the reason I said so was because the boys were doubtful, and didn't know which way they was going, and that is the time my mother's wisdom come in, and I said "Boys, come here and vote the ticket right, for this morning I wouldn't take a hat full of money for my principles." '

'Being unable to read or write, and having none of the ordinary sources of obtaining information, you looked to the Lord for it and got it?'

'Yes, sir.'

'The Lord heard your prayers?'

'Yes, sir; I can tell you where he fetched me.'

'Where?'

'He fetched me from hell's dark door to the marvelous light, so that things I thought in sinful days, when I came to the light of God, I said all that is fallen back of me, and now I start myself right before everybody.'

'Do you know of any other cases of colored people in this land where the Lord has instilled political knowledge into them?'

'Yes, sir. Many has come through the way, and some of them said the Lord sent them to preach the Gospel, but they can't read or write.'

'I can understand how He interferes with preaching, but what object did you think He had in interfering with politics and filling your mind with political wisdom?'

'Because why. I fought for my liberty and have been all through the Army, and what did my captain and colonel tell me? "George," he said, "the day you are turned out of service, be right, be pure to God and just to all men. Hold up your head; touch not and handle nothing of the unclean thing."'

'Whatever you know outside of what the Lord gave you, you picked up from other people's talk?'

'Not much from other poeple, because they can't learn me.'

'You can not read or write?'

'But the pureness of heart must come from God.' And the cross-examining congressman gave up.

There were numerous witnesses examined who were suspected of being members of the Ku Klux Klan; but, aside from those who had already confessed and turned state's evidence in some criminal suit, they mostly stood up well under cross-examination. They entered a blunt denial of any knowledge of the Ku Klux Klan or its works generally, and refused to be perturbed by pointed questioning; but occasionally one would lose his composure under the strain, as did Barnett Russell, a young farmer who lived in the country near Spartanburg, South Carolina. He was getting along swimmingly in his testimony until suddenly confronted with the information that a previous witness, a negro named Julius Cantrell, had sworn that Russell confessed to him that he was a member of the Ku Klux and had been out with them on several of their raids. When informed of Cantrell's accusation, Russell lost all his *sang-froid* and exploded in a Homeric tirade of profane indignation. 'He has sworn to a lie,' he burst out, 'as sure as God Almighty stands in heaven this day.' Then, rising from his seat on the witness stand, he continued excitedly and in a loud voice: 'I will stand up on a stack of Bibles and swear it till I die. If he has not sworn a lie essentially, God damn me. He swore a lie, the God damned nigger to hell. The niggers is here for nothing but to swear lies. Witnesses has been brung up to this place of the lowest-down character that can be brung up in Spartanburg district, and I can prove it by hundreds; I'll be God damn my soul.' Stunned by this torrent of irate and sulphuric incoherence, Chairman Scott could only admonish him weakly: 'That will do; sit down. Remember where you are. We have had enough of that.'

Some of the white witnesses were very plainly not telling all that they knew, notably General Forrest and other suspected leaders in the Ku Klux organization. As one of the members of the investigating committee caustically remarked, 'They practiced disguise in their sentiments and conversation as much as in their costume'; and there was abundant evidence of this in the testimony of many of those examined by the committee. Some of these were notoriously active in it and generally reputed to be officials in it; but the most rabid carpetbagger could not have been more emphatic in denial and censure than some of them.

The weaving circumlocution of General Forrest was by no means unique. General James H. Clanton, for example, an ex-general in the Confederate army, testified that he did not think there had ever been an organization in his state, Alabama, known as the Ku Klux Klan. There had been some disorders by disguised men, so he had heard; but, he said, 'I infer they

are reckless, irresponsible characters.' Pressed for specific
instances of outrages, he mentioned one or two of the more
notorious affairs, concerning which he said he knew none of the
details, and went on: 'I have heard of other outrages, but
mostly by negroes. In the county of Macon, Jim Allston, a
colored Republican member of the legislature, was shot in his
bed as he and his wife were retiring. He charged a colored rival
in the legislature and two accomplices with shooting him.' There
were white men who did such things, too, General Clanton admitted; but he declared: 'So help me, God; I have never known
one who was concerned in it.'

In view of this emphatic and unequivocal disavowal, there is
probably no foundation for the widely accepted theory that
General Clanton was the first Grand Dragon of the Realm of
Alabama in the original Invisible Empire — unless we bear in
mind the ingenious casuistry of the Ku Klux by which they
justified themselves in saying that they were not members of the
Ku Klux Klan because they themselves never called it by that
name. According to popular belief in Alabama General
Clanton was succeeded as Grand Dragon in that state by
General William H. Forney; but this also must have been a
popular error, as General Forney, when examined, disclaimed
all knowledge of it. Asked the point-blank question: 'Is there
any secret organization of disguised persons whose purpose it is
to resist the law?' General Forney blandly replied: 'There is no
organization (in Alabama) to resist the law.' Inasmuch as the
original Ku Klux Klan had been formally disbanded nearly
two years before this question was asked and answered, and inasmuch as no member of the Ku Klux would ever admit that
its purpose was to resist the law, General Forney was perhaps
technically truthful in his reply, even though he may have given
a slightly false impression.

Such denials, evasions and equivocations were characteristic
of the testimony of all the suspected leaders of the Ku Klux in

the various states and communities where hearings were held. For men so prominent in public life and well informed on all other topics, they displayed a surprising lack of knowledge about the operations of the Ku Klux Klan. 'See no evil; hear no evil; think no evil' was their motto; and they simply could not bring themselves to believe that there existed any such band of marauders as the Ku Klux Klan.

With all its inherent shortcomings and weaknesses, the published report of the investigating committee is a veritable treasure-house of information regarding the social and political conditions existing in the South during the Reconstruction; but to arrive at a proper appreciation of its value, the wheat of the truth must be carefully winnowed out of the chaff of rumor and mendacity; and the testimony of each witness must be considered and weighed in the light of his own background, character and personal interests.

It is also important to know something of the personnel of the committee itself, and for that purpose a brief sketch of each member is included in the Appendix.

XIV.   THE GRAND WIZARD OF THE EMPIRE

In any consideration of any organization, secret or otherwise, one of the first things we naturally want to know is: Who was at the head of it; who was its chief officer or guiding spirit? We have seen that in the formal organization of the Ku Klux Klan the ruler of the Empire was the Grand Wizard. But who was the Grand Wizard? It required an executive officer of more than ordinary ability to head such a movement as this and maintain it successfully in the face of the United States Government and an army of occupation. It required not only an able man, but a man of lion-hearted courage, a bold and unafraid spirit.

In the nature of things, such an organization as the Ku Klux Klan could have no written records. It left no archives to which the curious researcher may refer. There is, therefore, no documentary evidence to support it, but the statement may be safely and authoritatively made that the first, last and only Grand Wizard of the original and only Ku Klux Klan was General Nathan Bedford Forrest, the celebrated Confederate cavalry leader who was the idol of the South.

There is a story to the effect that when the Klan was first put on an organized basis there was a movement started to induce General Robert E. Lee to become its head, and that a committee went to Virginia to lay the matter before him. He, so the story goes, told the committee that he was physically unable to take an active part in such a movement but that he approved of the idea and would give it his support, although his support must be invisible. From this remark, according to this story, originated the designation 'The Invisible Empire' by which the order came to be known. This story has had more or less wide currency in the South; but Douglas S. Freeman, the foremost authority on the life of Lee, after studying and investigating the tradition dismissed it as having no credible foundation.

It has always been the understanding of all Southern people, however, that General Forrest was the head of the Ku Klux. Men known to have been members of the Klan have been unanimous in ascribing to him this office; his own family's traditions are to that effect; and at least one avowed member of the Klan in Nashville has left written testimony that he was present when the office was bestowed on Forrest.

Doctor John A. Wyeth, General Forrest's foremost biographer, said that in writing his biography he gave careful thought to the general supposition that Forrest was the Grand Wizard of the Ku Klux, but came to the conclusion that Forrest was not a member and took no part in the organization of the order. Doctor Wyeth expressed it as his opinion that Forrest was too shrewd to have placed himself in this position, since he was among the first who would have been suspected of complicity in such an activity. This, however, was only Doctor Wyeth's own personal and unsupported view.

Sharply at variance with Doctor Wyeth's opinion is the story that has always been told, and generally believed, in Tennessee. According to this story, General Forrest when he first heard of the activities of the organization called the Ku Klux in Middle Tennessee left his home in Memphis and journeyed to Nashville to look into the matter. In Nashville he straightway looked up Captain John W. Morton, who had been his chief of artillery during the war.

'John,' he said to Morton in his usual direct manner, 'I've heard about this Ku Klux Klan operating in Nashville or somewhere around here, and I know that if there is such a thing going on you are in it. I want to join.'

Captain Morton evaded the issue by inviting his old chieftain to go driving with him in his buggy before they started to talking about the Ku Klux. When they reached a secluded place on the outskirts of the city, Captain Morton suggested that they alight and take a walk through the woods. When they were completely out of sight of the road, Morton stopped and said: 'General, do you want to join the Ku Klux?' Forrest replied, somewhat testily: 'Didn't I tell you that that's what I came over here for?' Whereupon Morton, without further parley, said: 'Raise your right hand'; and then and there the preliminary oath of allegiance to the Invisible Empire was administered to its future Grand Wizard.

Morton explained that this was as far as he could go in the matter at that time, but told Forrest that that would be sufficient to admit him to the meeting of the Den to be held that night in Room No. 10 at the Maxwell House. Forrest attended the meeting that night, so the story goes, and was there made a full-fledged member of the order of which he was soon to be the recognized head.

A former member of the Ku Klux now living in Middle Tennessee relates a somewhat different version of this episode which he says he got from the lips of Captain Morton himself, who was an old crony of his. According to this story, one of the first initiates into the Klan at Pulaski was General George W. Gordon who, immediately recognizing its great possibilities as a regulatory body, went immediately to Memphis and told about it to General Forrest, who declared emphatically: 'That's a good thing; that's a damn good thing. We can use that to keep the niggers in their place.' Whereupon General Gordon not only swore Forrest in as a member of the order, but immediately conferred on him the office of Grand Wizard — by what authority is not quite clear. Later, so this story goes, Forrest visited Nashville and sought out Morton and, as a joke, started to quizzing him about 'this thing they call the Kookles or the Clucks or something like that.' Then when Morton took him to the secluded spot in the woods and offered to administer the oath to him, Forrest slapped him on the back, and, laughing uproariously, said: 'Why, you damned little fool, don't you know I'm the head of the whole damned thing?'

With all proper respect to the teller of this yarn, if Captain Morton told him any such story he doubtless did so with tongue in cheek or as a joke on himself; for that is certainly not the story he told when he started to putting things down in black and white. Morton wrote a book in 1909 entitled 'Forrest's Artillery' in which he tells the story, a highly colorful and dramatic one, of his services under the General during the war. No direct reference to his own or Forrest's connection with the Ku Klux Klan is included in the text of the book; but in the Appendix there is naïvely inserted an extraneous unsigned treatise entitled 'The Ku Klux Klan,' which includes a lengthy extract from an article written by Thomas Dixon, Jr., for the September, 1905, issue of the *Metropolitan Magazine,* in which is given a circumstantial story of Forrest's introduction into the mysteries of the Klan by Captain Morton as related. Mr. Dixon has since stated that he obtained his information directly from Captain Morton; and the fact that Morton included it in his book gives tacit endorsement to its authenticity, although even in 1909 it was not considered permissible for an ex-member of the mysterious brotherhood to admit openly that he had taken part in its activities forty years before or to give direct testimony as to the identity of the Grand Wizard. As a matter of fact, the extract from Doctor Dixon's article in Captain Morton's book is so amended with changes, corrections and interpolations as to be virtually Morton's own composition; and it certainly appears to have been his intention to give to the public this version of Forrest's initiation. Aside from Forrest himself, Captain Morton probably knew more about his former commander's connection with the order than any other person, as Forrest held him in the highest esteem and was his close friend and confidant; and there seems to be not the slightest reasonable doubt as to the fact that Forrest joined the Ku Klux Klan in Nashville, having gone there for that specific purpose, and that he later became its chief commanding officer.

Certain it is that when the Congressional Investigating Committee began to hold its series of hearings to get at the bottom of the Ku Klux matter, if they could, they lost no time in calling General Forrest before them to testify. They thought they had a pretty good idea of the identity of the head man of the order and they wanted to look him in the eye and talk with him. There is a tradition in Tennessee that shortly after General Forrest emerged from the ordeal of examination and cross-examination by the committee he was encountered by a friend who asked him what he had been doing and that he replied, promptly and proudly: 'I have been lying like a gentleman.' However much truth there may be in this reported conversation, it must be said that the printed record of the investigation shows that General Forrest was a good deal less than entirely frank with the committee, to put the mildest possible construction on his contradictions, evasions and strange lapses of memory. The various members of the committee pursued him relentlessly, but they were never able to pin him down.

Asked the point-blank question whether he had any actual knowledge of any such organization as the Ku Klux, General Forrest guardedly replied: 'I had, from information from others.' The committee, of course, was anxious to learn the names of these 'others'; but the best Forrest could do, after a lengthy round of verbal sparring, was to recall that one of those from whom he had received such information was a man by the name of Saunders. Mr. Saunders, however, it developed after a lot of questioning, had left Tennessee and moved to Asheville, North Carolina, where he had met the tragic fate of being poisoned by his wife. When the committee hopefully pressed on, seeking to ascertain the names of more of the 'others,' General Forrest by a stupendous effort of the memory recalled that he had also heard the matter discussed by two men who had 'gone out of the country.' The inquisitor bored in and the General finally recalled that 'one was named Jones.' Encouraged by this enlightening recollection, Chairman John Scott asked: 'What was his first name?' To which General Forrest replied, frankly and fearlessly: 'He has gone to Brazil, and has been there for two or three years.' Not dismayed, Senator Scott insisted: 'What was the name of the other?' But General Forrest could reply only: 'I am trying to think who he was; I can not call his name to mind now.'

At length recognizing the fact that this line of questioning was getting nowhere, Senator Stevenson interjected: 'I should like to have it understood that this witness will give us these names as soon as he can remember them. If he can not remember them in time to appear before the committee and give them, then he will send in writing to the chairman a list of such names as he may hereafter remember.' To this Chairman Scott responded dryly: 'That will be very desirable'; but the record does not disclose that General Forrest ever sent in any such list of names.

Under close and persistent questioning he admitted that there actually had been such an organization as the Ku Klux, but he attempted to minimize the significance of his admission by expressing the view that it did not exist anywhere except in Middle Tennessee and perhaps in a 'small portion of West Tennessee.' As to its name, he said: 'Some called them Pale

Faces; some called them Ku Klux. I believe they were under two names.' Then later, when the committee was trying to pin him down as to just where he had heard of the Ku Klux, this interesting colloquy ensued:

'Did you not hear of it in Louisiana?'

'No, sir.'

'Did you hear of the Knights of the White Camelia there?'

'Yes, they were reported to be there.'

'Were you ever a member of that order?'

'I was.'

'You were a member of the Knights of the White Camelia?'

'No, sir; I never was a member of the Knights of the White Camelia.'

'What order was it that you were a member of?'

'An order they called the Pale Faces, a different order from that.'

Having already testified that Pale Faces and Ku Klux were two names for the same thing, this seemed to identify General Forrest as being at least a member of the order of which he was the reputed chief officer, but it was impossible to trap him into making any such direct admission.

Had he ever seen a copy of the constitution of the Ku Klux? Yes, he saw one once in Memphis; some anonymous person sent it to him through the mails, he did not know why, and he had burned it.

'What was the name of the organization given in that constitution?'

'Ku Klux.'

'It was called Ku Klux?'

'No, sir; it was not called Ku Klux. I do not think there was any name given to it.'

'No name given to it?'

'No, sir; I do not think there was. As well as I recollect, there were three stars in place of a name.'

When the committee continued to quiz him insistently about this printed constitution, asking question after question concerning its provisions (his faulty memory failing to recall the desired information in each instance), General Forrest made one highly significant slip of the tongue.

After a long succession of 'I do not recollect,' 'I can not say,' 'I think not,' and similar evasions, he said: 'If I had thought that this thing would have come up in that shape, I would have tried to have gotten hold of one of these prescripts, as they were called, to give to you.'

The thoughtless use of the word 'prescript' provided evidence that the forgetful General knew more about the matter than he was willing to admit. Up to that time they had been talking about a 'constitution'; no use had been made of the word 'prescript,' the name by which it was known among the Ku Klux. The committee had in some way come into possession of one of the official Prescripts, and when General Forrest let his foot slip they pursued this line of attack with avidity.

'Did you act upon that prescript?' they asked him; to which he replied politely and positively: 'No, sir.' But the committee, with the Prescript in their hands, knew some of the duties of the Grand Wizard and they pressed him closely: 'Did you take any steps for organizing under it?' Whereupon Forrest burst out: 'I do not think I am compelled to answer any question that would implicate me in anything; I believe the law does not require that I should do anything of that sort.' 'Do you place your declination to answer upon that ground?' Chairman Scott asked suavely; but Forrest, recovering his composure, replied: 'I do not,' and continued his squirming, non-responsive answers to the committee's questions.

Asked if there were any organizations of the order in his neighborhood, he said he presumed there were but he could not recollect any of the members. Nettled by his continued vagueness, the chairman asked: 'Can you tell us who were the members, or any single member, of that organization?' 'Well, that is a question I do not want to answer now,' replied General Forrest.

Further pressed, he at length admitted that he knew the signs and passwords (somebody had told them to him) although he had 'never seen the organization together.' 'It was,' he said, 'a matter I knew very little about. I had very little to do with it. All my efforts were addressed to stop it, disband it, and prevent it.'

They pounced greedily on this. 'Did you want to suppress that organization?' he was asked. Then Forrest let his foot slip again and carelessly told the truth: 'Yes, sir; I did suppress it.' 'How?' 'Had it broken up and disbanded.' 'What influence did you exert in disbanding it?' But Forrest had had enough of his little experiment with telling the truth. Instead of stating what would have been the fact: 'I was the Grand Wizard of the Klan and, acting on my authority, I issued an order that the Klan be disbanded,' he said lamely: 'I talked with different people that I believed were connected with it, and urged its disbandment.' Perhaps exhausted by their unsuccessful efforts to wring any helpful information from him, the committee let it go at that.

Somewhat at variance with General Forrest's testimony before the committee, however, was an interview with him which was printed in the Cincinnati *Commercial* under date of September 1, 1868. This interview with the man who was popularly believed to be the head of the great Southern secret society created a nation-wide sensation; and Forrest promptly wrote a letter to the Cincinnati paper pointing out certain alleged inaccuracies in the interview — modifying certain too-frank admissions in it.

In the interview printed in the paper the correspondent stated that he asked General Forrest if there was such an organization as the Ku Klux in Tennessee at that time, to which Forrest was said to have replied:

'Well, sir, there is such an organization, not only in Tennessee but all over the South, and its numbers have not been exaggerated.'

'What are its numbers, General?'

'In Tennessee there are over 40,000; in all the Southern States about 550,000 men.'

That may have been a fairly accurate statement of the facts, so far as General Forrest knew at the time he was interviewed; but when he saw it printed in cold black and white he evidently realized that it indicated that he knew too much about the organization, and in his letter of correction to the paper he said: 'I said it was reported, and I believed the report, that there are 40,000 Ku Klux in Tennessee, and I believe the organization stronger in other states.' Confronted with this on the witness stand, General Forrest blandly said: 'So far as numbers were concerned, I made no statement.' But Senator Stevenson was not satisfied with this and, despite his denial, insisted on asking him if he had not told the interviewer that he believed there were forty thousand Ku Klux in Tennessee; General Forrest, however, stuck to his latest story: 'I did not, for I had no more idea than you have how many there were.'

The investigating committee's questioning of General Forrest brought them out the same hole they went in; but there was not a man on the committee who did not believe when Forrest stepped down from the stand that, despite his denials and evasions, they had been talking with the Grand Wizard of the Invisible Empire.

In the way of corroborative evidence, it is interesting to observe that the Prescript directly charges the Grand Wizard with the duty of establishing new Dens throughout the Empire; and, by some strange coincidence, new Dens seemed to blossom and flourish wherever General Forrest went in the South. His home was in Memphis, and the Ku Klux organization quickly fanned out through the counties of eastern Arkansas. He had some 'insurance business' in Athens, Alabama, shortly after his initiation, and the Ku Klux began to ride in that territory soon after Forrest had concluded his insurance business and gone home. While engaged in his railroad contracting business he had his business office in Aberdeen, in Mississippi, and Aberdeen is almost in the exact geographical center of the Ku Klux territory in that state. Forrest also had insurance business calling him to Atlanta early in 1868, and there was an outburst of Ku Klux activity immediately thereafter. Business of some mysterious nature took him to the Carolinas during this period, and his visit was closely followed by the appearance of the Klan in those states.

In fact, it was remarkable how General Forrest seemed to turn up at those places where the Ku Klux were prominently active. After the Klan had made a raid on Judge William T. Blackford in Greensboro, Alabama, and warned him to leave the state, Blackford testified, he was visited by 'a Confederate general, a warm personal friend' of his, who helped to protect him and who told him an impressive story of the powerful ramifications of the Ku Klux Klan and the impossibility of any individual's successfully opposing such a formidable organization. According to Blackford, this anonymous Confederate general stated that he had personally organized the Klan in Arkansas, and further told him of its extensive membership and its powerful connections. Every jury, the general was quoted as saying, had one or more Ku Klux on it; and one of the functions of the order was to provide an alibi for any member accused of any disorder. He also told of the Ku Klux practice of having its raids conducted by members of some Klan in another town or county, for the purpose of preventing identification. Pressed to reveal the identity of this ex-general who knew so much about the Ku Klux, Judge Blackford said it was a confidential matter, as his informant was a personal friend; and as far as he would go in the way of identifying him was to say that he was an ex-Confederate general and that his business brought him to that county a good deal of the time.

Judge Blackford, however, need not have been so punctilious about mentioning the name of his friend the Confederate general. General Forrest in his own testimony before the Investigating Committee referred to the Alabama incident without reservation, saying that 'Judge Blackford came to me for protection and I did protect him.' Blackford was a scala-wag, who had served for a while in the Confederate army; and although Forrest recognized him for what he was, a renegade and a trouble-maker, he maintained a semblance of friendly relations with him. 'He had given a great deal of bad advice to the negroes and kept them in confusion,' Forrest testified. 'He had large meetings of the negroes at his house, firing around and shooting, and it had become very dissatisfactory to the people. He was a drinking man, and when drunk would make threats.' The General, however, was a practical man and used Blackford to advantage in marshaling Republi-can support for his Memphis–Selma railroad. When eyebrows were raised at his making use of such a man and associating with him, Forrest said: 'I tried to excuse Blackford on the ground that he was drunk. I wanted the subscriptions and tried to carry all the votes I could. I set out by saying railroads had no politics.'

The fiery editor of the Tuscaloosa *Independent Monitor*, who was Cyclops of his local Den, vigorously criticized General Forrest for being seen in public with such a malodorous char-acter as Judge Blackford, and even went so far as to hint that Forrest had gone over to the Radicals. Forrest replied in a wrathful open letter that his critic did not know what he was talking about, and invited him to mind his own business.

Meanwhile, Captain John G. Stokes, the scalawag editor of
the Montgomery *State Journal*, launched an attack on Forrest
from another angle, charging that his railroad business was a
sham and a subterfuge and that while he was going about the
country stump-speaking, apparently for the purpose of furthering the prospects for his railroad, he was really engaged in
organizing the Ku Klux Klan throughout the South 'preparatory to pushing the country into another rebellion.' The
chastened and repentant editor of the *Monitor* rushed to the
defense of his Grand Wizard and former military commander
and denounced the Montgomery editor's story as a 'mare's
nest,' going on to say: 'What terror the scallawags must be in
of the great "Wizard of the Saddle" when their guilty consciences cause them to trump up such absurd notions. We
suggest that Stokes at once proceed to collect together his old
company of "rebels" that he never led before against realities,
except beyond the reach of "villainous saltpetre," and go in
pursuit of Forrest and his mythical klan.'

This thinly veiled reference to Stokes's reputed disgraceful
retreat from the bloody field of Shiloh, while commanding a
company of Confederate troops, silenced the Montgomery
editor temporarily; but all the knowing ones realized that
Captain Stokes was halfway right in his charges. Forrest's
interest in the proposed railroad was by no means a mere
blind. He was sincerely engaged in trying to promote the
road. The traveling around involved in the promotion work
did, however, provide an excellent opportunity for furthering
the Ku Klux work. That a goodly part of the General's time
was indeed devoted to Ku Klux affairs was emphasized by a
significant episode at about that time. It had been announced
that he would visit Tuscaloosa on a specified day in October
to speak in behalf of his railroad; but it was published in the
local paper that he would not be able to appear as he had received a telegram from Memphis making it necessary for him

to return to Tennessee, 'as Brownlow has called out his militia and great trouble is expected, as the Rads require riots to bolster up their fallen fortunes.' Evidently Forrest regarded the railroad as secondary to the demands of the Klan. Also it seems obvious that if he had been a mere innocent bystander he would hardly have abandoned his business and hurried back to Tennessee because of a threat against the Ku Klux Klan.

General Nathan Bedford Forrest was, beyond any reasonable doubt, the Grand Wizard of the Invisible Empire.

XV.   THE KU KLUX FEVER

ROBERT SOMERS, THE BRITISH TRAVELER who visited the South during the wild nightmare of the Reconstruction, commented on the complacency with which the people accepted the existence of the Ku Klux Klan as an active though invisible factor in their daily affairs to which they must adjust themselves. The extent to which this was true is impressively revealed by the ephemera and trivia of the times — things unimportant in themselves, but reflecting the attitude of the people in an intimate and interesting manner. Scanning the newspapers and periodicals of those years, it is obvious that the name of the Ku Klux — though nobody knew who they were — was apparently on every tongue, and they were talked about and written about and joked about as flippantly and familiarly as any other common phase of everyday life.

The newspapers of the South were full of Ku Klux news and comment, editorials and communications from 'Vox Populi' and 'Constant Reader' to the editor — nor was this comment confined entirely to the field of legitimate news. A reading notice in the Tuscaloosa *Independent Monitor* in April, 1868, said: 'If you wish to keep the Ku Kluxes off, buy a supply of the Grafton Mineral paint from John Glascock. We see by our exchanges that even low-down Rads and Nigs have been spared whose houses, wagons, etc., were coated with said paint.' Mr. Glascock, whose store was located in the ground floor of the building in which the *Monitor* was printed, carried an advertisement in the paper in which he mentioned and recommended this 'Anti-Radical Paint,' and there was evidently a harmonious working understanding between the editorial and advertising departments of this particular paper.

The mystic initials 'K K K' seemed to have an irresistible appeal to the imagination of all the people, and their use was by no means confined to those who had achieved citizenship in the Invisible Empire. Late in March, 1868, the citizens of Nashville woke up one morning to find the city plastered with posters on every available wall and corner, bearing the three dread letters, 'K K K,' prodigious in size and of deathly black, followed by an array of blood-red daggers, bleeding hearts and a profusion of hog-Latin gibberish. The enraged chief of police took one look and ordered them torn down instanter and without delay; whereupon, on closer examination, it developed that they were merely the clever advertisements of an extravaganza called 'The Ku Klux Klan' which was to be performed at a local theater, the St. Nicholas Varieties.

Use of the Ku Klux name in advertising was a common device in those days. In Nashville, as well as in other places, there was a Ku Klux Saloon. The Bay Horse Saloon in Memphis boldly advertised that it was Ku Klux headquarters (although that honor was disputed by the Pat Cleburne Bar-Room) and invited rural Ku Klux to pay the Bay Horse a sociable visit when visiting in Memphis. A Memphis lumberman gained attention by addressing his advertising appeal directly to the Ku Klux, advising them of special prices available to them on sash, doors and other building material. Even in *Harper's Weekly* the three K's were featured in the advertisement of J. H. Wickes, who was offering for sale a kind of kerosene for lamps said to be accident-proof. 'Kommon Kerosene Kills,'

declared Mr. Wickes, with the initial K's of large size, and
with grinning death's-heads to carry out the sinister motif.

The newspapers of the time evidently regarded the Ku Klux
as a good subject for jesting and the robustious humor of the
day; and one newspaper humorist of that period, an imitation
Josh Billings who signed himself 'Ally Gator,' dated all his
letters from the fictitious post-office, 'Ku Klux Cross Roads.'
Ku Klux jokes and witticisms were common; and, as might
have been expected, there were the inevitable reports of hens
who laid eggs bearing the plain and unmistakable marking
'K K K.' One Georgia hen, spurning such petty and ele-
mentary performances, was immortalized in an item which
told how 'A Ku Klux hen in the vicinity of Griffin has recently
been delivered of an egg upon whose shell in plain letters there
appear the remarkable words: "Woe unto R. B. Bullock." '
Bullock was the hated and oppressive carpetbagger Governor
of Georgia, who had a penchant for calling out the troops on
slight provocation, and the news item closed with: 'A large
detachment of troops will be ordered to that vicinity at once.'

The extent of the commercialization of the Ku Klux name
by progressive merchants was remarkable, a specimen being
provided by the following item which appeared in a Nashville
paper in June, 1868, under the heading 'K.K.K.K.':

'The genius and enterprise of some people is truly astound-
ing. Since the "Ku Klux fever" was at its highest pitch in
our midst, we have had "Ku Klux music" from the music
houses, "Ku Klux hats" from furnishing emporiums, "Ku
Klux cocktails" from the different saloons, together with the
many little "Ku Klux etceteras" not in mind. And to cap the
climax we now have the genuine "Ku Klux Klan Knife,"
with the cabalistic letters and the terrible symbols of the order
on its blade. That sterling firm, Craighead, Breast & Gibson,
exclusive wholesale hardware merchants, 45 Public Square,
conceived the happy idea several weeks since and yesterday a

large invoice of their express designing from the transatlantic manufacturers, Frederick Ware & Co., Sheffield, England, was received at their ware-rooms in this city.'

The Ku Klux Klan Knives found a ready sale among the young men of the South, and an occasional specimen of them might be seen occasionally in second-hand shops as late as a few years ago.

The 'Ku Klux music' mentioned in this connection afforded another evidence of the undisguised popularity of the Ku Klux Klan with the native population and the extent of the penetration of the Ku Klux fame into the cultural life of the times. In Nashville alone there were two pieces of popular music published which used the Ku Klux name in their titles; one of them, a waltz, was embellished with a lurid and fanciful illustration (printed in red ink) of a supposed Ku Klux initiation, the initiate, with a rope around his neck, quaking before a horrid array of skulls, alligators and other fearsome appurtenances. The other, the 'Ku Klux Klan Schottische and Mazurka' by R. L. Steinbagen, was more sedately printed in black and white, and received this grudgingly complimentary comment from the local Republican paper: 'The Ku Klux Klan Schottische and Mazurka, notwithstanding its name, is a sweet piece; and while we must acknowledge our disinclination to be too familiar with the K K K's, yet we really have fallen in love somewhat with the music. "A rose with any other name will smell as sweet." '

Practical jokers also found in the Ku Klux idea a fertile field for their misdirected energies. Mischievous boys delighted in scribbling warning and threatening letters, signed 'K K K,' and leaving them on the doorstep of innocent and inoffensive citizens. Not all the joking was done by boys, however, and although there was foundation enough for plenty of Ku Klux alarums during those troubled days, some of the serious Ku Klux scares originated in nothing more dangerous than the

elephantine pranking of some blithe spirit who thought he was
being funny. In Columbia, South Carolina, at one time there
was something approaching a panic as the result of the ingrow-
ing sense of humor of a prominent professional gambler there.
This gentleman, conscious of the hair-trigger nervousness of
the carpetbaggers then in control of the capital city and the
ease with which an alarming rumor might be kindled, induced
an old countryman named Sheldon to go to a merchant in
Columbia and tell him that he might want to engage feed for
fifteen hundred men and horses on Friday night of the following
week, and then go to a livery stable and inquire as to the possibility of engaging places for fifteen hundred horses for the
same night. Both the merchant and the livery-stable keeper
were enjoined to secrecy which, of course, insured their immediately telling everybody they knew, including the chief
of police, and soon the town was in a tumult of excitement
over the impending Ku Klux raid. The local paper took
cognizance of the incipient panic and attempted to allay the
people's fears by saying:

LOOKING FOR THE KU KLUX

There seems to be a general expectation or fear by the legislature that the dread and sepulchral Ku Klux Klan will pay
the state-house a visit to-night or to-morrow. A member of the
legislature told us with all gravity to-day that they were to
come to-morrow night, fifteen hundred strong; were to approach in four different ways, surround the Capitol and proceed
upon their bloody work. I heard another telling a crowd of
members standing in the hall of the House, in the most excited
manner, how a solitary horseman had rode into the state-house
yard this morning, galloped up to the front door and inquired
of parties standing there when the legislature would adjourn;
and, being informed, wanted to know if fifteen hundred horses
could be provided with food in town. Such tales are, of course,

absurd, but they plainly indicate the tremulous condition of our mighty rulers.

Despite this reassurance, however, it was several days before the carpetbagger legislature was relieved of the fear that they were to be overpowered and butchered in the halls of the Capitol by the invading Klansmen; and the gambler was so elated at the success of his prank that he closed his faro bank for three days in order to devote his undivided attention to a bacchanalian celebration of his own keen wit.

The members of the congressional committees themselves sometimes sought relief from the monotonous pro and con of murder, rape and arson by introducing a little levity into the proceedings. One of the members of the committee investigating the elections in Louisiana asked ironically of a negro who had testified that he was a Democrat: 'Are you a member of the Knights of the White Camelia?' This was a purely rhetorical and sarcastic question, since the basic tenet of the Knights of the White Camelia was the supremacy of the white race, but the ignorant negro took the question at face value and innocently answered: 'I don't know what that word means,' whereupon there ensued this exchange:

'You have seen the flower, the white camelia, haven't you?'

'No, sir; I don't know that word. I knew a girl once with a name like that; no, her name was just 'Melia.'

'But she was a Black Camelia, wasn't she?'

'No, sir, she was pretty near white.'

Another example of unconscious humor was supplied by a young man named E. A. Hightower, who lived in Warren County, Georgia. He testified that he joined the Ku Klux in that county in 1869 because he did not want the members to think he was opposed to it, but never took much active part in its work. He testified about the oath, the grip and the hailing signs, and when asked about the password said: 'If you were in distress you were to say "Ambulance"; "Ambulance" was the word of distress.' And probably 'Ambulance' was a more fitting word than the true word Avalanche, with which he had apparently confused it.

It is particularly interesting to observe the frequency with which the unsung and anonymous but prolific poets of the Reconstruction era were moved to lyrical composition in connection with the rise and fall of the Ku Klux. The Reverend A. W. Cummings of Spartanburg, South Carolina, was a carpetbagger preacher who added to his unpopularity by seeking and attaining the office of tax assessor and collector; and when the Federal troops were sent to Spartanburg by President Grant in 1871 the *Spartan* printed the following impious gibe:

A REVEREND GENTLEMAN'S EVENING PRAYER

(Supposed to have been uttered on the evening of the arrival of the United States cavalry at this place.)

Now I lay me down to sleep;
I pray thee, Grant, my body keep.
Just let the soldiers round me stand
And drive away the Ku Klux band,
That I may have one night of rest
With consciousness of safety blessed.
And though my conscience sting no more,
And keep me wakeful ever more,
I think I may make out to snore.
A grateful song I then will raise,
Thy soldiers and thy grace to praise.
Amen.

The subject of one poetic composition which gained considerable fame was a carpetbagger named Charles Morgan who settled in Yazoo County, Mississippi, and combined politics with the business of operating a sawmill. As the excesses of the Loyal League negroes intensified the antagonism of the native white people for the carpetbaggers, Mr. Morgan's popularity

in Yazoo City rapidly approached the irreducible minimum.
One day as he was leaving town to go to his sawmill across the
bayou, he was followed by a crowd of nagging boys who jeered
and taunted him with insulting cries of 'Polecat!' and other
choice epithets, and followed him onto the ferryboat, where
Morgan lost his self-possession and drew a pistol on them,
putting them to flight.

   This undignified episode, along with Morgan's other activities
in Yazoo County, were immortalized in a song composed by
some nameless native bard, sung to the tune of 'If You Belong
to Gideon's Band,' which was printed in the Yazoo *Banner*
in May, 1868:

I

Old Morgan came to the Southern land,
Old Morgan came to the Southern land,
Old Morgan came to the Southern land,
With a little carpet-bag in his hand.

Chorus

If you belong to the Ku Klux band
Here's my heart and here's my hand.
If you belong to the Ku Klux band
We are marching for a home.

II

Old Morgan thought he would get bigger
By running a sawmill with a nigger. — *Chorus.*

III

The crop it failed and the sawmill busted
And the nigger got very badly wusted. — *Chorus.*

IV

Old Morgan is a gay old rat
And the boys they called him a polecat. — *Chorus.*

V

But some close at his heels would tag
And call this hero scalawag. — *Chorus.*

VI

Old Morgan went to the bayou bridge
And with some little Ku Kluxes had a scrimmidge. — *Chorus.*

VII

Old Morgan stepped into the flat
And knocked a little Ku Klux into a cocked hat, and the little
Ku Klux didn't like that so very well, and another little Ku
Klux picked up a spike pole to hit old Morgan zip, and old
Morgan drew a horse pistol out of his pantaloons and cocked
it on the little coons, and the little Ku Klux that had picked
up the spike pole dropped it very soon, and old Morgan turned
and run out of the flat, and the little Ku Kluxes hollered 'Run,
polecat!' — *Chorus.*

Mr. Morgan, sad to relate, not only had to endure the
slings and arrows of Yazoo City's concentrated contumely,
but following the episode on the ferryboat he was arrested and
formally arraigned on the charges of carrying a concealed
deadly weapon, exhibiting a deadly weapon, violating a city
ordinance, disturbing the peace and assault. He was tried and
found guilty on all counts and fined sixty-one dollars — and
there are old folks in Yazoo County today who remember and
can sing this doggerel song commemorating the unfortunate
Mr. Morgan's difficulties.

There was an indefinable something about the Ku Klux
which seemed to inspire verse. When they first began to attract attention in General Meade's district early in 1868 he
issued a ukase against them in the form of a General Order
calling for their suppression and forbidding the newspapers to
print anything 'furthering the Ku Klux cause.' This aroused
the Augusta, Georgia, *Register and Chronicle* to the following
lyric production:

GENERAL ORDER NO. 30,721

Let every Ku Klux Klansman heed
The General Order of General Meade.
His Highness has received a fright
And can not sleep by day or night.
He sees in every Southern man
A member of the Ku Klux Klan,
And every time a ram's horn toots
(Poor fellow) trembles in his boots.
Oh, dear! Oh, dear! how they annoy him.
Hence his orders to destroy 'em.
So let every Klansman heed
The General Order of General Meade;
And all observe this General Rule,
Signed and sealed by Meade

DAMPHOOL

Not all the Ku Klux poetry was of a comic character, however. On March 19, 1868, there appeared in the Memphis *Avalanche* the following item: 'The following poem very mysteriously found its way upon our table yesterday. The writer is evidently a poet, a man of genius, and certainly knows something about the "Klan." We wish some member of the organization would tell us when, where and how to join the mysterious order, as from one to three hundred applications are made to us each day.'

DEATH'S BRIGADE

The wolf is in the desert
  And the panther in the brake.
The fox is on his rambles
  And the owl is wide awake;
For now 'tis noon of darkness
  And the world is all asleep,
And some shall wake to glory
  And some shall wake to weep.
      Ku Klux.

A river black is running
  To a blacker sea afar,
And by its banks is waving
  A flag without a star:
There move the ghostly columns
  Of the swift Brigade of Death
And every villain sleeping
  Is gasping now for breath.
                    Ku Klux.

Thrice hath the lone owl hooted
  And thrice the panther cried,
And swifter through the darkness
  The Pale Brigade shall ride.
No trumpet sounds its coming,
  And no drum-beat stirs the air,
But noiseless in their vengeance
  They wreak it everywhere.
                    Ku Klux.

Fly! fly! ye dastard bandits,
  Who are bleeding all the land,
The Dread Brigade is marching
  With viewless sword and brand;
Nor think that from its vengeance
  You in deepest dens may hide,
For through the darkest caverns
  The Dread Brigade will ride.
                    Ku Klux.

The misty gray is hanging
  On the tresses of the East,
And morn shall tell the story
  Of the revel and the feast.
The ghostly troop shall vanish
  Like the light in constant cloud,
But where they rode shall gather
  The coffin and the shroud.
                    Ku Klux.

This poem has been attributed to Albert Pike, the talented Arkansan who was at the head of the Ku Klux movement in that state and was a poet of no mean ability. Possibly he was the author, although, of course, he did not have the bravado to claim that honor publicly at that time.

An amusing item in the Norfolk, Virginia, *Journal* in February, 1869, told of the experience of Bishop Beckwith of the Episcopal Church when he made an episcopal visitation to a remote part of his diocese in Georgia. There were not many Episcopalians in that part of the state, especially in the rural sections; but few of the whites had ever seen a successor to the Apostles, and the negroes did not even know what sort of a creature a bishop was. There was no Episcopal church in the region; but, undeterred by all the obstacles in his way, the conscientious cleric announced that he would preach at a certain Baptist church on a given Sunday night. The whole neighborhood, members of all sects, were filled with curiosity to go and see the queer animal that read prayers out of a book. Of all the population, the negroes were more excited than any of the others — anything new or novel in the way of religion appealed to them. There were some qualms about visiting the vicinity of a graveyard after dark, but they determined to attend the service *en masse* and stand together in a group outside the front windows, thinking that however dangerous might be a graveyard generally, there would be no peril from Ku Klux where so large a congregation was assembled.

The rural Baptist church having no vestry room, the Bishop's host placed his vestments behind a tombstone in the churchyard during the afternoon, where he could conveniently don them upon his arrival there that night. At the appointed hour the church was thronged with whites, and the negroes stood packed, open-mouthed, before the door. Bishop Beckwith arrived on time, entered the graveyard by the back gate and there put on his episcopal vestures. There happened to be a

rather strong breeze blowing that night, and just as he came
around the corner of the church a gust spread out his white
robes like a billowing sail. Some of the negroes spied him and
yelled out: 'Ku Klux! Ku Klux!' At this they all looked
around, and when they beheld the flaunting white garments
approaching the whole crowd took to their heels shrieking
'Ku Klux!' 'In ten seconds not a single darkie could be seen,'
continued the newspaper account, 'but the sound of their foot-
steps in the distance fell upon the ear, and for half an hour
afterward could be heard the terrible words "Ku Klux! Ku
Klux!" far off in the country, as the affrighted negroes were
making for their homes.'

Allowing for the exaggeration sometimes deemed pardonable
in dressing up a humorous narrative, it does not seem entirely
unlikely that this episode actually occurred. A somewhat
similar incident happened in Nashville when a negro woman,
terrified by the sight of four Sisters of Mercy, fled down the
street shrieking: 'I seen 'em! I seen the Ku Klux! Promenadin'
in their grave clothes!'

Sometimes the Ku Klux themselves were the butt of the joke.
During the summer of 1869 a negro in Batesville, Mississippi,
had a white man arrested, charged with beating him, and then,
fearing possible reprisal by the Ku Klux, sent to the commander of the United States troops at Panola a request for
protection. A company of cavalry accordingly started for
Batesville, and that night about midnight when they were about
two miles from their destination, coming around a turn in the
road, they suddenly collided headlong with a body of mounted
Ku Klux 'in all their horrid paraphernalia.' The captain
of the cavalry company ordered his troopers to halt and draw
their carbines, and there was a brisk exchange of musketry
between the two bodies of men, several hundred shots being
fired. The Ku Klux soon realized, however, that they were
getting the worst of it and their leader ordered a retreat. One

luckless Klansman, named Jesse Rhoads, however, happened to be mounted on a mule, and the mule chose this unpropitious moment to exercise the historic prerogative of his genus to balk. His rider whipped and spurred him frantically, but the mule refused to budge; and as a result of this lack of co-operation from his stubborn mount Rhoads was ingloriously captured by the bluecoats and, 'horrid paraphernalia' and all, was exultantly hustled off to the jail at Vicksburg.

The pervasiveness of the Ku Klux influence extended even into the realm of sport. Baseball was just then beginning to get established as the national game, and local baseball clubs were springing up in all parts of the country, all of them tagged with more or less fancy appellations. In the South at this time it was perhaps inescapable that the Ku Klux name should be borrowed for this purpose, and in Nashville an ambitious group of embryo young Pop Ansons sought to terrify their opponents on the diamond by calling themselves the 'Young Ku Klux.' That the horrific name was not backed up by any corresponding talent was indicated by this sad report of their first game, as printed in the *Press and Times* in April, 1868: 'A baseball match took place yesterday between the Eclipse and the Young Ku Klux clubs. The following were the scores: Eclipse, 22; Young Ku Klux, 3.' And then the Radical editor of the paper added severely: 'The Ku Klux is a poor name for winning.' Perhaps the Young Ku Klux took the same view of the matter. At any rate, they seem to have changed their name to 'The Pale Faces,' which was a sort of current alias for the Ku Klux. The Pale Faces also turned out, however, to be 'a poor name for winning,' as the newspaper of May 1st carried this piece of news: 'The "Trix" and "Pale Faces" baseball clubs played a match game yesterday in which the former scored 19 and the latter 3.'

A more distant connection between the Ku Klux and the national game was revealed in an item which appeared in the Trenton, Tennessee, *Gazette* in August, 1868, headed: 'How Ku

Klux Stories are Manufactured.' This story related that 'The Tax Collector for the county, Mr. Parker, a few days ago visited Rutherford Station for the purpose of collecting the taxes for that district and, seeing a young man wearing a pair of red pants (the uniform of the members of the local Base Ball Club) at once concluding that he was a Ku Klux and that his presence was intended as an intimidation, left the place, declaring that he could not collect the taxes without the militia.' Mr. Parker's flight took him to Nashville, where his story was added to the swelling chorus of alleged Ku Klux outrages, while the innocent member of the Rutherford baseball club went on his way in his red pants, all unconscious of the furore precipitated by his gaudy garb.

An example of what passed for humor in those days is provided by a labored item in a Montgomery paper telling of an incident in connection with the banishment of several young men of Eutaw, Alabama, who were sentenced to a term in the military prison at Fort Jefferson on the Dry Tortugas for the offense of Ku Kluxing a carpetbagger. There was an uproar of protest at the severity of their punishment and they were eventually pardoned and returned triumphantly home, full of tales about their experiences, at which time this appeared:

A rich thing is told by one of the returned Tortured-guts victims, about an un-rekonstruckted

Ku Klux Mule

Which had been so R. E. Belyus as to kick one of the
Leeg-scented, loil 'woters' ov midnite Kompleckshun at New
Orleans, for which treezonable krime he was
Kourt-Marshaled
And sentenced to hard labor at Dry Tortured-guts, for life!
However, Long-ears managed to jump overboard on
the passage and swum defiantly off amid yells of
'Go it, Johnny; wish I was on your back, I'd go too,'
from the Eutaw boys!

That's nice
And now
Alabama Menagerie No. 2
is to exhibit at Montgumery on the 13th, and we look for
Jolly times — presently!
Free admission to kullered dam(n)sells who kin store a
carpetbag for the night. Montgumians are warned.

The Ku Klux were especially strong in Alabama, so much so
that in some parts of the state they came to be looked upon as an
established and quasi-legal factor in the administration of justice. In Jefferson County a negro man was arrested for stealing
cotton, and a white attorney who had raised him when he was a
slave and took an interest in him volunteered to defend him. He
discussed the matter with his dusky client and was told by him
that the Ku Klux had called on him some time before and interrogated him about the matter and, being convinced of his
guilt, had whipped him. The attorney forthwith went into the
court and demanded that the negro be released on constitutional grounds. The Constitution clearly provided, he said, that
no citizen should twice be placed in jeopardy for the same
offense. His client had already been tried, convicted and punished by the Ku Klux; to try him again was a clear case of
double jeopardy. Maybe it was the sheer audacity of the
theory; maybe the court was impressed by its sound logic; anyhow the bewildered but grateful negro was released.

XVI. KINDRED
ORGANIZATIONS

ALTHOUGH THE KU KLUX KLAN was by far the most widely known organization of its kind, it was by no means the only order in the South of similar purpose. Following the war, when the normal administration of the law collapsed and chaotic social and economic conditions prevailed, there was an instinctive movement among people of the South in the direction of banding together for common protection. There were scores of more or less local groups of this character, ranging in size and importance from the loose, informal neighborhood vigilance committees to such well-organized and well-regulated societies as the Knights of the White Camelia, for example.

Some of these existed as separate entities only during the months immediately following the war, and served as a nucleus around which the Ku Klux Klan was organized in those localities when it came into being. On the other hand, some of the most extensive and formidable of them were not active until after the decline and collapse of the Ku Klux Klan, at which time they blossomed out as secret societies based on the principle of 'white supremacy' and generally upholding the Democratic Party. In general, they had the same broad objectives as the Ku Klux Klan; but the fundamental difference was that they, as a rule, did not indulge in any deeds of violence and did not go about in disguise or make any secret of the fact of membership. They were 'secret societies' in the sense that the Masons or Odd Fellows are so called, in that they did not divulge their ritualistic procedure and confined their meetings to their own members; but membership was freely admitted, which was quite contrary to the basic principle of the Ku Klux Klan.

To the world at large, however, all these Southern secret societies of post-war times were loosely though inaccurately known as Ku Klux; and Doctor W. L. Fleming in his *Documentary History of the Reconstruction* groups all these organized protective organizations in what he aptly styles 'The Ku Klux Movement.' Granting that they were all actuated by the same basic motive, however, it should be borne in mind that the Ku Klux Klan as such had no official connection with any of these other organizations. The Klan was *sui generis*. It had more members and more advertising and more fearsome prestige than any of the other organizations, being approached only by the Knights of the White Camelia; and although the Klan, by its very pre-eminence, had its name used as a tag for all similar enterprises, they were all entirely independent of each other.

A thorough and detailed study of the Southern secret societies of Reconstruction days would constitute an interesting and valuable contribution to history. That, however, is another story; and for present purposes it must be sufficient to mention briefly some of the more outstanding activities along lines roughly parallel to the path of the Ku Klux Klan.

By long odds the most extensive and important of these post-war secret societies in the South, aside from the Ku Klux, was the Knights of the White Camelia. This order centered in Louisiana, but it extended into Texas and Arkansas, across southern Mississippi, Alabama and Georgia, and also to some extent in the other Southern states; and was said to have members even in the North and West.

'We have witnessed the revolting spectacle of excited negroes riding through our streets and on the public roads with guns on their shoulders, revolvers and dirks hanging at their sides, matches in their hands, yelling, cursing and threatening to shoot down and cut the throats of the whites and to destroy their property,' said Colonel Alcibiade de Blanc, later Grand Commander of the order in Louisiana and an active factor in its promotion. It was to offset such conditions, Colonel de Blanc declared, that the White Camelia was organized; and he went about the South making speeches on the subject of 'The Whites Must and Shall Rule,' which might be taken as the slogan of the organization. On the basis of this appeal it swept over Louisiana and the immediately adjacent territory. The specter of miscegenation was one of the principal concerns of the White Camelia, as black-and-tan legislatures were enacting laws permitting the intermarriage of the races, and every member of the Knights of the White Camelia was sworn never to marry any woman but of the white race. 'Nothing was asked about negro children,' a Northern commentator caustically remarked. 'If the applicant had not married the colored woman who bore his children, the White Camelia in its spotless purity was content.' But the members of the order were not disturbed by criticism. Racial solidarity was their fetish. 'We must all be united as are the flowers that grow on one stem,' was one of its declarations; and this was the idea persistently hammered into its members.

This order had grown to such proportions in Louisiana in 1872 that it embraced nearly all the Democratic voters in the state, and it had attained such power that General Rousseau, who commanded the district, advised the Republican leaders to abandon the campaign, as the organization had become too powerful for his command to subdue. In 1869 a Tennessee newspaper carried a news item from Texas stating that the Knights of the White Camelia had thirty-eight thousand members in that state; and, although this was probably an exaggeration, it was in fact immensely popular in that section.

In New Orleans, where there were eighteen Councils of the society, meetings were called by the simple process of inserting a single-line advertisement in the *Times:* 'K.W.C. No.——— Important,' and the members of the designated Council would thereupon assemble at the regular meeting place.

The sign of recognition of the Knights of the White Camelia was made by carelessly drawing the index finger of the left hand across the left eye, all the other fingers of that hand being closed. If the person addressed was a member, he would ask the question: 'Where were you born?' to which the proper answer was 'On Mount Caucasus.' Then: 'Are you free?' 'I am.' 'Were your ancestors free?' 'They were.' 'Are you attached to any order?' 'I am.' 'To what order?' 'To the Knights of the White Camelia.' 'Where does it grow?' 'On Mount Caucasus.'

Entrance to a Council was gained by giving four raps on the door; and for a general alarm in any town a bell was rung four times.

The Knights of the White Camelia appears to have grown out of a White Man's Club (also called the Caucasian Club) which was organized at Franklin, Louisiana, in May, 1867, by Colonel de Blanc. In the same month a local branch was established in New Orleans, which was later to be the headquarters of the organization; but there was no general convention of the order in New Orleans until 1868, at which time the leaders got together, adopted a constitution and began to extend its influence.

The Camelia society developed itself into a highly potent force in Reconstruction politics in the Southwest, particularly in Louisiana; and in that state it was directly through its instrumentality that the government was finally rescued from the plundering carpetbaggers and restored to responsible hands.

The White League was not organized until 1874, and then purely for political purposes, openly and avowedly. The Radicals called it 'Ku Klux without the disguise and secrecy'; but there was actually no connection whatever between the

White League and the Klan, and little similarity in their methods. The reason for the League was pretty well explained in its platform, which describes how the negroes 'voted like a body of soldiers obeying a command from unworthy and dishonest leaders,' and asserted that a 'league of the whites is the inevitable result of that formidable, oath-bound and blindly obedient league of the blacks.'

The political campaign in Louisiana for participation in which the White League was primarily organized was a wild and turbulent one, with frequent clashes between the rival forces. This violence culminated in the historic and bloody affray at the foot of Canal Street in New Orleans when the volunteer militia, largely composed of White Leaguers and commanded by Frederick N. Ogden, head of the League, clashed with the Kellogg black militia, made up largely of the metropolitan police of New Orleans, mostly negroes. There was a brisk battle, lasting for about ten minutes, in the course of which fifty-six men were killed — forty-four of the metropolitans and twelve of the White League. The White League continued as an active factor in Louisiana political affairs, and also spread to some of the other Southern States near-by, but gradually died out as the purpose for which it was organized was attained.

A post-war secret society which appears to have been organized in Tennessee, but which manifested itself to a lesser extent at various points throughout the South, was the 'Pale Faces.' Membership in the order was not a secret, and General Forrest freely admitted that he belonged to the Pale Faces while stoutly denying that he knew anything about the Ku Klux Klan — although in the next breath he declared that they were the same thing. This, however, was most likely a part of Forrest's general plan to obfuscate the issue as much as possible; for all other evidence indicates that they were not the same thing by any means. Roughly they had the same purpose in view, but the Pale Faces' plan of organization and method of operation were entirely different; and during the time of their activity they were quick and emphatic in denying that they had any connection with the Ku Klux Klan.

The first mention of this order in the press was in the Nashville *Union and Dispatch* of March 8, 1868, when in a news story telling of the organization of 'Silver Cycle No. 1' it was hailed, in the headline, as 'Another Mystic Brotherhood.' The news item went on to say: 'Another mysterious order, it would seem, has been organized in this city — the Pale Faces. This society, though looked upon by many as a myth, is said by others to be an auxiliary of the great Ku Klux Klan which is so rapidly spreading over the state and inaugurating terror among the negroes.' It was then related that an anonymous communication had been received the previous day telling of the organization of Silver Cycle No. 1 'at the shanty in Scylla's Den,' and that the following officers had been elected: 'Double Double Down — Mercury; Double Down — Knowledge; Assistant Double Down — Game Cock; Revolving Scribbler — Purity; Cash Swinger — Truth; Assistant Cash Swinger — Honesty; Walk Around — Charity; Deputy Walk Around — Truth; First Lookout — War; Second Lookout — Strength; Holy Youth — Virtue.' It was stated that the organization would meet every seventh Sunday 'at the shanty'; and in a postscript it was mentioned that its emblem was Justice, Purity and Truth.

Two days later the *Union and Dispatch* carried a card in which it was stated that they had been requested by an officer of the Pale Faces to make it plain that it had 'no connection whatever with the Ku Klux Klan,' as many supposed and as had been intimated in the previous news item. In June a prominent citizen of Nashville died, Captain Edward W. Clark, and his funeral was the occasion of the first public demonstration of the Pale Faces ever witnessed in that city, as they took part in the services and marched to the cemetery in the funeral procession.

In the newspaper account of the funeral it was stated that the
'Pale Face clans' gathered at the grave-side; and the next day
they had to publish an apology, pointing out that 'the Pale
Faces have no *clans*.' So fearful were they of confusion with the
notorious Ku Klux that the use of even the common noun 'clan'
was taboo.

By December, 1869, the Pale Faces had grown so strong that
they launched a paper of their own in Nashville known as 'The
Pale Face.' The first issue of this paper gave considerable information about the order, stating that it had sixty-one camps
in Tennessee, and that there were twenty thousand members on
its rolls, 'although it is not yet two years old.' W. J. Andrews of
Columbia was announced as Most Worthy State President.
This publication lived a very brief and uneventful life; in fact
the order itself did not long survive the restoration of popular
government in the state, which was fully attained shortly thereafter.

Another minor organization of this kind in Tennessee was the
'Red Jackets,' which had a chapter in Johnsonville on the
Tennessee River and at other points in that vicinity. A newspaper comment about the order stated that 'The objects of this
conclave, which seems to be quite numerous in that section, are
similar to those of the Ku Klux Klan.' The Red Jackets, however, survived but briefly and made no visible impress on the
affairs of the state.

In Mississippi there were a number of organizations of this
kind after the war. About the most active of them was a society
known as the Native Sons of the South, which was centered in
Monroe County, where it was said to have more than eight
hundred members. Initiates into this order took the following
oath:

'I do solemnly swear, in the presence of Almighty God and
this band of faithful brethren, that I will never reveal or make
known, except when authorized to do so by proper authority,

any of the secrets, signs, passwords, grips or other obligations, so help me God, and keep me steadfast therein.'

The following catechism ensued after the oath:

'Who will protect the rights of all men?'

'The Native Sons of the South.'

'Whom do we in this most solemn hour swear vengeance against?'

'The carpetbagger and all who affiliate with him.'

'What is to be done with the carpetbaggers and their friends?'

'They are to be driven from the borders of the state.'

'Who is to accomplish this most noble work?'

'The Native Sons of the South.'

Members of the order were enjoined to keep the fact of their membership a profound secret, but this injunction was rendered somewhat absurd by the fact that they were immediately furnished with a glazed cap, across the front of which was lettered 'Native Sons,' which they wore publicly on the occasion of their parades. The most ambitious undertaking of the Native Sons was a campaign to organize the negroes to vote the Democratic ticket, but this proved abortive. The leading figures were soon arrested by the United States officers; and, although they were later released from custody, the organization shriveled up and disappeared.

Another Mississippi organization was known as 'The Society of the White Rose,' which preceded the Ku Klux Klan and apparently was absorbed into the Klan when the latter was introduced into Mississippi. John B. Taliaferro stated that he joined the Society of the White Rose in Brooksville, being under the impression that its purpose was to bring thieves to justice. It was an oathbound organization, but there was no penalty prescribed for a violation of the oath. Taliaferro said that about six or eight months after he joined he was invited to a meeting in the woods, and when he got there he found all those in attendance in disguise. They formed a circle, he said; the captain, standing in the center, swore in some new members; they all put on their disguises, and then fell to discussing various individuals who were reported to need regulatory attention. When they demanded of Taliaferro that he take a new oath of membership in the Ku Klux Klan, stating that his White Rose oath wasn't strong enough for the sterner business of the Klan, he refused, so he said, and when they insisted he fled to Jackson.

J. F. Sessions of Franklin County, Mississippi, told of an organization in that county known as the Knights of the Black Cross, which dressed in a white robe and a white cap, but no mask. Members of the Black Cross took an oath of fidelity to the Constitution of the United States and swore to endeavor to secure the success of the Conservative or Democratic Party. It was active in the elections of 1868; but after the elections it faded out of sight. Apparently there was some overdoing of the organization of secret societies at that time, for Mr. Sessions also testified that when an organizer came to town and attempted to start something else of the same kind the impetuous young men of the town rode him out of town on a rail.

Another organization in Mississippi which showed a spurt of activity in 1870, when the Ku Klux Klan was beginning to wane, was the order known as the Seventy-Six Association, or simply as the Seventy-Six. The organizer and head man was said to be Doctor Thomas G. Gathright, who operated the Somerville Institute at Somerville in Noxubee County. This was purely a political order, in the interest of the Democratic Party, and was planned to be active throughout the whole country, with General Frank Blair at one time mentioned as its leader. So far as can be learned, however, it was never active to any great extent except in Mississippi and Louisiana; and did not exert its influence for a very long time even in those states. It had some prominent members, including such prominent ex-Confederates as General Braxton Bragg, General S. B. Buckner,

General Dabney H. Maury, General Cadmus Wilcox and others of similarly high standing. The preamble of the constitution of the order, as quoted by Doctor Fleming, set out its objectives as follows:

'To oppose by all peaceful and lawful means within our power the usurpations of the Radical party.

'To uphold the principles of the United States Constitution as established and interpreted by its framers.

'To vindicate the history of the South from the malignant and systematic assaults and aspersions of the Press, Pulpits and Politicians of the Radical party.

'To place before the world the true condition of the South during the recent war, and her condition at the present time.

'To form a nucleus around which the true men of the South may rally in contending for these great ends.

'To promote the material interests of the South.

'And, further, as an auxilliary to this association, to establish and maintain in the City of New Orleans a newspaper which shall be devoted to the advancement, advocacy and dissemination of these principles.'

It is not of record that any such newspaper was ever established in New Orleans, and probably the association collapsed before this ambitious project could be realized.

'The Robertson Family' was the odd name of another Mississippi organization (said by some to be identical with The Seventy-Six) which took its name from its password, which consisted of this dialogue:

'Do you know Robertson?'

'What Robertson?'

'Squire Robertson.'

'Yes, I know him,' this latter response being accompanied by drawing the right hand rapidly across the brow and back over the right ear as though brushing back the hair.

This gesture with the hand was suspiciously similar to the

sign of the Ku Klux; and it was said by some Mississippi writers that the Robertson Family was 'an offshoot of the Ku Klux Klan and affiliated with it.' This supposition, however, appears to be entirely gratuitous and unsupported, as there is no evidence anywhere that they were in any way connected, except that possibly some of the members of one might also have been members of the other.

In Mississippi at the same time there was also 'The White Brotherhood,' which never amounted to very much. There were branches of this organization at two or three places in Alabama, just over the Mississippi line; and in Alabama the White Brotherhood and the Ku Klux were considered synonymous — which they probably were not.

Immediately following the close of the war there was a small but active local organization in the northeastern part of Mississippi known as 'Dow Blair's Regulators.' At that time there were a great deal of horse-stealing and other outrages being perpetrated on the citizens, in the absence of any official restraint, and this band of regulators was formed for the purpose of stamping out this disorder, which it pretty effectively did.

C. L. Casey, deputy United States marshal in Spartanburg, South Carolina, testified that as early as 1865 there was an organization of regulators in that part of the state who called themselves 'Slickers,' although he was unable to explain the significance or origin of the name. 'They would just go about hanging,' he explained vaguely; and then added, in terrified retrospect: 'God! they killed in those days.' But he was emphatic in his declaration that they were not Ku Klux, although they were 'disguised with some kind of faces.'

No other reference to the 'Slickers' is found in any other of the records pertaining to Reconstruction conditions in South Carolina; although soon after the war in some of the up-country counties there were some self-constituted bands of regulators who were bluntly styled 'bushwhackers' by the citizens, and whose marauding was looked upon as reprehensible by the law-abiding people regardless of political inclination.

A South Carolina organization surrounding whose aims and plans there was considerable mystery was the Council of Safety, which was organized following the elections in 1870 when it was feared that there was imminent danger from the belligerent black militia. It was a so-called secret society, but copies of its constitution were widely and publicly distributed and even printed in the newspapers. It was openly charged by the Radicals that it was just another name for the Ku Klux; but this charge was hotly denied by E. W. Seibels, a prominent Democratic leader who was one of the Council's admitted leaders. That the Council had in mind something more definite, and probably more drastic, than a mere political organization was indicated by the clause of its oath where the initiate swore never to reveal any of the secrets of the Council 'or the organization of which it may become a part,' and the further obligation to obey all its rules and mandates, specifically mentioning Articles II and III of the constitution. These articles read:

II

The objects of this organization are, first, to preserve the peace, enforce the laws, and protect and defend the persons and property of the good people of this state; and, second, to labor for the restoration of constitutional liberty, as taught by our forefathers, and to reform abuses in the government, state and national.

III

Its operations shall be two-fold:

1. Political, social and moral, under the forms of established laws.

2. Physical, according to the recognized principles of self-defense.

This reference to physical self-defensive operations aroused some curiosity, and some apprehension on the part of the Radicals; but the exact meaning of this clause was never publicly defined, and soon the necessity for definition disappeared as the Council of Safety faded from existence.

Mention of some of the pre-Ku Klux organizations in the state of Georgia was included in the official report of General Davis Tillson, head of the Freedmen's Bureau in that state, dated November 1, 1866. 'Bands of men styling themselves "Regulators," "Jayhawkers" and "Black Horse Cavalry,"' said Gen. Tillson, 'have infested different parts of the state, committing the most fiendish and diabolical outrages on the freedmen. I am unaware of a single instance where one of these villains has been arrested and brought to trial by the civil authorities. . . . I am led to believe that in some instances the civil authorities and well-disposed citizens have been over-awed by these organizations. In others, I fear the civil authorities have sympathized with them. Whenever they have neglected or refused to act, troops have been despatched to arrest the guilty parties; but, as the outlaws are generally well mounted, have the sympathy of more or less of the inhabitants, are familiar with the country, and have numerous opportunities for concealment, they generally escape.'

An organization which flourished in the Florida parishes of Louisiana after the disbandment of the Ku Klux, between 1872 and 1877, was known by its members simply as 'No. 298.' This order had branches or 'conclaves' throughout this part of Louisiana, notably in the parishes of East and West Feliciana, East Baton Rouge and Livingston, and it numbered among its membership some of the prominent men of that region, including the commanding officer of the United States troops in that district. In Volume I of the *Mississippi Valley Historical Review* is printed the ritual of this order as it was preserved in the records of the conclave at Jackson, Louisiana. 'No. 298,' like the other post-Ku Klux societies, had for its main purpose the ascendancy of the white natives over the negroes and carpetbaggers; but there is no record of its resorting to any deeds of violence, nor did its members affect any form of disguise.

This was just one of a scattering lot of post-Ku Klux organizations which after the final dissolution of the Ku Klux Klan sprang up in those parts of the South where the Ku Klux objectives had not been entirely accomplished. Long after the Klan had been disbanded and the last rumor of its activities had died away, there were societies and organizations in the South, working in the open and without disguise, but willing to resort to force if necessary to accomplish the preservation of what they considered the rights of the white people.

Aside from the White League in Louisiana and that vicinity, there were in South Carolina the numerous local 'Rifle Clubs,' 'Sabre Clubs' and 'Artillery Clubs' which had roughly the same purpose. The outstanding organization of the kind in South Carolina was the famous 'Red Shirts' commanded by General Wade Hampton, which finally swept the carpetbagger government out of South Carolina and by the decisiveness of its victory freed the South of the last lingering traces of the blight of Reconstructionism. The Red Shirt movement was virtually a revolution, accomplishing its objectives by armed force, though it resorted to no concealment.

These latter organizations, however, all came after the Ku Klux era. They worked in the open and without disguise, as conditions no longer made concealment necessary. In a way they were, to use the modern military parlance, 'mopping up' where the Ku Klux shock troops had made the initial successful assault against carpetbaggery. They consolidated the Ku Klux gains and helped to make permanent the improvements in political and social conditions effected by the decidedly irregular and violent methods of the Ku Klux.

XVII. DECLINE AND DISBANDMENT

Just when and under what circumstances the Ku Klux Klan was dissolved it is impossible to say exactly. As a matter of fact, it is hardly accurate to say that it was disbanded at all; it would be a closer approximation of the facts to say that it gradually melted away — and the melting process proceeded more rapidly in some sections than in others.

The popularly accepted story of the Klan's final days is that Nathan Bedford Forrest, the Grand Wizard of the Invisible Empire, issued a formal disbandment order and that the Klan forthwith destroyed its regalia, burned its rituals and ceased to exist. Forrest himself, in testifying before the Congressional Committee, made the broad statement that he suppressed the Ku Klux; but when pressed for details he was singularly vague as to how he accomplished this and just when he did it. It was early in 1868, he said at first; then he said that it must have been after the fall of 1868. A surviving member of the Klan in Memphis stated that his Den received the dissolution order in August, 1869, fixing the date with reference to the election of that year.

What is generally referred to as the disbandment order was issued by Grand Wizard Forrest late in January, 1869. The document is dated, in the Ku Klux code: 'Dismal Era, Fourth

Green Day, Last Hour, C.A.R.N.'; which, being interpreted, means January, fourth Monday, 12 o'clock, 1869. This order, however, is decidedly ambiguous in its wording, possibly intentionally so; and although it directly instructs that all uniforms and regalia be forthwith destroyed, it also specifically states that 'This order is not to be understood to dissolve the Order of the Ku Klux Klan, but it is hereby held more firmly together and more faithfully bound to each other in any emergency that may come.' This so-called order is in the form of a resolution, and starts off with 'Whereas, the Order of the Ku Klux Klan is in some localities being perverted from its original honorable and patriotic purposes,' going on to say that public sentiment was against masked organizations, and ordering that 'the masks and costumes of this order be entirely abolished and destroyed.' It was also decreed that there be no more 'demonstrations' until they were ordered by 'a Grand Titan or higher authority.'

The Ku Klux handbook, written in 1884 by D. L. Wilson and J. C. Lester, the latter one of the organizers of the original Pulaski society, stated that the disbandment was effected by a proclamation from Grand Wizard Forrest, the date of which is placed at 'a short while after Brownlow's order declaring martial law,' which was February 20, 1869. Concerning it they say:

'This proclamation recited the legislation directed against the Klan, and stated that the order had now, in large measure, accomplished the objects of its existence. At a time when the civil law afforded inadequate protection to life and property, when robbery and lawlessness of every description were unrebuked, when all the better elements of society were in constant dread for the safety of their property, persons and families, the Klan had afforded protection and security to many firesides, and, in many ways contributed to the public welfare. But greatly to the regret of all good citizens, some members of the Klan had violated positive orders; others, under the name and disguises of the organization had assumed to do acts of violence, for which the Klan was held responsible. The Grand Wizard had been invested with the power to determine questions of paramount importance to the interests of the order. Therefore, in the exercise of that power, the Grand Wizard declared that the organization heretofore known as the Ku Klux Klan was dissolved and disbanded.

'Members were directed to burn all regalia and paraphernalia of every description, and to desist from any further assemblies or acts as Ku Klux. The members of the Klan were counseled in the future as heretofore, to assist all good people of the land in maintaining and upholding the civil laws, and in putting down lawlessness. This proclamation was directed to all Realms, Dominions, Provinces and "Dens" in "the Empire." It is reasonably certain that there were portions of the Empire never reached by it. The Klan was widely scattered and the facilities for communication exceedingly poor. The Grand Wizard was a citizen of Tennessee. Under the statute just now quoted (Tennessee's anti-Ku Klux law, enacted by the Brownlow legislature) newspapers were forbidden to publish anything emanating from the Klan. So that there was no way in which this proclamation could be generally disseminated.

'Where it was promulgated, obedience to it was prompt and explicit.

'Whether obeyed or not, this proclamation terminated the Klan's organized existence as decisively and completely as Gen. Lee's last general order on the morning of the 10th (*sic*) of April, 1865, disbanded the Army of Northern Virginia.

'When the office of Grand Wizard was created and its duties defined, it was explicitly provided that he should have "the power to determine questions of paramount importance, and his decision shall be final." To continue the organization or to disband it was such a question. He decided in favor of disbanding and so ordered. Therefore the Ku Klux Klan had no organized existence after March, 1869.'

This book was written nearly twenty years after the event, and it is possible that Mr. Lester, despite his opportunity for inside information, may have been the victim of some confusion of memory as to this disbandment order and its provisions; also there seems a strong probability that the order to which he refers, despite the date he ascribes, may have been the same as the order issued in January, 1869, in which the destruction of the masks and costumes was ordered. It seems hardly reasonable that such an order should have been issued in January and then followed up with another proclamation a month later, again issuing the same instructions. Also, despite the rather sophistical reasoning advanced by Mr. Lester, the matter of the disbandment was hardly as simple and clean-cut a matter as he would make it appear. There were Ku Klux activities in Mississippi and the Carolinas long after the date of Forrest's disbandment order; and in at least one instance in Mississippi a Den was organized as late as 1870 by a man who had gone to Memphis (Forrest's home) for the purpose of getting the oath and ritual.

It is interesting to observe in this connection that the Original Prescript provided that the Grand Wizard was elected for a term of three years, his term beginning 'the first Monday in May, 1867'; and that there should be a new election of officers at the expiration of the initial term. Forrest's term as Grand Wizard, therefore, expired in May, 1870; and, since no steps were ever taken to re-elect him or to elect a successor, it seems safe to assume that the organization had officially ceased to exist at least by that time.

Some students of Reconstruction history have advanced the view that Forrest by his so-called disbandment order was merely playing a trick on the Radicals, using this means to lead them to believe that the Klan was disbanded when it really was not. This might possibly be so; but it is difficult to see how any such strategy could have been expected to be effective when the order itself was not publicly announced. Forrest was a master of deceit and trickery in his military operations; but no such scheme, however clever, could be expected to work unless the enemy were permitted to know something about it. A trap can't operate unless the bait is accessible.

There is an interesting piece of folklore in Tennessee to the effect that the disbandment of the Ku Klux came about as a result of a personal interview and understanding between Forrest and President Grant. According to this story, Forrest went to Washington to see Grant soon after the national elections of 1868, and then and there made a deal with the President-elect whereby he promised to return to Tennessee and disband the Ku Klux immediately in return for Grant's promise to withdraw all the Federal troops from the Southern States and end the Reconstruction oppression. If Forrest did make any such deal, however, he was very badly out-traded, as there was never the slightest indication that Grant had any intention of carrying out his alleged part of such a bargain. The last Federal troops were not withdrawn from the South until 1876, more than eight years after Grant's election; and the worst part of the oppression of Reconstruction, including the enactment of the vicious anti-Ku Klux Law and the inquisition conducted by the Congressional Committee, was during the eight years Grant sat in the White House. The picture of Grant and Forrest sitting in Washington, smoking their cigars and amiably negotiating for the peace of the Southern States, makes the background for a pretty story; but there probably is not an atom of fact in it.

In most sections of the South the dissolution of the Ku Klux was governed solely by local conditions; and, generally speaking, the Klan's end was more in the form of a spotty, slow and gradual disintegration than a formal and decisive disbandment.

In a great many places the more respectable members of the organization began to withdraw as the Klan's acts of violence increased under the influence of the wilder, desperate young men who infiltrated into its membership or adopted its disguise. Freed of this restraint, this younger and more irresponsible element frequently moved on to deeds of even greater violence, until sometimes the more mature and responsible members stepped in again and restrained them, or tried to restrain them.

David Schenck, reputed high official of the organization in North Carolina, told the investigating committee how the Klan disintegrated in that state: 'I heard that the Klan was committing some of these outrages, or were connected with them. I asked Mr. Summey, the marshall of the town, if he would not request Mr. Berrier to come to my office. He came, and I told him that these things were unlawful, and wrong morally, upon principle and every other way; and I advised him to disband these organizations if he could. I told him I thought that they were wrong. He went home, and as he afterwards told me, and as it has come out since in evidence, he did leave the Klan and several others did. They then reorganized, with Hobbes as chief. Hobbes came to me during the latter part of January, 1871, while the Ku Klux bill was under discussion in Washington, and told me the men he was connected with were committing this violence, and what should he do about it. I told him I had only to say what I had always said, that I was opposed to all that violence, and advised him to break it up if he could. He went home and left it. They then organized a third time, and I think Anderson Davis and nine men were left in it. Those are the remnants of that society; they are the last dregs of that concern.'

Asked the direct question: 'Whatever may have been your original idea of this organization and its purpose, you say it has been used in North Carolina for the purpose of committing these outrages?' to which he replied: 'Yes, sir. I can not shut my eyes to that fact. I think it has been very grossly perverted to improper purposes.'

A good statement of this prostitution of the Ku Klux in some sections during those latter days was included in a dispatch from a Georgia correspondent printed in the New York *World* in January, 1870: 'When the Ku Klux Klan was first introduced into Georgia, it seemed more like a sort of organized practical joke upon the negroes than any serious enterprise. . . . But before long the low-downers took to "Ku Klucking," as they call it, and then cruelties began to be practiced, and decent men withdrew from the organization altogether. Whenever a set of low, disorderly fellows feel inclined to commit a rascality, they put on masks and call themselves Ku Klux. A true statement of the case is not that the Ku Klux are an organized band of licensed criminals, but that men who commit crimes call themselves Ku Klux.'

One of the foremost factors tending to contribute to the breaking up of the original Ku Klux Klan and the destruction of its influence was this appearance throughout the South of groups of counterfeit Ku Klux who used the convenient and familiar disguise as a cloak for robbery, assault, assassination and other crimes. During its later days a good part of the real Klan's work consisted in seeking out and punishing these imitators; and, as these spurious Ku Klux were suppressed, the genuine members of the order gradually came to realize that they had set in motion a piece of machinery whose power they had not foreseen and which was rapidly getting beyond their control.

Misuse of the Ku Klux regalia by impostors was reported as early as 1868. In the neighborhood of Nashville there developed a gang of outlaws who operated in the Ku Klux disguise and who came to be known as 'the Black Ku Klux.' Their operations were resented and resisted by the genuine Klansmen of Middle Tennessee, and a sort of guerrilla warfare was maintained for several months between the Black Ku Klux and the real Ku Klux.

The spurious Ku Klux were also active in Maury County, Tennessee, as early as March, 1868, when three men in the disguise of the Klan went to the negro quarters on the Potter place a few miles west of Columbia and robbed the negroes. While they were passing through the premises of Mr. Clayton Abernathy (a reputed Ku Klux) he saw and stopped them and made them unmask, when, as he reported, he found them to be 'three notorious, negro-loving Brownlowites.' Two other counterfeit Ku Klux who committed an outrage on a negro in Maury County at this time were captured by genuine members of the Klan and turned over to the authorities at Columbia for punishment. The June 20 issue of the Columbia *Herald* told of a negro man who had been called to his door and shot, going on to say: 'The persons were in the disguise of Ku Klux, but it is the belief of all that they were counterfeit. They are represented as having been drunk and disorderly.' In the same issue of this paper it was related that 'some persons in the disguise of Ku Klux' had fired at some negroes playing marbles in the road by moonlight. 'Everybody is convinced that these men were not Ku Klux,' the editor said, 'and it is time that the real Ku Klux were exonerating themselves of the contumely and odium being cast upon them by counterfeits.'

The editor of the *Herald* must have had powers of clairvoyance as to what the Ku Klux would do in the circumstances, or else he got remarkably prompt reaction from his advice, for that very same day he issued an 'Extra' carrying a screaming headline of 'Warning to Bogus Ku Klux' in which it was stated: 'This morning we find inside our window the following important order. Last night there was a large body of men in town, in a singular uniform, and it is probable that it was their intention to leave the order so that it would appear in to-day's *Herald*. The *Herald*, however, was made up last night, and so we issue an extra for the benefit of our readers. It speaks for itself':

GENERAL ORDER NO. 1

Headquarters Province No. 1
Frightful Era, Crimson Epoch
Alarming Hour

'Fiat justitia ruat coelum'

To All Whom it May Concern:

Paragraph I. — Parties in Ku Klux and various other disguises have at different times and places made their appearance and committed unlawful acts. *This shall be stopped.*

Members of former Ku Klux Klans are ordered to *destroy* their disguises, *say nothing* and remain at home. If they are true to their oaths, and friends to the cause they swore to support, they will obey this order, as it emanates from the superior in rank to their Great Grand Cyclops; if they do not obey it, they shall be treated as *traitors, enemies and perjurers.*

Parties assuming masks or disguises for amusement, or for unlawful purposes, are ordered from this 20th day of May [June?], 1868, never to do so within the limits of this county. If they are good citizens who may desire doing so, they will at once see the propriety of attending to this command; if they are not, and if they disobey it, they shall be punished for their misdeeds, as an example to others, *by hanging.*

Members of this province are ordered never to appear in uniform or any disguise upon any pretext whatever, unless by order of the Den Commander; and the Den Commander will not order out any member or members without special orders from these headquarters. Any violation of this shall be punished by the highest penalty known in our constitution.

The persons who assumed disguises to perpetrate outrages, thereby bringing disgrace and discredit upon an organization formed for the benefit of our people, are known. This order is especially intended for them, *et id omne genus.*

There are true and tried members of this organization in each civil district of this county. Hundreds of well-armed and determined men can in two hours be rallied to any point in the county. They are well organized. They are not banded together to whip and abuse negroes, Rebels or Radicals, to molest or annoy the soldiers of the Union, nor to resist in any way the laws of the land. They are organized to preserve law and order, and their purpose shall not be defeated by outside parties, be they friends or foes.

Paragraph II — Members and officers of other Provinces have no right, and shall not — without written permission from the chief officer of the Dominion, or by request of the commander of this Province — enter into the same. *No infringement of this shall be allowed under any circumstances.*

Paragraph III — A detail is ordered out to-night to show that the above can be carried out, and to assure the citizens of this community that their lives, persons and property shall be protected by those who have their interest and the interest of our country at heart.

By order of the G.G., Province No. 1.

GRAND SCRIBE.

The 'G.G., Province No. 1' was the Grand Giant of Maury County, and it will be observed that his edict is addressed to three different classes of people: former members of the Ku Klux who, for some reason, had severed their connection with the order; persons innocently appearing in disguises for amusement; and those assuming the disguise to perpetrate outrages. The demonstration ordered — a parade through the streets of Columbia — was held that night; and apparently the warning was of some effect, for it seems that it was never necessary for the Klan to carry out its threat of punishing miscreants by hanging.

A somewhat similar admonitory proclamation was issued in the fall of 1868 by the Grand Dragon of the Realm of Tennessee, presumably General George W. Gordon, in which he expressed great indignation because 'outrages have been perpetrated by irresponsible parties in the name of the Klan.' This order in full was as follows:

Headquarters Realm No. 1
Dreadful Era, Black Epoch,
Dreadful Hour

General Order No. 1

Whereas, Information of an authentic character has reached these headquarters that the blacks in the counties of Marshall, Maury, Giles and Lawrence are organized into military companies, with the avowed purpose to make war upon and exterminate the Ku Klux Klan, said blacks are hereby solemnly warned and ordered to desist from further action in such organizations, if they exist.

The G.D. regrets the necessity of such an order. But this Klan shall not be outraged and interfered with by lawless negroes and meaner white men, who do not and never have understood our purposes.

In the first place, this Klan is not an institution of violence, lawlessness and cruelty; it is not lawless; it is not aggressive; it is not military; it is not revolutionary.

It is, essentially, originally and inherently a protective organization. It proposes to execute law instead of resisting it; and to protect all good men, whether white or black, from the outrages and atrocities of bad men of both colors, who have been for the past three years a terror to society, and an injury to us all.

The blacks seem to be impressed with the belief that the Klan is especially their enemy. We are not the enemy of the blacks, as long as they behave themselves, make no threats upon us, and do not attack or interfere with us.

But if they make war upon us they must abide the awful retribution that will follow.

The Klan, while in its peaceful movements and disturbing no

one, has been fired into three times. This will not be endured any longer; and if it occurs again, and the parties be discovered, a remorseless vengeance will be wreaked upon them.

We reiterate that we are for peace and law and order. No man, white or black, shall be molested for his political sentiments. This Klan is not a political party; it is not a military party; it is a protective organization, and will never use violence except in resisting violence.

Outrages have been perpetrated by irresponsible parties in the name of this Klan. Should such parties be apprehended, they will be dealt with in a manner to insure us future exemption from such imposition. These imposters have, in some instances, whipped negroes. This is wrong! wrong! It is denounced by this Klan, as it must be by all good and humane men.

The Klan now, as in the past, is prohibited from doing such things. We are striving to protect all good, peaceful, well-disposed and law-abiding men, whether white or black.

The G.D. deems this order due to the public, due to the Klan, and due to those who are misguided and misinformed. We therefore request that all newspapers who are friendly to law, and peace, and the public welfare, will publish the same.

By order of the G. D., Realm No. 1.

By the Grand Scribe.

In northern Alabama there was a flurry of trouble with imitation Ku Klux after the Klan had been formally disbanded in 1869 by public pronouncement in the Athens papers. The Ku Klux disguise offered so convenient and effective a medium for cloaking criminal deeds that the outlaw element of that part of the state boldly began to operate in Ku Klux raiment. Illicit distillers and horse-thieves and other law-breakers organized gangs which wore the standard disguise of the Klan; but there was no co-operation between the different gangs; in fact they not infrequently made raids on each other. It was a highly com-

plex situation — the spurious Ku Klux were fighting among
themselves, during intervals between their raids on the law-
abiding citizens; and meanwhile the respectable members of
the original Klan were trying to formulate some plan for bringing these unauthorized depredations to an end, something which
the regular law-enforcing officials and the soldiers seemed unable to do.

The situation grew so intolerable that there was eventually
held in Athens a mass-meeting of the citizens of that section in
which the outlawry of the masked bands was roundly denounced
and a determination was expressed to 'put down lawlessness.'
This meeting was participated in by a number of prominent
citizens of Athens who were known to have been active in the
original Ku Klux, and their participation in the meeting was
accepted as evidence of the true Klansmen's indignation at
crimes committed in their name.

Such meetings as this were not uncommon in the South at
this time. When Major Merrill took a detachment of United
States troops to Yorkville, South Carolina, in February, 1871,
following the disturbance there, he called a conference with the
leading men of the town and expressed his regret concerning the
activities of 'bands of disguised men' in that community, asking
for their co-operation in repressing these disturbances. As a
result of this conference, there was a meeting of the citizens at
which it was decided to publish in the Yorkville *Enquirer* a 'card'
setting forth their opposition to unlawful activities. Accordingly
the following statement, to which were appended some six
hundred signatures, was published:

'The undersigned citizens of York County, earnestly desiring
the preservation of the public peace and for the purpose of
guaranteeing to all citizens the protection of life and liberty,
respectfully urge it as a duty for every citizen to discourage all
acts of violence. We do not desire to dictate to others, but are
convinced that a repetition of violence must disorganize society

and result in a general state of insubordination, the consequences of which may be deplored when too late to be remedied.
As members of the community whose common interest is imperiled, we pledge our individual efforts and influence to prevent further acts of violence, and will aid and support the civil
authorities in bringing offenders to justice. We respectfully
solicit a hearty co-operation of our fellow-citizens throughout the
county in our efforts to preserve the peace and to prevent further
acts of violence and domestic disorder.'

The *Enquirer* carried a report of the conference with Major
Merrill, and in an editorial deploring the disturbances which
had brought the troops there referred to the Ku Klux Law
which had recently been enacted by Congress. The editorial
concluded: 'The Ku Klux Act comprehends all persons found
in disguise, or in unlawful assemblies on the highways, or on
the premises of another. This act will be enforced, and rigidly
enforced; and unless our people at once determine that there
must be no further acts of violence in the county, we will soon
have occasion to observe the practical operations of the law in
its utmost severity and with all its unpleasant consequences.'

Evidently this appeal was in vain, however, for on March 9
there appeared in the *Enquirer* what the editor designated as a
'Ku Klux Manifesto,' which he stated had been received by him
through the mail. This document was headed 'Extract of Minutes,' and said:

Article 1. Whereas there are malicious and evil-disposed persons who endeavor to perpetrate their malice, serve notices, and
make threats under the cover of our august name, now we warn
all such bogus organizations that we will not allow of any interference. Stop it!

Article 2. There shall be no interference with any honest,
decent, well-behaved person, whether white or black; and we
cordially invite all such to continue at their appropriate labor,

and they shall be protected therein by the whole power of this organization. But we do intend that the intelligent, honest white people (the tax-payers) of this county shall rule it! We can no longer put up with negro rule, black bayonets, and a miserably degraded and thievish set of law-makers, (God save the mark!) the scum of the earth, the scrapings of creation. We are pledged to stop it; we are determined to end it, even if we are 'forced by force to use force.'

Article 3. Our attention having been called to the letter of one Rose, county treasurer of York, we brand it as a lie! Our lieutenant was ordered to arrest him, that he might be tried on alleged charges of incendiarism (and if convicted he will be executed). But there were no shots fired at him and no money stolen; that is not in our line; the legislature of the state of South Carolina have a monopoly in that line.

By command of our chief

Official   K.K.K., A.A.G.

The activities of the false Ku Klux gave the true Klan much trouble in South Carolina, as in other parts of the South, and a good part of their time was spent in looking after offenses of this kind. In the spring of 1870 two unscrupulous white men in Union County sold a set of tools to a negro blacksmith, and then went to his shop one night, along with two of their friends, all dressed in Ku Klux disguise, and took the tools away from the negro. The genuine Ku Klux heard about this and they promptly ascertained the identity of the guilty white men, went to them and made them give the tools back to the negro blacksmith.

Two desperadoes named James R. Mullens and F. R. Cudd, living in the Pacolet River district of the state, were reported to be operating at the head of a band of counterfeit Ku Klux, whipping negroes and levying blackmail. This brought forth a public proclamation from the Cyclops of the local Den stating that there were spurious Ku Klux at work in that territory and that if they did not desist they would be violently dealt with. The depredations continued, whereupon the official Ku Klux visited the homes of Mullens and Cudd one night, called them out and said to them: 'You have been disguising yourselves and going over the county whipping negroes and alarming the people, and we intend to stop it. Bring your disguises here.' They took the disguises and burned them, and then took them out and administered a severe beating of 150 lashes to each of them.

'They claim a monopoly of that kind of rough justice, apparently,' commented one of the investigating Senators dryly when told of this episode; and this was indeed the fact. The Ku Klux of Union County, for example, stopped at nothing in carrying out their own decrees; but they were extremely jealous of their self-constituted authority, and when spurious Ku Klux began to make their appearance in that section the genuine Klan posted the following stern notice on the courthouse door:

Headquarters K. K. K.
Department of S. C.

General Order No. 49 from the G. G. C., SS —

We delight not in speech, but there is language which, when meant in earnest, becomes desperate. We raise the voice of warning, 'Beware! Beware!' Persons there are (and not unknown to us) who, to gratify some private grudge or selfish end, like Wheeler's men, so-called, are executing their low, paltry and pitiful designs at the expense not only of the noble creed we profess and act, but also to the great trouble and annoyance of their neighbors in various communities. We stay our hand for once; but if such conduct as frightening away laborers, robbery and connivance at the secrets of our organization is repeated, then the mockers must suffer and the traitors meet their merited doom. We dare not promise what we do not perform. We want no substitutes or conscripts in our ranks. We can be as generous as we are terrible; but stand back. We've said it; there shall be no interference.

By order of the grand chief,

A. O., GRAND SECRETARY.

One of the strangest manifestations of the counterfeit Ku Klux was the surprising prevalence of such practices by the negroes. In April, 1871, a negro man named Tom Durham was killed in Mississippi while disguised as a Ku Klux; and it was no uncommon thing in that state for the negroes to assume the Klan's regalia for the purpose of Ku Kluxing each other for personal reasons. The first arrest made under Mississippi's Ku Klux law was that of a carpetbagger white man and a band of negroes who Ku Kluxed one of their own race.

In January, 1871, a negro named Bill Garrison, who had been pardoned from the South Carolina state penitentiary, returned to his home in York County and organized a gang of negroes who disguised themselves like Ku Klux and, armed with shotguns, raided and plundered a store owned by a white man named Douglas, near Yorkville. Garrison and three of the men escaped, but four of them were captured and, after one had confessed, three were sentenced to prison for the counterfeit Ku Klux raid.

There were negro Ku Klux also reported in Alabama and Georgia; and in Haywood County, Tennessee, a Democratic negro named William Johnson was Ku Kluxed by some Radical negroes in an effort to make him vote the Radical ticket. Tennessee also had Radical Ku Klux of white skins, and it was reported from Paris in 1868 that James Guthrie, the commissioner of registration there, and a leading Radical politician, was discovered to have a Ku Klux disguise hidden in his office which he frequently donned as a cover for some of his nocturnal mischief. Guthrie was also accused of sending Ku Klux warning notices to himself, permitting him thereby to pose as a martyr.

In April, 1868, one of the Tennessee papers boldly stated that 'Brownlow sent one of his Ku Klux in the shape of a negro preacher to burn a meeting house of the Loyal Leagues. Brownlow intended to lay the blame on the Ku Klux, but unfortunately for him his pet was caught by some negroes who now have him in charge.'

It was about this time that the Radical *Press and Times* in Nashville carried a news item telling of the burning of a negro school near Carthage, definitely charging it to the Ku Klux, who, they said, 'notified the teachers in a bloody handwriting,' with a coffin at the head of the letter, 'that they should suffer death unless they went north where they belonged.' Investigation revealed, however, so another Nashville paper reported, that the schoolhouse was burned by members of the Loyal League as a result of a quarrel with another faction of negroes in the community. A Carthage committee investigated the matter and reported that 'It is a mixed fight of negroes and their white assistants.' But it was reported in the Northern press as another horrible Ku Klux outrage.

It is a matter of speculation to what extent the demise of the Klan was hastened by the restrictive legislation aimed at it. Practically all the states embraced in the Invisible Empire passed Ku Klux laws of varying severity, and in 1871 the United States Congress enacted similar legislation modeled after the North Carolina law. Seldom has a more despotic piece of legislation disgraced the statute books of the United States. By this act the Constitutional guarantees of the states were ruthlessly set aside; the Federal courts were given jurisdiction over the charges of assault, robbery and murder, with means provided through which the juries could be (and were) effectively packed; and the President was authorized to declare martial law and to suspend the writ of habeas corpus when-

ever he chose. This infamous 'Force Bill' was roundly denounced in Congress and elsewhere, North and South, by
Democrats and also by Republicans. Senators Schurz and
Trumbull, partisans though 'they were, spoke strongly against it
while it was under consideration in the Senate; and James A.
Garfield assailed it in the House. Joining in the chorus of
criticism was General W. T. Sherman, then commander of
the United States Army, who at a public entertainment in
New Orleans said: 'I probably have as good means of information as most people in regard to what is called the Ku Klux. . . .
If Ku Klux bills were kept out of Congress and the Army kept
at their legitimate duties, there are enough good men in the
South to put down all Ku Klux or other marauders.'

Hundreds of alleged Ku Klux were arrested under the terms
of this Federal law, most of whom were never brought to trial,
although a handful were finally convicted and sent to prison
for short terms. The rigorous enforcement of this law, along
with the terror created by the wholesale arrests, may have
served to dampen the ardor of the Ku Klux in some localities,
especially in the Carolinas; but, in general, the Klan's disintegration closely paralleled the disappearance of the conditions
which brought it into being. The Ku Klux Klan could hardly
be accused of fear or timidity. They had operated under the
noses of an army of occupation for three years or more, in successful disregard of all efforts to confound and frustrate them.
The mere enactment of a proscriptive law would not in itself
have served suddenly to strike terror into the hearts of an
organization of such hardihood and cause them to curl up and
quit. As conditions began to right themselves, however, and
as irresponsible members and non-members of the Klan began
to use the Ku Klux disguise improperly, the leaders in the
organization, as well as those originally in sympathy with its
purposes, began to express doubts as to the advisability of
continuing it.

The feeling of the conservative and responsible people of the South at this time was reflected in an open letter addressed 'To the Ku Klux Organization' which ex-Governor Neill S. Brown published in the Nashville *Banner* early in 1869, urging them to desist and disband. 'I do not know the purpose of your organization,' wrote Governor Brown, 'nor am I aware of your masters. I never saw one of your body to know him. I have heard a thousand and one stories of your outrages, very many of which I believe to have been exaggerated.' But, he went on, whatever may have been their motives at the beginning, admitting the insecurity of life and property, those times had passed away and, he concluded: 'We must have peace, and law and order.'

Even such a stalwart Southerner as B. H. Hill of Georgia, in an interview given to a traveling correspondent of the Cincinnati *Commercial* in November, 1871, said: 'The Ku Klux business ... is the greatest blunder our people ever committed.' He expressed the belief that men originally went into the Klan believing that was the only way to protect themselves and their families against criminals; but, he said, bad men had taken advantage of the situation and had used the Ku Klux cloak for private vengeance, robbery and plunder, negroes as well as white men engaging in such outrages. Going a step further he said: 'I believe that some of these outrages were actually perpetrated by the political friends of the parties slain, for the purpose of manufacturing a feeling at the North against the South and producing a reconstruction of the state.'

This was a serious charge of heinous and almost unbelievable depravity, but there were a good many people who believed it. Also, there was a widespread belief, in the North as well as in the South, that the reports of Ku Klux outrages were very greatly exaggerated in the North, for political purposes. Following the election of Grant in November, 1868, there was a sudden and noticeable falling off in the reports of Ku Klux

activities. The Radicals ascribed this to the righteous fear that
was thrown into the Rebels' hearts by the victory of the Republicans; but the Conservative press boldly charged that the
pre-election reports of terror and maltreatment had been
largely manufactured for political purposes. The Louisville
Courier Journal remarked that 'The Radicals have a large
supply of "Ku Klux" outrages left over after the election,'
going on to say that 'the St. Louis *Democrat* accounts for having
exhausted its quota of outrages by noticing the report of the
Ku Klux having closed the assassination department of their
concern and being about to hold on a while until they can
learn the wishes of the High Morose Cyclops.'

But gradually the reports of Ku Klux outrages grew less and
less frequent until mention of them finally disappeared from
the pages of the daily papers, this for the simple reason that
the Klan itself had ceased to exist and with it its works. For
the date of its death, as for its birth, it is impossible to ascribe a
specific day and month and year. It was; and then it was not —
no man could say when the one condition ended and the other
began.

It was organized for a definite purpose — the protection of
the Southern white people during the years when they had no
other protection, and the prevention of the political over-
mastery of the white citizens by the blacks. In achieving its
purposes it adopted sometimes heroic, illegal methods; but
there was no question in their minds as to the fact that the end
justified the means. Realizing the inherent dangers of such a
powerful engine of regulation, they ceased its use as soon as it
had served their purpose, their original objectives fairly well
attained.

So lived and so died the Ku Klux Klan. It made its name a
symbol of terror and desperation. There are today many thousands of Americans who think of it as an indefensible gang of
outlaws and murderers. But ask any person who lived in the

South during that wild nightmare called the Reconstruction and who saw the Klansmen as they went about their self-appointed task, ask such a one and from the light in his eyes it will be easy to see that the Klan in his memory is clad in shining armor, *sans peur et sans reproche.*

378

APPENDIX

Damnant quod non intelligunt.

PRESCRIPT

OF THE

❀   ❀

———•—•—•———

What may this mean,
That thou, dead corse, again, in complete steel,
Revisit'st thus the glimpses of the moon,
Making night hideous; and we fools of nature,
So horridly to shake our disposition,
With thoughts beyond the reaches of our souls?

———•—•—•———

An' now auld Cloots, I ken ye're thinkin',
A certain *Ghoul* is rantin', drinkin',
Some luckless night will send him linkin',
       To your black pit;
But, faith! he'll turn a corner jinkin',
       An' cheat you yet.

382

1800'S

CREED

We, the * * , reverently acknowledge the Majesty and Supremacy of the Divine Being, and recognize the Goodness and Providence of the Same.

PREAMBLE

We recognize our relations to the United States Government, and acknowledge the supremacy of its laws.

APPELLATION

ARTICLE I. This organization shall be styled and denominated the * *

TITLES

Art. II. The officers of this * shall consist of a Grand Wizard of the Empire and his ten Genii; a Grand Dragon of the Realm and his eight Hydras; a Grand Titan of the Dominion and his six Furies; a Grand Giant of the Province and his four Goblins; a Grand Cyclops of the Den and his two Night Hawks; a Grand Magi, a Grand Monk, a Grand Exchequer, a Grand Turk, a Grand Scribe, A Grand Sentinel, and a Grand Ensign.

Sec. 2. The body politic of this * shall be designated and known as 'Ghouls,'

DIVISIONS

Art III. This * shall be divided into five departments, all combined, constituting the Grand * of the Empire. The second department to be called the Grand * of the Realm. The third, the Grand * of the Dominion. The fourth, the Grand * of the Province. The fifth, the * of the Den.

DUTIES OF OFFICERS

GRAND WIZARD

Art. IV. Sec. 1. It shall be the duty of the Grand Wizard, who is the Supreme Officer of the Empire, to communicate with and receive reports from the Grand Dragons of Realms, as to the condition, strength, efficiency and progress of the *s within their respective Realm. And he shall communicate from time to time, to all subordinate *s, through the Grand Dragons, the condition, strength, efficiency, and progress of the *s throughout his vast Empire; and such other information as he may deem expedient to impart. And it shall further be his duty to keep by his G Scribe a list of the names (without any caption or explanation whatever) of the Grand Dragons of the different Realms of his Empire, and shall number such Realms with the Arabic numerals, 1, 2, 3, &c., *ad finem*. And he shall instruct his Grand Exchequer as to the appropriation and disbursement which he shall make of the revenue of the * that comes to his hands. He shall have the sole power to issue copies of this Prescript, through his Subalterns and Deputies, for the organization and establishment of subordinate *s. And he shall have the further power to appoint his Genii; also, a Grand Scribe and a Grand Exchequer for his Department, and to appoint and ordain Special Deputy Grand Wizards to assist him in the more rapid and effectual dissemination and establishment of the * throughout his Empire. He is further empowered to appoint and instruct Deputies, to organize and control Realms, Dominions, Provinces, and Dens, until the same shall elect a Grand Dragon, a Grand Titan, a Grand Giant, and a Grand Cyclops, in the manner hereinafter provided. And when a question of paramount importance to the interest or prosperity of the * arises, not provided for in this Prescript, he shall have power to determine such question, and his decision shall be final, until the same shall be provided for by amendment as hereinafter provided.

GRAND DRAGON

Sec. 2. It shall be the duty of the Grand Dragon who is the Chief Officer of the Realm, to report to the Grand Wizard when required by that officer, the condition, strength, efficiency, and progress of the * within his Realm, and to transmit through the Grand Titan to the subordinate *s of his Realm, all information or intelligence conveyed to him by the Grand Wizard for that purpose, and all such other information or instruction as he may think will promote the interests of the *. He shall keep by his G. Scribe a list of the names (without any caption) of the Grand Titans of the different Dominions of his Realm, and shall report the same to the Grand Wizard when required; and shall number the Dominions of his Realm with the Arabic numerals, 1, 2, 3, &c., *ad finem*. He shall instruct his Grand Exchequer as to the appropriation and disbursement of the revenue of the * that comes to his hands. He shall have the power to appoint his Hydras; also, a Grand Scribe and a Grand Exchequer for his Department, and to appoint and ordain Special Deputy Grand Dragons to assist him in the more rapid and effectual dissemination and establishment of the * throughout his Realm. He is further empowered to appoint and instruct Deputies to organize and control Dominions, Provinces and Dens, until the same shall elect a Grand Titan, a Grand Giant, and Grand Cyclops, in the manner hereinafter provided.

GRAND TITAN

Sec. 3. It shall be the duty of the Grand Titan who is the Chief Officer of the Dominion, to report to the Grand Dragon when required by that officer, the condition, strength, efficiency, and progress of the * within his Dominion, and to transmit, through the Grand Giants to the subordinate *s of his Dominion, all information or intelligence conveyed to him by the Grand Dragon for that purpose, and all such other information or instruction as he may think will enhance the interests of the *. He shall keep, by his G. Scribe, a list of the names (without caption) of the Grand Giants of the different Provinces of his Dominion, and shall report the same to the Grand Dragon when required; and he shall number the Provinces of his Dominion with the Arabic numerals, 1, 2, 3, &c., ad finem. And he shall instruct and direct his Grand Exchequer as to the appropriation and disbursement of the revenue of the * that comes to his hands. He shall have power to appoint his Furies; also to appoint a Grand Scribe and a Grand Exchequer for his department, and appoint and ordain Special Deputy Grand Titans to assist him in the more rapid and effectual dissemination and establishment of the * throughout his Dominion. He shall have further power to appoint and instruct Deputies to organize and control Provinces and Dens, until the same shall elect a Grand Giant and a Grand Cyclops, in the manner hereinafter provided.

GRAND GIANT

Sec. 4. It shall be the duty of the Grand Giant, who is the Chief Officer of the Province, to supervise and administer general and special instruction in the formation and establishment of *s within his Province, and to report to the Grand Titan, when required by that officer, the condition, strength, progress and efficiency of the * throughout his Province, and to transmit, through the Grand Cyclops, to the subordinate *s of his Province, all information or intelligence conveyed to him by the Grand Titan for that purpose, and such other information and instruction as he may think will advance the interests of the *. He shall keep by his G Scribe a list of the names (without caption) of the Grand Cyclops of the various

Dens of his Province, and shall report the same to the Grand Titan when required; and shall number the Dens of his Province with the Arabic numerals, 1, 2, 3, &c., *ad finem*. And shall determine and limit the number of Dens to be organized in his Province. And he shall instruct and direct his Grand Exchequer as to what appropriation and disbursement he shall make of the revenue of the * that comes to his hands. He shall have power to appoint his Goblins; also, a Grand Scribe and a Grand Exchequer for his department, and to appoint and ordain Special Deputy Grand Giants to assist him in the more rapid and effectual dissemination and establishment of the * throughout his Province. He shall have the further power to appoint and instruct Deputies to organize and control Dens, until the same shall elect a Grand Cyclops in the manner hereinafter provided. And in all cases, he shall preside at and conduct the Grand Council of Yahoos.

GRAND CYCLOPS

Sec. 5. It shall be the duty of the Grand Cyclops to take charge of the * of his Den after his election, under the direction and with the assistance (when practicable) of the Grand Giant, and in accordance with, and in conformity to the provisions of this Prescript, a copy of which shall in all cases be obtained before the formation of a * begins. It shall further be his duty to appoint all regular meetings of his * and to preside at the same — to appoint irregular meetings when he deems it expedient, to preserve order in his Den, and to impose fines for irregularities or disobedience of orders, and to receive and initiate candidates for admission into the * after the same shall have been pronounced competent and worthy to become members by the Investigating Committee. He shall make a quarterly report to the Grand Giant, of the condition, strength and efficiency of the * of his Den, and shall convey to the Ghouls of his Den, all information or intelligence conveyed to him by the Grand Giant for that purpose, and all such other information or instruction as he may think will conduce to the interests and welfare of the *. He shall preside at and conduct the Grand Council of Centaurs. He shall have power to appoint his Night Hawks, his Grand Scribe, his Grand Turk, his Grand Sentinel, and his Grand Ensign. And he shall instruct and direct the Grand Exchequer of his Den, as to what appropriation and disbursement he shall make of the revenue of the * that comes to his hands. And for any small offense he may punish any member by fine, and may reprimand him for the same: And he may admonish and reprimand the * of his Den for any imprudence, irregularity or transgression, when he is convinced or advised that the interests, welfare and safety of the * demand it.

GRAND MAGI

Sec. 6. It shall be the duty of the Grand Magi, who is the Second Officer, in authority, of the Den, to assist the Grand Cyclops and to obey all the proper orders of that officer. To preside at all meetings in the Den in the absence of the Grand Cyclops; and to exercise during his absence all the powers and authority conferred upon that officer.

GRAND MONK

Sec. 7. It shall be the duty of the Grand Monk, who is the third officer, in authority, of the Den, to assist and obey all the proper orders of the Grand Cyclops and the Grand Magi. And in the absence of both of these officers, he shall preside at and conduct the meetings in the Den, and shall exercise all the powers and authority conferred upon the Grand Cyclops.

GRAND EXCHEQUER

Sec. 8. It shall be the duty of the Grand Exchequers of the different Departments of the * to keep a correct account of all the revenue of the * that shall come to their hands, and shall make no appropriation or disbursement of the same except under the orders and direction of the chief officer of their respective departments. And it shall further be the duty of the Grand Exchequer of Dens to collect the initiation fees, and all fines imposed by the Grand Cyclops.

GRAND TURK

Sec. 9. It shall be the duty of the Grand Turk, who is the Executive Officer of the Grand Cyclops, to notify the ghouls of the Den of all informal or irregular meetings appointed by the Grand Cyclops, and to obey and execute all the lawful orders of that officer in the control and government of his Den. It shall further be his duty to receive and question at the Out-Posts, all candidates for admission into the *, and shall *there* administer the preliminary obligation required, and then to conduct such candidate or candidates to the Grand Cyclops at his Den, and to assist him in the initiation of the same. And it shall further be his duty to act as the Executive officer of the Grand Council of Centaurs.

GRAND SCRIBE

Sec. 10. It shall be the duty of the Grand Scribes of the different departments to conduct the correspondence and write the orders of

the chiefs of their departments, when required. And it shall further
be the duty of the Grand Scribes of the Den to keep a list of the
names (without caption) of the ghouls of the Den — to call the Roll
at all regular meetings and to make the quarterly report under the
direction of the Grand Cyclops.

GRAND SENTINEL

Sec. 11. It shall be the duty of the Grand Sentinel to detail, take
charge of, post and instruct the Grand Guard under the direction
and orders of the Grand Cyclops, and to relieve and dismiss the
same when directed by that officer.

GRAND ENSIGN

Sec. 12. It shall be the duty of the Grand Ensign to take charge
of the Grand Banner of the *, to preserve it sacredly, and protect
it carefully, and to bear it on all occasions of parade or ceremony,
and on such other occasions as the Grand Cyclops may direct it to
be flung to the night breeze.

ELECTION OF OFFICERS

ART. V. Sec. 1. The Grand Cyclops, the Grand Magi, the Grand
Monk, and the Grand Exchequer of Dens, shall be elected semi-
annually by the ghouls of Dens. And the first election for these
officers may take place as soon as seven ghouls have been initiated
for that purpose.

Sec. 2. The Grand Wizard of the Empire, the Grand Dragons
of Realms, the Grand Titans of Dominions, and the Grand Giants
of Provinces, shall be elected biennially, and in the following manner,
to wit: The Grand Wizard by a majority vote of the Grand Dragons
of his Empire, the Grand Dragons by a like vote of the Grand Titans
of his Realm; the Grand Titans by a like vote of the Grand Giants
of his Dominion, and the Grand Giant by a like vote of the Grand
Cyclops of his Province.

The first election for Grand Dragon may take place as soon as
three Dominions have been organized in a Realm, but all subsequent
elections shall be by a majority vote of the Grand Titans throughout the Realm, and biennially as aforesaid.

The first election for Grand Titan may take place as soon as
three Provinces have been organized in a Dominion, but all subsequent elections shall be by a majority vote of all the Grand Giants
throughout the Dominion and biennially as aforesaid.

The first election for Grand Giant may take place as soon as three
Dens have been organized in a Province, but all subsequent elections

shall be by a majority vote of all the Grand Cyclops throughout the Province, and biennially as aforesaid.

The Grand Wizard of the Empire is hereby created, to serve three years from the First Monday in May, 1867, after the expiration of which time, biennial elections shall be held for that office as aforesaid. And the incumbent Grand Wizard shall notify the Grand Dragons, at least six months before said election, at what time and place the same will be held.

JUDICIARY

ART. VI. Sec. 1. The Tribunal of Justice of this * shall consist of a Grand Council of Yahoos, and a Grand Council of Centaurs.

Sec. 2. The Grand Council of Yahoos, shall be the Tribunal for the trial of all elected officers, and shall be composed of officers of equal rank with the accused, and shall be appointed and presided over by an officer of the next rank above, and sworn by him to administer even handed justice. The Tribunal for the trial of the Grand Wizard, shall be composed of all the Grand Dragons of the Empire, and shall be presided over and sworn by the senior Grand Dragon. They shall have power to summon the accused, and witnesses for and against him, and if found guilty they shall prescribe the penalty and execute the same. And they shall have power to appoint an Executive officer to attend said Council while in session.

Sec. 3. The grand Council of Centaurs shall be the Tribunal for the trial of ghouls and non-elective officers, and shall be composed of six judges appointed by the grand Cyclops from the ghouls of his Den, presided over and sworn by him to give the accused a fair and impartial trial. They shall have power to summon the accused, and witnesses for and against him, and if found guilty they shall prescribe the penalty and execute the same. Said Judges shall be selected by the Grand Cyclops with reference to their intelligence, integrity and fair mindedness, and shall render their verdict without prejudice or partiality.

REVENUE

ART. VII. Sec. 1. The revenue of this * shall be derived as follows: For every copy of this Prescript issued to the *s of Dens, Ten Dollars will be required. Two dollars of which shall go into the hands of the Grand Exchequer of the Grand Giant; two into the hands of the Grand Exchequer of the Grand Titan; two into the hands of the Grand Exchequer of the Grand Dragon, and the remaining four into the hands of the Grand Exchequer of the Grand Wizard.

Sec. 2. A further source of revenue to the Empire shall be ten per cent of all the revenue of the Realms, and a tax upon Realms, when the Grand Wizard shall deem it necessary and indispensable to levy the same.

Sec. 3. A further source of revenue to Realms shall be ten per cent of all the revenue of Dominions, and a tax upon Dominions when the Grand Dragon shall deem such tax necessary and indispensable.

Sec. 4. A further source of revenue to Dominions shall be ten per cent of all the revenue of Provinces, and a tax upon Provinces when the Grand Titan shall deem such tax necessary and indispensable.

Sec. 5. A further source of revenue to Provinces shall be ten per cent, on all the revenue of Dens, and a tax upon the Dens, when the Grand Giant shall deem such tax necessary and indispensable.

Sec. 6. The source of revenue to Dens, shall be the initiation fees, fines, and a *per capita* tax, whenever the Grand Cyclops shall deem such tax indispensable to the interests and purposes of the * .

Sec. 7. All of the revenue obtained in the manner herein aforesaid, shall be for the exclusive benefit of the *. And shall be appropriated to the dissemination of the same, and to the creation of a fund to meet any disbursement that it may become necessary to make to accomplish the objects of the *, and to secure the protection of the same.

OBLIGATION

ART. VIII. No one shall become a member of this *, unless he shall take the following oath or obligation:

'I, ——— of my own free will and accord, and in the presence of Almighty God, do solemnly swear or affirm that I will never reveal to any one, not a member of the *   * by any intimation, sign, symbol, word or act, or in any other manner whatever, any of the secrets, signs, grips, pass-words, mysteries or purposes of the *   *, or that I am a member of the same or that I know any one who *is* a member, and that I will abide by the Prescript and Edicts of the *   *. So help me God.'

Sec. 2. The preliminary obligation to be administered before the candidate for admission is taken to the Grand Cyclops for examination, shall be as follows:

'I do solemnly swear or affirm that I will never reveal anything that I may this day (or night) learn concerning the *   *. So help me God.'

ADMISSION

Art. IX. Sec. 1. No one shall be presented for admission into this *, until he shall have been recommended by some friend or intimate, who *is* a member, to the Investigating Committee, which shall be composed of the Grand Cyclops, the Grand Magi and the Grand Monk, and who shall investigate his antecedents and his past and present standing and connections, and if after such investigation, they pronounce him competent and worthy to become a member, he may be admitted upon taking the obligation required and passing through the ceremonies of initiation. *Provided*, That no one shall be admitted into this * who shall have not attained the age of eighteen years.

Sec. 2. No one shall become a member of a distant * when there is a * established and in operation in his own immediate vicinity. Nor shall any one become a member of any * after he shall have been rejected by any other *.

ENSIGN

Art. X. The Grand Banner of this * shall be in the form of an isosceles triangle, five feet long and three wide at the staff. The material shall be Yellow, with a Red scalloped border, about three inches in width. There shall be painted upon it, in black, a Draco-volans, or Flying Dragon,[1] with the following motto inscribed above the Dragon, 'QUOD SEMPER, QUOD UBIQUE, QUOD AB OMNIBUS.'[2]

AMENDMENTS

Art. XI. This Prescript or any part or Edicts thereof, shall never be changed except by a two-thirds vote of the Grand Dragons of the Realms, in Convention assembled, and at which Convention the Grand Wizard shall preside and be entitled to a vote. And upon the application of a majority of the Grand Dragons, for that purpose, the Grand Wizard shall appoint the time and place for said Convention; which, when assembled, shall proceed to make such modifications and amendment as it may think will advance the interest, enlarge the utility, and more thoroughly effectuate the purposes of the *.

INTERDICTION

Art. XII. The origin, designs, mysteries and ritual of this * shall never be written, but the same shall be communicated orally.

[1] See Webster's Unabridged Pictorial.

[2] 'What always, what every where, what by all is held to be true.'

REGISTER

I.	1st—Dismal.	7th—Dreadful.
	2nd—Dark.	8th—Terrible.
	3rd—Furious.	9th—Horrible.
	4th—Portentous.	10—Melancholy.
	5th—Wonderful.	11—Mournful.
	6th—Alarming.	12th—Dying.
II.	I—White.	IV—Black.
	II—Green.	V—Yellow.
	III—Blue.	VI—Crimson.

VII—Purple.

III.	1—Fearful.	7—Doleful.
	2—Startling.	8—Sorrowful.
	3—Awful.	9—Hideous.
	4—Woeful.	10—Frightful.
	5—Horrid.	11—Appalling.
	6—Bloody.	12—Last.

EDICTS

I. The Initiation Fee of this * shall be one dollar, to be paid when the candidate is initiated and received into the *.

II. No member shall be allowed to take any intoxicating spirits to any meeting of the * Nor shall any member be allowed to attend a meeting when intoxicated; and for every appearance at a meeting in such a condition, he shall be fined the sum of not less than one nor more than five dollars, to go into the revenue of the *.

III. Any member may be expelled from the * by a majority vote of the officers and ghouls of the Den to which he belongs, and if after such expulsion such member shall assume any of the duties, regalia or insignia of the * or in any way claim to be a member of the same, he shall be severely punished. His obligation of secrecy shall be as binding upon him after expulsion as before, and for any revelation made by him thereafter, he shall be held accountable in the same manner as if he were then a member.

IV. Every Grand Cyclops shall read or cause to be read, this Prescript and these Edicts to the * of his Den, at least once in every three months — And shall read them to each new member when he is initiated, or present the same to him for personal perusal.

V. Each Den may provide itself with the Grand Banner of the *

VI. The *s of Dens may make such additional Edicts for their control and government as they shall deem requisite and necessary. *Provided*, No Edict shall be made to conflict with any of the provisions or Edicts of this Prescript.

VII. The strictest and most rigid secrecy, concerning any and everything that relates to the * shall at all times be maintained.

VIII. Any member who shall reveal or betray the secrets or purposes of this * shall suffer the extreme penalty of the Law.

Hush, thou art not to utter what I am. Bethink thee; it was our covenant. I said that I would see thee once again.

L'ENVOI

To the lovers of Law and Order, Peace and Justice, we send greeting; and to the shades of the venerated Dead, we affectionately dedicate the * *

REVISED AND AMENDED

PRESCRIPT

OF THE

ORDER

OF THE

＊

＊   ＊

Damnant quod non intelligunt.

APPELLATION

This Organization shall be styled and denominated, the Order of the * * *.

CREED

We, the Order of the * * *, reverentially acknowledge the majesty and supremacy of the Divine Being, and recognize the goodness and providence of the same. And we recognize our relation to the United States Government, the supremacy of the Constitution, the Constitutional Laws thereof, and the Union of States thereunder.

CHARACTER AND OBJECT OF THE ORDER

This is an institution of Chivalry, Humanity, Mercy, and Patriotism; embodying in its genius and its principles all that is chivalric in conduct, noble in sentiment, generous in manhood, and patriotic in purpose; its peculiar objects being,

First: To protect the weak, the innocent, and the defenceless, from the indignities, wrongs, and outrages of the lawless, the violent, and the brutal; to relieve the injured and oppressed; to succor the suffering and unfortunate, and especially the widows and orphans of Confederate soldiers.

Second: To protect and defend the Constitution of the United States, and all laws passed in conformity thereto, and to protect the States and the people thereof from all invasion from any source whatever.

Third: To aid and assist in the execution of all constitutional laws, and to protect the people from unlawful seizure, and from trial except by their peers in conformity to the laws of the land,

ARTICLE I

TITLES

SECTION 1. The officers of this Order shall consist of a Grand Wizard of the Empire, and his ten Genii; a Grand Dragon of the Realm, and his eight Hydras; a Grand Titan of the Dominion, and his six Furies; a Grand Giant of the Province, and his four Goblins; a Grand Cyclops of the Den, and his two Night-hawks; a Grand Magi, a Grand Monk, a Grand Scribe, a Grand Exchequer, a Grand Turk, and a Grand Sentinel.

SEC. 2. The body politic of this Order shall be known and designated as 'Ghouls.'

ARTICLE II

TERRITORY AND ITS DIVISIONS

SECTION 1. The territory embraced within the jurisdiction of this Order shall be coterminous with the States of Maryland, Virginia, North Carolina, South Carolina, Georgia, Florida, Alabama, Mississippi, Louisiana, Texas, Arkansas, Missouri, Kentucky, and Tennessee; all combined constituting the Empire.

Sec. 2. The Empire shall be divided into four departments, the first to be styled the Realm, and coterminous with the boundaries of the several States; the second to be styled the Dominion, and to be coterminous with such counties as the Grand Dragons of the several Realms may assign to the charge of the Grand Titan. The third to be styled the Province, and to be coterminous with the several counties; *provided*, the Grand Titan may, when he deems it necessary, assign two Grand Giants to one Province, prescribing, at the same time, the jurisdiction of each. The fourth department to be styled the Den, and shall embrace such part of a Province as the Grand Giant shall assign to the charge of a Grand Cyclops.

ARTICLE III

POWERS AND DUTIES OF OFFICERS

GRAND WIZARD

Section 1. The Grand Wizard, who is the supreme officer of the Empire, shall have power, and he shall be required to, appoint Grand Dragons for the different Realms of the Empire; and he shall have power to appoint his Genii, also a Grand Scribe, and a Grand Exchequer for his Department, and he shall have the sole power to issue copies of this Prescript, through his subalterns, for the organization and dissemination of the Order; and when a question of paramount importance to the interests or prosperity of the Order arises, not provided for in this Prescript, he shall have power to determine such question, and his decision shall be final until the same shall be provided for by amendment as hereinafter provided. It shall be his duty to communicate with, and receive reports from, the Grand Dragons of Realms, as to the condition, strength, efficiency, and progress of the Order within their respective Realms. And it shall further be his duty to keep, by his Grand Scribe, a list of the names (without any caption or explanation whatever) of the Grand Dragons of the different Realms of the Empire, and shall number such Realms with the Arabic numerals 1, 2, 3, etc., *ad finem*; and he shall direct and instruct his Grand Exchequer as to the appropriation and disbursement he shall make of the revenue of the Order that comes to his hands.

GRAND DRAGON

Sec. 2. The Grand Dragon, who is the chief officer of the Realm, shall have power, and he shall be required, to appoint and instruct a Grand Titan for each Dominion of his Realm, (such Dominion not to exceed three in number for any Congressional District) said appointments being subject to the approval of the Grand Wizard of the Empire. He shall have power to appoint his Hydras; also, a Grand Scribe and a Grand Exchequer for his Department.

It shall be his duty to report to the Grand Wizard, when required by that officer, the condition, strength, efficiency, and progress of the Order within his Realm, and to transmit, through the Grand Titan, or other authorized sources, to the Order, all information, intelligence, or instruction conveyed to him by the Grand Wizard for that purpose, and all such other information or instruction as he may think will promote the interest and utility of the Order. He shall keep by his Grand Scribe, a list of the names (without caption) of the Grand Titans of the different Dominions of his Realm, and shall report the same to the Grand Wizard when required, and shall number the Dominion of his Realm with the Arabic numerals 1, 2, 3, etc., *ad finem*. And he shall direct and instruct his Grand Exchequer as to the appropriation and disbursement he shall make of the revenue of the Order that comes to his hands.

GRAND TITAN

Sec. 3. The Grand Titan, who is the chief officer of the Dominion, shall have power, and he shall be required, to appoint and instruct a Grand Giant for each Province of his Dominion, such appointments, however, being subject to the approval of the Grand Dragon of the Realm. He shall have the power to appoint his Furies; also, a Grand Scribe and a Grand Exchequer for his Department. It shall be his duty to report to the Grand Dragon when required by that officer, the condition, strength, efficiency, and progress of the Order within his Dominion, and to transmit through the Grand Giant, or other authorized channels, to the Order, all information, intelligence, instruction or directions conveyed to him by the Grand Dragon for that purpose, and all such other information or instruction as he may think will enhance the interest or efficiency of the Order.

He shall keep, by his Grand Scribe, a list of the names (without caption or explanation) of the Grand Giants of the different Provinces of his Dominion, and shall report the same to the Grand Dragon when required; and shall number the Provinces of his Dominion with the Arabic numerals 1, 2, 3, etc., *ad finem*. And he shall direct and instruct his Grand Exchequer as to the appropriation and disbursement he shall make of the revenue of the Order that comes to his hands.

GRAND GIANT

SEC. 4. The Grand Giant, who is the chief officer of the Province, shall have power, and he is required, to appoint and instruct a Grand Cyclops for each Den of his Province, such appointments, however, being subject to the approval of the Grand Titan of the Dominion. And he shall have the further power to appoint his Goblins; also, a Grand Scribe and a Grand Exchequer for his Department.

It shall be his duty to supervise and administer general and special instructions in the organization and establishment of the Order within his Province, and to report to the Grand Titan, when required by that officer, the condition, strength, efficiency, and progress of the Order within his Province, and to transmit through the Grand Cyclops, or other legitimate sources, to the Order, all information, intelligence, instruction, or directions conveyed to him by the Grand Titan or other higher authority for that purpose, and all such other information or instruction as he may think would advance the purposes or prosperity of the Order. He shall keep, by his Grand Scribe, a list of the names (without caption or explanation) of the Grand Cyclops of the various Dens of his Province, and shall report the same to the Grand Titan when required; and shall number the Dens of his Province with the Arabic numerals 1, 2, 3, etc., *ad finem.* He shall determine and limit the number of Dens to be organized and established in his Province; and he shall direct and instruct his Grand Exchequer as to the appropriation and disbursement he shall make of the revenue of the Order that comes to his hands.

GRAND CYCLOPS

SEC. 5. The Grand Cyclops, who is the chief officer of the Den, shall have power to appoint his Night-hawks, his Grand Scribe, his Grand Turk, his Grand Exchequer, and his Grand Sentinel. And for small offenses he may punish any member by fine, and may reprimand him for the same. And he is further empowered to admonish and reprimand his Den, or any of the members thereof, for any imprudence, irregularity, or transgression, whenever he may think that the interests, welfare, reputation or safety of the Order demand it. It shall be his duty to take charge of his Den under the instruction and with the assistance (when practicable) of the Grand Giant, and in accordance with and in conformity to the provisions of this Prescript — a copy of which shall in all cases be obtained before the formation of a Den begins. It shall further be his duty to appoint all regular meetings of his Den, and to preside at the same; to appoint irregular meetings when he deems it expedient; to preserve order and enforce discipline in his Den; to impose fines for irregularities or disobedience of orders; and to receive and initiate candidates for admission into the Order, after the same shall have been pronounced competent and worthy to become members, by the Investigating Committee herein after provided for. And it shall further be his duty to make a quarterly report to the Grand Giant of the condition, strength, efficiency, and progress of his Den, and shall communicate to the Officers and Ghouls of his Den, all information, intelligence, instruction, or direction, conveyed to him by the Grand Giant or other higher authority for that purpose; and shall from time to time administer all such other counsel, instruction or direction, as in his sound discretion, will conduce to the interests, and more effectually accomplish, the *real* objects and designs of the Order.

GRAND MAGI

SEC. 6. It shall be the duty of the Grand Magi, who is the second officer in authority of the Den, to assist the Grand Cyclops, and to obey all the orders of that officer; to preside at all meetings in the Den, in the absence of the Grand Cyclops; and to discharge during his absence all the duties and exercise all the powers and authority of that officer.

GRAND MONK

SEC. 7. It shall be the duty of the Grand Monk, who is the third officer in authority of the Den, to assist and obey all the orders of the Grand Cyclops and the Grand Magi; and, in the absence of both of these officers, he shall preside at and conduct the meetings in the Den, and shall discharge all the duties, and exercise all the powers and authority of the Grand Cyclops.

GRAND EXCHEQUER

SEC. 8. It shall be the duty of the Grand Exchequers of the different Departments to keep a correct account of all the revenue of the Order that comes to their hands, and of all paid out by them; and shall make no appropriation or disbursement of the same except under the orders and direction of the chief officer of their respective Departments. And it shall further be the duty of the Exchequers of Dens to collect the initiation fees, and all fines imposed by the Grand Cyclops, or the officer discharging his functions.

GRAND TURK

SEC. 9. It shall be the duty of the Grand Turk, who is the executive officer of the Grand Cyclops, to notify the Officers and Ghouls

of the Den, of all informal or irregular meetings appointed by the
Grand Cyclops, and to obey and execute all the orders of that
officer in the control and government of his Den. It shall further
be his duty to receive and question at the outposts, all candidates
for admission into the Order, and shall *there* administer the preliminary obligation required, and then to conduct such candidate or
candidates to the Grand Cyclops, and to assist him in the initiation
of the same.

GRAND SCRIBE

SEC. 10. It shall be the duty of the Grand Scribes of the different
Departments to conduct the correspondence and write the orders
of the Chiefs of their Departments, when required. And it shall
further be the duty of the Grand Scribes of Dens, to keep a list of
the names (without any caption or explanation whatever) of the
Officers and Ghouls of the Den, to call the roll at all meetings, and
to make the quarterly reports under the direction and instruction
of the Grand Cyclops.

GRAND SENTINEL

SEC. 11. It shall be the duty of the Grand Sentinel to take charge
of post, and instruct the Grand Guard, under the direction and
orders of the Grand Cyclops, and to relieve and dismiss the same
when directed by that officer.

THE STAFF

SEC. 12. The Genii shall constitute the staff of the Grand Wizard;
the Hydras, that of the Grand Dragon; the Furies, that of the Grand
Titan; the Goblins, that of the Grand Giant; and the Night-hawks,
that of the Grand Cyclops.

REMOVAL

SEC. 13. For any just, reasonable and substantial cause, any appointee may be removed by the authority that appointed him, and
his place supplied by another appointment.

ARTICLE IV

ELECTION OF OFFICERS

SECTION 1. The Grand Wizard shall be elected biennially by the
Grand Dragons of Realms. The first election for this office to take
place on the 1st Monday in May, 1870, (a Grand Wizard having
been created, by the original Prescript, to serve three years from

the 1st Monday in May, 1867); all subsequent elections to take place every two years thereafter. And the incumbent Grand Wizard shall notify the Grand Dragons of the different Realms, at least six months before said election, at what time and place the same will be held; a majority vote of all the Grand Dragons *present* being necessary and sufficient to elect a Grand Wizard. Such election shall be by ballot, and shall be held by three Commissioners appointed by the Grand Wizard for that purpose; and in the event of a tie, the Grand Wizard shall have the casting-vote.

SEC. 2. The Grand Magi and the Grand Monk of Dens shall be elected annually by the Ghouls of Dens; and the first election for these officers may take place as soon as ten Ghouls have been initiated for the formation of a Den. All subsequent elections to take place every year thereafter.

SEC. 3. In the event of a vacancy in the office of Grand Wizard, by death, resignation, removal, or otherwise, the senior Grand Dragon of the Empire shall immediately assume and enter upon the discharge of the duties of the Grand Wizard, and shall exercise the powers and perform the duties of said office until the same shall be filled by election; and the said senior Grand Dragon, as soon as practicable after the happening of such vacancy, shall call a convention of the Grand Dragons of Realms, to be held at such time and place as in his discretion he may deem most convenient and proper. *Provided*, however, that the time for assembling such Convention for the election of a Grand Wizard shall in no case exceed six months from the time such vacancy occurred; and in the event of a vacancy in any other office, the same shall immediately be filled in the manner herein before mentioned.

SEC. 4. The Officers heretofore elected or appointed may retain their offices during the time for which they have been so elected or appointed, at the expiration of which time said offices shall be filled as herein-before provided.

ARTICLE V

JUDICIARY

SECTION 1. The Tribunal of Justice of this Order shall consist of a Court at the Head-quarters of the Empire, the Realm, the Dominion, the Province, and the Den, to be appointed by the Chiefs of these several Departments.

SEC. 2. The Court at the Head-quarters of the Empire shall consist of three Judges for the trial of Grand Dragons, and the Officers and attachés belonging to the Head-quarters of the Empire.

SEC. 3. The Court at the Head-quarters of the Realm shall consist of three Judges for the trial of Grand Titans, and the Officers and attachés belonging to the Head-quarters of the Realm.

SEC. 4. The Court at the Head-quarters of the Dominion shall consist of three Judges for the trial of Grand Giants, and the Officers and attachés belonging to the Head-quarters of the Dominion.

SEC. 5. The Court at the Head-quarters of the Province shall consist of five Judges for the trial of Grand Cyclops, the Grand Magis, Grand Monks, and the Grand Exchequers of Dens, and the Officers and attachés belonging to the Head-quarters of the Province.

SEC. 6. The Court at the Head-quarters of the Den shall consist of seven Judges appointed from the Den for the trial of Ghouls and the officers belonging to the Head-quarters of the Den.

SEC. 7. The Tribunal for the trial of the Grand Wizard shall be composed of at least seven Grand Dragons, to be convened by the senior Grand Dragon upon charges being preferred against the Grand Wizard; which Tribunal shall be organized and presided over by the senior Grand Dragon *present;* and if they find the accused guilty, they shall prescribe the penalty, and the senior Grand Dragon of the Empire shall cause the same to be executed.

SEC. 8. The aforesaid Courts shall summon the accused and witnesses for and against him, and if found guilty, they shall prescribe the penalty, and the Officers convening the Court shall cause the same to be executed. *Provided* the accused shall always have the right of appeal to the next Court above, whose decision shall be final.

SEC. 9. The Judges constituting the aforesaid Courts shall be selected with reference to their intelligence, integrity, and fair-mindedness, and shall render their verdict without prejudice, favor, partiality, or affection, and shall be so sworn, upon the organization of the Court; and shall further be sworn to administer even-handed justice.

SEC. 10. The several Courts herein provided for shall be governed in their deliberations, proceedings, and judgments by the rules and regulations governing the proceedings of regular Courts-martial.

ARTICLE VI

REVENUE

SECTION 1. The revenue of this Order shall be derived as follows: For every copy of this Prescript issued to Dens, $10 will be required; $2 of which shall go into the hands of the Grand Exchequer of the Grand Giant, $2 into the hands of the Grand Exchequer of the Grand Titan, $2 into the hands of the Grand Exchequer of the

Grand Dragon, and the remaining $4 into the hands of the Grand Exchequer of the Grand Wizard.

SEC. 2. A further source of revenue to the Empire shall be ten per cent of all the revenue of the Realms, and a tax upon Realms when the Grand Wizard shall deem it necessary and indispensable to levy the same.

SEC. 3. A further source of revenue to Realms shall be ten per cent of all the revenue of Dominions, and a tax upon Dominions when the Grand Dragon shall deem it necessary and indispensable to levy the same.

SEC. 4. A further source of revenue to Dominions shall be ten per cent of all the revenue of Provinces, and a tax upon Provinces when the Grand Giant shall deem such tax necessary and indispensable.

SEC. 5. A further source of revenue to Provinces shall be ten per cent of all the revenue of Dens, and a tax upon Dens when the Grand Giant shall deem such tax necessary and indispensable.

SEC. 6. The source of revenue to Dens shall be the initiation fees, fines, and a *per capita* tax, whenever the Grand Cyclops shall deem such tax necessary and indispensable to the interests and objects of the Order.

SEC. 7. All the revenue obtained in the manner aforesaid, shall be for the *exclusive* benefit of the Order, and shall be appropriated to the dissemination of the same and to the creation of a fund to meet any disbursement that it may become necessary to make to accomplish the objects of the Order and to secure the protection of the same.

ARTICLE VII

ELIGIBILITY FOR MEMBERSHIP

SECTION 1. No one shall be presented for admission into the Order until he shall have first been recommended by some friend or intimate who *is* a member, to the Investigating Committee, (which shall be composed of the Grand Cyclops, the Grand Magi, and the Grand Monk,) and who shall have investigated his antecedents and his past and present standing and connections; and after such investigation, shall have pronounced him competent and worthy to become a member. *Provided,* no one shall be presented for admission into, or become a member of, this Order who shall not have attained the age of eighteen years.

SEC. 2. No one shall become a member of this Order unless he shall *voluntarily* take the following oaths or obligations, and shall *satisfactorily* answer the following interrogatories, while kneeling, with his right hand raised to heaven, and his left hand resting on the Bible:

PRELIMINARY OBLIGATION

'I —— solemnly swear or affirm that I will never reveal any thing that I may this day (or night) learn concerning the Order of the * * *, and that I will true answer make to such interrogatories as may be put to me touching my competency for admission into the same. So help me God.'

INTERROGATORIES TO BE ASKED:

1st. Have you ever been rejected, upon application for membership in the * * *, or have you ever been expelled from the same?

2d. Are you now, or have you ever been, a member of the Radical Republican party, or either of the organizations known as the 'Loyal League' and the 'Grand Army of the Republic?'

3d. Are you opposed to the principles and policy of the Radical party, and to the Loyal League, and the Grand Army of the Republic, so far as you are informed of the character and purposes of those organizations?

4th. Did you belong to the Federal army during the late war, and fight against the South during the existence of the same?

5th. Are you opposed to negro equality, both social and political?

6th. Are you in favor of a white man's government in this country?

7th. Are you in favor of Constitutional liberty, and a Government of equitable laws instead of a Government of violence and oppression?

8th. Are you in favor of maintaining the Constitutional rights of the South?

9th. Are you in favor of the re-enfranchisement and emancipation of the white men of the South, and the restitution of the Southern people to all their rights, alike proprietary, civil, and political?

10th. Do you believe in the inalienable right of self-preservation of the people against the exercise of arbitrary and unlicensed power?

If the foregoing interrogatories are satisfactorily answered, and the candidate desires to go further (after something of the character and nature of the Order has thus been indicated to him) and to be admitted to the benefits, mysteries, secrets and purposes of the Order, he shall then be required to take the following final oath or obligation. But if said interrogatories are not satisfactorily answered, or the candidate declines to proceed further, he shall be discharged, after being solemnly admonished by the initiating officer of the deep secresy to which the oath already taken has bound him, and that the extreme penalty of the law will follow a violation of the same.

FINAL OBLIGATION

'I ——— of my own free will and accord, and in the presence of Almighty God, do solemnly swear or affirm, that I will never reveal to any one not a member of the Order of the * * *, by any intimation, sign, symbol, word or act, or in any other manner whatever, any of the secrets, signs, grips, pass-words, or mysteries of the Order of the * * *, or that I am a member of the same, or that I know any one who *is* a member; and that I will abide by the Prescript and Edicts of the Order of the * * *. So help me God.'

The initiating officer will then proceed to explain to the new members the character and objects of the Order, and introduce him to the mysteries and secrets of the same; and shall read to him this Prescript and the Edicts thereof, or present the same to him for personal perusal.

ARTICLE VIII

AMENDMENTS

This Prescript or any part or Edicts thereof shall never be changed, except by a two-thirds vote of the Grand Dragons of the Realms, in convention assembled, and at which convention the Grand Wizard shall preside and be entitled to a vote. And upon the application of a majority of the Grand Dragons for that purpose, the Grand Wizard shall call and appoint the time and place for said convention; which, when assembled, shall proceed to make such modifications and amendments as it may think will promote the interest, enlarge the utility, and more thoroughly effectuate the purposes of the Order.

ARTICLE IX

INTERDICTION

The origin, mysteries, and Ritual of this Order shall never be written, but the same shall be communicated orally.

ARTICLE X

EDICTS

1. No one shall become a member of a distant Den, when there is a Den established and in operation in his own immediate vicinity; nor shall any one become a member of any Den, or of this Order in any way, after he shall have been once rejected, upon application for membership.

2. No Den, or officer, or member, or members thereof, shall operate beyond their prescribed limits, unless invited or ordered by the proper authority so to do.

3. No member shall be allowed to take any intoxicating spirits to any meeting of the Den; nor shall any member be allowed to attend a meeting while intoxicated; and for every appearance at a meeting in such condition, he shall be fined the sum of not less than one nor more than five dollars, to go into the revenue of the Order.

4. Any member may be expelled from the Order by a majority vote of the Officers and Ghouls of the Den to which he belongs; and if after such expulsion, such member shall assume any of the duties, regalia, or insignia of the Order, or in any way claim to be a member of the same, he shall be severely punished. His obligation of secrecy shall be as binding upon him after expulsion as before, and for any revelation made by him thereafter, he shall be held accountable in the same manner as if he were then a member.

5. Upon the expulsion of any member from the Order, the Grand Cyclops, or the officer acting in his stead, shall immediately report the same to the Grand Giant of the Province, who shall cause the fact to be made known and read in each Den of his Province, and shall transmit the same, through the proper channels, to the Grand Dragon of the Realm, who shall cause it to be published to every Den in his Realm, and shall notify the Grand Dragons of contiguous Realms of the same.

6. Every Grand Cyclops shall read, or cause to be read, this Prescript and these Edicts to his Den, at least once in every month; and shall read them to each new member when he is initiated, or present the same to him for personal perusal.

7. The initiation fee of this Order shall be one dollar, to be paid when the candidate is initiated and received into the Order.

8. Dens may make such additional Edicts for their control and government as they may deem requisite and necessary. *Provided*, no Edict shall be made to conflict with any of the provisions or Edicts of this Prescript.

9. The most profound and rigid secrecy concerning any and everything that relates to the Order, shall at all times be maintained.

10. Any member who shall reveal or betray the secrets of this Order, shall suffer the extreme penalty of the law.

ADMONITION

Hush! thou art not to utter what I am; bethink thee! it was our covenant!

REGISTER

I

1. Dismal,
2. Mystic,
3. Stormy,
4. Peculiar,
5. Blooming,
6. Brilliant,

7. Painful,
8. Portentous,
9. Fading,
10. Melancholy,
11. Glorious,
12. Gloomy.

II

I. White, II. Green, III. Yellow, IV. Amber, V. Purple, VI. Crimson, VII. Emerald.

III

1. Fearful,
2. Startling,
3. Wonderful,
4. Alarming,
5. Mournful,
6. Appalling,

7. Hideous,
8. Frightful,
9. Awful,
10. Horrible,
11. Dreadful,
12. Last.

IV

Cumberland.

L'ENVOI

To the lovers of law and order, peace and justice, we send greeting; and to the shades of the venerated dead we affectionately dedicate the Order of the * * *.

Resurgamus

APPENDIX III

INTERVIEW WITH GENERAL N. B. FORREST
Printed in the *Cincinnati Commercial*, August 28, 1868, with his reply

In August, 1868, a mild sensation was created by the publication in the Cincinnati *Commercial* of a news-letter from its traveling correspondent who was then in Memphis, and who reported an interview with General Nathan Bedford Forrest on the subject of the Ku Klux Klan, then a subject of absorbing interest throughout the entire country. This news article was as follows:

Memphis, Tenn., August 28, 1868.

To-day I have enjoyed 'big talks' enough to have gratified any of the famous Indian chiefs who have been treating with General Sherman for the past two years. First I met General N. B. Forrest, then General Gideon A. Pillow, and Governor Isham G. Harris. My first visit was to General Forrest, whom I found at his office, at 8 o'clock this morning, hard at work, although complaining of an illness contracted at the New York convention. The New Yorkers must be a bad set indeed, for I have not met a single delegate from the Southern States who has not been ill ever since he went there. But to General Forrest. Now that the southern people have elevated him to the position of their great leader and oracle, it may not be amiss to preface my conversation with him with a brief sketch of the gentleman.

I cannot better personally describe him than by borrowing the language of one of his biographers. 'In person he is six feet one inch and a half in height, with broad shoulders, a full chest, and symmetrical, muscular limbs; erect in carriage, and weighs one hundred and eighty five pounds; dark-gray eyes, dark hair, mustache and beard worn upon the chin; a set of regular white teeth, and clearly cut features'; which, altogether, make him rather a handsome man for one forty-seven years of age.

Previous to the war — in 1852 — he left the business of planter, and came to this city and engaged in the business of 'negro trader,' in which traffic he seems to have been quite successful, for, by 1861, he had become the owner of two plantations a few miles below here, in Mississippi, on which he produced about a thousand bales of cotton each year, in the meantime carrying on the negro-trading. In June, 1861, he was authorized by Governor Harris to recruit a regiment of cavalry for the war, which he did, and which was the nucleus around which he gathered the army which he commanded as lieutenant general at the end of the war.

After being seated in his office, I said:

'General Forrest, I came especially to learn your views in regard to the condition of your civil and political affairs in the State of Tennessee, and the South generally. I desire them for publication in the Cincinnati Commercial. I do not wish to misinterpret you in the slightest degree, and therefore only ask for such views as you are willing I should publish.'

'I have not now,' he replied, 'and never have had, any opinion on any public or political subject which I would object to having published. I mean what I say, honestly and earnestly, and only object to being misrepresented. I dislike to be placed before the country in a false position, especially as I have not sought the reputation I have gained.'

I replied: 'Sir, I will publish only what you say, and then you can not possibly be misrepresented. Our people desire to know your feelings toward the General Government, the State government of Tennessee, the radical party, both in and out of the State, and upon the question of negro suffrage.'

'Well, sir,' said he, 'when I surrendered my seven thousand men in 1865, I accepted a parole honestly, and I have observed it faithfully up to to-day. I have counseled peace in all the speeches I have made. I have advised my people to submit to the laws of the State, oppressive as they are, and unconstitutional as I believe them to be. I was paroled and not pardoned until the issuance of the last proclamation of general amnesty; and, therefore, did not think it prudent for me to take any active part until the oppression of my people became so great that they could not endure it, and then I would be with them. My friends thought differently, and sent me to New York, and I am glad I went there.'

'Then, I suppose, general, that you think the oppression has become so great that your people should no longer bear it.'

'No,' he answered, 'It is growing worse hourly, yet I have said to the people "Stand fast, let us try to right the wrong by legislation." A few weeks ago I was called to Nashville to counsel with other gentlemen who had been prominently identified with the cause of the confederacy, and we then offered pledges which we thought would be satisfactory to Mr. Brownlow and his legislature, and we told them that, if they would not call out the militia, we would agree to preserve order and see that the laws were enforced. The legislative committee certainly led me to believe that our proposition would be accepted and no militia organized. Believing this, I came home, and advised all of my people to remain peaceful, and to offer no resistance to any reasonable law. It is true that I never have recognized the present government in Tennessee as having any legal existence, yet I was willing to submit to it for a time, with the hope that the wrongs might be righted peaceably.'

'What are your feelings towards the Federal Government, general?'

'I loved the old Government in 1861; I love the Constitution yet. I think it is the best government in the world if administered as it was before the war. I do not hate it; I am opposing now only the radical revolutionists who are trying to destroy it. I believe that party to be composed, as I know it is in Tennessee, of the worst men on God's earth — men who would hesitate at no crime, and who have only one object in view, to enrich themselves.'

'In the event of Governor Brownlow's calling out the militia, do you think there will be any resistance offered to their acts?' I asked.

'That will depend upon circumstances. If the militia are simply called out, and do not interfere with or molest any one, I do not think there will be any fight. If, on the contrary, they do what I believe they will do, commit outrages, or even one outrage, upon the people, they and Mr. Brownlow's government will be swept out of existence; not a radical will be left alive. If the militia are called out, we can not but look upon it as a declaration of war, because Mr. Brownlow has already issued his proclamation directing them to shoot down the Ku Klux wherever they find them; and he calls all southern men Ku Klux.'

'Why, general, we people up north have regarded the Ku Klux as an organization which existed only in the frightened imaginations of a few politicians.'

'Well, sir, there is such an organization, not only in Tennessee but all over the South, and its numbers have not been exaggerated.'

'What are its numbers, general?'

'In Tennessee there are over forty thousand; in all the Southern States about five hundred and fifty thousand men.'

'What is the character of the organization, may I inquire?'

'Yes, sir. It is a protective, political, military organization. I am willing to show any man the constitution of the society. The members are sworn to recognize the Government of the United States. It does not say anything at all about the government of the State of Tennessee. Its objects originally were protection against Loyal Leagues and the Grand Army of the Republic; but after it became general it was found that political matters and interests could best be promoted within it, and it was then made a political organization, giving its support, of course, to the democratic party.'

'But is the organization connected throughout the State?'

'Yes, it is. In each voting precinct there is a captain, who, in
addition to his other duties, is required to make out a list of names
of men in his precinct, giving all the radicals and all the democrats
who are positively known, and showing also the doubtful on both
sides and of both colors. This list of names is forwarded to the
grand commander of the State, who is thus enabled to know who
are our friends and who are not.'

'Can you, or are you at liberty to, give me the name of the commanding officer of this state?'

'No; it would be impolitic.'

'Then I suppose there would be no doubt of a conflict if the militia
interfere with the people; is that your view?'

'Yes, sir; if they attempt to carry out Governor Brownlow's proclamation by shooting down Ku Klux — for he calls all southern men
Ku Klux — if they go to hunting down and shooting these men,
there will be war, and a bloodier one than we have ever witnessed.
I have told these radicals here what they might expect in such an
event. I have no powder to burn killing negroes. I intend to kill
the radicals. I have told them this and more. There is not a radical
leader in this town but is a marked man; and if a trouble should
break out, not one of them would be left alive. I have told them
that they were trying to create a disturbance and then slip out and
leave the consequences to fall upon the negro; but they can't do it.
Their houses are picketed, and when the fight comes not one of
them would ever get out of this town alive. We don't intend they
shall ever get out of the country. But I want it distinctly understood
that I am opposed to any war, and will only fight in self-defense.
If the militia attack us, we will resist to the last; and, if necessary,
I think I could raise 40,000 men in five days, ready for the field.'

'Do you think, general, that the Ku Klux have been of any benefit
to the State?'

'No doubt of it. Since its organization the leagues have quit
killing and murdering our people. There were some foolish young
men who put masks on their faces and rode over the country frightening negroes; but orders have been issued to stop that, and it has
ceased. You may say further that three members of the Ku Klux
have been court-martialed and shot for violations of the orders not
to disturb or molest people.'

'Are you a member of the Ku Klux, general?'

'I am not; but am in sympathy and will cooperate with them.

I know they are charged with many crimes they are not guilty of. A case in point is the killing of Bierfield at Franklin, a few days ago. I sent a man up there especially to investigate the case, and report to me, and I have his letter here now, in which he states that they had nothing to do with it as an organization.'

'What do you think of negro suffrage?'

'I am opposed to it under any and all circumstances, and in our convention urged our party not to commit themselves at all upon the subject. If the negroes vote to enfranchise us, I do not think I would favor their disfranchisement. We will stand by those who help us. And here I want you to understand distinctly I am not an enemy to the negro. We want him here among us; he is the only laboring class we have; and, more than that, I would sooner trust him than the white scalawag or carpetbagger. When I entered the army I took forty-seven negroes into the army with me, and forty-five of them were surrendered with me. I said to them at the start: "This fight is against slavery; if we lose it, you will be made free; if we whip the fight, and you stay with me and be good boys, I will set you free; in either case you will be free." These boys stayed with me, drove my teams, and better confederates did not live.'

'Do you think the Ku Klux will try to intimidate the negroes at the election?'

'I do not think they will. Why, I made a speech at Brownsville the other day, and while there a lieutenant who served with me came to me and informed me that a band of radicals had been going through the country claiming to be Ku Klux, and disarming the negroes, and then selling their arms. I told him to have the matter investigated, and, if true, to have the parties arrested.'

'What do you think is the effect of the amnesty granted to your people?'

'I believe that the amnesty restored all the rights to the people, full and complete. I do not think the Federal Government has the right to disfranchise any man, but I believe that the legislatures of the States have. The objection I have to the disfranchisement in Tennessee is, that the legislature which enacted the law had no constitutional existence, and the law in itself is a nullity. Still I would respect it until changed by law. But there is a limit beyond which men can not be driven, and I am ready to die sooner than sacrifice my honor. This thing must have an end, and it is now about time for that end to come.'

'What do you think of General Grant?' I asked.

'I regard him as a great military commander, a good man, honest and liberal, and if elected will, I hope and believe, execute the laws honestly and faithfully. And by the way, a report has been published in some of the newspapers, stating that while General Grant and lady were at Corinth, in 1862, they took and carried off furniture and other property. I here brand the author as a liar. I was at Corinth only a short time ago, and I personally investigated the whole matter, talked with the people with whom he and his lady lived while there, and they say that their conduct was everything that could be expected of a gentleman and lady, and deserving the highest praise. I am opposed to General Grant in everything, but I would do him justice.'

The foregoing is the principal part of my conversation with the general. I give the conversation, and leave the reader to form his own opinion as to what General Forrest means to do. I think he has been so plain in his talk that it can not be misunderstood.

As soon as General Forrest read this account of the interview with him, he addressed the following letter to the correspondent who wrote it:

Memphis, September 3, 1868.

Dear Sir:

I have just read your letter in the Commercial, giving a report of our conversation on Friday last. I do not think you would intentionally misrepresent me, but you have done so and, I suppose, because you mistook my meaning. The portions of your letter to which I object are corrected in the following paragraphs:

I promise the legislature my personal influence and aid in maintaining order and enforcing the laws. I have never advised the people to resist any law, but to submit to the laws, until they can be corrected by lawful legislation.

I said the militia bill would occasion no trouble, unless they violated the law by carrying out the governor's proclamation, which I believe to be unconstitutional and in violence of law, in shooting men down without trial, as recommended by that proclamation.

I said it was reported, and I believed the report, that there are forty thousand Ku Klux in Tennessee; and I believe the organization stronger in other states. I meant to imply, when I said that the Ku Klux recognize the Federal Government, that they would obey all State laws. They recognize all laws, and will obey them, so I have been informed, in protecting peaceable citizens from oppression from any quarter.

I did not say that any man's house was picketed. I did not mean to convey the idea that I would raise any troops; and, more than that, no man could do it in five days, even if they were organized.

I said that General Grant was at Holly Springs, and not at Corinth; I said the charge against him was false, but did not use the word 'liar.'

I can not consent to remain silent in this matter; for, if I did so, under an incorrect impression of my personal views, I might be looked upon as one desiring a conflict, when, in truth, I am so averse to anything of the kind that I will make any honorable sacrifice to avoid it.

Hoping that I may have this explanation placed before your readers, I remain, very respectfully,

N. B. FORREST

APPENDIX IV

PERSONNEL OF THE JOINT SELECT COMMITTEE TO INQUIRE INTO THE CONDITIONS OF AFFAIRS IN THE LATE INSURRECTIONARY STATES

John Scott, Senator from Pennsylvania, was born in that state in 1824, was elected as a Republican in 1868 and served from March, 1869, to March, 1875, not being a candidate for re-election.

Zachariah Chandler, Senator from Michigan, was born in New Hampshire in 1813, and was prominent in the organization of the Republican Party in 1854. He served in the Senate from 1857 to 1875, being defeated for re-election that year, but was re-elected again in February, 1879, and served until his death in November of the same year.

Benjamin Franklin Rice, Senator from Arkansas, was born in New York State in 1828. He was admitted to the bar in Kentucky, and later moved to Minnesota. He served as captain and adjutant general in the Minnesota volunteers during the Civil War, but settled in Little Rock, Arkansas, in 1864, taking up the practice of law there. He helped organize the Republican Party in Arkansas, and was elected to the Senate in 1868, serving until 1873, when he resumed his law practice in Arkansas.

John Pool was born in North Carolina in 1826, and was elected to the Senate as a Republican from that state, serving from 1868 to 1873, and not being a candidate for re-election.

Daniel Darwin Pratt, Senator from Indiana, was born in Maine in 1813 and moved to Indiana in 1832; he was elected to the Senate in 1869 and served until 1875.

Francis Preston Blair, Jr., Senator from Missouri, was born in Kentucky in 1821. He served in the Mexican War, and resigned from the House of Representatives in 1861 to become a colonel in the Union army, advancing to the rank of brigadier general. He was an unsuccessful candidate for Vice-President on the Democratic ticket in 1868, but was elected to the Senate in 1871 to fill the unexpired term of Charles D. Drake, resigned. He served until 1873, and was not a candidate for re-election.

Thomas Francis Bayard, Sr., was a native of Delaware and was elected to the Senate from that state as a Democrat in 1869, serving until 1885, when he resigned to become Secretary of State.

Luke Potter Poland, Representative (and previously Senator) from Vermont, was born in that state in 1815. He was elected to the House as a Republican, serving from 1867 to 1875, being an unsuccessful candidate for re-election.

Horace Maynard, Representative from Tennessee, was born in Massachusetts in 1814, moving in 1839 to Tennessee, where he became active in politics as a Whig. He was elected to the House as a Republican, serving from 1866 to 1875, not being a candidate for re-election.

Glenni William Scofield, Representative from Pennsylvania, was born in New York State in 1817. He was elected to Congress as a Republican, serving from 1863 to 1875; he was not a candidate for re-election.

John Franklin Farnsworth, Representative from Illinois, was born in Canada in 1820, later moving to Michigan and then to Chicago. He was elected as a Republican in 1857 and served until 1861, not standing for re-election. He served in the Union army during the Civil War, reaching the rank of brigadier general, but was elected to Congress again in 1863 and resigned his commission to take up his duties in the House. He served until 1873, being an unsuccessful candidate for re-election.

John Coburn, Representative from Indiana, was born in that state in 1825; he served in the Union Army, being breveted brigadier general in 1865, and was elected to Congress in 1867. He served until 1875, an unsuccessful candidate for re-election.

Job Evans Stevenson, Representative from Ohio, born in that state in 1832, was elected to Congress as a Republican and served from 1869 to 1873, when he resumed his practice of law in Cincinnati.

Benjamin Franklin Butler, Representative from Massachusetts, was born in New Hampshire in 1818, moving to Massachusetts in 1828. He was a delegate to the Democratic national conventions in Charleston and Baltimore in 1860; he entered the Union army as a brigadier general in 1861, and rose to be a major general, resigning in 1865, after commanding at New Orleans, Fortress

Monroe, etc. He was elected to Congress as a Republican in 1867 and served until 1875, also from 1877 to 1879, declining to stand for renomination.

William Esselstyne Lansing, Representative from New York, was born in that state in 1821. He was elected to Congress as a Republican in 1861, serving until 1863; he was not a candidate for re-election, but was elected again in 1871 and served until 1875, when he retired voluntarily to practice law.

Samuel Sullivan Cox was born in Ohio in 1824; he was elected to Congress from that state as a Democrat and served from 1857 to 1865, being an unsuccessful candidate for re-election. He moved to New York City in 1865, and was elected to the House from that state in 1869, serving until 1873, when he was defeated for re-election, but was subsequently elected to fill out a vacancy caused by the death of James Brooks, and then served in the House until 1885, when he resigned to accept a diplomatic position. In 1886 he was again re-elected to Congress, and served until his death in 1889.

James Burnie Beck, Representative (and later Senator) from Kentucky, was born in Scotland in 1822. He was elected to Congress as a Democrat and served from 1867 to 1875, then served in the Senate from 1876 until his death in 1890.

Philadelph Van Trump, representative from Ohio, was born in that state in 1810; was elected to Congress as a Democrat and served from 1867 to 1873; he was not a candidate for re-election.

Alfred Moore Waddell, Representative from North Carolina, was born in that state in 1834; he was elected to Congress as a Democrat and served from 1871 to 1879, being an unsuccessful candidate for re-election.

James Carroll Robinson, Representative from Illinois, was born in that state in 1823. He was elected to Congress as a Democrat in 1859, serving until 1865 and not seeking re-election. He was elected to the House again in 1871 and served until 1875, when he voluntarily retired.

James Millander Hanks, Representative from Arkansas, was born in Arkansas in 1833. He was elected to the House as a Democrat in 1871 and served until 1873, not seeking re-election.

Charles Waldron Buckley, Representative from Alabama, was born in Unadilla, New York, in 1835. He served in the Union army as chaplain of a colored regiment, and after he was mustered out settled in Alabama, where he became superintendent of education for the Bureau of Education and Freedmen. Upon the readmission of Alabama to the Union he was elected to Congress and served in the House from 1868 to 1873; he was not a candidate for re-election.

Burton Chauncey Cook, Representative from Illinois, was born in New York State in 1819, moving to Illinois in 1835. He was elected to Congress as a Republican and served from 1855 to 1871, when he resigned and resumed the practice of law.

Daniel Wolsey Voorhees, Representative and Senator from Indiana, was born in Ohio in 1827, moving to Indiana in early childhood. He was elected to the House as a Democrat and served from 1861 to 1865 and from 1869 to 1873. He later served Indiana as a Senator from 1877 to 1897, and was an unsuccessful candidate for re-election.

REFERENCES

Avary, Mrs. Myrta (Lockett): *Dixie After the War.* New York, 1906.
Beard, James Melville: *K.K.K. Sketches, Humorous and Didactic.* Philadelphia, 1877.
Bowers, Claude G.: *The Tragic Era.* Boston, 1929.
Brewster, James: *Sketches of Southern Mystery, Treason and Murder.* Milwaukee, 1903.
Brown, William G.: *The Lower South in American History.* New York, 1902.
Bryant, Benjamin: *Experience of a Northern Man among the Ku Klux.* Hartford, 1872.
Clayton, Powell: *The Aftermath of the Civil War in Arkansas.* New York, 1915.
Cox, Samuel S.: *Three Decades of Federal Legislation.* Providence, 1885.
Damon, Eyre: *When the Ku Klux Rode.* New York, 1912.
Dixon, Edward H.: *The Terrible Mysteries of the Ku Klux Klan.* New York, 1868.
Fertig, James Walter: *The Secession and Reconstruction of Tennessee.* Chicago, 1898.
Ficklen, John Rose: *History of Reconstruction in Louisiana.* Baltimore, 1910.
Fleming, Walter L.: *Civil War and Reconstruction in Alabama.* New York, 1905.
Fleming, Walter L.: *Documents Relating to Reconstruction.* Morganton, West Virginia, 1904.
Fleming, Walter L.: *Documentary History of Reconstruction.* Cleveland, 1906.
Garner, James W.: *Reconstruction in Mississippi.* New York, 1901.
Henry, Robert Selph: *The Story of Reconstruction.* Indianapolis, 1938.
Herbert, Hilary A.: *Why the Solid South? Of Reconstruction and Its Results.* Baltimore, 1890.
Leland, John A.: *A Voice from South Carolina.* Charleston, 1879.
Lester, J. C., and Wilson, D. L.: *Ku Klux Klan, Its Origin, Growth and Disbandment.* Nashville, 1884.
Lester, J. C., and Wilson, D. L. (with Introduction by Walter L. Fleming): *Ku Klux Klan.* New York, 1905.
Lonn, Ella: *Reconstruction in Louisiana after 1868.* New York, 1918.

McNeily, J. S.: 'War and Reconstruction in Mississippi,' in *Proceedings of the Mississippi Historical Society.*

Morgan, A. T.: *Yazoo, or the Picket Line of Freedom.* Washington, 1884.

Pike, J. S.: *The Prostrate State; South Carolina under Negro Government.* New York, 1874.

The Nation's Peril; Twelve Years' Experience in the South. Published by the friends of the compiler, New York, 1872.

The Papers of Randolph Abbott Shortwell. North Carolina Historical Commission, Raleigh, 1929.

United States Congress: Report of Joint Select Committee to Inquire into the Condition of Affairs in the Late Insurrectionary States. Government Printing Office, Washington, 1872. 13 vols.

Warmoth, H. C.: *War, Politics and Reconstruction.* New York, 1930.

FICTION

Dixon, Thomas: *The Clansman.* New York.

Krey, Laura: *And Tell of Time.* Boston, 1938.

Tourgee, Albion W.: *A Fool's Errand, by One of the Fools.* New York, 1902.

Tyler, Charles W. *The K.K.K.* New York, 1902.

EPILOGUE

EPILOGUE

THE PUBLISHERS OF THIS NEW EDITION OF *Invisible Empire,* issued thirty years after the first edition, have thought it appropriate and desirable to have the author write an additional chapter, or Epilogue, telling something of the conception of the book and the extensive research on which it is based, and also clarifying any misconception which may have existed as to its purpose. This I have gladly consented to do.

First, it seems important to point out and emphasize that the complete title of the book is: *Invisible Empire: The Story of the Ku Klux Klan, 1866-1871.* The wording of the title was intended to make it entirely clear that the book is devoted solely to a discussion of the organization that mushroomed in the South during the troubled days of the Reconstruction, following the Civil War — just this and nothing more.

Unfortunately, a surprising number of people, including many of those who reviewed the book at the time of its original publication, either did not notice the subtitle or else chose to disregard it. At any rate, many of the reviews and comments were devoted largely to the denunciation of a then active organization calling itself "Knights of the Ku Klux Klan," which was receiving much unfavorable publicity. Unaccountably, some, who evidently had not read it, instinctively jumped to the erroneous conclusion that it was intended as a defense of this latter-day Klan, although, as a matter of fact, the modern Klan is not even mentioned in *Invisible Empire.*

It can not be too strongly stressed that this pseudo-Klan, as well as other subsequent organizations with similar names, had not the slightest, remotest connection with the original Ku Klux Klan which was organized at Pulaski, Tennessee, in 1866, and which was formally and officially disbanded in 1871, thus ending its existence. *Invisible Empire,* being devoted solely and exclusively to that original Pulaski-born Klan, was not intended to discuss the purposes or activities of any modern organization, nor was it concerned with other aspects of the Reconstruction.

It should also be emphasized that the purpose of this book was neither to justify nor to condemn the activities of the Ku Klux Klan of the 1860's, but simply to tell the factual story of what took place in that turbulent era of our country's history. The idea of such a book originated with its first publishers, the Houghton Mifflin Company of Boston. Impressed by the fact that no authoritative and accurate book on the subject existed, they thought it highly desirable that the true story of this dramatic chapter in the history of the nation should be recorded. Knowing of my extensive interest and research in Tennessee and Southern history, they offered me a contract to write such a book, which offer I accepted. Their only requisite was that the book should be entirely objective in its treatment of the subject — not condemning and not approving, but simply presenting an unadorned account of what actually happened. Having accepted their contract, I devoted more than a year to an intensified program of research, supplementing my existing knowledge of the subject gained in my previous research in Civil War and postwar history.

A primary and fruitful source of information was the Congressional "Report of the Joint Select Committee to Inquire Into the Condition of Affairs in the Late Insurrectionary States," which was published by the Government Printing Office in 1872. In this voluminous official report (thirteen volumes in small type) was printed a word-for-word transcript of all the testimony developed by the searching investigation conducted by the members of this Congressional committee, all of which I read.

I also researched all the available files of contemporaneous newspapers, some of which provided current accounts of the Klan's activities at that time. Even locating these old newspaper files was often difficult. For instance, I knew that one of the organizers of the original Klan at Pulaski was the editor and publisher of a local newspaper, the *Citizen*; but when I went to Pulaski to examine the early files I found that they had been sold to a university library in North Carolina, where necessarily my research had to be conducted. Similarly, the files of the *Independent,* published in Tuscaloosa, Alabama, by the admitted leader of the Klan there, had been acquired by the State Library and Archives in Montgomery. When I went to Montgomery to examine these files, I was given the most hospitable reception by Mrs. Owen, the State Archivist. Not only did she give me un-limited access to the files, but to expedite my research she permitted me to work in the archives as late at night as I cared to stay, despite the official closing hour. (The friendly and courteous night watchman assured me that he was by experience familiar with the zealous pertinacity of historical researchers. Months later I learned that he was a trusty from the State Penitentiary, serving a life term for murder.)

At the time of my research in 1938-39, there were still a few members of the original Klan alive; but most of them, even seventy years after taking their oath of secrecy, still felt so firmly bound by it that they were generally unwilling to admit their mem-bership or participation. In spite of this, it was often possible to extract from them information relating to specific episodes which strongly suggested that it was based on first-hand experience.

Typical was the attitude of a highly respected nonagenarian I interviewed in one Southern town. When first approached as a possible source of Ku Klux information he said (but with the suggestion of a twinkle in his eye) : "What could have made you think that a reputable citizen like me would have been a member of such an illegal organization?" I admitted that it was of course unthinkable to suspect him of any lawbreaking; but I went on to say that I thought it possible that at some time he might have heard some actual member of the Ku Klux tell something about it. On this basis he was willing to talk freely; but I noticed that in relating some of his stories he at times unconsciously lapsed into using the first-person pronoun "I" instead of the anonymous "he" or "they," to whom these escapades were being attributed.

It is understandably difficult for law-abiding people of the present time to realize the prevalence of the provocative conditions existing in the South in the Reconstruction days, conditions so intolerably severe as to move the afflicted people to resort to the desperate expedient of such extralegal measures as those practiced by the Ku Klux Klan. Abundant evidence that such provocation did exist is to be found in the Congressional Joint Committee Report. This committee's membership of twenty-one Senators and Representatives was carefully selected to preclude any likelihood of pro-Southern bias. Thirteen members of the Committee signed the majority report, which was of the condemnatory nature expected. Eight conscientious members, however, brought in a minority report which, though not justifying the Klan's acts of violence, did imply frankly that in their opinion it was understandable.

"Had there been no wanton oppression in the South," they said, "there would have been no Ku Kluxism. Had there been no rule of the tyrannical, corrupt carpetbagger or scalawag rule, there would have been no secret organizations. From the oppression and corruption of the one sprang the vice and outrage of the other. . . . When even the courts were closed, and the Federal officers ignored, insulted and trampled upon the rights of the ostracized and disfranchised white man, . . . many of them took the law into their own hands and did deeds of violence which we neither justify nor excuse. But all history shows that bad government will make bad citizens; and when the corruptions, extortions and villainies of the governments which Congress has set up and maintained over the Southern states are thoroughly understood and made known, as we trust they will some day, the world will be amazed at the long-suffering and endurance of that people."

An impressive example of the stunning impact of this oppression and corruption on even an unfriendly observer is to be found in a book entitled *The Prostrate State,* written by James S. Pike of New York (D. Appleton & Company, 1873). Pike was a prominent and talented writer of that era, a member of the staff of the New York *Tribune* who became a part owner and associate editor of that influential newspaper. He was an avowed abolitionist and a Republican of such status that President Lincoln had appointed him Minister of the United States at The Hague, where he served until his return to this country in 1866. Although rejoicing in the emancipation of the slaves, he was fully cognizant of the problems created by this abrupt change in the relationship of the former slaves and slaveholders. "We only disposed of one phase of the negro question in abolishing slavery," he wrote. "The great perplexity of establishing just relations between the races is yet to be encountered."

In going to South Carolina for the firsthand observation on which his book was based, the Maine-born Pike's natural inclination was one of sympathy for the freedmen rather than for the defeated and disfranchised citizens of South Carolina. But he was astonished and shocked by the incredible irresponsibility and dishonesty of the state legislature which was then ruling the state, and as an honest reporter he dutifully set down the facts in his book, even though his findings were distasteful and probably greatly at variance with his expectations. He bluntly described the legislators' sessions as a "shocking burlesque upon legislative proceedings," going on to say that "scoundrelism is dominant and all legislation is in the hands of unscrupulous knaves who belong in the penitentiary." In justification of his strong language, Pike said: "It is not harsh to criticise members of this 'Black Parliament' in the way we do, for we only say of them what they say of themselves. They are in the habit of charging one another with ignorance and venality and corruption without stint, and it is not deemed any offense." Summing up his impressions he wrote:

"Here is the outcome, the ripe perfected fruit of the boasted civilization of the South, after two hundred years of experience. A white community that had gradually risen from small beginnings till it grew into wealth, culture and refinement and became accomplished in all the arts of civilization . . . lies prostrate in the dust, ruled over by this strange conglomerate, gathered from the ranks of its own servile population. It is the spectacle of a society suddenly turned bottom-side up. . . . It is the dregs of the population habilitated in the robes of their intelligent predecessors and asserting over them the rule of ignorance and corruption through the inexorable machinery of a majority of numbers. It is barbarism overwhelming civilization by physical force." And if it seemed so to an uninvolved visitor, how galling must it have been to the suffering victims of such barbarism?

In reviewing *Invisible Empire* in the New York *Herald Tribune* in 1939, Henry Steele Commager wrote disparagingly: "The time is past when the historian can speak, without elaborate qualifications, of 'the wild nightmare called the Reconstruction.' . . . [*Invisible Empire*] repeats all the hackneyed charges of corruption, extravagance and misrule." Apparently time had passed very fast indeed for Prof. Commager: only four years earlier in his Introduction to a new edition of *The Prostrate State,* he was referring as follows to Reconstruction conditions in South Carolina:

"Here was presented in its most extreme form the actualization of the theory of racial equality. . . . Here was fulfilled, in fantastic fashion, the degradation of the democratic dogma. Here were revealed the temptations to which victors are exposed when not restrained by public opinion, the dangers to which the vanquished are subjected when not protected by law. Here were displayed, in grotesque form, the inevitable results of power without responsibility, authority without tradition, administration without intelligence or training. . . . There ensued such a travesty upon government as had never before been witnessed in an Anglo-Saxon state. . . . Graft and corruption and extravagance became the order of the day; . . . convictions were almost impossible to obtain, and justice was prostituted in the courts." And, to emphasize that such conditions were then prevalent in the South, Prof. Commager added: "It must be remembered, too, that the experience of South Carolina during the period of Reconstruction was far from unique. Other Southern states had their tales of woe, and the sufferings of Louisiana were no less extravagant than those of the Palmetto State."

Possibly historians who in later years had difficulty appreciating the social and political conditions during Reconstruction which gave rise to the original Klan were unconsciously influenced by the widespread disapproval incurred by the twentieth-century organizations which appropriated its name. Certainly there is today much confusion of the first Ku Klux Klan with the pseudo-Klans which arose after a lapse of several decades. The confusion is perhaps a natural error on the part of the uninformed public whose knowledge of (and interest in) the subject extends no further than a recognition of the similarity in name and a vague recall of the sinister connotations of that name. No well-informed person, however, should be so misled. That the old and the new organizations were totally different in motivating cause and in objective is apparent when they are examined and understood.

The primary difference has always been in motivation. The original Klan sprang into being in 1866 to meet the chaotic, abnormal and intolerable conditions of that era for which no normal and lawful remedy seemed immediately available. None of the modern organizations using the name of the Klan would pretend, however, that there is now or ever was any such impelling reason for their existence. Another conspicuous difference has been that whereas there was never any suspicion or accusation of commercial motive in the original Klan, pecuniary gain seems to have been obviously a strong and prominent factor in the formation and promotion of many of the modern users of the name.

The first, and financially most successful, of the modern pseudo-Klans was the brainchild of William Joseph Simmons of Atlanta. Simmons was a man of imposing appearance and a fluent speaker and writer. Born on a farm in Alabama, he had been in his adult life successively a dropout medical-school student, a Methodist minister, and eventually a professional organizer of fraternal insurance orders. While engaged in the latter occupation, he acquired the honorary title of Colonel, to which he clung tenaciously in his subsequent activities.

Simmons attributed the germ of his inspiration for the creation of his Knights of the Ku Klux Klan to a "vision." In this vision clouds drifting in front of the moon assumed the shape of white-robed riders of horses galloping across the horizon, with an outline of a map of the United States in the background. In the words of one of his friendly and ecstatic biographers, Simmons then and there "registered a vow that a great patriotic fraternal order should be builded as a memorial to the heroes of our nation." Apparently the translation of his vow into action was a slow process, as it was not until fifteen years later (in 1915) that he took the steps leading to the incorporation of the Knights of the Ku Klux Klan.

His biographer stated that "There was no thought in the mind of Colonel Simmons to revive in any way the night-riding, masked operations of the original Ku Klux Klan, for conditions in the South do not justify such an organization to-day, but the principal thought around which centered the idea of reestablishing the Ku Klux Klan was its lofty spiritual purpose, to be manifested in the new organization which would constitute a great American patriotic and fraternal order." Despite this disclaimer, however, the canny Colonel did seek to fortify his position for profitable purposes by declaring that his K. K. K. K. was "the only legitimate heir of the parent organization of reconstruction days, and therefore possessed of the sole rights to all of its regalia, ritual and symbols," including the "official white costumes" — a reservation which was to bear golden fruit in the future.

Colonel Simmons announced his new organization to the world in a verbose and flowery Proclamation, which opened with these words:

> To all Nations, Peoples, Tribes and Tongues, and to the Lovers of Law and Order, Peace and Justice, of the Whole Earth, Greetings: I, and the citizens of the Invisible Empire through me, proclaim to you as follows:
>
> We the members of this Order, desiring to promote real patriotism toward our civil government; honorable peace among men and nations; protection for and happiness in the homes of our people; love, real brotherhood, mirth and manhood among ourselves, justice and fraternity among all mankind; and believing that we can best accomplish these noble purposes through the channel of a high-class mystic, social, patriotic, benevolent association, having a perfected lodge system, with an exalted ritualistic form of work and an effective form of government, not for selfish profit but for

the mutual betterment, benefit and protection of all our oath-bound associates, their welfare physically, socially, morally and vocationally, and their loved ones, do proclaim to the whole world that we are dedicated to the sublime and pleasant duty of providing generous aid, tender sympathy and fraternal assistance in the effulgence of the light of life and amid the sable shadows of death; amid fortune and misfortune, and the exalted privilege of demonstrating the practical utility of the great, yet most neglected, doctrine of the Fatherhood of God and Brotherhood of Men as a vital force in the lives and affairs of men. In this we invite all men who can qualify to become citizens of the Invisible Empire, to approach the portal of our beneficent domain and join us in our noble work of extending its boundaries . . . to bless mankind, and to keep eternally ablaze the sacred fire of a fervent devotion to pure Americanism.

Despite his turgid eloquence and his promotional experience, however, the Simmons version of the Klan, perhaps because of the vagueness of its declared lofty objectives, did not seem to appeal very strongly to the people who were expected to join. After five years of the organizer's most earnest and vigorous efforts, the Knights of the Ku Klux Klan had only a few thousand members and was reported to be experiencing financial difficulties. It was at this juncture, however, that the Klan as a potentially profitable business enterprise attracted the attention of a talented professional promoter, Edward Young Clarke, of Atlanta. Clarke had been notably successful in promoting fund-raising campaigns for more or less deserving activities, and he made a businessman's deal with Simmons to employ himself and his organization for the expansion of the Klan's membership.

Clarke went to work promptly, and his activities were attended with remarkable success. Within a year the membership of the Klan had spurted to more than 100,000, and within a few more years it was reported to have swelled to a million or more. It

was Clarke who invented the nomenclature of the additional subordinate officials and workers who provided the steam for the
membership drive. The low man on the titular totem-pole, but
actually the key man responsible for the success or failure of the
drive, was the house-to-house salesman whose function it was to
persuade new members to sign on the dotted line. He bore the
resoundingly alliterative title of "Kleagle of the Knights of the Ku
Klux Klan." The head of the organization in each of the forty-
five states in which it operated was called the King Kleagle. Above
all the King Kleagles, at the top of the pole was the one supreme
ruler of the promotional phase of the organization, the Imperial
Kleagle, which title was assumed by Clarke himself. Simmons
was considerately permitted to continue calling himself the Grand
Wizard, the title given General Nathan Bedford Forrest when he
was the head of the original Klan. When a Kleagle signed up a
new member he collected an initial membership fee of ten dollars.
Of this the Kleagle retained four dollars for himself; one dollar
went to the King Kleagle of his state; the remaining five dollars
went to the headquarters in Atlanta. Just how this five dollars
was divided was never publicly revealed, but during the peak
years of the Knights of the Ku Klux Klan the Grand Wizard and
the Imperial Kleagle seemed to be enjoying a comfortable af-
fluence as the fruits of the well-paid Kleagles came pouring in.

An important and significant difference between the old Klan
and the new Knights of the Ku Klux Klan was that the old Klan
never solicited or invited members; membership was attained only
by voluntary application. The cornerstone of the new Klan's struc-
ture was the effective campaign of vigorous and persistent solicita-
tion of members, and the prepayment of a substantial membership fee.

The membership appeal of the two organizations was also
entirely different. Although, in the nature of things, the member-

ship of the original Klan was composed almost entirely of white
men, it was not a racist organization in the modern sense of the
word: its victims included white carpetbaggers and scalawags as
well as black freedmen. Nor was there ever any mention or suspicion of religious prejudice or exclusion from membership in the
old Klan on religious grounds; in fact, it was commonly understood that a Jewish citizen of Pulaski was secretary of the original
Klan there. On the other hand, the Klan organized by Simmons
publicly admitted that "We bar from membership Jews, Catholics
and negroes." In pursuing its campaign for new members, its
promoters soon discovered that its all-white policy had little appeal
outside the South, and so the emphasis in its promotional material
soon shifted to an emotional appeal for 100 percent Americanism,
reaching back to the "Know-Nothingism" of the 1850's for some
of its basic philosophy. The success of this shrewd shift in emphasis
is shown by the surprising support achieved by the new Klan in
the North, Midwest and Far West, with remarkably large membership and political power in such states as Indiana and Oregon,
where "white supremacy" is a meaningless shibboleth.

In his audacious declaration in 1915 that his Knights of the
Ku Klux Klan was the legitimate heir of the Klan of Reconstruction days, and thereby was the possessor of "the sole right to
all of its regalia, ritual and symbols," including "the official white
costumes," Mr. Simmons cleverly paved the way for what developed into a highly profitable sideline, the sale of "the official
white costumes" to the members. Actually, however, the original
Klan had no "official costumes," white or otherwise. Each member was more or less a law unto himself as far as his costume was
concerned. They were invariably homemade by the mothers, wives
or sisters of the members, and there was wide variation in their
color and style. The robes were generally made of calico — some
red, some black and some white — the only requirement being

that they should be large enough to envelop the whole body of the wearer and effectively conceal his identity. The style and shape of the accompanying headdress, including a mask, was also left to the whim of the wearer. There was no central headquarters, like that of Simmons in Atlanta, from which the members were required or able to purchase an "official" costume. Nor did the original Klan have any paid officers or solicitors of members.

The only thing in the way of regalia or symbols that the old Klan had was an official flag, with which each local group or "Den" was supposed to supply itself, made to the following specifications: "The Grand Ensign or Banner of the Ku Klux shall be in the form of an isosceles triangle, five feet long and three feet wide at the staff. The material shall be yellow, with a red scalloped border, about three inches in width. There shall be painted upon it in black a Dracovolans, or Flying Dragon, with the following motto inscribed on it: 'Quod semper, quod ubique, quod ab omnibus.' [What always, what everywhere, what by all, is held to be true.]" Incidentally, the original flag of the original Den at Pulaski, made precisely to these specifications, has been presented to the Tennessee Historical Society by the last living descendant of one of the organizers. So far as is known, the Simmons Klan did not use this or any other flag.

It is interesting to trace the origin and background of the "fiery cross," the popularly accepted symbol of the modern Klan. Apparently the promoters of the Simmons Klan derived much of their inspiration from the vividly impressive presentation of the original Klan's supposed activities in D. W. Griffith's spectacular motion picture, "The Birth of a Nation" (1915). This film was based on a work of fiction entitled *The Clansman* (1905), written by the Reverend Thomas Dixon of North Carolina. In Dixon's novel, one of the demonstrations staged by his fictional Klan featured the burning of a fiery cross, and this flaming symbol became a sort of showy trademark of the latter-day Ku Klux Klan.

When I had concluded my rather extensive research into the origin and practices of the original Ku Klux Klan, it suddenly dawned on me that there had not been any mention of any use of a "fiery cross" in any of the recorded public appearances of the Ku Klux of the 1860's, either in the newspaper accounts of parades or demonstrations or in the testimony of any of the cloud of witnesses who testified in the Congressional Inquiry in 1872.

This seemed strange, so I wrote to Dixon and asked him what authority, if any, he had for introducing this feature in his novel. He replied that his uncle, reputed to be a member of the old Klan in North Carolina, had told him that he had made use of a burning cross in one of the demonstrations of his group, having been told by his grandfather of the use of this symbol by one of the early Scottish clans. I pressed Dixon for further information on the subject, but my subsequent letters to him were unanswered. Griffith, probably not knowing (and not caring) about the attenuated basis for associating the fiery cross with the actual activities of the actual Ku Klux Klan, certainly recognized the dramatic possibilities of this gimmick and made it an outstanding and impressive feature of his motion picture.

Thus the fiery cross became erroneously but indelibly fixed in the public mind as an essential feature of the official ceremonies of the original Ku Klux Klan, and through its widespread use by the modern imitation Klans became firmly established as synonymous with the Ku Klux. It seems safe to assert, however, that (with the possible exception of Dixon's uncle) no member of the original Ku Klux Klan ever made use of any such symbol. At any rate, no single mention of such a manifestation appears in any contemporaneous newspaper, or in the voluminous record of the Congressional investigation, nor was it ever mentioned to me in any conversations with supposed survivors of the original Klan.

Unquestionably the idea of a flaming cross appealed strongly to the myth-loving public and even to some of those who purported to write authoritatively about the original Klan. For instance, a book entitled *Authentic History, Ku Klux Klan, 1865-77* (by Susan L. Davis, New York, 1924) was embellished on its cover with a lurid and imaginative drawing of a ghostly equestrian in flowing robe on a galloping horse, fearlessly holding in his hand a large blazing cross. This drawing was repeated in a startling frontispiece in color. Far from being "authentic," this history is now generally recognized by historians as one of the most inaccurate historical works ever produced. Illustrated with a large number of irrelevant photographs, it includes some unbelievable as well as manifestly impossible statements attributed to prominent Confederate personages (all of whom were deceased at the time of publication).

A true account of the original Ku Klux Klan, aside from its historical contribution, should make sufficiently interesting reading without fictional embellishments. It is such an account that I attempted to present in writing *Invisible Empire*. Allan Nevins, reviewing the work in the *Saturday Review of Literature* thirty years ago, described it as "a history that is well organized, thorough, judicious in tone and interesting throughout its 400 pages." My hope is that in this publication of a second edition, a new generation of readers may also find it so.

INDEX

INDEX

Index

Newberry County, S.C., 217, 221, 227, 235, 238
New Orleans *Times*, 345
New York *Evening Mail*, 95
New York *Herald*, 26, 236–238
New York *Illustrated News*, 43–44
New York *Sun*, 209–210
New York *Tribune*, 174, 250–251
New York *World*, 200, 362
News, see Savannah *News*
'Night Hawks,' 10, 34, 50
Norfolk *Journal*, 337
Norris, 'Chap,' 180–183

Oath of Allegiance to K.K.K., 36, 54–56; *see also* Shotwell Oath, Yorkville Oath, and Leach Oath
Obion County, Tenn., 86–87, 105
Odd Fellows, 343
Officers of K.K.K., names of, 10, 34; duties of, 34–35; election of, 35, 113
Officers of Pale Faces, 347
Ogden, Frederick N., 346
Oglethorpe County, Ga., 175
Oliver, Thomas, 199
Orange County, N.C., 197
Ord, Gen., 148, 149
Organizer of K.K.K., *see* Forrest, Gen. N. B.
Origin of K.K.K., fantastic theories, 7–8, 19; social club in Pulaski, 9–10; 21–22; 44; 77; in Ala., 116
Orr, Gov. James L., 214–216
Ouachita Parish, La., 288
Outlaw, Wyatt, 197
Overton County, Tenn., 80, 107
Owens, A. B., 224
Owens, William K., 51, 223
Oxford, trial in, 162–166

Page, Aleck, 163–166
Page, Fanny, 164
Pale Face, 348
Pale Faces, 318, 346–348
Palmer, Jos. B., 103
Parker, Albert H., 253–257
Parker, Tenn. Tax Collector, 340
Penalties imposed by K.K.K., 45, 69–70
Perry, Gov. Benjamin Franklin, 214, 216
Pickens County, Ala., 117, 124
Pickens, Judge, 157
Pickett, Lt., 151
Pickett, Col. A. C., 261
Pike, Gen. Albert, 245–246, 337
Pillow, Gideon J., 103
Pine Bluff *Republican*, 246–247
Planters Banner, see Franklin *Planters Banner*

Poland, Rep. Luke P., 296, 297
Pollard, Judge Austin, 152–154
Pontotoc *Equal Rights*, 152
Pontotoc Raid, 152–155
'Pontotoc Times,' 154
Pool, Sen. John, 192, 296, 297, 299
Pope, Gen. John, 168–169, 263
Portentous month, 37
Porter, Dr. H. H., 154–155
Postle, Isaac A., 301
Postle, Mrs., wife of Isaac the Apostle, 301
Pousser, Richard, 275
Pratt, Sen. Daniel P., 296, 299
Prescript of 1867 (original), 33–37, 54, 281, 357
Prescript of 1868, opening declaration of purpose, 1, 38; revision of original Prescript, 38; territory covered, 39; article on elegibility for membership, 39–40; change in code, 40; use of stars for name, 2, 41; changes in oath of allegiance, 54–55; no reference to banner, 58; preserved copy of, 113; duty of Grand Wizard, 321
Press and Times, see Nashville *Press and Times*
Price, Daniel, 156–159
Publications of the Mississippi Historical Society, 146
Public Ledger, see Memphis *Public Ledger*
Pulaski *Citizen*, 13, 21, 23–25, 33, 41, 83
Purman, Maj. W. J., 271–275
Purpose of K.K.K., 16, 18, 20, 31, 38, 45, 366

Quarles, Wm. A., 103

Rainey, Jim, *see* Williams, Jim
Randolph, Ryland, 60, 116–120, 129–131, 139, 140, 323–324
Rapides Tribune, see Alexandria *Rapides Tribune*
Rattlesnake Den, 221–222
Recognition, sign of, 51–54
Reconstruction Act, 32, 168, 215, 244–246
Reconstruction, Documentary History of the, Dr. W. L. Fleming, 343
Reconstruction in Louisiana, History of, John Rose Ficklen, 286–287
Reconstruction legislature, *see* anti-Ku Klux law of Ga.; Federal Ku Klux law; Reconstruction Act; Shoffner Law
Reconstruction, Story of, Henry, 264
Red Jackets, 348
Red Shirts, 355

PATTERSON SMITH REPRINT SERIES IN
CRIMINOLOGY, LAW ENFORCEMENT, AND SOCIAL PROBLEMS